PLANNING
ATLANTA

Harley F. Etienne and Barbara Faga, eds.

American Planning Association
Planners Press

Making Great Communities Happen

Chicago | Washington, D.C.

Also available in this series
Planning Los Angeles, David C. Sloane, ed.
Planning Chicago, J. Bradford Hunt and Jon B. DeVries, eds.

Copyright © 2014 by the American Planning Association

205 N. Michigan Ave., Suite 1200, Chicago, IL 60601
1030 15th St., NW, Suite 750 West, Washington, DC 20005

www.planning.org/plannerspress

ISBN: 978-1-61190-126-9

Library of Congress Control Number: 2014936581

Publication of this book was made possible in part by generous support from several contributors. Financial support was provided by the University of Michigan's Taubman College of Architecture and Urban Planning; the Land Economics Foundation and Lambda Alpha International—the Honorary Society of Land Economics; and the Georgia Planning Association. In kind support was provided by LAI's Atlanta Chapter.

Printed in the United States of America

FOR DOUGLAS ALLEN AND HARRY L. WEST,
AND ALL OF THE PLANNERS AND DREAMERS
WHO WORKED FOR A BETTER ATLANTA

CONTENTS

ACKNOWLEDGMENTS

Books are never easy to complete, and this one is no exception. Volumes that bring together voices from across a discipline and practice such as planning face a real challenge in trying to speak to multiple audiences while also creating meaningful and insightful results. We believe that we have accomplished this and hope that readers feel the same way.

First, we must thank the generous support and prodding of the editorial staff at the American Planning Association, specifically Sylvia Lewis, director of publications, and Camille Fink, senior editor, who stepped in at a critical point and helped carry this project to the finish line. Although he is no longer with the press, we also want to mention Tim Mennel, who brought this project to us in the first place.

We must also acknowledge and sincerely thank the Office of the Vice President for Research and the Taubman College of Architecture and Urban Planning at the University of Michigan for their generous subvention grant to support this book project. Steve French, dean of the College of Architecture at the Georgia Institute of Technology, deserves special thanks for his support of this project as well.

We gratefully acknowledge the Georgia Planning Association for its early and generous support and Lambda Alpha International (LAI), especially Ian Lord, president of LAI, Steven Gragg, president of the Land Economics Foundation, and Joan Herron, president of the LAI Atlanta chapter. We also thank Laurie Marston, LAI Executive Committee member, and Jon B. DeVries, chair of the Land Economic Foundation Research Committee, for continuing the collaboration between LAI and the American Planning Association.

There are many others who deserve mention for their support of this project. Of course, we are thankful to the contributors to this volume who graciously responded to our numerous requests for revisions and fact-checking, and Kit Sutherland for her perspectives on the nearly completed full draft. Others who helped include our Georgia Institute of Technology colleagues Dan Immergluck, Bruce Stiftel, Brian Stone, and Dana Habeeb; the staff at the Georgia Tech Center for Quality Growth and Regional Development and the Georgia Tech Center for Geographic Information Systems; and University of Michigan colleagues Monica Ponce de Leon, Jean Wineman, Barbara Tiejen, Sandra Patton, Lesli Hoey, Scott Campbell, June Thomas, Margaret Dewar, and Joe Grengs.

Carl Patton deserves special recognition for sharing his knowledge of Georgia State University and Downtown Atlanta, and A.J. Robinson for his in-depth understanding of Downtown. Others who contributed valuable information or images include the staff at Central Atlanta Progress, notably Wilma Sothern and Lynn Williamson; the Atlanta History Center; Paul Morris and the Atlanta BeltLine; Doug Shipman and the National Center for Civil and Human Rights; James Shelby and the Atlanta Department of Planning and Community Development; Shannon Powell and the Midtown Alliance; and Dan Reuter and the Atlanta Regional Commission. Thanks also to George Berry, Tina Arbes, and Karen Huebner, who provided their time and knowledge of Atlanta history.

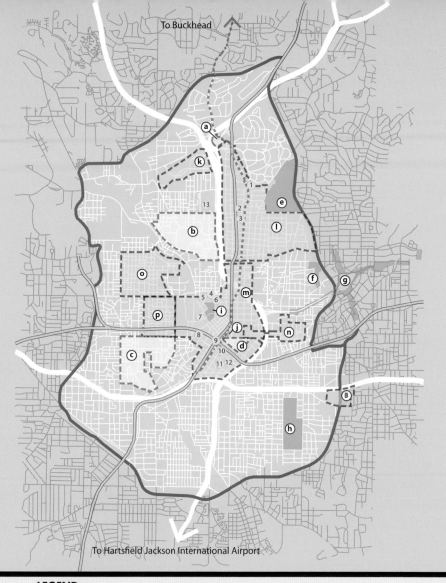

To Buckhead

To Hartsfield Jackson International Airport

LEGEND

	Interstate Highways
	Peachtree Street
	Beltline Corridor
	MARTA

POINTS OF INTEREST
1. Lindbergh Center
2. Woodruff Arts Center
3. Colony Square
4. Turner Headquarters
5. Federal Reserve Building
6. Margaret Mitchell House
7. Fox Theatre
8. Emory Midtown Hospital
9. Center of Civil and Human Rights
10. Georgia Aquarium
11. Children's Museum of Atlanta
12. Georgia World Congress Center
13. CNN Center

14. The Gulch
15. Five Points MARTA Station
16. Underground Atlanta
17. Grady Hospital
18. Georgia State Capitol
19. Atlanta City Hall
20. Turner Field

UNIVERSITIES
a. SCAD
b. Georgia Institute of Technology
c. Atlanta University Center
d. Georgia State University

PARKS
e. Piedmont Park
f. Old Fourth Ward Park
g. Freedom Park & Carter Center
h. Grant Park

i. Centennial Olympic Park
j. Woodruff Park
k. Washington Park

NEIGHBORHOODS
l. Atlantic Station
m. Midtown
n. Virginia Highland
o. Downtown
p. MLK Jr. Historic District
q. Glenwood Park
r. English Avenue
s. Vine City
t. West End

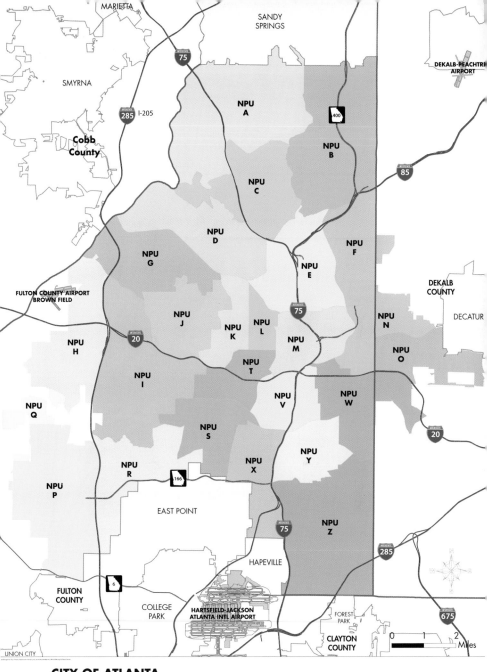

CITY OF ATLANTA
NEIGHBORHOOD PLANNING UNIT (NPU) MAP

INTRODUCTION

Harley F. Etienne and Barbara Faga

As the story goes, in the summer of 1864, Union Army Major General William Tecumsah Sherman invaded and nearly completely destroyed the city of Atlanta. On September 2, the Confederate Army abandoned the city and ordered all Confederate assets destroyed. The aftermath of these events was a significant morale boost for the Union Army and the North and contributed to the reelection of Abraham Lincoln a few months later. Any student of Atlanta's history knows about Sherman's Atlanta campaign and the indelible mark it left on the city's psyche. As the city rebounded from the war, the devastation that it had suffered became one of its many calling cards and a defining feature of the city's emblem: a phoenix rising from flames. The city's official motto is simply the Latin word, *resurgens*, which means "rising again."

Perhaps more than any other major U.S. city, Atlanta continually charts its future by redefining and reshaping itself. The city's history is marked by periods of ruin and resurgence. After each era, the city can be characterized by its misfortunes and dogged effort to leave them behind. From the devastation of the American Civil War to the pre-Olympic boom, to the current housing crisis, the practice of planning in Atlanta reflects the city's struggle to find a core identity and chart a course to its future. It also reflects the city's effort to become and remain economically dominant, connected, and competitive at the regional, national, and global levels.

It is perhaps important to note early in this volume that the city is really only a part of the story. Unlike Los Angeles and Chicago, Atlanta proper actu-

Figure A.1. Atlanta from the Ashes (also known as "Phoenix Rising") was designed by Jim Seigler, fabricated by Gamba Quirino and Feruccia Vezzoni, and commissioned by the Rich Foundation in 1969.

ally occupies a very small piece of the larger region that casually and freely uses its name. The U.S. Census places the city's 2012 population at 443, 775, which represents only a bit more than eight percent of the metropolitan region (U.S. Census Bureau 2013). While the city's population is growing, it is not keeping pace with the region's growth and certain long-standing populations—namely African Americans—are abandoning the city for neighboring suburbs in significant numbers.

This edited volume has brought together some of Atlanta's most highly regarded planning practitioners and thought leaders to assess how planning has shaped the city's growth and creates challenges and opportunities in the present. There has never before been a view of this city through the various subfields that make up the profession of planning. By bringing together a diversity of perspectives and approaches, this book aspires to combine rigorous analysis with accessible ideas and practical knowledge about how planning and development have happened here and continue to occur.

Market Triumphalism and Mythmaking

In the introduction to the first book of this series, *Planning Los Angeles*, David C. Sloane makes a point of discussing the many myths that make up the City of Angels. In Atlanta, Los Angeles, and many other cities, myth is an important part of city-making. Charles Rutheiser's book *Imagineering Atlanta: The Politics of Place in the City of Dreams* (1996) challenged Atlanta to face the extent to which the city has been built by dreams and perhaps to some extent "puffery." But then, what is planning but the gap between dreams and current reality? In planning places, planners often must sell the idea of what they hope a city to be to its occupants. Even if the vision for a new place comes from the people themselves, the planner must assemble and present the idea of what could be to a community of people. Atlanta's destruction during the Civil War allowed for a particular myth narrative of a city to be written and believed—one of being rebuilt from little to nothing into a global and regional gateway and hub of finance, entertainment, education, and services over the course of a century.

One of the most dominant public images of Atlanta is the one created by Tom Wolfe in his book *A Man in Full* (1998). All fiction is based partly on reality. The plot of that novel intersects with planning in what we learn about the city's aspirations and the delicate balance of race relations that are unique to any American city—south or north. The trials and tribulations of the characters in the book are actually fairly prescient given what came our way in 2008.

The stories of Atlanta's largest corporations are in many ways symbolic of how cities succeed or fail in a capitalist system. A small, drugstore concoction leads to the existence of one of the most powerful and important corporations on the planet. A little more than a mile to the north of the Coca-Cola headquarters is the home of the media giant Turner Broadcasting that manages content on virtually every media platform available today. Ten miles to the south, the city manages one of the busiest passenger and air cargo freight airports in the world that is dominated by one of the largest airlines and one of the largest shippers anywhere else on earth. With Delta Air Lines, Turner Broadcasting, Coca-Cola, and UPS, we find four dominant and important multinational corporations that are as important to the world as they are to Atlanta. The services and goods they provide are essential to the functioning of the global economic system, and yet they grew up alongside the city of Atlanta like siblings.

Our challenge as editors has been to assemble chapters that speak to the reality of planning in Atlanta and provide a thorough narrative of how the city and region have come to be what they are today without appearing to gloat or brag. The abovementioned companies have changed how we get news, what we watch, what we drink, how we travel, and how commerce ships its goods. So, the city and region do have bragging rights. However, there is much to critique and question in this anomaly of urban growth and resilience.

Ongoing Tensions and Injustices

Many who read this volume will no doubt be familiar with former Atlanta mayor Ivan Allen's famous quip about the city's relative lack of civil rights era struggle and controversy when he called Atlanta, "the city too busy to hate" (Bayor 1997, 42; Hein 1972). This did not however mean that there were not real challenges to overcome in terms of the city's racial climate and integration. Georgia state law required the immediate suspension of funding or tax-exempt status at any college or university with an integrated student body. Whereas the integration of the University of Georgia was controversial and violent, Atlanta's Georgia Institute of Technology and Emory University integrated without court order or violent unrest (McMath 1985). It is also noteworthy that Atlanta elected progressive mayors who were sympathetic and, in some cases, openly support- ive of the civil rights movement from 1942 until 1974, when it elected its first African American mayor, Maynard Jackson.

In the northern sections of the city, and their nearby suburban counter- parts of Dunwoody, Sandy Springs, and Johns Creek, metropolitan Atlanta is nearly perfect, aside from the sweltering summer heat and daily traffic jams along Peachtree Road, the Georgia 400 Freeway, and virtually every inter- state that runs through, around, or out of the city. In these communities, there is wonderful housing, relatively low crime, abundant shopping and dining amenities, and racial integration that should be the envy of the nation.

To live, shop, and operate in Buckhead is to live at the center of metro- politan Atlanta's paradoxes. In the halls of the historic Lenox Mall, the well- heeled shop at high-end and exclusive brand name stores alongside gay men in stilettos and pearls, while visitors from all over the state converge to take traditional Christmas photos with Santa Claus and ride the "Pink Pig" holiday coaster, a holdover from a South of not-so-long ago. Here they all compete to belong and own this space. It is a private, lavish space that is a paragon of conspicuous consumption and the living room to a region whose identity is as distinguishable as its growth boundary.

Very close to this world of paradoxes is the stretch of land that rests between Buford Highway and Interstate 85, an alternate universe of middle- to low-income Asian and Latino communities that seems almost bucolic in comparison to the lower-income communities on the west side of Atlanta, just south of the railroad tracks that separate them from the southwestern edge of Buckhead. These heavily industrial and post-industrial spaces are yielding to apartment lofts and condominium communities that cater to recent college graduates and young transplants, coming to enjoy the most cosmopolitan city in the American southeast.

To shop, dine, or live in Buckhead or its counterparts means having the option to have very little contact or exposure to the dilapidated and post-industrial parts of the metropolitan region that have not yet caught up. On the city's southeast, southwest, and western edges are communities with housing abandonment rates and crime rates comparable to some of the most danger-ous and blighted cities in the United States. And the evidence suggests that this gulf is widening, not shrinking.

Atlanta's story of growth and dynamism would appear to be nothing short of miraculous, if not for the weaknesses that revealed themselves dur-ing the Great Recession of 2008. The city and region have benefitted from "growing by growing." The premise of the entire regional economy has been that in-migration would fuel housing demand, which would then create de-mand for jobs and services, which would in turn inspire more migration, and lead to even greater housing demand.

As we brought the writing of this book to a close, Atlanta's major league baseball franchise announced its plans to leave Turner Field for a yet-to-be constructed stadium in nearby Cobb County (Bradley 2013). What few commentators have offered is a connection to another fairly quiet event that took place in 2010, when the city's daily paper moved its headquarters for suburban Dunwoody (Henry 2010). This followed another even quieter move of the Atlanta Opera Company to "Sminings" in 2006.[1] So perhaps there is a slow but increasingly loud trickling of amenities and resources out of the city. And as some commentators have noted, these moves may be couched in terms of competitive pricing or transportation but may in part be due to underlying and long-standing racial tensions that put the central city and its issues beyond the interest or attention span of many suburban dwellers (Brown 2013).

Overview of the Book

The volume is divided into five distinct sections representing eras or themes in Atlanta's planning history and development. Part I, *Terminus to International City*, discusses the city's early beginnings and growth with particular attention to how its transportation infrastructure played a major part in creating the context in which Atlanta would grow. Part II, *Diversity and Development*, presents different perspectives on how identity, neighborhoods, power, and access determined which planning projects moved forward, who drove them, and who benefited from their success or failure. Part III, *Travel, Traffic, and Transit Define a City*, provides readers with views of current regional and local transportation planning projects, including the airport, the recent reintroduction of streetcars to the downtown area, and the auspicious Beltline project. Part IV, *Boom and Bust*, speaks to the city and region's reliance on growth through discussions about the 1996 Olympics, notable mixed use communities, and housing and economic development policy. Part V, *Innovation and Challenges Shape the Future*, discusses some of the environmental risks and innovations that may shape the city and region in the decades to come.

No book can possibly incorporate all topics, perspectives, or ideas, and this one similarly does not profess to do this. However, we have gathered chapters that appeal to a larger audience interested in learning about the city and to practitioners wanting to understand how Atlanta has come together and how it struggles to sustain its growth in the face of environmental, demographic, social, and policy challenges. Since this volume contains contributions from academic researchers and practitioners, writing styles and ideological perspectives vary widely. Instead of forcing the book to cater to one audience or another, we sought to reach several audiences. Some chapters contain empirical research, while others are largely historical and descriptive. A few others are highly personal accounts of planning practice that would only make sense if told by the planning practitioner himself or herself. To that end, each section contains discussions on particular topics, "Practitioner Perspectives," that provide an opportunity for well-regarded and experienced planners to speak about their work in Atlanta.

As many other writers have noted, Atlanta is a city of aspirations. Perhaps, then, its ability to transcend its internal tensions and challenges embodies the idea that planning is the "organization of hope." For the conclusion to this volume, former Atlanta Mayor Shirley Franklin shows that she understands the ways in which planning is central to Atlanta's story. In her epilogue, she provides some thoughts about how Atlanta will need planning to chart its path for the next century.

PART 1

Terminus to the International City

From the 1830s through today, Atlanta has been all about growth. What began as "Terminus," a small settlement at the crossroads of four rail lines, has evolved two centuries later into an international city with the world's busiest airport and cache enough to be awarded and host the 1996 Centennial Olympic Games. Suffice it to say that problems occurred along the way. We are a dichotomy in regard to location and form. Acknowledged as the capital of the south, we are often regarded as an East Coast city but ironically located at a longitude (84° west) that is one degree west of the Midwestern city of Detroit (83° west). Unlike the more traditional cities local business leaders admire—Chicago, Boston, and New York to name a few—the physical plan is similar to the western cities built along rail lines. Roads follow topography leading to street patterns that are indecipherable to visitors.

These chapters, written by planning leaders, practitioners, and scholars, characterize the planning process, which is in essence a *local way* of doing things. The phrase *you dance with the one that brung you* illustrates how alliances are formed. Just as Stone (1989) described, Atlanta remains coalition-based. Successful planning practice in Atlanta requires the insight to look beyond what people are saying to understand their realities. Issues of race, location, background, and intentions are often not as they appear. The community speaks in code, and practice here involves listening intently to understand the real issues.

Figure B.1. Peachtree Street looking south

Douglas Allen's "Learning from Atlanta" examines the topography, land lots, and railroads that initially formed the city. Allen describes Atlanta's development pattern as having more in common with cities of the "wild west" than with the more traditionally planned southern towns of Savannah, Charleston, and Richmond. Without an Oglethorpe, Burnham, or L'Enfant to guide design, the geometry of this city was set by businessmen, and businessmen have continued throughout each century to reshape the form of the city through their projects.

In "Changing Demographics and Unprecedented Growth", Ellen Heath and John Heath illustrate the changes over time in the population due to fast growth. Race, income, immigration, and education have repositioned population throughout the city and counties as Atlanta established its reputation as an international city. Like many U.S. cities, Atlanta has turned itself inside out. White suburban residents are moving back to the city as African American residents, along with a growing Hispanic community, are moving to the suburbs. The Heaths combine their private and public sector experience to put together this insightful overview of regional demographics.

Mtamanika Youngblood describes her experience and the success of planning and financing tools such as the Historic District Development Corporation (HDDC) in "The Historic District Development Corporation and the Challenge of Urban Revitalization." Youngblood's personal account describes the strategic planning and funding needed to guide development, mitigate gentrification, and address displacement in the Old Fourth Ward neighborhood. Fighting to keep residents in their homes is a priority for the intown neighborhoods, in light of years of displacement due to urban renewal and big projects including sports facilities and public housing redevelopments. Old Fourth Ward is home to the legacies of Martin Luther King Jr., community activist Marie Cowser, the "Sweet Auburn" district, and a litany of residents and entities that have collaborated as pioneers for intown neighborhood planning.

Paul Kelman, in "Creating Urban Reinvention: Downtown Atlanta," describes the planning that in some cases guide—and in many times follow development projects. Kelman relates his experience with big downtown projects, including transportation improvements, the Centennial Olympic Park Area, and Georgia State University's growth from a Georgia Tech night school in the 1970s to a city university of 32,000 students.

Leslie Sharp's "Crazy Like The Fox: Atlanta's Preservation Schizophrenia" recounts Atlanta's significant preservation wins, including the Fox Theatre and the Margaret Mitchell House, as well as its tragic losses, including four majestic rail stations, major downtown department stores, grand theaters, and numerous mansions and public buildings. Atlanta's struggle to retain historic structures is constantly under pressure from new development projects. Atlantans are impressed by the next new thing, which Sharp refers to as the tension of past value compared to worshiping the future. In other words, General Sherman's legacy of demolition reigns in regard to historic structures. The unfortunate tendency is to value new construction over iconic buildings, a preference that confounds residents who value important structures and places.

Joseph G. Martin Jr. discusses how the public and private sector work together on projects where such collaborations might seem impossible. In "Public-Private Partnerships: Atlanta Style," Martin outlines the methods used to redevelop the Underground Atlanta entertainment complex, the civic center, mixed use housing at Bedford Pine, and venues for the 1996 Olympics. Atlanta is home to many public-private partnerships that highlight the organizational and management complexity of these relationships.

"Building Public Transit in Atlanta: From Streetcars to MARTA" by Harry West is the history of transit over the last two centuries. From the crossroads founded on transportation to this century's city of sprawl, the issues are explained in detail. Starting with the railroads and Joel Hurt's first streetcar, expanded by the age of the automobile and highway construction, strengthened by federal funding for MARTA, the city's transportation situation has evolved into a dream or a nightmare depending on where you live. West's intriguing first-person account of the evolution of transit is detailed and insightful.

These chapters explain how Terminus evolved into a region of over six million. We anticipate that you will come to understand how planning built this city as you enjoy these chapters.

CHAPTER 1

Learning from Atlanta

Douglas Allen

In the history of city planning, the significance of Atlanta is its insignificance. Unlike Savannah, Atlanta was not the product of a plan devised by speculative intellectuals in a West London drawing room. In contrast to the Puritan towns of New England, it was not the creation of a visionary religious community. Nor was it the result of idealistic philanthropy, as was Philadelphia. The city never had a L'Enfant, a Haussmann, or a Burnham. It was never planned as a capital city, becoming one only because of its strategic location during the American Civil War. For city planners and urban designers, however, it is arguably one of the best cities to study precisely for this reason—it never had any great plan at all. Yet with only a few rudimentary elements, it developed into the nation's ninth-largest metropolitan area and its sixth-largest urban economy. How the city grew, and the forces underlying its patterns of growth, make Atlanta the perfect case study. It is a living laboratory for understanding urban formation and the powerful resilience of a constitutional framework of streets, blocks, infrastructure, and public space as the vicissitudes of social and economic forces shaped cities in nineteenth-century America.

The focus of this essay will be how circumstantial topography combined with the initial pattern of streets, blocks, lots, and infrastructure has influenced the city over time, despite the absence of any overall plan. This pattern remains as the present governing condition of Atlanta's downtown. This pattern not only persisted to the present but shaped further patterns of growth in extraordinary ways, constraining and forming a variety of land uses into a coherent whole. An examination of each geometric circumstance and how they interacted to produce the physical structure of Atlanta is the subject of this chapter.

Topography

Atlanta sits on the southern slope of the Appalachian Piedmont. Here, during the Cambrian period, an underlayment of granitic intrusions into the metamorphic substrata folded the piedmont along a northeast strike of 25 degrees. This fold captured the Chattahoochee River and redirected its course away from the Savannah River watershed and the Atlantic Ocean into the Apalachicola and the Gulf of Mexico. The watershed of the Chattahoochee, Atlanta's only source of fresh water, is the narrowest of any major river, with its eastern limit only seven miles from the riverbed. This limit is the eastern continental divide, splitting rainfall between the Atlantic and the Gulf. This divide, Peachtree ridge, is now the alignment of Peachtree Street (Figure 1.1).

The ridgeline became a major trail, and the original path predates European or colonial settlement. Today Peachtree Street remains the oldest human artifact in Atlanta, and the ridge that it followed generated much of the formal structure of the city. Further, it generated a host of "Peachtrees," including Peachtree Way, Peachtree Circle, Peachtree Place, and West Peachtree Street, a portion of which actually lies to the east of Peachtree Street. At last count, Atlanta has 71 streets that incorporate the name Peachtree. Especially considering that peach trees are not native to North America, the plethora of Peachtrees has jokingly been called a planned attempt to confuse everyone, especially visitors. In fact, it offers a glimpse into the patchwork process of subdivision that characterizes the absence of an overall plan.

At the southern tip of the Peachtree ridge, just south of present-day Marietta Street, the land flattened out into a saddle, then re-formed into a ridge a few hundred yards to the south. A small spring erupted into the flattened area as it dipped down into the natural saddle; it would be here that three major railroads, each following high ground orthogonal to the Peachtree ridge, would intersect (Figure 1.1).

Land Lots: Creek and Cherokee Cessions

Though Georgia was a colonial enterprise, predating the formation of the United States by almost fifty years, the part of the state that Atlanta is now in was frontier as late as the 1820s. In fact, it was not even part of Georgia. The land where the future city would form belonged to a loose confederation of Creek Indian tribes. To the north and northwest, across the Chattahoochee, lay the Cherokee Nation, one of the Five Civilized Tribes, with a written language, a legislature, and a capital city at New Echota.

Creek and Cherokee land cessions in Georgia had begun as early as 1763 and continued through the eighteenth century. In 1802 colonial Geor-

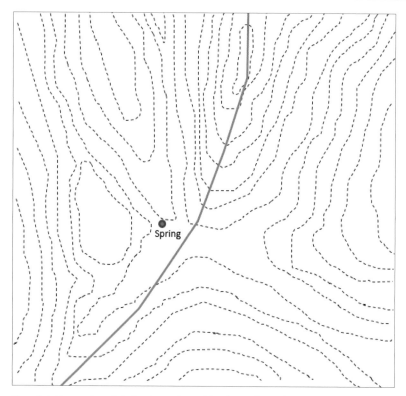

Figure 1.1. Topography with the Peachtree ridge and Peachtree Ridge Trail. (Source: Map by author.)

gia's western territory (in today's northern Alabama and northern Mississippi) was claimed by the United States. In return for Georgia ceding its claim, the federal government promised to remove the Creeks and Cherokees from Georgia soil. By 1804, with the cessions of land secured for the state, Georgia changed the colonial headright system to one it deemed fairer, where any white man with four dollars could enter a lottery for land taken or ceded from Native Americans (Coleman 1977). In 1827 land lots were surveyed over the former Creek lands extending northward to the Chattahoochee. These lots, ranging between 160 and 202.5 acres in size, were distributed via lottery and surveyed between 1827 and 1832.

Georgia, as one of the 13 original states, was exempt from the National Land Ordinance of 1785 that produced the great grid of the American Midwest and West. Under that system, square-mile sections, quartered into 160-acre squares and further subdivided into 330-foot blocks, produced both the family farms of the Midwest prairies and the urban blocks of its cities. Though Georgia's land lots developed with the land ordinance as a precedent, their size varied considerably. The core of the future Atlanta would develop in Land Lots 51, 52, 77, and 78 of the former Creek territory, each with the peculiar dimension of 202.5 acres. Each owner then subdivided these individual land lots into streets, blocks, and building lots as he or she saw fit.

Shortly after the lottery of 1827, two events signaled the end of the Cherokee Nation in Georgia. In 1828, 50 miles to the northeast of today's Atlanta in what is now White and Lumpkin Counties, gold was discovered on land that was part of the Cherokee Nation. Mining operations grew and the gold attracted speculators, increasing the pressure to claim the Cherokee lands in total. Second, the state of Georgia wanted to construct a railroad to connect the expanding settlements of the upper Midwest with the Gulf and Atlantic ports of Mobile, Charleston, and Savannah. In 1830 the Georgia legislature initiated a plan for the removal of the region's original inhabitants. It did so by simply annexing the Cherokee Nation, calling upon the U.S. government to enforce its earlier agreement.

Having no great army, and believing naively in the courts, the Cherokees filed suit against the state of Georgia. In Worcester v. Georgia in 1832, the U. S. Supreme Court ruled that the laws of Georgia were invalid in Cherokee lands. President Andrew Jackson and Vice President John C. Calhoun, who had interests in one of the gold-mining enterprises near what is now Dahlonega, refused to abide by the ruling, resulting in the removal of the Cherokee in the dark chapter of our history that became known as the Trail of Tears.

To facilitate the settlement of the Cherokee lands, the Georgia legislature extended a land lottery to cover the recently ceded territories. According to a law passed in 1838, assignment of the lots had been by a draw open to any free citizen over the age of eighteen, with the following exceptions:

> *Any fortunate drawer in any previous Land Lottery who has taken out a grant of said Land Lot; any person who mined, or caused to be mined, gold or other metal in the Cherokee Territory; any person who has taken up residence in said Cherokee Territory; or any person who is a member of or concerned with a horde of thieves known as the Pony Club.* (Georgia General Assembly 1831)

Railroads

In 1836 the legislature authorized the construction of a railroad at state expense, which would be known as the Western and Atlantic Railroad. The establishing act called for a survey to be conducted from the Tennessee River near Ross's Landing (now Chattanooga) to a practical crossing point on the Chattahoochee (Garrett 1954). From there, a route would be surveyed to connect the cities of Athens, Madison, Milledgeville, and Forsyth to the east and south. Once the point of crossing was established, a well-watered area was

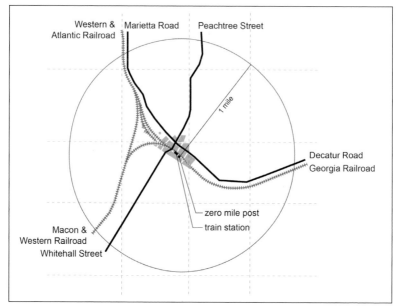

Figure 1.2. Central Atlanta, primary roads and railroad lines, 1847. (Source: Map by Elizabeth Ward and Douglas Allen.)

needed that was also flat enough to turn cars around at the intersection, with future lines to be extended from the Gulf and Atlantic ports. The plan was for three railroads— the Western and Atlantic Railroad, the Georgia Railroad, and the Macon and Western Railroad—to intersect at the terminus in the land lot identified by the survey.

On May 22, 1836, Colonel Stephen Harriman Long, formerly a topographical engineer under the command of General Andrew Jackson, crossed the small creek at Fort Peachtree on the Chattahoochee River, heading in a southeasterly direction (Johnston 1931). Commissioned by the legislature, Long and his surveying crew sought the tract of land required by the railroad. To his north, south, and east lay the recently ceded lands of the Creek Nation, vacated by cessions in 1802, 1822, 1826, and 1828. To his west across the river was the Cherokee Nation. Fort Peachtree stood at the border of the two territories. After four months, working his way southward and eastward from Fort Peachtree, Long found what he had been looking for, the flat saddle that split the central portion of the Peachtree ridge: a plain of about 20 acres fed by a small spring in Land Lot 78 of the recently platted but unsettled territory of the former Creek Nation. In November of 1836, Long filed his report with the legislature, referring to the site as "Terminus," and the future city of Atlanta was born.

Figure 1.3. Western and Atlantic roundhouse, Land Lot 78, 1864

By 1839 John Thrasher had built a home and a general store at this location, and the settlement was nicknamed Thrasherville. By 1842 the settlement at the terminus had six buildings and thirty residents (Garrett 1954). In the face of dissatisfaction with the name Terminus, a petition was sent to Governor Wilson Lumpkin to rename the settlement in honor of his daughter, Martha, and for three years the new town was known as Marthasville. By 1845 the chief engineer of the Georgia Railroad, J. Edgar Thomson, suggested that Marthasville be renamed to the feminine form of Atlantic, and in 1847 a one-mile radius was drawn from a "zero mile post" and the area was incorporated as Atlanta (Figure 1.2) (Garrett 1954).

In 1846 the Georgia Railroad, originally known as the Monroe Railroad, completed tracks to Atlanta from the east. The two railroads spurred growth and by 1850, the year of the city's first census, the population was 2,569. Wagon roads paralleled the rail lines to the northwest (presently Marietta Street) and to the east (presently Decatur Street). They intersected the Peachtree ridge in Land Lots 77 and 78 (Figure 1.3).

In 1851 a third rail line, the Macon and Western, was finally connected to the earlier two; once the three railroads were joined, the settlement began to grow rapidly. With the economic growth brought by the railroads, the city commissioned its first map in 1853. Edward Vincent, a British surveyor and architect, was given the job, along with a commission to design a rail depot. The potential importance of the junction of three rail lines was not lost on the legislature, and a part of DeKalb County was carved out and renamed Fulton County, with Atlanta as its county seat. The following year, a county court-

TABLE 1.1	City of Atlanta, Early Employment Sectors
Employment Sector	Percentage of Population
Construction-related trades	46
Railroad-related	23
Mercantile	10
Prostitutes and barkeepers	6
Medical and legal	6
All else	9
Source: Garrett 1954	

house combined with a city hall was constructed on the site of the present state capitol. In 1854 a fourth rail line, the Atlanta and LaGrange Rail Road (later Atlanta and West Point Railroad) arrived, connecting Atlanta with La-Grange, Georgia, to the southwest. This sealed Atlanta's role as a rail hub for the entire South, with lines to the northwest, east, southeast, and southwest.

Despite the images made popular by books and movies, Atlanta shared more with western cities than it did with the older cities of Charleston, Savannah, and Richmond. Its economy was driven entirely by the railroad; the city's first detailed census, in 1860, reveals much about the character of the place. From its earliest period, Atlanta was associated with transportation and construction. Almost 80 percent of the population was engaged in construction-related activities, transportation, and the mercantile functions that naturally followed (Table 1.1).

By the outbreak of the Civil War, Atlanta had grown to a total population of 7,741 (Garrett 1954). The nature of the city as a transportation hub made it of vital importance; Atlanta would become one of the chief military supply centers for the South, which made it a major target of federal military strategy. After a two-month march against heavy opposition, General William Tecumseh Sherman arrived on the outskirts of Atlanta in early July of 1864. Camped to the north and west, he encircled the city and a prolonged siege ensued. The strategy was to outflank the entrenched defenses and cut rail lines to the east and south, the Western and Atlantic line having already been rendered useless. Realizing the importance of Atlanta's transportation network, Georgia Governor Joseph E. Brown had written to Confederate President Jefferson Davis that "this place is to the Confederacy as the heart is to the body" (Foote 1974, 411). Sherman's strategy had been to hold positions on the east, north, and west and to forego a direct assault on the city in favor of seizing the rail lines to the south. If all three main lines could be severed, the city had no choice but to surrender, though his intent was, in his own words, to "destroy Atlanta and make it a desolation." Sherman's flanking strategy worked, and on September 2,

1864, the city found itself isolated (Foote 1974). Sherman, now fifteen miles to the south of the city, heard a series of enormous explosions at 4:00 a.m. in the early morning following the surrender. General Hood, the commanding general of the Confederate army in charge of the defense of the city, had blown up 82 carloads of ammunition and five locomotives when he realized that the city was lost (Foote 1974). The ensuing fire destroyed virtually everything and became part of the city's identity and mythology, though General Sherman had little to do with it. The official seal of the city would be changed from a locomotive engine to a phoenix, the mythological bird that obtains new life by rising from the ashes of its predecessor.

Urban Form

As the Vincent Map of 1853 (Figure 1.4) shows, the form of the city was derived entirely from the circumstantial collision of square land lots, Peachtree ridge, Peachtree Street, the flat topographic saddle used to form both the intersection

Figure 1.4. Vincent's subdivision map of the city of Atlanta, DeKalb County, Georgia, 1853

and the terminus of the three main rail lines, and the rail lines themselves radiating east, south, and northwest from the terminus. In the absence of prior streets or a governing plan, the only connection to the rest of the world was through the rail lines that followed topographic high ground and the wagon roads that traveled along the Peachtree ridge to the north and south and paralleled the railroads to the east and west. Each land lot owner was free to subdivide the land as he or she saw fit, and although a tacit convention was reached concerning orthogonal geometry and rectangular blocks, each owner used a different street width and block size. Streets and blocks adjacent to a rail line ran orthogonal to the railroad. Those on the edges of the three land lots that contained rail lines ran orthogonal to Peachtree Street.

Land Lot 78

Of the four land lots, number 78 was the most significant. The original owner, Jane Doss, sold it to Matthew Henry of Gwinnett County for fifty dollars. Henry held onto it for twelve years and then sold it to Reuben Cone for $300 dollars (Garrett 1954). This land lot was bounded by Peachtree Street on the northeast and would later contain the railroad terminus, the spring, and the small early settlement known as Thrasherville (Garrett 1954, 165). The irregular geometries of both its boundaries and the elements it contained would lead Cone to use a 200-by-200-foot block in his land lot. This small block grid, rotated almost 45 degrees from north, was driven by the angle that the Marietta Road created as it paralleled the Western and Atlantic Railroad to the northwest. Peachtree Street sliced through the southwestern corner of the land lot, and the alignment of Marietta Street followed the Western and Atlantic line to the northwest. Today this area of Downtown Atlanta is known as the Fairlie-Poplar Historic District; the land lot contains the Georgia World Congress Center, Atlanta Merchandise Mart, Phillips Arena, CNN Center, Woodruff Park, and Centennial Olympic Park. The irregularly shaped triangular lots that take up the rotation of the grid at Peachtree Street as a seam with Land Lot 51 would later be occupied by Woodruff Park.

Land Lot 77

In 1842 Samuel Mitchell donated five acres of Land Lot 77 to the state for the railroad right-of-way (Cagle 1991). This tract, known as "State Square," became the site of the depot designed by Edward Vincent, and the official terminus point was moved to its eastern edge (Figure 1.5). Earlier, Samuel Mitchell, Frederick Arms, and former governor Wilson Lumpkin subdivided Land Lot 77 into 17 blocks, 400 feet by 400 feet, with streets aligned orthogonal to the eastern rail line. This created a second orientation within the original four land lots. Land Lot 77 would contain the original depot and market, and would later hold the present state capitol, the Fulton County Courthouse and Administration

Figure 1.5. State Square, Land Lot 77, 1864

Building, and Atlanta's City Hall. The intersection of Peachtree Street and the wagon roads to Marietta and Decatur would become known as Five Points and would function as the center of the downtown commercial city until the interstate highways reordered commercial functions.

Land Lot 52
Along the eastern boundary of Land Lot 77, the streets continued the block pattern into Land Lot 52. As the eastern rail line curved to the north, however, the street pattern rotated with the curve, creating trapezoidal blocks. In 1844 Land Lot 52 was purchased by L.P. Grant. A civil engineer and surveyor, Grant would donate a substantial suburban tract to the south of the city in 1881 as its first park and planned suburb. In the mid-1960s, the construction of Interstates 75 and 85 cut through this rotated section and erased the block geometries present at the initial subdivision. Today Georgia State University occupies most of the remainder the land lot.

Land Lot 51
Along the northern edge of Land Lot 52, the streets rotated again to meet those in Land Lot 51. The owner, Hardy Ivy, had acquired the land lot from the origi-

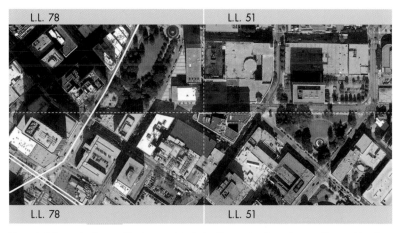

Figure 1.6 Present land uses with relation to historic land lots, railroads, and streets. (Source: Map from Google Earth; analysis by Douglas Allen.)

nal owner, James Paden, for $225 in 1833. Considered by many to be the first settler in what would later become Atlanta, Ivy originally constructed only his own home. As the city grew northward along the Peachtree ridge, however, he soon subdivided Land Lot 51 into streets and blocks. Following his own logic, and perhaps because other land lots had been subdivided, Ivy seemed obligated to the north-south alignment of Peachtree Street, as no rail line was tangent to any point within boundaries of the land lot. This meant that the streets running north from Land Lot 52 had to rotate approximately 45 degrees along the seam, creating triangular parcels at its northern edge. Ivy's blocks were also not square but rectangular. The blocks varied in size as they expanded or contracted in their north-south alignment to connect to the rotated grids of Cone's Land Lot 78. The first row of blocks was set at 500 feet east-to-west and 525 feet north-to-south, with three 175-foot parcels facing the streets aligned north-south. In the second row the block dimension was compressed to 400 feet in the north-south orientation, while the full 525 feet was maintained east to west. In 1880 the developer of Atlanta's second planned suburb, Joel Hurt, would insert Edgewood Avenue along the seam between Land Lots 51 and 52. The 45-degree rotation remains today (Figure 1.6).

Land Lot 51 would later contain some of the most heterogeneous land uses in the city. To the north, John Portman would construct Peachtree Center, the mixed use development, between 1959 and 1990, while on the south the famous Auburn Avenue (Wheat Street on the Vincent Map of 1853) would extend eastward into what would later become the Old Fourth Ward. This street would see the birth of the Southern Christian Leadership Conference (SCLC), as well as the breakout of rhythm and blues into mainstream white America. This major African American business district from the late 1870s to the abolition of Jim Crow in the early 1960s is now the national landmark, the Sweet Auburn Historic District. On Saturday night in 1953, Ray Charles among others would change the face of American music at the Royal Peacock nightclub at 186 Auburn Avenue. Then, on the following Sunday, down the street at 407 Auburn Avenue, Martin Luther King Jr. would begin to change the face of social justice from the pulpit of Ebenezer Baptist Church.

As the city grew, the presence of the railroad dividing north from south made crossing difficult. In 1854 a wooden viaduct was constructed across the tracks, connecting Alabama Street on the south to Marietta Street on the north. This would remain the only connection across the tracks until 1899, when the viaduct connecting Peachtree Street to Whitehall Street (now South Peachtree) was constructed (Garrett 1954). Between 1900 and 1920, additional viaducts would span the tracks and by 1950, the eastbound tracks were covered completely. This area became known as Underground Atlanta despite the fact that it was never actually underground. This bifurcation of the city by railroads into a northern portion in Land Lots 51 and 78 seems to have affected the movement of wealth as well. Wealthy residential areas clustered to the north along the Peachtree ridge as early as the 1870s (Preston 1979). The area immediately south of the railroad in Land Lots 77 and 52 contained most of the state and local government functions. The residential areas immediately adjacent to Land Lots 77 and 52 to the south, east, and west ranged from working class to poor. This pattern continued well into the twentieth century and at a macro level continues today.

Conclusion

These rudimentary elements combined to form a patchwork of squares and streets with anomalies at the edges where the land lots joined. In this way, the core of the city had six distinct geometric conditions. The Peachtree ridge ran due north and south at its high point between Land Lots 78 and 51, then departed from true north as it moved south through Land Lot 78 at an angle of approximately 28 degrees. The land lots were abstractly placed as political lines, subdividing undifferentiated territory into 202.5-acre squares running north-south and east-west. The geometry of the railroads followed their own logic: a combination of high ground for drainage and flat land for intersection.

This collision between topographic circumstance, the arc and tangent geometries of railroad construction, and the political overlay of land lots ordered by the Georgia legislature as a tool of occupation, resulted in a remarkably resilient pattern. The subdivision of the land lots in the absence of rules or regulations resulted in an amalgam of rotated blocks of varying sizes and streets of varying widths. The extent to which any of the streets within each land lot actually connected, or aligned with others, appears to be governed only by a pragmatic necessity to be a part of some larger whole. The result was a city that, while neither physically beautiful nor socially just, contained within its constituent parts a latent potential for civic virtue.

Stephen Harriman Long, shortly after surveying the initial rail lines from which the city would develop, was offered a land lot for the princely sum of $100. In a letter refusing the offer, he stated that "the Terminus will be a good location for one tavern, a blacksmith shop, a grocery store and nothing else" (Shingleton 1985, 12). In a similar way, it is impossible to think that Hardy Ivy, owner of Land Lot 51, could ever have imagined a world where John Portman's Peachtree Center or the Royal Peacock Club would occupy any of the simple blocks laid out shortly after 1836. Nor could he have imagined that the street he designated as Wheat Street would one day be home to the headquarters of the SCLC or Ebenezer Baptist Church. Nor could Reuben Cone have possibly foreseen that in Land Lot 78, John Pemberton would open a drugstore in 1886 serving a carbonated elixir called Coca-Cola. Nor could he have known that the interstitial and leftover spaces of his rotated grids would one day contain Centennial Olympic Park, Woodruff Park, or the global headquarters of CNN.

Atlanta contains lessons, and they are clear. The simple subdivision of land lots into streets and blocks varying between 200 and 525 feet, with resulting geometric anomalies, formed scaffolding that could accommodate enormous changes in land use over time. The leftover areas produced by the circumstantial rotation of streets and blocks, to meet up with topographic features such as the Peachtree ridge or the railroad alignments, were later filled in with parks and public spaces. Collectively, this arrangement projected a public frame prior to occupation or use, whose stability allowed land uses to fluctuate according to the vicissitudes of social and economic change in land use, while assuring continuity between past and future. Each successive generation, subject to its own circumstances and needs, its sense of justice and economic benefit, conditioned by the simplest of urban constitutional and infrastructural elements, was able to write its own story into a place as a coherent whole. In so doing, they built a good city. Imagine if a Burnham or a L'Enfant had been involved.

CHAPTER 2

Changing Demographics and Unprecedented Growth

Ellen Heath, FAICP, and John Heath, AICP

For many of the millions of newcomers to the Atlanta region in the 1970s through the 1990s, the electronic, changing "Atlanta Population Now" sign at the Darlington Apartments on Peachtree Street was a symbol of the dynamism and excitement that brought them to the new capital of the South. The definition of "Atlanta" was not clear, and people wondered how they could keep track of who was really moving here and how many babies were being born. The truth apparently is a bit more prosaic: the owners of the sign looked at population projections for the region and set the counter to automatically increase at a fixed rate in accordance with the projections (Freaney 1997). Nonetheless, the sign was an affirmation that this was a great place to be and that big things were in store for Atlanta.

City of Atlanta

Often recognized as the commercial and cultural center of the American South, the city of Atlanta is, in absolute terms, not a large city, with approximately 133 square miles and a 2010 population of about 420,000. The city is a major transportation hub, with extensive rail and road networks, and it is the site of the world's busiest airport, Hartsfield-Jackson Atlanta International Airport (Airports Council International 2012).

The 1996 Centennial Olympic Games in Atlanta served as a catalyst for many planned improvements that has encouraged the redevelopment of many in-town neighborhoods and the in-migration of younger professionals from the suburbs. The concentration of colleges and universities also attracts young people, many of whom stay as young professionals. The Georgia

Institute of Technology, Georgia State University, Emory University, Atlanta University Center (including Morehouse and Spelman Colleges), and other institutions of higher learning play a large role in attracting new residents and businesses to the city.

Atlanta Metropolitan Area

The Atlanta metropolitan area encompasses 20 northern Georgia counties and includes development patterns that range from very urban to very rural. The metro area has a land area of approximately 6,100 square miles with a 2010 population of nearly 5,260,000. Fulton County, in which the majority of the city of Atlanta is located, had a 2010 population slightly greater than 900,000. The next largest counties are the inner-ring suburbs of Gwinnett, Cobb, and DeKalb, with 2010 populations of 805,000, 690,000, and 688,000, respectively. The remaining counties that make up the metro area had populations that ranged from 260,000 persons (Clayton County) to 64,000 (Spalding County). The Atlanta metropolitan area was the ninth-largest metropolitan statistical area (MSA) in the United States in 2010. (All population figures are from the U.S. Census Bureau's "DP-1: Profile of General Population and Housing Characteristics" tabulations.)

Other significant cities in the region include Decatur and Dunwoody (DeKalb County), Marietta (Cobb County), Sandy Springs and Roswell (Fulton County) and Lawrenceville (Gwinnett County). Decatur, Marietta and Roswell all date back to the mid-nineteenth century and have distinct identities separate from Atlanta and the Atlanta suburbs. Characterized by historical, charming downtowns, these cities are regional commercial centers that functioned mostly independently of Atlanta, only becoming suburbs in the second half of the twentieth century as metro Atlanta's population spread to their borders and beyond.

Atlanta's Role in the Region

Atlanta's total population of approximately 420,000 represents only eight percent of the metropolitan statistical area total (Table 2.1). This is one of the lowest central city to metro population ratios in the United States and reflects explosive growth in the suburbs since the 1980s, while the city's population was shrinking and then stabilizing. Of the 20 largest MSAs in the country, only two—Miami-Ft. Lauderdale-Pompano Beach and Riverside-San Bernardino-Ontario—have smaller central cities. (Notably, both of these metro areas have two major urban centers, Miami/Fort Lauderdale and Riverside/San Bernardino, while Atlanta is the sole traditional central city in the Atlanta-Sandy Springs-Marietta MSA.)

As noted by historians Darlene Roth and Andy Ambrose, the trend of suburban growth in Atlanta has been underway since the middle of the last century, the result of the relocation of employment centers and the expansion of the regional highway system (Roth and Ambrose 1996).

TABLE 2.1.	Largest Metropolitan Areas in the U.S. and Central City Populations, 2010			
Rank	Metropolitan Statistical Area	2010 Census	Central City	Percent of MSA
1	New York–Northern New Jersey–Long Island, NY–NJ–PA	18,897,109	8,175,133	43.3
2	Los Angeles–Long Beach–Santa Ana, CA	12,828,837	3,792,621	29.6
3	Chicago–Joliet–Naperville, IL–IN–WI	9,461,105	2,695,128	28.5
4	Dallas–Fort Worth–Arlington, TX	6,371,773	1,197,816	18.8
5	Philadelphia–Camden–Wilmington, PA–NJ–DE–MD	5,965,343	1,526,006	25.6
6	Houston–Sugar Land–Baytown, TX	5,728,143	2,099,451	36.7
7	Miami–Fort Lauderdale–Pompano Beach, FL	5,564,635	399,457	7.2
8	Atlanta–Sandy Springs–Marietta, GA	5,268,860	420,003	8.0
9	Washington–Arlington–Alexandria, DC–VA–MD–WV	5,582,170	601,723	10.8
10	Boston–Cambridge–Quincy, MA–NH	4,522,858	617,594	13.7
11	Detroit–Warren–Livonia, MI	4,296,250	713,777	16.6
12	Phoenix–Mesa–Glendale, AZ	4,281,899	1,455,632	34.0
13	San Francisco–Oakland–Fremont, CA	4,335,391	805,235	18.6
14	Riverside–San Bernardino–Ontario, CA	4,115,871	303,871	7.4
15	Seattle–Tacoma–Bellevue, WA	3,439,809	608,660	17.7
16	Minneapolis–St. Paul–Bloomington, MN–WI	3,279,833	382,578	11.7
17	San Diego–Carlsbad–San Marcos, CA	3,095,313	1,307,402	42.2
18	St. Louis, MO–IL	2,812,896	319,294	11.4
19	Tampa–St. Petersburg–Clearwater, FL	2,783,243	335,709	12.1
20	Baltimore–Towson, MD	2,710,489	620,964	22.9

Source: Data from U.S. Census Bureau 2010

City of Atlanta Demographics

Founded in 1847 as Terminus, the end point of three railroad lines, Atlanta quickly grew, increasing by 271 percent in the 1850s and 128 percent in the 1860s. The city continued to grow steadily until 1950, when the total population was 331,314 (Atlanta 2011). In 1952 the city annexed portions of Fulton and DeKalb Counties, nearly tripling the size of the city from

TABLE 2.2	Population Change, City of Atlanta, 1850–2010		
Year	Population	Population Change	Percent Change
1850	2,572		
1860	9,554	6,982	271
1870	21,789	12,235	128
1880	37,409	15,620	72
1890	65,533	28,124	75
1900	89,872	24,339	37
1910	154,839	64,967	72
1920	200,616	45,777	30
1930	270,366	69,750	35
1940	302,288	31,922	12
1950	331,314	29,026	10
1960	487,455	156,141	47
1970	496,973	9,518	2
1980	425,022	(71,951)	-14
1990	394,017	(31,005)	-7
2000	416,474	22,457	6
2010	420,003	3,529	1

Source: Data from U.S. Census Bureau 2010

37 to 118 square miles and bringing the total population to 428,299 (Roth and Ambrose 1996). The city's population peaked in 1970 at 496,973 and declined by more than 100,000 people (more than 20 percent) between 1970 and 1990; during the same period, the population of the Atlanta region grew by more than a million people, or more than 70 percent (Roth and Ambrose 1996; Atlanta Regional Commission 2011b). Since 1990 the overall population has stabilized, growing by just over one percent during 1990 to 2010. Table 2.2 shows a summary of Atlanta's decennial census numbers from 1850 to 2010. The general population numbers only tell part of the story, however, as the characteristics of Atlantans have changed while their numbers have remained steady.

Race
In the early and mid-twentieth century, the racial composition of Atlanta remained relatively stable. From 1900 to 1960, African Americans comprised between 30 and 40 percent of the city's total population, and whites made up 60 to 69 percent. Atlanta has always attracted African Americans and other non-whites be-

cause of educational and employment opportunities. However, until the 1970s, housing options for African Americans and other non-white residents were limited because costs, restrictive zoning practices, and the unwillingness of realtors to sell to African Americans. The consequence of these actions was that African American populations tended to concentrate in poorer, less desirable locations. Following World War II, Atlanta experienced a housing shortage. This was especially true within the African American community, which in 1946 made up a third of the city's population but were restricted by residential segregation to only 10 percent of the city's developed land. In 1952, recognizing the need to increase housing opportunities for minorities, the Metropolitan Planning Commission proposed a plan that identified new areas for the expansion of African American homes. Additionally, agreements were reached among the real estate community, city government, and various civic organizations that would allow for the selling of homes to African Americans in traditional white neighborhoods. Under this agreement, nearly 800 homes in the Mozley Park neighborhood and nearly 300 units in Collier Heights were sold in 1953 and 1954.

By the 1960s these formal agreements disappeared and many neighborhoods in the southern and western parts of Atlanta changed from all white to all black. In the 20 years between 1950 and 1970, the number of Atlanta census tracts in which African Americans constituted at least 90 percent of the population more than tripled and many traditionally white neighborhoods became almost entirely African American (Harmon 1996). As opportunities for black families increased, many middle-class white families migrated to areas on the edge of the city or to nearby suburbs. Highway construction made it easier to live on the periphery of the city or in the suburbs and work in the central city. This "white flight" resulted in a 20 percent decline in the proportion of whites in the city's population between 1960 and 1970 (Gibson and Jung 2005).

Improving economic conditions within the African American community, tied to increased access to municipal employment and private sector jobs, provided new housing opportunities. For middle-class African Americans, traditionally white single-family neighborhoods such as Kirkwood or Mozley Park were good choices. Unfortunately, for the inner-city poor, the options continued to be substandard public or private housing with unhealthy living conditions and high crime rates (Harmon 1996).

During this period, the city's urban renewal program also had a significant impact on the urban poor by destroying substandard but affordable housing and causing the relocation of nearly 5,000 families to either public housing or other low-income areas. Increasingly the urban poor, who were predominantly African American, were concentrated in public housing communities on Atlanta's west side (a 1968 report by the Atlanta Housing Authority indicated that 83 percent of all public housing units were located on the west side of Atlanta) (Harmon 1996).

TABLE 2.3.	Historical Racial Characteristics, City of Atlanta, 1850-2010	
Year	Total Population White	Total Population Black/African American
1850	80.1	19.9
1860	79.7	20.3
1870	54.4	45.6
1880	56.3	43.7
1890	57.1	42.9
1900	60.2	39.8
1910	66.4	33.5
1920	68.7	31.3
1930	66.7	33.3
1940	65.4	34.6
1950	63.4	36.6
1960	61.7	38.3
1970	48.4	51.4
1980	32.4	66.6
1990	31.0	67.1
2000	33.2	61.4
2010	38.4	54.0

Source: Data from Gibson and Jung 2005; U.S. Census Bureau 2013

By 1970, 51.4 percent of Atlantans were African American. Atlanta's first African American mayor, Maynard Jackson, was elected in 1973. For the next 20 years, the proportion of African Americans in the city continued to increase, peaking at 67.1 percent in 1990. This trend reversed after 1990. The 2000 census revealed that the percentages of African Americans and whites were 61.4 and 33.2, respectively. The trend of the percentage of blacks decreasing and whites increasing continued after 2000: the 2010 Census shows that 54 percent of Atlantans were African American and 38.4 percent were white. (Hispanics made up slightly more than 5 percent of Atlanta's population in the year 2010.) Table 2.3 illustrates the racial characteristics of Atlanta's population since 1900 (Gibson and Jung 2005).

Why is Atlanta's white population now increasing while the African American population is shrinking? Several events may explain the dynamic. Atlanta benefited greatly from the announcement of the 1990 International Olympic Committee decision to stage the 1996 Olympic Games in Atlanta.

The impending games, along with the general national economic boom of the mid-1990s, attracted many new people of all races to Atlanta, and mostly white neighborhoods such as Buckhead and Midtown (and most areas in-between) experienced an influx of jobs and new housing. Intown neighborhoods, characterized by streetcar suburbs such as Inman Park, Virginia-Highland, Brookwood Hills, Garden Hills, and many others, continued to revive and densify. An analysis conducted by the City of Atlanta's Department of Planning and Development indicated that the total population of the Buckhead area increased by nearly 19,000 between 2000 and 2010, with the Midtown area's population increasing by more than 14,000 during this same period (Atlanta 2011b).

While northside Atlanta neighborhoods were redeveloping and densifying, the city's public housing projects in the south and west were also undergoing a major transformation. In the early 1990s, almost 10 percent of Atlantans lived in more than 40 public housing projects, owned by the Atlanta Housing Authority (AHA) (Newman 2002; Atlanta Housing Authority 2010). The vast majority of these residents were African American. In 1994, responding to the attention that would be on the city of Atlanta in 1996, and that would reveal the poor physical and social conditions in Atlanta's large housing projects, AHA embarked on an ambitious program to redevelop more than a dozen large sites. The earliest redevelopment efforts, Techwood Homes (adjacent to the Olympic Village at Georgia Tech) and Eastlake Meadows (near the historic Bobby Jones-designed golf course in East Atlanta), became the model for the national Hope VI Program and subsequent efforts to redevelop outdated single-income public housing projects into modern, mixed income communities (Atlanta Housing Authority 2010). While many original residents of Techwood Homes, Eastlake Meadows, and the other redeveloped communities returned to public housing in Atlanta, or other housing in Atlanta, others chose to leave the city. For example, in the first wave of redevelopment, 1,442 units of mixed income apartments in Centennial Place (the former Techwood/Clark Howell Homes) and the Villages of East Lake (former Eastlake Meadows) replaced 1,845 units of public housing. Only 56 percent of the new units were set aside for low-income families. These three projects – which were just the beginning of AHA's ambitious redevelopment program – resulted in the net loss of more than 1,000 public housing units. Many residents moved out before the demolition of the units occurred and their subsequent whereabouts were not traced (Newman 2002).

The redevelopment of and reduction in the number of public housing units, which tend to have relatively large household sizes, combined with the influx of young professionals, resulted in a different population in Atlanta. The average household size decreased slightly from 2.30 to 2.29 persons between 2000 and 2010, and the percentage of nonfamily households increased from 51 percent to 56 percent of all households. In 2010, of these nonfamily households, 76 percent were headed by non-elderly persons living alone (U.S. Census Bureau 2000, 2010).

Income

In 2000 median household income in Atlanta was $34,770, which was 82.8 percent of the national median income of $41,994 (U.S. Census Bureau 2000). Over the next 10 years, the household incomes of Atlantans remained higher than the nation as a whole but increasingly less so. The 2011 median household income in Atlanta was $43,903, or 86.9 percent of the median national income of $50,502. (These numbers not adjusted for inflation.) The greatest increases in income were recorded in the northern portion of the city, with modest increases seen in other areas.[1]

On the other hand, the number of families in poverty increased slightly between 2000 and 2010, rising from 21.3 percent in 2000 to 22.4 percent in 2010. Nearly half of these families in 2010 were headed by females, with dependent children present in 60 percent of the households in poverty.

Metropolitan Atlanta Demographics

Without a large body of water or mountain range nearby, the Atlanta metropolitan area has no physical barriers to growth. Accordingly, the urbanized area has continued to grow in all directions, as once-rural counties have become urbanized or suburbanized and fully integrated into Atlanta's economic orbit. As a result, the official definition of metropolitan Atlanta has changed dramatically over the years. Figures 2.1 and 2.2 illustrate the growth since 1950 of the Atlanta MSA as defined by the U.S. Census Bureau.

As the urbanized area has grown so, of course, has the population. Table 2.4 shows the growth since 1970 in the 10-county region of the Atlanta Regional Commission (ARC).[2] As illustrated by the table, the growth has been continuous, with the 1980s and 1990s seeing the largest growth. During the 1970s, when Atlanta was experiencing population decline, the 10-county region almost doubled in population. During the 1980s, 86 percent of the metropolitan area's population growth came from the suburbs, especially in Cobb and Gwinnett Counties. In the 1980s, these two counties were in the top 10 fastest growing in the country and by 1999 both counties had populations greater than the city of Atlanta (Kruse 2005).

The economic strength of the suburbs was also growing in relation to the city of Atlanta. For example, between 1963 and 1972, Atlanta's share of metropolitan retail sales declined from approximately 66 percent to 44 percent, with sales in the central business district (CBD) declining to just 7 percent. Jobs in the CBD followed a similar pattern, falling from 20 percent to 12 percent of total metropolitan employment between 1960 and 1975 (Kruse 2005). Most recently, between the years 2000 and 2010, the Atlanta MSA's population increased from approximately 4.2 million to 5.3 million, a 24.4 percent increase. Gwinnett County, located northeast of the city of Atlanta, had the greatest absolute increase in population, adding 217,000 new residents, a 37 percent increase since 2000. However, population growth occurred north, south, east, and west

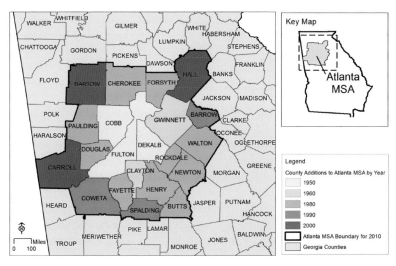

Figure 2.1. Atlanta metropolitan statistical area counties by year of addition, 1950–2010. (Source: Map by Atlanta Regional Commission and AECOM.)

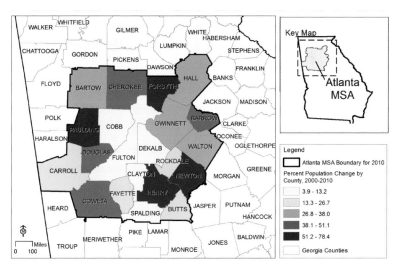

Figure 2.2. Atlanta regional population change by county, 2000-2010. (Source: Data from U.S. Census Bureau; analysis by authors; map by AECOM.)

TABLE 2.4.	Atlanta Regional Population Change, 1970-2010					
Year	1970	1980	1990	2000	2010	Total Change 1970-2010
Population	1,500,823	1,896,182	2,557,800	3,429,379	4,107,750	2,606,927
Percent change		26	35	34	20	174

Source: Atlanta Regional Commission 2012a

of the central city. Forsyth County, north of Atlanta, had the greatest percentage increase, from 98,407 to 175,511, a 78.4 percent in population. Close behind was Paulding County, west of the city, which increased from 81,678 to 142,324, a 74.3 percent increase. Other rapidly growing exurban counties included Henry to the south of Atlanta (71 percent population increase), Newton to the east (61 percent increase), Cherokee in the northwest (now more traditionally suburban than exurban) (51 percent increase), and Barrow also in the northwest (50 percent increase).

In 2000 whites made up 60 percent of the metro area's population, African Americans made up 28 percent, and Hispanics (any race) made up 7 percent. By 2010 the population mix had changed, with the percentage of the population white decreasing to 57 percent) and the percentages of the population made up of African Americans and Hispanics increasing to 34 percent and 10 percent, respectively. The increase in the percentage of Hispanics was especially significant in Gwinnett County and is discussed in greater detail later in this chapter.

The face—and sound—of metro Atlanta is changing in other ways as well. Many new Atlantans are arriving from other countries. In 2000, 86.7 percent of metro Atlantans spoke only English. In 2010 there was a small drop in the percentage of English-only speakers to 82.6 percent of the total population. Approximately 9.5 percent of metro Atlantans spoke Spanish. No other single language accounted for more than one percent of non-English languages spoken by metro Atlantans, but other languages represented included (in order of magnitude) Hindi, Urdu, and other Indic languages; Ibo, Yoruba, and other African languages; Korean; Vietnamese; Chinese; and French. By 2012 approximately 13.1 percent of the region's population was foreign-born (U.S. Census Bureau 2000; 2010; 2012).

Median household incomes of metro Atlantans are generally higher than those in the city of Atlanta; in 2000, the metro median household income was $51,948, significantly higher than the national median income of $41,994. By 2010, the metro Atlanta income was $53,182, which was still higher than the U.S. median income of $50,046 but less so than in 2000 (U.S. Census Bureau 2000, 2010, 2012).

The metro area certainly did not escape the effects of the Great Recession, and metro Atlantans have been faced with an unfamiliar economic reality. Between 1990 and 2000, the ARC 10-county region added 87,158 people every year. In the next decade, the growth decreased to an annual average of 67,837, no doubt due to smaller-than-average numbers at the end of the 2000–2010 decade. Between 2010 and 2012, the average annual growth slowed further to 35,875. In the 1990s, jobs grew at four or five percent per year; in 2008 and 2009, the region lost 2.9 percent and 5.3 percent of its jobs, respectively. Most of the lost jobs were in finance, government, and construction. Employment has rebounded slightly, with an average growth of 1.3 percent annually in 2010-2012, but the gains have yet to compensate for earlier losses (Skinner 2013).

Gwinnett County: A Case Study in Change

Perhaps no area in the metro Atlanta region tells the story of the region's change over the years more than Gwinnett County. While each county in the metro area has its own story, Gwinnett exemplifies the trajectory of growth and change in most suburban counties. Before the interstate highway system was built, Gwinnett was a rural, agricultural community with few economic ties to the rest of the region. As suburban Atlanta began to grow, Gwinnett's easy access to and from Atlanta, low land costs, and reputation for good schools resulted in a population explosion, and the county became the stereotypical white bedroom community. One of the authors attended a planning public hearing in the late 1980s, when the character of the community was changing rapidly, and many long-time Gwinnett residents were profiting from the sale of agricultural and forest lands while lamenting the changes in their rural lifestyles and pastoral character of the county. Newcomers, too, lured by inexpensive housing and uncongested roads, didn't necessarily welcome their newer neighbors. At the public hearing, one woman rose to bemoan the changing landscape: "When I moved here from the Northeast *two years ago*, Gwinnett was really nice. Now you've let all these other people in, and traffic is horrible and everything is ruined!"

Today, the same attributes that attracted white residents in the late twentieth century have attracted a more diverse population, and the county is the new face of metro Atlanta. According to a recent diversity study, Gwinnett's diversity index of 76.2 percent placed it in the top two percent of all counties in the nation; this means that two randomly chosen people in Gwinnett County would be from different racial or ethnic backgrounds 76 percent of the time (Abdullahi 2013; Schuder 2013).

Overall population growth in Gwinnett County has been explosive since the 1970s. Table 2.5 illustrates the growth of the county's population during this time period. As described in the county's 2030 Unified Plan, Gwinnett's population

TABLE 2.5.	Population Growth, Gwinnett County, Georgia, 1970-2010					
Year	1970	1980	1990	2000	2010	Total Change 1970-2010
Population	72,349	166,808	356,500	588,448	805,321	732,972
Percent change		131	114	65	37	1013

Source: Atlanta Regional Commission 2012a

has changed significantly since 1990. Between 1990 and 2000, the number of non-white residents increased at 10 times the rate of the white population, with non-white residents accounting for 27 percent of the total population in 2000, compared to 11 percent in 1990 (Gwinnett County 2009). By 2010, fully 46.7 percent of "Gwinnetians" were non-white (U.S. Census Bureau 2010). The growth of Gwinnett's Hispanic population is emblematic of the diversity trend in the county's population. Since 1980, the Hispanic population has exploded from .08 percent of the total to over 20 percent (Table 2.6). Similarly, the percentage of Gwinnett's population that is Asian has also increased dramatically. In 2010, 10.6 percent of the county's population was Asian, up from 7.2 percent in 2000 (U.S. Census Bureau 2000, 2010). In 2012, 24.7 percent of Gwinnett's population was foreign-born, compared to 13.1 percent foreign-born in the MSA (U.S. Census Bureau 2012).

Unfortunately, as the county's population has diversified, economic prosperity has waned a bit. In 2000, the county's median household income was $60,537, approximately 20 percent higher than the metro Atlanta median household income, and roughly 50 percent higher than the national median income. By 2010, the county's median income had actually decreased in non-inflation adjusted dollars to $57,548, still higher than but much closer to the median income for metropolitan Atlanta ($53,182) and the U.S. ($50,046) (U.S. Census Bureau 2000, 2011, 2012).

Conclusion

This chapter gives a general picture of Atlanta and the Atlanta metropolitan area covering key demographic indicators, primarily for the years 2000 and 2010. The picture that emerges is a central city experiencing slower growth in comparison to most of the counties in the metro area. Numbers, however, do not tell the complete story. With more than 70 combined years of living in the city, the authors have seen remarkable changes. In the 1970s, we saw Atlanta as an up-and-coming regional hub, but with the personality of a smallish southern town (and very traditionally southern white-and-black, despite being heralded as "the next great international city" by its most enthusiastic boosters). During the next decades numerous trends and activities—changes in political leadership,

TABLE 2.6.	Hispanic Population Growth, Gwinnett County, Georgia, 1980-2010			
Year	1980	1990	2000	2010
Hispanic population	1,426	8,470	61,439	162,035
Percent Hispanic	0.8	2.4	10.9	20.1

Source: Data from Gwinnett County 2009; U.S. Census Bureau 2010

a visionary development community, the continued growth of a large African American middle class, a commitment by city government and a group of "urban pioneers" to revitalize the many intown neighborhoods, and a welcoming attitude toward members of the gay community—have resulted in a city in which good restaurants abound, cultural opportunities are varied and abundant, young people are attracted from the suburbs and elsewhere to enjoy intown living, and the pace of life is brisk yet still retains its southern personality. Forecasts of future growth suggest that in the foreseeable future the population of the city may grow by more than 200,000 residents and that the population will continue to diversify in terms of age, education, and ethnicity (Atlanta 2011). For the metro area, ARC forecasts that the 20-county region's population will increase to more than eight million by 2040, with Gwinnett leading the region by adding almost 413,000 people. ARC notes that the expected population growth will resemble the growth in the region between 1980 and 2010 in terms of numbers, but that the characteristics of the new population will be different, older, and more diverse (Atlanta Regional Commission 2011b).

CHAPTER 3

The Historic District Development Corporation and the Challenge of Urban Revitalization

Mtamanika Youngblood

The Martin Luther King Jr. (MLK Jr.) Historic District is the historic heart of the Old Fourth Ward, once a prominent, prosperous Atlanta community. The Old Fourth Ward and the MLK Jr. Historic District—bounded by Courtland Street at the edge of Downtown on the west, the railroad tracks that separate the neighborhood from Inman Park on the east, Decatur Street on the south, and North Avenue on the north—encompassed a population that was mainly African American and economically diverse. Large homes built by successful professionals stood alongside more modest working-class bungalows and traditional shotgun houses. Manufacturing companies such as Scripto and the John Harland Company provided accessible, well-paid employment. A strong network of religious institutions such as Ebenezer Baptist Church, Big Bethel AME Church, and Wheat Street Baptist Church, as well as educational and social institutions, provided a vibrant cultural milieu. The confidence and dynamism of the area was symbolized in the nickname given to its nationally known business district, "Sweet Auburn."

Beginning in the 1960s, Sweet Auburn and the Old Fourth Ward experienced sudden and prolonged decline. Desegregation created new housing opportunities on the west side of Atlanta, which many middle-class African Americans found appealing. They relocated in large numbers, leaving behind stately homes that became rental properties. Desegregation also proved to be an economic one-way street, sending African American dollars to white businesses without the reciprocal benefit of white dollars flowing back to the African American community or its businesses. The loss of middle-class dollars stripped much of the luster from Sweet Auburn as a business district, and when the neighborhood was bisected by an expressway during a mid-sixties urban renewal program, its fate was sealed. Over the next 25 years, absentee ownership, disinvestment, rising unemployment, and escalating crime combined to transform one of Atlanta's proudest communities into a classic urban slum. It was into this deterioration that community activists and leaders, including Coretta Scott King, strode and created the Historic District Development Corporation (HDDC) to rehabilitate and revitalize the Sweet Auburn/ Martin Luther King Jr. Historic District.

In 1983, just as the HDDC was beginning its work to reverse the neighborhood's decline, it took advantage of an opportunity to form an important, defining partnership with the Trust for Public Lands (TPL), the National Park Service, and the City of Atlanta. The TPL acquired three dilapidated structures on the edge of the Martin Luther King Jr. National Historic Site, and then sold the properties to the HDDC for one dollar. In turn, the HDDC applied for and received community development block grant funding to rehabilitate the structures. When the rehabilitation was complete, the HDDC sold the structures, containing eight units of housing, to the National Park Service at market rate. This partnership resulted in seed funding for the HDDC to begin its revitalization efforts in the neighborhood and to give the National Park Service the ability to temporarily relocate the mostly elderly residents living in the properties being restored.

In 1984, after agreeing we did not want to spend another year in the suburbs, my husband, George Howell, and I decided to buy a large, rundown house in the MLK Jr. Historic District. After many months, we finally decided that if all the little old ladies we had come to know when we kept returning to the house as part of our decision-making process could live in the neighborhood, then so could we. We moved into our rehabbed home in March of 1985, with a one-month-old daughter in tow. We thought that surely, given the presence of the MLK Jr. National Historic Site and the proximity to Downtown, someone was going to revitalize the neighborhood. We had no idea it would be *us*.

We began suing recalcitrant landlords and encouraging our frightened, elderly neighbors to call the police when they needed. Eventually, we were asked to join the board of the HDDC. By the late 1980s, even with a National Historic Site showcasing the Martin Luther King Jr. Center for Nonviolent Social Change, King's birth home, and Ebenezer Baptist Church and attracting hundreds of thousands of visitors each year, it was clear that unless the HDDC strategically approached the revitalization of the neighborhood, the community that nurtured King was going to be lost. Lost either to increasingly sophisticated, property-acquiring drug dealers, or to market driven buyers who would soon realize that despite its vacant lots and dilapidated houses, the neighborhood—wedged between Downtown Atlanta and Inman Park, one of the city's most affluent neighborhoods—had the *potential* to be a very attractive place to live.

So, supported by the new leadership we provided and a small grant from Fulton County, neighborhood residents came together and created a strategic plan. The planning process helped the HDDC define more clearly its major goal and primary mission: restoring the area to the proud, economically diverse and viable community that once existed, while preventing displacement of existing residents and maintaining the historic character.

The process also helped the HDDC's leaders to understand that the way the organization had operated in the past was not very effective. Instead of acquiring and rehabilitating a property based on a "for sale" sign or an intolerably high level of criminal activity regardless of where it was in the neighborhood, HDDC began very carefully acquiring property in the same manner it had decided to revitalize the neighborhood—one block at a time.

This "block-by-block" strategy was a way of assuring existing residents, new residents, and investors that the HDDC was taking a holistic approach to physical redevelopment by building on vacant lots, rehabilitating dilapidated structures, and assisting owner-occupants, all in close proximity to one another. So, to the extent possible, anyone renting or buying a newly rehabilitated house would not be living next door to a trash-strewn, overgrown vacant lot, nor would the buyer of a newly constructed infill home be living next to a vacant dilapidated structure.

This approach was absolutely key because, in order for the HDDC to implement its mission, it relied on three guiding principles:

- The first principle was *non-displacement of existing residents.* Mostly low income and elderly, these existing residents were integral to the HDDC's efforts to revitalize the community, and protecting their interests and right to benefit from the neighborhood's rebirth was, and remains, of paramount concern to the HDDC.
- The second principle was *historic preservation.* The HDDC preserves structures—whether shotgun houses, large Victorians, or commercial buildings—because they reflect the unique fabric and identity of the neighborhood.
- The third principle was *economic diversity.* The HDDC believes that a mix of incomes is necessary for the economic viability of a community. The existing housing patterns reflected the area's mixed income legacy.

While these guidelines were notable, the HDDC also understood that unless it "controlled the dirt" it could not guarantee the preservation of historic structures or the economic diversity of neighborhood. The other sobering reality faced by the HDDC was the market, which left on its own would always seek its highest level[1]. Low-income elderly residents generally do not constitute the "highest level" in a market-driven revitalization effort, and they are often the first to go as a result.

By 1993, when then NationsBank Community Development Corporation (CDC) was looking for a neighborhood partner, it looked closely at the HDDC. Despite having no staff, the all-volunteer, board-run organization had developed 12 units of housing, created a strategic plan, developed a detailed neighborhood plan, and served as the impetus behind lobbying the Corporation for Olympic Development in Atlanta to implement a comprehensive redevelopment plan for the entire Old Fourth Ward. The HDDC's board was composed of neighborhood residents, community leaders, neighborhood business persons, and professional advisors. And, it had recently applied to the newly funded Atlanta Neighborhood Development Partnership (ANDP) for operational support, which would provide resources for the organization's first full-time paid staff.

NationsBank CDC, which had successfully developed affordable infill housing in Charlotte, North Carolina, decided its objectives and interests were aligned with the block-by-block approach the HDDC had outlined in its 1988 strategic plan. The HDDC recognized the opportunity to partner with an organization with the resources and expertise to advance its residential development efforts, as well as to gain the capacity to eventually do its own new construction.

By the end of 1993, the two organizations formed the Historic District Redevelopment Partnership (HDRP) and immediately began the strategic acquisition of vacant lots throughout the neighborhood. While the HDRP was acquiring vacant property, the HDDC continued to acquire vacant dilapidated structures and poorly maintained and managed absentee-landlord-owned rental property. The HDDC tried to convince these slumlords to improve their properties as part of the neighborhood's revitalization, but in every case, they were uninterested. They had an approach that drained just enough from low-income, often elderly residents living in deplorable conditions, but that worked for them. So, when they refused to participate in its efforts, HDDC exerted a great deal of community pressure by consistently complaining to code enforcement to ensure that the property was maintained in standard condition or to law enforcement if there was any public safety infraction. Because of their unwillingness to invest in these properties, eventually they agreed to sell.

Once a significant portion of the target area had been acquired, the HDRP began building infill housing on the vacant lots while the HDDC rehabilitated existing structures on the same block at the same time. This was particularly important because now the HDDC could temporarily relocate the residents of a rental property previously owned by an absentee landlord to a newly rehabbed house on the same block, for the same rent they were paying the slumlord. Once their former residences were completed, the residents were offered the opportunity to move back at no cost to them. Not one ever did. At some point, when asked why she did not want to move back to her renovated home, a resident named Mrs. Brown said "Honey I lived in that house for 40 years. Now I get to live in this new house. Why would I want to move back?"

The beauty of this strategy was that because the entire block was being redeveloped, the temporary relocation could always occur on that block. This created a very important sense of security and trust, especially with long-term elderly tenants.

How did the HDDC do this? Essentially, the HDDC looked at every possible source of subsidy to maintain affordability for existing and new residents. In addition to the partnership with NationsBank (eventually Bank of America), the HDDC used City of Atlanta HOME[2] funds to subsidize the acquisition and rehabilitation of existing houses and the Low Income Housing Tax Credit (LIHTC) on the multifamily units. The HDDC worked with the Fulton County/City of Atlanta Land Bank Authority to acquire tax-delinquent property. It made strategic use of the City of Atlanta's Housing Enterprise Zone Ordinance and applied for and received a Rehabilitated Historic Tax Abatement on every rehabilitated historic structure. It also made an all-out effort to ensure that low-income, elderly owner-occupants took advantage of the property tax exemption that was created for them. At some point it became apparent that if the HDDC did not develop market-rate housing in the neighborhood, someone else was surely going to do so. So it did and it used the proceeds to cross-subsidize more affordable units.

Additionally, the HDDC worked diligently to become involved in and provide leadership to the local Neighborhood Planning Unit, which provides official neighborhood input to the city on zoning, land use, urban design, and the use of public funding for projects within the community. In short, it was important for the HDDC to have a voice in what got built and for whom.

Using the "block-by-block" strategy, the HDDC had to address the problems it found as it encountered them.[3] In addition to its single-family housing efforts, it rehabilitated crime-ridden multifamily dwellings; converted a site previously occupied by a scrap metal yard to a mixed use condominium complex with live-work units; and converted a 225,000-square-foot, historic cotton compress warehouse on the eastern end of Auburn Avenue into a mixed income, mixed use creative complex called Studioplex. The HDDC was also instrumental in the development of a 300-unit mixed income, mixed use complex within minutes of Downtown Atlanta.

Rehabbing existing structures and building new housing in the MLK Jr. Historic District in the mid-nineties was not an easy task. Shootings and theft of building materials, appliances, and copper at night was matched by the confrontations with prostitutes and drug dealers during the day. While there was general support for the HDDC's efforts, there was also a strong resistance to change from the negative forces in neighborhood. The HDDC's Residents Advisory Committee (RAC) did all the things residents could do to combat these negative forces. The RAC formed a neighborhood watch; worked closely with the Fourth Ward Neighbors, a neighborhood organization that successfully focused on criminal activity at the time; and worked closely with the city and the Atlanta Police Department. Over time, as more vacant properties that served as havens for criminal activity were rehabbed and more residents moved in, the negative forces began to dwindle and move on.

In the early 1990s, the HDDC was approached by a group that had recently formed an organization to revitalize the Sweet Auburn commercial corridor at the western end of the MLK Jr. Historic District. The idea was that this group would concentrate on the commercial end of the district while the HDDC would concentrate on the residential property at the eastern end. While the HDDC's mission was the revitalization of both the residential and commercial portions of the Historic District, this proposed approach appeared to be a way to get more done faster, especially since visitors from around the world were coming to Atlanta for the Olympics in 1996. Unfortunately, while the residential portion of the Historic District continued to revitalize and eventually provided the catalyst for the revival of the Old Fourth Ward in general, these efforts resulted in no progress toward the rebirth of the commercial portions of Sweet Auburn.

But, there appeared to be hope for Sweet Auburn, when in the late nineties Atlanta was awarded an Empowerment Zone designation. Atlanta's application to the federal government specifically identified the Auburn Avenue area as a prime target for the kind of poverty-alleviating funds and tax credits offered by the Empowerment Zone. Using the Old Fourth Ward and Butler/Auburn redevelopment plans as guides, the HDDC pulled together 35 organizations as diverse as Grady Hospital and Operation P.E.A.C.E. (affiliated with the Bedford-Pine Section 8 housing community) to create a comprehensive, neighborhood-based request to the Atlanta Empowerment Zone Corporation (AEZC). The application sought to address the myriad human and economic development needs of the broader Old Fourth Ward/Butler Auburn community in a way that truly empowered the community. Despite valiant efforts on the part of neighborhood organizations and activists, that goal apparently was not the AEZC's intention. Fifteen years, $100 million, and several criminal convictions later, the investment in Sweet Auburn has been miniscule.[4]

The HDDC went on to acquire the historic Atlanta Life properties at Auburn and Piedmont Avenues and continued to lobby for public funding, private investment, and the preservation of Sweet Auburn. However, by 2010, the crash of the housing and credit markets and the subsequent recession had taken its toll on the organization. Coupled with the synonymous decrease in philanthropic support and the loss of critical leadership, the HDDC slipped into decline.

The vacuum left by the HDDC's inactivity was filled by those less committed to its ideal of the importance of community and affordable housing in the residential section of the neighborhood and the need to preserve its historic architecture on the commercial end. Despite these setbacks, the 33-year-old organization is beginning to turn around. The same spirit that led its early all-volunteer board pervades its current board of directors. The board, along with key long-time neighborhood partners, has kept the organization alive.

In 2011 new staff leadership provided the needed impetus just as the markets were beginning to rebound. By 2012, when the historic Atlanta Daily World building was threatened with demolition, HDDC rallied supporters to oppose it. With the help of a broad coalition of residents, neighborhood, and civic and preservation organizations, the application for demolition was denied. This effort garnered national attention for a city not known for recognizing the value of its historic structures.

In June 2012, the National Trust for Historic Preservation recognized Sweet Auburn as a national treasure and added the commercial portion of the Historic District to its "America's 11 Most Endangered Places" list at an event on the corner of Auburn and Piedmont Avenues. The HDDC had begun advocating for a Main Street Program on Sweet Auburn as early as 1998 when it included the creation of an Auburn Avenue Main Street in the Empowerment Zone application. Now, with the broad coalition of stakeholders that had continued to meet after saving the Atlanta Daily World building from the wrecking ball, coupled with the interest of the National Trust, the time to create a Main Street program for Auburn Avenue seemed right.

At the end of 2012, the HDDC—along with its partners and with technical assistance from the National Trust and the National Main Street Center created a new organization, Sweet Auburn Works (SAWorks) to lead the preservation-based economic resurgence of Auburn Avenue. The revitalization of Sweet Auburn requires three things: leadership, political will, and resources. At various times one or even two of those requirements have been met, but never all three at once. With a board comprising elected officials, major property and business owners, and civic and community organizations and some early fundraising success, SAWorks is the potential nexus of those three requirements. Development of the Atlanta Streetcar and the expansion of Georgia State University offer new opportunities that, if tethered to SAWorks' preservation-based economic and business development approach, could be real catalysts for revitalization.

The HDDC owes much of its success to leadership at both the board and staff levels, a commitment to good planning internally within the organization and externally in the broader community, and the recognition of the importance of strategic partnerships and collaborations with other neighborhood and preservation organizations, government entities, and nonprofit and for-profit developers.

The HDDC's efforts have led to the development or rehabilitation of 112 single-family homes, nearly 500 units of multifamily housing, and 40,000 square feet of commercial space, and, most importantly, the revitalization of one of the most significant neighborhoods, not just in Atlanta, but in the country. With nearly one million visitors from across the nation and around the world coming to the Historic District each year, the HDDC's work needed to reflect the legacy of the neighborhood that nurtured Martin Luther King Jr. and the economic vibrancy that defined it.

The HDDC continues to work to fulfill its mission, but the journey has not been flawless. The organization is now dealing with the results of its success, having to contend with rising property values and—in what has become one of the hottest neighborhoods in Atlanta—the constant challenge of maintaining affordability. While the organization prides itself on managing to revitalize the neighborhood without displacing its low-income indigenous residents, the HDDC did not put in place the kind of protections (beyond the affordable housing it owns and manages) that would insure affordability in the neighborhood over time. As a result, the HDDC is currently considering a community land trust as a way to address the need for a long-term affordable housing solution.

The HDDC is the oldest surviving community development corporation in Atlanta. It is part of a community development industry that continues to struggle to survive and remain relevant, despite its successful revitalization of inner city neighborhoods in Atlanta and the affordable housing it has created. There are two trade associations, the Atlanta Housing Association of Neighborhood Based Developers and the Georgia State Association of Nonprofit Developers that over the years have advocated for more funding support, affordable housing subsidies, and public policy aligned with community-based economic development. The ANDP provided operational funding and project financing in the past, as did Enterprise Community Partners, which has once again begun to provide support. Organizations like NeighborWorks (formerly the Neighborhood Reinvestment Corporation) provide training and funding to its network members. The City of Atlanta, utilizing U.S. Department of Housing and Urban Development resources, provides some operational support and project financing for community housing development organizations. Fulton County and the State of Georgia also provide funding and financing. The Community Foundation for Greater Atlanta and United Way—along with various national, and to a limited extent local, foundations, financial institutions, and corporations—have also over time provided resources to community development.

However, none of this funding is significant, sustained, or substantial enough to support the kind of robust community development industry needed in Atlanta. As market rate housing development resurges in Atlanta, the need for affordable housing is growing at the same time the amount of affordable housing is decreasing. There is no affordable housing delivery system in Atlanta. There is no priority placed on affordable housing development that in any way matches the need for it in the city.

An effort to create community land trusts that would ensure affordability long-term is currently focusing on neighborhoods that adjoin the Atlanta BeltLine. This effort was created with a broad base of stakeholders and has received national attention. Despite this and the fact that there are over 250 community land trusts in the country and it is recognized as a superior approach to extending the lifecycle of housing subsidies, the program's implementation in Atlanta is stalled.

There is no question that community development corporations need to work harder and smarter to expand and maintain the affordability they have been able to create. However, it is also clear that only by analyzing and anticipating the growth potential of inner city neighborhoods—then strategically planning for and controlling that growth—can we mitigate gentrification and the resulting displacement it causes. Unless Atlanta finds the political will to address the inequitable way it is allowing its inner city neighborhoods to develop, the result will be a sad tribute to its political legacy.

CHAPTER 4

Creating Urban Reinvention: Downtown Atlanta

Paul B. Kelman, FAICP

Change is one of the constants in Atlanta, and the Downtown area is no exception. Visitors today, returning after 25 years, would hardly recognize the place. The impact of the Centennial Olympic Games on Atlanta was huge because most of the events, and the development that enabled the city to host those events, were centered Downtown. However, the Olympic Games were just part of the story as government and the private sector worked together to reinvent Downtown. Physical changes are most certainly noticeable, but institutional and social changes are evident as well. Dramatic residential growth has reshaped neighborhoods: lofts in Castleberry Hill, high-rise condos in the Centennial Olympic Park area, repurposed office buildings at Five Points, student housing along Piedmont Avenue, mid-rise buildings in the Auburn-Edgewood corridor, and mixed income communities in Centennial Place and Capitol Gateway.

New and improved transportation infrastructure has enabled Downtown to remain viable in the region and accessible to the world's busiest airport. Transportation demand management practices, smarter zoning, development codes, and an increased emphasis on the pedestrian environment have led to a more livable downtown. Construction of the Atlanta Streetcar is energizing long-dormant areas on the east side of Downtown.

New and improved parks and open spaces, heavily programmed with activities throughout the year, make the Downtown area more attractive to residents as well as visitors. Special events at Underground Atlanta and Centennial Olympic Park—along with the millions of visitors to the Georgia Aquarium, World of Coca-Cola, CNN Center, and the Children's Museum—add vitality to the city center. The National Center for Civil and Human Rights and the College Football Hall of Fame will add to the synergy.

Atlanta is one of the nation's top convention and professional sports cities, and the expanded Georgia World Congress Center, Georgia Dome, and Philips Arena draw millions of patrons each year. They stay in the more than 12,000 hotel rooms within walking distance of the convention center and dine in the more than 300 Downtown restaurants. Funding has been secured to replace the Georgia Dome in 2017 with a new multipurpose retractable-roof stadium. Of the one billion dollar total budget, close to $100 million is slated to improve adjacent neighborhoods and transportation infrastructure.

Increased economic activity and employment are critical to success. Marketing and economic development strategies have been instrumental in maintaining a strong market for office space, even as suburban competition has increased markedly. Creative approaches to financing and development have facilitated new development in both traditionally strong areas and in underdeveloped ones. Challenges remain with competition between aging office buildings Downtown and newer buildings in Midtown, Buckhead, and the suburbs. The conversion of older buildings to residential and university uses has been helpful, but the Downtown share of the metropolitan office market continues to drop. An improved regulatory structure for future growth has been put in place to take advantage of the next wave of activity as Atlanta and the nation recover from the Great Recession. A greener, smarter development pattern is emerging as long-planned changes affect the design and development process.

Public safety is paramount in making the Downtown a desirable place to live, work, and play. Crime has fallen dramatically over the last 15 years as the Ambassador Force and cooperating police agencies have made a real difference, but visitors continue to be wary because of the perception of crime.

Georgia State University (GSU) is the Southeast's leading urban research institution (Georgia State University 2013). Over 32,000 graduate and undergraduate students are enrolled in more than 100 fields of study. Founded in 1913, GSU was characterized as a "commuter school" for most of its 100 years. All that changed in 1996, when part of the Olympic Village built for the Olympic athletes was transformed into GSU student housing. Over the next two decades, more than 4,100 units of student housing were built in Downtown Atlanta, dramatically changing the look and feel of the campus. Private companies are currently developing additional housing to fill future student housing needs. As GSU continues to grow, more buildings are poised to be repurposed for academic, housing, and support needs. Fairlie-Poplar, the Piedmont Avenue corridor, other eastside locations, Underground Atlanta, and Turner Field are likely areas for additional expansion.

GSU's impact is growing. New facilities for research, athletics, and classroom education are needed and planned. As its student population includes fewer commuters, more areas are becoming revitalized as students walk and bike between classes, housing, and restaurants. Downtown's continuing strength is its institutions. Public and private organizations work closely together to advance their collective agenda for civic progress. An energized business community, a committed group of charitable foundations, and a receptive local political climate have all served Atlanta well in the past and left a proud legacy of achievement. Future advances will depend even more on these institutions to continue to innovate. Atlanta remains the center of government, tourism, transportation, education, and sports. Its dominance in employment and shopping diminished as the rest of the region grew dramatically.

Starting in the 1970s, private and public leaders worked jointly to develop and put in place strategies to enhance and grow Downtown. Central Atlanta Progress, Inc. (CAP), the Downtown business association, has been the prime driver of planning due to the business community's strong association with elected officials. Until the 1972 election of Maynard Jackson, Atlanta's first African American mayor, most of the city's elected leaders were from the business community. Several authors have studied the downtown power structure in Atlanta during the last 60 years. Floyd Hunter wrote *Community Power Structure* in 1953, and Clarence Stone's 1989 book *Regime Politics* is a classic on the politics of governing. Both elaborated upon the important role that Atlanta's top business leaders played in growing the city.

Planning Processes

Since the early 1970s, a number of comprehensive plans for Downtown Atlanta have been developed. What follows is an annotated list of the studies and plans drafted by CAP and its partners over the past 40 years.

Central Area Study I and Central Area Study II

The Central Area Study I (CAS I) explored the economic drivers of the Southeast's largest metropolitan region as it grew past 1.5 million people. Completed in 1971, the plan proposed key infrastructure and policy initiatives to accommodate the new residents and the expected activity in central Atlanta (CAP 1971). Primarily focused on physical improvements, CAS I identified new urban design projects to build upon the then proposed Metropolitan Atlanta Rapid Transit Authority (MARTA) rail system, downplayed the addition of new freeways beyond those already planned, and anticipated a more pedestrian-oriented downtown by promoting dense development around the future transit stations.

The Central Area Study II (CAS II) planning was released in 1988. The geographic scope of the planning effort expanded to include most of the area inside the historic railroad corridor that ringed the central city and that now forms the Atlanta BeltLine. The priority was to make the area more livable and inviting to people. Improvements in pedestrian areas, retailing, housing, public safety, transportation infrastructure, the arts and entertainment, recreation, business retention and recruitment, maintenance, and marketing were identified as desirable to the central city. A general obligation bond issue was proposed along with a special tax district. (CAP 1988).

Central Atlanta Action Plan

The *Central Atlanta Action Plan* (CA²P) kicked off in 2002 with a summit that resulted in a vision for Downtown. Community forums and online dialogues produced recommended strategies (CAP 2000). The plan was notable for its attention to quality-of-life issues, the growing importance of Downtown's residential community and surrounding neighborhoods, and issues affecting the city's homeless population.

Imagine Downtown and the Encore

Downtown's current comprehensive plan was adopted in 2004 and updated in 2009. The plan promotes responsible growth and development with options for transit, sidewalks, and open space. New construction was directed towards dense mixed use development incorporating a variety of retail, office, and residential uses in a 24-hour community (CAP 2004). Specific initiatives included: a multimodal transportation hub; an improved Peachtree Street corridor; expanded options for urban living; a revitalized SoNo (South of North) area to connect the Downtown and Midtown neighborhoods; attractions, including the National Center for Civil and Human Rights, and the College Football Hall of Fame in the Centennial Olympic Park area; redevelopment of vacant land and parking lots in the South Central Business District; the Green Line plan; and improvements in the Sweet Auburn neighborhood (CAP 2009).

Green Line Plan

The Green Line is a vision for the east-west corridor of Downtown stretching from the State Capitol to Philips Arena. Dominated by a linear park ringed by pedestrian-oriented development and hallmarked by increased multimodal connectivity, the plan provides a comprehensive look at the future. Recommendations include: capping the railroad gulch to introduce open space and air rights development sites above with transit and parking underneath; developing a Multimodal Passenger Terminal in conjunction with the Five Points MARTA station; transforming the Five Points MARTA station into an integrated and activated open space plaza; adding new entrances to Underground Atlanta along with expanded retail and entertainment uses; and revitalizing the vacant World of

Coca-Cola building with attraction and hospitality uses, including possibly a state-operated museum.

The 2007 plans were orientated toward physical improvements and the recommended strategies leaned heavily toward economic, and marketing of the area. Most of the planning processes and subsequent improvements have been joint ventures between CAP and entities including the City of Atlanta, the State of Georgia, and the Atlanta Regional Commission.

Key Organizations

Although many public and private entities are involved in planning and implementation in Downtown Atlanta, the following have been very instrumental in the ongoing success of Downtown.

Central Atlanta Progress, Inc.

CAP, founded as the Central Atlanta Improvement Association in 1941, is a private not-for-profit community development organization providing leadership, programs, and services to preserve and strengthen economic vitality. With a board of directors made up primarily of business leaders, CAP is funded through the investment of businesses and institutions. Throughout the course of over 60 years of explosive growth in Downtown, CAP has worked behind the scenes integrating ideas, building partnerships, and coordinating efforts to improve the central city.

Downtown Atlanta Community Improvement District

Authorized by the Georgia Constitution, a community improvement district (CID) is a mechanism for funding certain governmental services, including street and road construction and maintenance, parks and recreation, and public transportation systems (Georgia Cities Foundation 2013). The Downtown Atlanta Community Improvement District was formed in 1995 by the City of Atlanta. The board of the CID then entered into an agreement with Atlanta Downtown Improvement District, Inc. (ADID) to act as the administrative body for the Downtown Atlanta CID.

Invest Atlanta

Invest Atlanta comprises the Urban Residential Finance Authority, the Downtown Development Authority, and the Atlanta Economic Renaissance Corporation. Subsidiaries include Atlanta BeltLine, Inc. Until 2012, Invest Atlanta was known as the Atlanta Development Authority (Invest Atlanta 2013a).

Atlanta Housing Authority

The Atlanta Housing Authority (AHA) is considered a national leader in the transformation of public housing. In 1996, the AHA created the financial and legal model for mixed income, mixed finance transactions that include publicly assisted housing as a component. This model is used by the U.S. Department of Housing and Urban Development's HOPE VI revitalization program. In Atlanta, it has resulted in six mixed income communities, with three more in the predevelopment phase. The first of these is Centennial Place, located in Downtown Atlanta and within the ADID area.

Strategies
Atlanta Downtown Improvement District
Founded in 1995, the ADID is a public-private partnership to make Downtown cleaner, safer, and more hospitable. The ADID is funded through a CID similar to a business improvement district. Expanded via several annexations, the district currently contains 220 blocks. The ADID is financed through a $5 million levy on commercial property within the district boundaries. Several major programs are supported: the Ambassador Force, the Clean Team, which provides information to tourists and periodic street clean-up; management of Woodruff Park; and, a capital improvement program. In effect, the ADID is the action arm of CAP, enabling it to carry out an extensive program to implement its strategic plans.

The ADID is arguably the most important entity in Downtown apart from the City of Atlanta itself. While some councilpersons and neighborhood advocates have opposed initiatives, a generally positive relationship exists among the concerned parties. In recent years, the growing residential population in Downtown has supported CAP and ADID initiatives with its neighborhood association.

Tax Increment Finance Districts
Most of Downtown falls within one of two tax allocation districts (TADs), the eastside and westside TADs. In most of the U.S., these are called tax increment finance districts, or TIFs. These TIF districts offer developers a method of paying for public improvements within the area through increases in tax revenue resulting from revitalization of the area. Tax allocation bonds are used to finance redevelopment costs within a TAD. The bonds are issued to support a pledge of the projected increase in *ad valorem* revenues from the proposed TAD redevelopment for their repayment (Invest Atlanta 2013b). As TADs have proliferated throughout the city, they have become more controversial due to increased competition among target areas and concern about the experience of TIFs in other states.

Centennial Olympic Park Area Redevelopment
A grand legacy of the 1996 Summer Olympic Games is Centennial Olympic Park, a 21-acre gathering place for the city. While plans for the park were in development in the years leading up to the Olympics, CAP saw the opportunity

to create a public-private partnership to revitalize the underdeveloped land adjacent to the future park. A new not-for-profit entity, Central Olympic Park Area, Inc. (COPA), was created with the mission to revitalize the area around the park. COPA was successful in bringing about positive change in a short period of time. Accomplishments include catalytic land assembly in the area northeast of Centennial Olympic Park, Centennial Hill, that would ultimately become home to the Children's Museum and the mixed use Allen Plaza development; land assembly in the area northwest of the park that led to development of Northyards Business Park; and new mid-rise housing and hotels built on the park edges. Funding for adjacent affordable housing was generated from a percentage of land sales (Invest Atlanta 2013a).

Notable Public-Private Projects

Numerous programs have targeted Fairlie-Poplar, Atlanta's turn-of-the-nineteenth-century central business district. Most notable were creation of the Fairlie-Poplar Task Force, special design guidelines, and targeted capital improvements (CAP 2013b). CAP partnered with the City of Atlanta to review and update the zoning regulations, a need that had been identified repeatedly in many CAP plans. CAP managed a group of stakeholders and a consultant team to draft a proposed unified zoning code, as well as supporting documents that became recommendations to the City of Atlanta regarding specific changes to existing Downtown districts. The new Special Public Interest Zoning District was adopted by city council in 2010.

An economic development program was created in 2001 as part of the city and state economic development network. The program is dedicated to promoting economic vitality through retention of existing businesses, recruitment of new businesses, encouragement of private and public investment in new development, adaptive reuse of existing real estate, and provision of data and information about Downtown (CAP 2013c).

Civic leaders in Atlanta had thought about building a civil and human rights museum for years (CAP 2013d). In 2005 Mayor Shirley Franklin and former mayor Andrew Young asked CAP and the Boston Consulting Group to research existing museums and institutes. A working group comprising community and business leaders, scholars, and public officials convened in 2006 to research, analyze, and consider the establishment of a Center for Civil and Human Rights in Atlanta. The group reported that a center should be established to commemorate the groundbreaking contributions of Atlantans and Georgians to the historic struggle for African American freedom and equality. It would also serve as a space for dialogue and action around the struggles for freedom in the U.S. and around the world.

The streetcar on Peachtree Street and Edgewood and Auburn Avenues has been part of many plans dating back to 1990. As a result of a $48 million TIGER II grant in 2010 from the federal government and significant funding commitments from the City of Atlanta, the ADID, and MARTA, the first phase of the Atlanta Streetcar was authorized as a $93 million project. Construction has been underway since 2012, with completion and operation likely in 2014 (CAP 2013e).

One of the most difficult challenges Atlanta has faced—and continues to face—is homelessness. Numerous public-private initiatives have been launched to deal with the complex situation, but no one is pleased with the outcomes. Mayors have pledged an end to homelessness, and thousands have received help through supportive housing, social services, shelters, and employment and medical programs. Dozens of provider and advocate organizations work together, but no solution is on the horizon.

Conclusion

Downtown Atlanta has evolved and changed over the past 45 years and now stands ready to reclaim its place as the metro area's most important tourist, business, and shopping destinations. Central Atlanta Progress, the Downtown Atlanta Community Improvement District, and Invest Atlanta have led Downtown's progress through many comprehensive plans and various public-private ventures that facilitated considerable investment. Much of this happened because of their understanding of Downtown as a transportation hub and geographic nexus of the region that was too important to ignore. Adding to Downtown's progress alongside the work of CAP, the ADID, and Invest Atlanta were Olympic-era improvements and Georgia State University's expansion that complemented work happening in other quarters of Downtown. Although much work remains to make Downtown Atlanta even more vibrant and dynamic, the area is well positioned to capitalize on past investments and interest.

CHAPTER 5

Crazy Like The Fox:
Atlanta's Preservation Schizophrenia

Leslie N. Sharp

Although only a young child, I still remember the "Save the Fox" campaign. I remember the buttons people wore and the news stories. Later I remember going to see the "Best Little Whorehouse in Texas" at the Fox Theatre in high school and wondering how could anyone ever have considered tearing down this beautiful place. While I did not know then that my career would be spent trying to document and preserve historic places, I did know that the Fox was special and that Atlanta was lucky to have it—a fact which now should be considered beyond debate. Over the ensuing decades, I would see many preservation fights around Atlanta—many won and many lost. Looking back, I am struck by how Atlanta views its history and its historic built environment as almost separate entities—one celebrated and the other almost disposable.

This chapter provides a snapshot of historic preservation in Atlanta, Georgia. With both successes and dismal defeats, Atlanta is a city with a rich history whose record saving its notable buildings reflects its complicated relationship with the past and its continued hope for a brighter future. This tension is reflected in the Atlanta Urban Design's 1987 statement: "Atlanta is the Capital City of the Southeast, a city of the future with strong ties to its past. The old in new Atlanta is the soul of the city, the heritage that enhances the quality of life in a contemporary city. Without these artifacts of our culture, Atlanta would simply not be Atlanta. In the turbulent 60's, Atlanta was "the city too busy to hate." It must never become "the city too busy to care" (Atlanta Urban Design Commission 1987, 11).

So what was going on in the 1980s that led the authors to even consider that Atlanta did not care about its past or rather its "soul?" This period followed three decades of unprecedented growth in Atlanta and around the country, while at the same time there was a preservation awakening that resulted in a public framework for the modern historic preservation movement. For example, the National Historic Preservation Act was passed in 1966 and amended to better address local issues and needs in 1980; the Georgia State Historic Preservation Office was founded out of the Georgia Historical Commission in 1969 as mandated by the National Preservation Act; the state's preservation non-profit Georgia Trust for Historic Preservation was founded in 1973;

Figure 5.1. The Fox Theatre marquee

the Atlanta Urban Design Commission in 1975; and the Atlanta Preservation Center in 1979. Although these preservation-centered organizations formed, this period would continue to be marked by widespread razing of and threats to Atlanta's historic built environment and a lack of preservation planning (Atlanta Preservation Center 2014; Georgia Trust for Historic Preservation 1999; Spalding 1979).

In 1987 the Atlanta Urban Design Commission published *Atlanta's Lasting Landmarks*, which listed and described the historic resources that had been locally designated, and captured the context in which these organizations had formed. In it, the authors observed: "One fact cannot be denied: Atlanta is now facing a crisis in historic preservation. The pace of the destruction of buildings, even entire blocks of buildings, has accelerated in recent years. To some, older buildings seem to have outlived their usefulness; to others, these same structures offer unlimited opportunities for preservation and reuse" (Atlanta Urban Design Commission 1987, 6). This sounding of alarm following thirty years of destruction and expansion in Downtown and Midtown Atlanta witnessed many of Atlanta's landmark buildings being threatened and dozens of irreplaceable buildings lost as the passage above suggests.[1] While the signing of a strong local preservation ordinance in June 1989 served to bolster preservation efforts, there would still be more losses—both intentional and unintentional—to come.

Using vignettes representing successes and failures, this chapter will explore the schizophrenic nature of Atlanta's historic preservation consciousness marked by an appreciation for its own history but an often blatant disregard for its historic fabric representing this history. Like Atlanta's past, its historic preservation past reflects tensions associated with race, politics, and wealth, and its identity as a progressive, modern city. These preservation stories represent the complicated psyche of Atlanta.

Preservation Vignettes
The Fox Theatre
When the American Institute of Architects (AIA) were planning their 1975 conference in Atlanta, the mood must have been a little bleak if the guide to Atlanta's architecture prepared for the conference is an indication, as it was dedicated to the Fox Theatre, a building that the authors thought was surely going to be demolished. In describing it, Elizabeth Lyon wrote, "Possibly the most important and interesting building of this period [1920s], and certainly the most significant to the present culture of the city, is the endangered Fox Theatre. At this time, this incredible architectural puzzle, as Professor Frank Beckum of the Georgia Institute of Technology has aptly called it, is scheduled for demolition in May, 1975, and strenuous efforts to preserve it are underway" (1975, 39).

The Fox Theatre opened on Christmas Day in 1929, first as the Yaarab Temple, then the Shriners meeting hall, and, when the scale and budget for

Figure 5.2. The Fox Theatre interior

the project got out of control, as a second theatre to be run by movie tycoon William Fox (Figure 5.1). The national depression had already begun, and it would not be long before the Shriners were forced to relinquish their interest in the building, which would eventually be owned by Fox. Between the 1940s and 1960s, the Fox would remain a viable entertainment site; however, the rapid expansion of Atlanta and the demise of the Fox as a happening venue would lead to talks of its demolition. Facing Peachtree Street at the corner of Ponce de Leon Avenue, Southern Bell wanted this prominent real estate for their international headquarters. Atlantans formed the organization Atlanta Landmarks, Inc. in 1974 and fought against its razing. That same year it received National Register of Historic Places designation, which helped bring recognition to its significance. Atlanta Landmarks, a non-profit organization, began the now infamous "Save the Fox" campaign. It was able to borrow funds to buy the building in 1975 and actually pay off the mortgage six months early in 1978. Since taking it over, Atlanta Landmarks has remained in the black every year and reinvested its surplus into the restoration of the building and to outreach. The theatre hosts over 300 performances, concerts, and movies every year and is now a National Historic Landmark. In addition to being an important economic and cultural driver in Atlanta, the Fox adheres to the strictest of preservation principles and is meticulous in its on-going restoration efforts (Figure 5.2). The Fox has also created the Fox Theatre Institute, which is the nation's only comprehensive preservation organization dedicated to theatre preservation. The Institute provides resources, mentoring, and education to help promote theatre preservation and restoration across the state (American Institute of Architects 1975; Fox Theatre 2014; Gournay 1993; McKaughan 2014).

The Margaret Mitchell House

In 1989 then mayor Andrew Young supported the Margaret Mitchell House's designation as an Atlanta Landmark in order to help preserve it following four years of efforts by local preservationists to save it. This was an intermediate step to prevent its demolition, but in 1994 it was set afire under suspicious circumstances. In preparation for the Atlanta Olympic Games, the German Daimler-Benz Corporation put up $5 million in 1996 to restore the Margaret Mitchell House, where Mitchell wrote *Gone with the Wind*. Inexplicably the house caught fire again about a month before its restoration was complete. Many have suggested that the fires were racially motivated due to the "Old South" attitudes found in Mitchell's best known work, *Gone with the Wind*. After the burnings of the house, the owners, with the support of the State Historic Preservation Office, pursued listing of the building—the Crescent Avenue Apartments—in the National Register of Historic Places for its historical significance, as Mitchell's ground floor apartment mysteriously remained intact. Considered by some to be a preservation success, the Margaret Mitchell House is now operated by the Atlanta History Center and is open for tours (Figure 5.3). The Margaret Mitchell Literary Center is affiliated with the house and hosts numerous events throughout the year. The focus on Mitchell provides the opportunity to tell visitors the full story of Mitchell's life and her commitment to advocating education for African Americans rather than just *Gone with the Wind* which, for many, represents a depiction of Southern past best forgotten and contrary to Atlanta's branding as a progressive Southern city (Cloues 1996; Thomas 2014).

Auburn Avenue and the Martin Luther King Jr. Historic District

The mecca for African American commercial, political, and social activity in Atlanta, if not the United States, was Auburn Avenue, home of the Atlanta Daily World (Figure 5.4) and the surrounding area known as Old Fourth Ward. The Auburn Historic District became a National Historic Landmark in 1976, but the area has since declined. In 1992, the area was listed as one of the National Trust for Historic Preservation's 11 Most Endangered Places and in 2012 the National Trust for Historic Preservation once again recognized its great significance, as well as its potential loss, by naming it a National Treasure (National Trust for Historic Preservation 2014; Poole 2012; Youngblood 2012).

The building of Interstate 75/85 in the early 1970s divided the commercial area in half and separated the residential portion of the neighborhood on the east from Downtown Atlanta and a large portion of the commercial district. Decline and decay followed and since then, what had been one of

Figure 5.3. Historically known as the Crescent Avenue Apartments because the building once faced Crescent Avenue, the Margaret Mitchell House has a complex story of destruction and preservation.

the wealthiest African American enclaves in the country, now appears to be impoverished. It is the west side of the neighborhood adjacent to downtown and Georgia State University where significant commercial and community landmark buildings are crumbling and vacant, threatened by development, or already gone (Youngblood 2012).

Conversely, the residential portion of the neighborhood further east has seen major investment and represents a preservation success, in a large part due to the Historic District Development Corporation (HDDC) (Newman 1999).[2] While the historic commercial part of Auburn Avenue continues to decline, the residential portion of the neighborhood to the east continues to see reinvestment, including hip new restaurants, bars, and galleries. However, gentrification remains a concern as both the location and housing stock are desirable (Kirk 2007).

While the presence of the Martin Luther King Jr. Historic Site in the Old Fourth Ward has contributed to bringing investment and visitors to the area, there have been issues with its preservation and interpretation (Figures 5.5 and 5.6). As stated by the United States Congress in 1980, "The places where Martin Luther King Jr. was born, where he lived, and worshiped, and where he is buried should receive special attention to protect and interpret these areas for the benefit, inspiration, and education of present and future generations" (National Park Service 1985). The National Park Service has had a mixed record when it comes to the preservation of the area even while they have restored houses, the firehouse, and Ebenezer Church and created educational programs that millions of people participate in each year.

For the 1996 Atlanta Olympic Games, Congress allocated $11.8 million to expand the interpretation of the Martin Luther King Jr. Historic Site, resulting in the creation of a visitor's center where a community center had been and an extremely large parking lot on the former site of the Scripto Pen and Ink factory. This is where in 1964 Scripto workers (600 of the 800 workers were black and most were women), under the leadership of King, successfully waged a strike for better wages (Hooper and Hooper 1999). Unfortunately, the National Park Service would support demolishing the building significant in civil rights and labor history to build a new parking lot in the 1990s (Blythe et al. 1994; Crimmins and White 1989; Newman 2001).

In addition to the building of new facilities often at the expense of historic ones, the National Park Service's preservation and interpretation of Reverend King's life and legacy has been criticized by scholars. Inwood states that "the focus on King and the decision to concentrate on the events central to his life reinforces normative histories of the US Civil Rights struggle. The NPS presentation of King as the preeminent figure of the US Civil Rights struggle glosses over deeply entrenched divisions that emerged during the US Civil Rights Struggle" (Inwood 2009, 98). He adds that "the NPS pre-

Figure 5.4. *Atlanta Daily World Building, circa 1979*

Figure 5.5. The birth home of Martin Luther King Jr. at 501 Auburn Avenue is a centerpiece of the visitor experience to the Martin Luther King Jr. National Historic Site, which is operated by the National Park Service.

sentation of King delegitimizes other leaders (Malcolm X for example) who presented alternatives to the goals laid out by King and his organizations. The Park Service Memorials also omit mention of the role gender played in the Civil Rights Struggle...The official history of Civil Rights serves to silence the voices and contributions made by countless women during the Civil Rights struggle"(Inwood 2009, 98).

The expansion of the federal government in downtown also would result in losses in addition to the Scripto factory. Founded in Atlanta in 1891, the Rich's Department Store, referred to as "the symbol of Atlanta" and home to the Crystal Bridge, the Pink Pig monorail ride, and a liberal exchange and credit policy, was the setting for the integration of downtown businesses led by Dr. King. The downtown Rich's department store was also the site of the only arrests related to a sit-in in Atlanta after the Student Nonviolent Coordinating Committee (SNCC), under the leadership of Julian Bond and Lonnie

Figure 5.6. The tomb of King and his wife Coretta Scott King is surrounded by a reflecting pool and represents some of the modern additions to the historic site.

King (no relation to Dr. King), convinced Martin Luther King Jr. to participate to garner national attention. The SNCC leaders knew that Rich's was lynchpin in integrating businesses, and their plan with the arrest of Dr. King and others was critical (Allen 1996). Significant in terms of commerce, architecture, and its role in Civil Rights, the Downtown store building became the centerpiece of a preservation compromise that resulted in the United States government demolishing a large portion—the Store for Homes—for use as a new Sam Nunn Federal Center (Figure 5.7). Extensively documented, the General Services Administration hosted an exhibit on the history of this Atlanta institution and the new federal use. In addition, the Federal Center has been much celebrated for its incorporation of a historic building. The Richard B. Russell Federal Building (1979) now stands on the site of the 1905 Terminal Station Building (razed 1972), which was designed by architect P. Thornton Marye, the architect who designed the Fox Theatre (Clemmons 2012; Rose 2001).

The Highways Versus the Neighborhoods

Perhaps the most significant preservation battle that Atlanta has faced and won was over the proposed Interstate 485 and Stone Mountain Tollway, both of which would have destroyed multiple intown neighborhoods. In 1964, the Georgia Department of Transportation (then the Highway Department) unveiled plans for an extensive freeway system that would connect 400 with 685 on the South with a second roadway connecting 75/85 to the Stone Mountain Freeway. Morningside, Virginia Highlands, Inman Park, Candler Park, Old Fourth

Ward, Druid Hills, and other neighborhoods would have been decimated. Over the next decade, the neighborhoods organized themselves to fight the proposed roads, filing multiple lawsuits, getting political support, and negotiating designs and route alternatives. Although hundreds of houses were demolished (particularly in the Old Fourth Ward district), the neighborhoods (aided by several federal actions such as the passage of the National Environmental Policy Act in 1969 and the Supreme Court's ruling to stop the Tennessee DOT from building a highway through the historic Overton Park in Memphis) were successful in killing these highway projects. The neighborhoods also maintained their organizations and now have significant influence and power in local decision making (Newman 2001).[3]

While some of the vacant land from the destruction of houses was turned into parks (John Howell Memorial Park, Sidney Marcus Park, and Freedom Park), a large swath of the vacant land would be ripe for another proposed four-lane roadway. Known as the Presidential Parkway, this proposal set off another battle involving the former President Jimmy Carter, who wanted an east-west roadway to connect major thoroughfares to his presidential library (Pousner 1986). Citizens once again united to form the group Citizens Against Unnecessary Thoroughfares in Older Neighborhoods (CAUTION) and would eventually be successful in shaping and limiting the roadway. The road became the Freedom Parkway and connected I-75/85 to the Carter Center and gave easy access to the Martin Luther King Jr. Historic Site. After much negotiation, the road

Figure 5.7. The south side of the Rich's Department Store Crystal Bridge in downtown Atlanta

was designed to meander through the Freedom Park, have a maximum speed of 35 miles per hour, and provide access to Ponce de Leon Avenue and Moreland Avenue (as well as to the King and Carter Centers). The residents of the Candler Park and Druid Hills neighborhoods were successful in preventing the road from extending through their neighborhoods and instead got an extension of the Freedom Park to be built on the still-vacant land from the earlier highway battle (Applebome 1993; Carlson 1995; Freedom Park Conservancy 2014; Harris 1982; Newman 2001).

Conclusion

Atlanta's preservation schizophrenia remains as the community's commitment to both progress and its historic roots continues to result in complicated preservation projects. Recently, the Savannah College of Art and Design (SCAD) saved Ivy Hall, the Victorian-era home of Atlanta Railway Company president Edward Peters on Ponce de Leon in Midtown. However, in preventing its demolition, the land was developed as a major apartment complex within feet of the restored house (Bierig 2009; Saporta 2013).[4] This project, an extension of their nearby main campus, does not diminish SCAD's increasingly significant role in preservation on the city, as the acquire-and-rehabilitate philosophy allowed it to occupy the former Atlanta School of Art and Design.

Just on the other side of Midtown on Spring Street, the Georgia Tech Foundation has been battling the city and the preservation community over the Crum and Forster Building, an Atlanta landmark building designed by architect Ed Ivey, one of the Georgia Tech students who helped found the architecture program in 1908. The most recent compromise between the city and the foundation is that the front one-third of the property will be preserved and a high performance computing building will be built behind it (the demolition of the back two-thirds was completed in October 2013).

Two of the most talked about preservation-related issues today are the historic Friendship Baptist Church and the Atlanta Beltline. The city agreed to purchase the Reconstruction-era church for approximately $19.5 million to make way for a new football stadium for the Atlanta Falcons (the Georgia Dome is the current home to the Falcons and was completed in 1992) (Leslie 2013). The Atlanta BeltLine, a massive urban design project dreamed up by Ryan Gravel while an architecture and planning student at Georgia Tech, is a 22-mile, historic rail corridor that circles the heart of the city. It connects 45 historic neighborhoods and is an economic development and transportation enhancement project—potentially the largest scale preservation/revitalization project in the state (Atlanta BeltLine 2014; Brown 2013; Dewan 2006).

These contemporary projects are reminiscent of Atlanta's past preservation projects where the government, preservation groups, and various neighborhood organizations and activists have worked to combat developers, vandals, and the many layers of government who have differing visions of what is important, what should be saved, and what should be built. The saving of the Fox Theatre in the 1970s arguably remains the greatest single preservation victory as the Fox appeared doomed. Others, such as the stopping (and eventual reshaping) of the Presidential Parkway and the opening of Margaret Mitchell's apartment as a historic museum, demonstrate how even Atlanta's successes were fraught with complexities. Losses such as the 1906 Terminal Station (demolished in 1972), a large portion of the Downtown Rich's Building (demolished in 1995), and the ongoing disintegration of the Sweet Auburn Historic District leave scars upon the landscape, as well as in the hearts of longtime residents. Journalist Maria Saporta observed the following about the demolition of I.M. Pei's Gulf Oil building: "Atlanta can be such a disorienting city. One day a building can be standing on a corner waiting for you like an old friend. And the next day it's gone. No warning. Just gone... It's enough to drive you crazy if you're from Atlanta. Block after block is filled with ghosts of buildings past. Your mind begins to play tricks on you as you try to remember a piece of history that's been replaced by a surface parking lot waiting for that next wave of frenzied development" (Saporta 2013).

The April 1975 issue of the *AIA Journal,* focusing on Atlanta, contained an article titled "An Accidental City with a Laissez-Faire Approach to Planning," which described the city as seeming to be the result of a "series of spontaneous developmental explosions." Atlanta's historic built environment has suffered from this same phenomenon as urban renewal, wealth and poverty, transportation issues, the growth of the federal government's presence in the city, and the Olympics have resulted in major landmarks being razed as well as preserved. Crimmins and White (1989, 240) observed, "But for all of its hankering after the glitter of northern growth, Atlanta remains a city of the South, rooted for better and for worse, in the economy, culture, and history of the region." It is this tension between valuing the past and worshiping the future that has created Atlanta's preservation schizophrenia, but it is also this tension that makes Atlanta an interesting place to live and visit.

CHAPTER 6

Public-Private Partnerships: Atlanta Style

Joseph G. Martin Jr.

PRACTITIONER PERSPECTIVE

Public-private partnerships have been crucial to Atlanta's development. Although this approach has been used throughout the United States and around the world, it has been particularly important to Atlanta in achieving civic goals that neither the public nor the private sector could have done alone. Business and government working together for a common purpose has been one of the distinctive aspects of Atlanta's progress over the years. This relationship has not always been easy or pleasant, and neighborhood groups have sometimes been left out. Nevertheless, Atlanta would not be the great city it is today without the effective use of public-private partnerships.

Nature of Public-Private Partnerships

Perhaps the first public-private partnership (PPP) in the United States was the Lewis and Clark Expedition (Summers 2012). This venture had all the characteristics of a PPP as that term is used today. The U.S. government and a private company joined forces to undertake a mission that neither could have done on its own. A PPP is different from simply privatizing or outsourcing a public service. When a city contracts with a private entity to collect its garbage or operate its water system, this is nothing more than hiring someone to perform a task that the city could presumably do itself. Likewise, a PPP is more than selling publicly owned assets to a private entity, even if the transaction includes an incentive for the purchaser to do something in the public interest.

Instead, a public-private partnership entails a working relationship between a governmental body and a private entity to perform a task for their mutual benefit. Usually, this concept is intended to take advantage of what each sector can do best. A sound PPP requires a full understanding of the goals of the venture and a mutual commitment to fulfill each party's obligations. The agreement should be based on clearly defined roles and include an evaluation of the outcomes.

What does each side bring to the table? The public sector, which can take the form of a quasi-public entity as well as a unit of government, is empowered to articulate the public interest and must abide by various laws on public disclosure. The public sector also has an inherent regulatory responsibility. Usually in the U.S., but not always in the rest of the world, a government has greater financial resources and can borrow on more favorable terms than the private sector. Under certain circumstances, it can even condemn land for a public purpose.

On the other hand, a private entity, whether for profit or not for profit, is usually able to act with greater flexibility, since it is not bound by the laws that apply to governmental bodies or required to reveal its decision-making process. It may be able to employ or retain specialized expertise by offering higher compensation than the public sector can pay. Private entities are also subject to various forms of taxation, although such taxes may be abated or reduced as part of an agreement with a governmental unit.

The public goals may range from creating jobs to encouraging desired development. On the private side, the usual incentive is the income that can be earned from the project, but a non-profit entity can also benefit from the accomplishment of one or more of its goals. Public-private partnerships have taken many different forms in Atlanta, as illustrated by the following examples of projects in which I have been involved.

Public Housing

One of the simplest applications is the "turn-key" development of public housing by private developers. In one instance, the Atlanta Housing Authority (AHA) entered into an agreement in 1972 with an entity that Alvin Barge, Herb Millkey Sr. and his son, Herb Millkey Jr., and I had formed for this purpose. Our responsibility was to find a site where public housing could be built in Buckhead; to get the site rezoned if necessary; to design, construct, and finance the entire project; and ultimately to sell the completed units to AHA for a fixed price by a certain date.

The private developer performed all of these tasks, including a contentious rezoning, and eventually transferred the ownership of what was then known as the 3601 Piedmont High Rise to AHA. To this day, few people realize it is actually public housing. AHA gained an attractive residential project that it could not have developed on its own because of the staunch resistance to public housing in this area, and the developer earned a reasonable profit. The overall community benefited from the dispersal of public housing.

Urban Redevelopment

In the early 1970s, AHA, which was then the redevelopment agent for the City of Atlanta, announced its intention to sell 78 acres of land in the Bedford-Pine Urban Redevelopment Area around the Atlanta Civic Center. This sale was prompted by pressure from the U.S. Department of Housing and Urban Development (HUD) to dispose of all of the land that AHA still owned from its urban renewal projects (Grable 1979). The City of Atlanta and AHA decided to divide the site into several tracts to expedite the sale, but Dan Sweat, the president of Central Atlanta Progress (CAP), and other leaders of CAP realized that this property represented a unique opportunity to encourage mixed income housing at a close-in location. This goal could be accomplished only by keeping all of the property together and using the value of the commercial land to subsidize the cost of the land for residential development.

Since AHA was required to sell each of the parcels to the highest bidder, CAP asked six major real estate developers in Atlanta to form a non-profit development company, called Park Central Communities (PCC), to consolidate the property by purchasing each of the parcels separately. However, when AHA decided it would not sell any of the land to a non-profit, PCC was changed to become a for-profit entity, with a non-profit corporation owned by CAP as the majority owner. Joel Cowan agreed to chair the board of this company, and I later became its president.

When the formal bidding was held in 1973, PCC was able to acquire the entire tract by submitting the highest offer for each of the individual parcels. The total amount was $11 million. Because of the intense politics at that time, AHA delegated its approval of the required Comprehensive Development Plan to the local Project Area Committee (PAC), a community group then headed by Ted Clark. The negotiations between PCC and the PAC ultimately bogged down over issues like the number of publicly assisted housing units, the extent and location of open space, and other community goals, primarily because the PAC had little incentive to compromise its positions. Maynard Jackson, who was in his first term as mayor, intervened to arrange a mediation process which finally produced an agreement.

Shortly after the bids were submitted to purchase this land, Atlanta plunged into a severe real estate recession, which prevented PCC from borrowing the funds it needed to post the required down payment. PCC was saved by an unexpected event. A lawsuit against AHA led to the local requirement of an environmental impact statement, which delayed the closing to a time when PCC could make the down payment. The disposition agreement was finally signed in 1975.

Meanwhile, PCC began confidential discussions with a real estate company representing an unidentified client, which turned out to be the Georgia Power Company. These discussions eventually resulted in the sale of a site on

Piedmont Avenue to Georgia Power for its corporate headquarters. With the proceeds from this sale, PCC was able to cover nearly all of the cost of the entire tract and could sell the other sites to individual developers for residential use at a feasible price. In addition to a prominent structure for Georgia Power, the project has produced over two thousand residential units, a shopping center, parks, and other community facilities. This success could not have been achieved without a public-private partnership and enlightened leadership from both the public and private sectors.

Nevertheless, important lessons can be learned from this project. AHA relinquished its own public responsibility by allowing PCC to define the overall goals for the project and delegating many of its approval powers to the PAC. At the same time, the staff of AHA participated in many aspects of the technical planning and design that should have been left to the private developers.

Economic Development

In the early 1980s, the City of Atlanta created the Atlanta Economic Development Corporation (AEDC), largely as an initiative by both Maynard Jackson and Dan Sweat (even though they disagreed over many of the implementing steps, including my selection as its second president). AEDC was formed as a non-profit entity to act as the development arm of the city with a broad-based board of directors, chaired by the mayor. In that sense, AEDC was not a public-private partnership itself, but it has undertaken many projects that do fit the definition of a PPP. (AEDC later became the Atlanta Development Authority and is now Invest Atlanta).

One of the best of these projects was the development of the Atlanta Industrial Park just off Interstate 285 at the Chattahoochee River near Cobb County. This was an area with high unemployment, and Bankhead Courts, a troubled public housing community, was located nearby. Bill Hare, a visionary real estate broker, obtained a listing for a large tract of land with 240 acres that had been used by the Chattahoochee Brick Company for the mining of shale products. The site had been scalped, leaving behind an environmental blight with no apparent value or feasible reuse potential.

AEDC saw the opportunity to develop a close-in industrial park but also recognized the obstacles. Real estate taxes were much higher in the city of Atlanta than in unincorporated Cobb County across the river, and significant funding would be needed to reclaim the land and develop an attractive industrial park. The city government responded by establishing an enterprise zone to abate property taxes under a law enacted by the state for this purpose, and a group of Atlanta banks purchased bonds issued by the Fulton County Development Authority (FCDA) to acquire the land and develop sites. When the city built the streets (with the aid of a federal grant), AEDC worked with the city to grade the adjacent sites at the same time.

In reality, AEDC never owned anything, since the title to the land was held by the FCDA, but it arranged contracts with private developers to construct industrial buildings on a speculative or preleased basis. The entire site has been developed for companies offering well over a thousand jobs. The glue holding everything together was AEDC, which had a pivotal role as the intermediary for all transactions.

Mixed Use Development

When Andrew Young was elected mayor in 1982, he was determined to bring back Underground Atlanta as a retail and entertainment center at the heart of the city. Underground Atlanta had flourished for several years, but it closed by the end of the 1970s, largely because of fears about crime and problems resulting from the fragmented ownership of the site. Moreover, the Metropolitan Atlanta Rapid Transit Authority (MARTA) had cut a broad swath through this area when building its East Line, creating a huge chasm in the middle of downtown. Something had to be done.

So Atlanta did what it does best by forging a partnership between the public and private sectors. The mayor enlisted the help of Dan Sweat and CAP, which then formed a committee of experts to evaluate the feasibility of reviving Underground Atlanta. With its expertise in other "festival marketplaces" across the county, the Rouse Company was a natural partner.

However, a need still existed for an entity to act on behalf of the public and private sectors. The Underground Festival Development Company (UFDC) was created for this purpose. Several of Atlanta's most respected business leaders agreed to serve on its board. Cecil Conlee chaired the board, and I became its president.

Working closely with the city, UFDC designed a complex plan to achieve multiple goals, including a large plaza over the MARTA tracks, a new retail and entertainment center, a hotel, and the museum that would become the "World of Coca-Cola." All of the land had to be assembled for a coherent project. The city would own the plazas, the streets above and below the viaducts, and the parking deck; and a newly formed investment group would own the commercial facilities. The Rouse Company would lease the tenant spaces and manage the center upon its opening.

Interestingly, UFDC coordinated the design and construction of both the public and private improvements using a single architect and a single contractor (both of which were joint ventures). Atlanta's Downtown Development Authority (DDA) issued $85 million in bonds, with 75 percent being spent on public improvements and 25 percent on the commercial facilities. HUD awarded an Urban Development Action Grant of $10 million, and the city used some of its other federal funds for loans and some of its local sales tax funds for land acquisition. Fulton County paid $6 million for the right to use a large portion of the parking, and Atlanta businesses invested $17 million as the final piece in an overall budget of $142 million.

Although the development team considered many alternatives, the intent was always to take advantage of the historic character of this area, especially in terms of the streets that had been covered by viaducts more than 100 years earlier. The existing structures were renovated, and new structures were designed with the original motif in mind. Representative statues and historic markers were placed at appropriate locations along with antique vehicles.

However, the outside plazas had to be more contemporary in design, while creating gathering places on a platform over the rail tracks. The absence of any nearby harbor or river made it essential to add water features in the main plaza. Much of the need for outside lighting was addressed by a tower near the center of the main plaza. Few people realize that a modern radio tower was retrofitted for this purpose.

One of the toughest hurdles was acquiring a large number of privately owned parcels. It would have been legally possible to condemn such parcels, but all of them were purchased through negotiations, sometimes in complex transactions that included a share of future revenues from the project. During the validation of the bonds, the original financing plan was rejected by the Georgia Supreme Court, but the reasons cited by the court provided a guide for revising the plan to meet the constitutional test. The city insisted on an ambitious affirmative action plan, which was implemented in good faith and helped to nurture minority-owned firms that have gone on to be very successful. Meanwhile, the economics of the project required constant value engineering at every stage and led to rental rates which were based on levels of sales projections that turned out to be overly optimistic.

The skills of the development team produced an award-winning design, but the social dynamics affecting the project turned out to be much more difficult. The public-private partnership was very effective during the development phase, in large part because of Mayor Young's leadership, but became less and less of a shared enterprise during the operating phase because subsequent city administrations were less interested in supporting the project as a civic endeavor.

Underground Atlanta got off to a spectacular start when it opened in 1989, but the center has faltered in subsequent years. The highly publicized disturbance that followed the 1992 acquittal of the police officers in the beating of Rodney King and the annual Freaknik weekends—a spring break weekend which, at its height, attracted more than 250,000 students and revelers—created the impression that Underground Atlanta was unsafe. The unkempt conditions outside the Five Points MARTA station made many visitors to the center feel uncomfortable. Further, the national chain stores and upscale restaurants that are typical of other festival marketplaces may not have been the appropriate mix of tenants for Underground Atlanta.

In any event, Underground Atlanta is a classic example of a public-private partnership, which was formed by enlightened civic leaders and implemented through an ingenious plan. The overall setting is still physically attractive after nearly 25 years of operation. The greatest challenge is drawing a mix of local residents which is representative of the entire community as well as tourists and conventioneers. The riddle of Underground is one of Atlanta's most perplexing questions and unfulfilled opportunities.

Centennial Olympic Games

Hosting the Centennial Olympic Games in 1996 was the biggest and boldest civic event in Atlanta's history, but opinions differ as to whether this undertaking was a public-private partnership. Billy Payne and the Atlanta Organizing Committee (AOC) conceived of the games as a private venture that could pay for itself. That aspect was very appealing to everyone. Indeed, AOC's successor, the Atlanta Committee for the Olympic Games (ACOG), operated as a private entity and financed the games though an amazing array of funding sources. The fact remains, however, that the 1996 Olympic Games were "awarded to the City of Atlanta" in the immortal words broadcast from Tokyo on a large screen at Underground Atlanta. Despite the pronouncements, the city and even the state were still ultimately responsible for the all aspects of the games.

A public entity, the Metropolitan Atlanta Olympic Governing Authority (MAOGA), headed by George Berry was organized to provide public oversight and protect the public interest if anything should go wrong. The significant legacy from the 1996 games is found not only in international recognition but also in major public improvements, including Turner Field and Centennial Olympic Park.

This legacy includes a host of other public and private initiatives and types of community improvements, although I had hoped more could have been done for the neighborhoods around the venues. One of the most imaginative projects to benefit the community was the development of Greenlea Commons —with planning input from the Urban Land Institute—near the Olympic Stadium, in which the rents from leasing these townhouses for hospitality suites during the games provided enough equity to sell them to future residents at affordable prices. John Wieland Homes developed this project, and the Summerhill Neighborhood Development Corporation arranged the financing.

Although there was an array of official documents, the roles of the AOC, the MAOGA, and the city were not always clear, and the various goals were not always neatly aligned. As a vivid example of conflicting actions, the city decided to allow entrepreneurs to place vending stands throughout the Olympic venues, much to the consternation of ACOG. Nevertheless, the staging of the 1996 Olympic Games certainly would not have happened without the extraordinary initiative of a private group and the strong support of the public sector.

Civic Projects

Hope House, a transitional residence for homeless men, was developed by Progressive Redevelopment, Inc., a non-profit developer, on land owned by the city on Washington Street near Memorial Drive. The financing included an intricate combination of ground leases tied to the income of the project, several layers of loans, and some "groans" (loans that turn into grants under certain conditions). Hope House opened in 2005 and continues to provide valuable assistance to many formerly homeless men.

In addition to its role in Hope House, the Capitol Hill Neighborhood Development Corporation (CHNDC) guided the development of a large parking deck in the same block, using the proceeds of bonds issued by DDA. (CHNDC is an ecumenical community development corporation formed by the three churches on Capitol Hill.) The city needed parking, and CHNDC wanted to enhance the block across from City Hall and create an attractive site for future mixed use development. The parking deck opened in late 2007, but the rest of the site has not been developed for its intended use.

Atlanta Habitat for Humanity worked with SunTrust Banks in developing its new Family Support Center, which includes a major warehouse and a retail store as well as its administrative offices and educational center. SunTrust used New Markets Tax Credits to make the project feasible. As a result, Atlanta Habitat for Humanity will be able to meet its facility needs; SunTrust earned a reasonable return on its investment; and the federal government achieved its goal of encouraging new development in a distressed area.

Education

In 1991 the Atlanta Board of Education could not find a way to provide critically needed facilities for its students. The formation of a non-profit corporation, which issued $50 million in revenue bonds, resulted in development of new facilities for lease to the school system. This technique has been used by other school systems in Georgia, but is no longer needed with the advent of a sales tax for school facilities.

Charter schools represent a new twist in the evolution of PPPs. They are public schools in the sense that they are open to all students without tuition and are supported by public funds. Nevertheless, each of these schools is operated by a non-profit corporation under a contract with the host school system. A charter management company may also be involved. Several charter schools have been approved by the Atlanta Public Schools and other school systems in Georgia.

The Verdict

So, what is the verdict? A public-private partnership is not enough by itself to make a project work if the underlying economics are not feasible, and the basic principles for a sound partnership have to be followed. However, Atlanta is an excellent case study of how this technique has been used to accomplish civic goals that neither the public nor the private sectors could have done on their own, with the larger city and region being the beneficiaries of these efforts.

CHAPTER 7

Building Public Transit in Atlanta: From Streetcars to MARTA

Harry L. West

The Metropolitan Atlanta Rapid Transit Authority (MARTA) has very deep roots in Atlanta. It was initially conceived of in 1960 as part of a six-point growth and development program for the city proposed by Ivan Allen, Jr., then president of the Atlanta Chamber of Commerce. Touted as an elixir for Atlanta's 1960s era transportation crisis, MARTA's path to materialization in 1979 represents an interesting journey of regime politics and conflict management (Stone 1989; Toon 2007). As an urban planner in Atlanta starting in the late 1960s, I present a firsthand account of the ebbs and flows of the process of making MARTA a reality. In this chapter, I tell a story of this journey beginning with an early history of public transit in Atlanta.

Public Transit in Atlanta: 1866–1969

The Atlanta City Council franchised the city's first public transit company, the Atlanta Street Railway Company, in 1866 (Carson 1981). However, it was not until 1871 that the first line began operating from Downtown to the West End neighborhood with horses and mules pulling transit cars on steel rail tracks. The success of this endeavor prompted other entrepreneurs to enter the arena of public transportation. These were all private companies franchised by the city with very little oversight.

By 1886 five companies were operating on very specific lines and many others had been franchised to begin operation. Some were successful while others were not, leading to the first consolidation of transit companies in 1891. Over the years many more consolidations, bankruptcies, buyouts and failures would occur. Many of the Atlanta business elite were involved, names revered in the development and leadership of the city as financiers and supporters or directly involved in the management and development of the operations. Many of the larger sums of money, however, came from Baltimore and Boston.

The game as well as the playing field changed forever when Joel Hurt developed Inman Park as a suburban residential area. Hurt built and paved Edgewood Avenue, a "straight-as-an-arrow" street, to provide access to Downtown from this new development. More importantly, the avenue included double rail track in the street and introduced the operation of Atlanta's first electric streetcars in 1891. The Atlanta & Edgewood Street Railroad Company began service in 1889. To provide the power to run his electric cars, Hurt constructed his own electric power generating plant. This placed him in direct competition with Henry Atkinson, an engineer, who had started an electric light company and was already competing with the Atlanta Gas Light Company. Quickly, the nature of the competition grew from monopolizing public transit to monopolizing electric power as well. As Atkinson moved into transit, a 10-year open competition ensued.

During the period 1891 to 1902, other transit companies continued to operate, but the primary contenders were Atkinson and Hurt. They operated with changing company names, some so similar they were difficult to distinguish at times, and camouflaged behind other companies as well. For example, Hurt became the head of Trust Company of Georgia and installed Ernest Woodruff as head of his transit operation, even though Hurt made the decisions. Looking for any advantage wherever it might be found, the two protagonists contended in the Georgia legislature, before the Atlanta City Council, in both state and federal courts, in the news media (at one point Atkinson purchased a one-third ownership of *The Atlanta Journal*), and of course in the delivery of services.

While the goal for each man was monopoly of the utilities and its attendant perquisites, publicly both railed loudly and often against the very idea. Most of Atlanta's leaders both public and private had aligned with one side or the other, but they were also growing tired of the confrontation and were concerned with the impact on the future of the city. Not surprisingly, access to capital became the determining factor in who would dominate the race.

It has been suggested that behind the scenes Samuel Inman, after whom Hurt had named his development, quietly contacted banks in Boston, New York, and Baltimore to discuss the Atlanta situation (Carson 1981). For reasons known only to them, the banks collectively decided to back Atkinson. All Hurt's interests were purchased and he agreed to stay out of the transit and electric power business. The Georgia Railway and Electric Company was incorporated in 1902 and proceeded to consolidate electric, natural gas, and rail transit into one utility. The Hurt Building and Georgia Power's Plant

Atkinson are existing physical legacies of their namesakes' contributions to Atlanta's landscape.

For the next 48 years, the rail transit system in Atlanta was owned and operated by a power company, known successively as the Georgia Railway and Electric Company, the Georgia Railway and Power Company, and finally the Georgia Power Company. One would have hoped that after so many years of struggle and turmoil some smooth sailing would be in the offing, but problems—including unregulated competition, political inconsistency, fare controls, labor strikes, and racial issues—continued to impede the process.

Competition came from an unanticipated direction in the late teens and early 1920s. With the growing availability of automobiles, two of Atlanta's largest auto dealers, Hanson Oakland Company and Hopkins Cadillac, encouraged the creation of a jitney service. They not only sold vehicles to entrepreneurs but also operated their own jitneys, privately owned automobiles modified for passenger service. The jitneys operated along the most profitable rail corridors and undercut the transit fare. The jitneys were more flexible and for the most part unregulated, which obviously reduced trolley revenue. Suffice it to say, the transit forces were not passive in their response to this latest business threat. With gradually increasing regulation and some concern regarding illegal procurement activities, some jitney drivers were finally pushed out of business after the better part of a decade (Chambliss 2008).

Transit was also undergoing political transformation in response to new regulations and regulators, inconsistent treatment, and at times outright hostility. The transit system originally was subject only to regulation through the city's franchise agreement. Subsequently, the State of Georgia created the Public Service Commission whose activities not only impacted the transit system but also power production and rates. Arguably, the most difficult time politically for transit in Atlanta was during the two terms of Mayor James L. Key. Personally opposed to transit and backed by an entire administration that was anti-transit and hostile to the power company, the mayor was a force to contend with.

To say that obtaining fare increases was difficult is a gross understatement even when the transit company was required to contribute to the costs of street paving and bridge construction. The level of fares and transfers were kept unreasonably low through most of this period. Also contributing to the financial issues were two very difficult and extensive labor strikes. While operating under Jim Crow laws like all other systems in the South, transit became inadvertently embroiled in the Atlanta race riot of 1906 when some passengers were pulled from a transit vehicle in Downtown and subjected to the rioting.

Later the transit company once again faced competition, this time from coaches and buses. With the able assistance of his attorney, William B. Hartsfield, John Steinmetz created the Suburban Coach Company. Unlike its predecessors, Suburban was careful not to compete directly with the rail system but instead developed routes not served by rail. Georgia Power and Suburban worked together in some ways to improve transit service until the rail system and Suburban were sold in 1950. Another short-lived effort at competition came in the form of rogue taxi cabs. Local proprietor and garage owner A. L. Belle Isle organized the cabs, and he instructed his drivers to select a route into the city and—in effect—ride around until the taxi was full. As might be expected, the service would not be very satisfactory and thus did not last long.

Any discussion of Atlanta's rail transit during this pre-MARTA time would not be complete without mentioning the interurban rail lines. What was the difference between trolley service and interurban lines? Longer distances, city-to-city service, fewer stops, larger vehicles, and higher speeds. Atlanta's first interurban line ran from downtown Atlanta to Marietta Square in 1905. The line was an almost immediate success, with heavy patronage. The line began at Marietta and Walton Streets with stops at Hills Park, Bolton, Gilmore, Smyrna, Fair Oaks, and terminated in Marietta, an 18-mile-long trip. This line bears the unfortunate distinction having had the most disastrous accidents in Atlanta's transit history. On the morning of January 2, 1928, a head-on collision involving an empty northbound train and a southbound commuter train killed six people (Carson 1981; Smith 2010). The line continued to operate and drew new riders during World War II when the Bell Bomber Plant was in operation in Marietta. Shortly after the war and during the time the line was still operating with patronage greater than pre-war volumes, Steinmetz persisted with efforts to acquire the line with the stated intention of reconfiguring it to bus service. Steinmetz acquired ownership and the interurban rail system ceased operations in 1947.

The Stone Mountain interurban line was announced in 1911 and began service in 1913. Disagreement ensued as to whether the line qualified as an interurban line and therefore could use the same fare structure as the Marietta line, even though the two lines covered approximately the same distance. Ultimately the Stone Mountain line was deemed to be not an interurban line and the one-way fare was set at 25 cents, compared with the 35 cents fare on the Marietta line. The service almost folded in 1939, and the Georgia Power Company considered replacing it with buses. Fortunately, the rail service was continued, as shortly thereafter the country was engaged in World War II and fuel rations pushed people to use the rail service. By 1946 Steinmetz was negotiating to purchase the line, again with the intention of converting the service to buses. A legal technicality was discovered that prohibited the sale without Georgia Power first obtaining authority to convert the service. The conversion was approved by the Public Service Commission and the sale to Steinmetz's Suburban Coach took place. The rail service continued into 1948 until buses on order could be delivered.

The third and last foray into interurban service was one that the Georgia Power Company had not been contemplating. Georgia Power had planned to extend trolley service as far as Oglethorpe University and had already applied for the necessary DeKalb County authorization. Then in 1917, the U.S. Army announced plans to construct a training center to be known as Camp Gordon. The camp would be located near Chamblee (on the site of present day DeKalb Peachtree Airport) to support World War I needs. Atlanta's business community immediately began pressing for a quick and easy way for soldiers to get to and from businesses. At the time, the rail line went through Buckhead and continued on Peachtree Road as far as the Fulton-DeKalb County line, with the planned Oglethorpe extension in process. The extension to Oglethorpe with double tracks and the single track to Camp Gordon was in service by October 1917. A War Department grant to improve Peachtree Road, which the Atlanta Chamber of Commerce had helped to obtain, assisted the extension. The service was so overwhelmed with servicemen and civilians that the company added trailer cars, used skip stops, and maxed out the line. However, the company would not incur the expense of double-tracking the line past Oglethorpe University for what it considered to be a temporary use. As the war ended the following year and patronage declined rapidly, the company's decisions seemed appropriate, at least in the short term. Indeed the Camp Gordon service was completely discontinued in 1921. Oglethorpe University remained the end of the line even for bus service until the privately owned transit service was purchased by MARTA.

After considering all the issues and problems one might ask: Why did the Georgia Power Company want to stay in the transit business? For one, it was able to address the challenges over time. Plus the transit businesses provided a critical outlet for the company's electricity with very good profit margins. At the same time, the Georgia Power Company came to consider transit to be a service that improved the city, helping it to prosper and grow and resulting in more customers for electricity. Shortly after the end of World War II, however, the decline of rail transit service in larger cities, with some notable exceptions, was obvious.

The decline of urban rail transit systems across the country was apparent in the post-war period but has particular differences in Atlanta due to local issues. In his effort to acquire the Marietta interurban service and convert the trains to buses, Steinmetz disclosed that Mayor William Hartsfield told him that he wanted all rail out of Atlanta's streets by the end of 1947. The mayor was known to be a strong advocate of limited-access highways and buses. Georgia Power's own introduction of electric buses (trackless trolleys) on some lines provided a more comfortable travel experience for its riders. Then there was the major labor strike that was not settled until after Georgia Power sold the system to the Atlanta Transit Company (ATC) in 1950.

These local concerns may have been in addition to or assisted by some other issues that were affecting rail transit systems all over the United States. One of these was the Public Utility Holding Act of 1935. Many electric street-car systems, such as the one in Atlanta, were owned by electric utilities. The 1935 law, among many other regulatory issues, in effect prohibited owner-ship of streetcar systems by public electric utilities. The law also prohibited the sale of products between utilities, so even if the previous condition had been somehow inapplicable, the electric utility could not have provided subsidized electricity to the streetcars. The law allowed for voluntary submission of di-vestiture plans to the Securities and Exchange Commission. By 1948 most electrical utilities had complied, and the resulting impact was the effective removal of electric transit systems in most cities.

By 1950, the city was without streetcars with the Georgia Power Company having previously sold its interurban lines to Steinmetz and Sub-urban Coach ceasing its streetcar operations in 1949. Georgia Power was in the process of selling the remaining system to the Atlanta Transit Company (ATC) while embroiled in a damaging five-week strike by the transit union. At the time of the sale, more than 450 trackless trolleys were available for service and shortly afterward were rolling again with the ac-tive support of the union. The system was gradually expanded under the guidance of the new owners with some service line extensions and new service. One ATC innovation was the implementation of express service on eight of the electric bus lines; for express service to work, slip sidings were constructed for the local service buses to pull over and allow the express bus to pass. The trackless trolleys were slowly replaced over a 13-year period with diesel engine powered city buses. ATC never pur-chased an electric bus, possibly because after 1959 there were no North American manufacturers of electric buses. By 1963 the active inventory of trackless trolleys in Atlanta was down to less than 300, and by September of that year the entire system was converted to diesel-powered buses, en-abling the removal of the overhead power lines in the city. ATC operated its bus-only system as a private company serving mostly the same area that had been served by the previous owners. ATC later changed its name to the Atlanta Transit System (ATS) and operated under that name until it was acquired by MARTA in 1972 for $13 million.

Public ownership of the transit system in Atlanta had been discussed and anticipated for many years, but not until 1965 was formal action taken in that direction. As early as 1946, a transportation plan for Atlanta prepared under the auspices of the Georgia Highway Department (later the Department of Transportation, GDOT) recommended that the land beneath Peachtree Street be protected for future use as a tunnel for a public transit system. In the early 1960s, the Atlanta Region Metropolitan Planning Commission (ARMPC), later renamed the Atlanta Regional Commission (ARC) had started planning for a system of rapid transit for the Atlanta region.

Legislation approved in the 1965 session of the Georgia General Assembly authorized the creation of a public transit system for five counties: Clayton, Cobb, DeKalb, Fulton, and Gwinnett. Those counties at that time represented the metropolitan area as defined by the U.S. Census Bureau. Each county held a referendum to determine whether or not to participate in the new organization. Cobb voted not to participate, but the other four counties voted yes. MARTA was created by Clayton, DeKalb, Fulton and Gwinnett Counties and became a fledgling organization under the wing of the ARMPC. Planning efforts involved developing a specific system that could be taken to the electorate for financing support.

The referenda to finance the proposed system failed in all four counties in 1968. It was generally thought that proposing an additional property tax to finance the system was the Achilles' heel of the referenda (Basmajian 2008). While disappointed, MARTA staff and supporters went back to the drawing board and began to rethink options for a more acceptable financing mechanism.

MARTA: 1969 Onwards

In 1969 I was appointed Acting County Manager of Fulton County (I did not meet the minimum age requirement, so I remained "acting" until the law could be amended) and as a result became more directly involved in the discussions. I particularly remember Stell Huie, MARTA's attorney, and Pope McIntyre, the financial advisor, and their contributions to solving the financial, legal, and political issues related to the authorization of a second set of referenda in 1971.

After much deliberation and soul-searching, the group had decided that a one percent sales tax in each county would best provide the necessary funding and had the best chance of being approved by the voters (as the total sales tax at the time was only three percent). To say there were obstacles to this approach would be a major understatement, but we agreed to proceed. Individual counties could assess a property tax increase as had been proposed in the first set of referenda, but only the state legislature had the authority to approve a sales tax. Convincing the Georgia General Assembly to set a precedent on any subject was difficult enough, but to prompt them to relinquish their control of sales taxes was a monumental task. This is the part of a successful effort where Huie and his colleagues had their greatest moment. Ultimately the Georgia legislature authorized referenda in the four counties to approve or deny the imposition of a one percent sales tax for the purpose of providing the local support for MARTA. Concessions were made, with the most onerous in the long run being that no more than 50 percent of the sales tax proceeds could be used for maintenance and operations.

With the legal issues overcome, attention now turned to the remaining political issues and how best to convince the voters to support the proposal. I remember participating in strategy sessions held in the upstairs storage area of the J.J. Haverty furniture store in downtown Atlanta. These sessions featured the use of probably every known tactic of political campaigns and public relations promotional efforts. I recall Mayor Sam Massell advocating a free fare but ultimately accepting and supporting a fare reduction to 15 cents. One of the most significant actions prior to the referenda was a visit to Atlanta by John Volpe, the U.S. Secretary of Transportation. During one of his public presentations, either ad lib or purposefully, Volpe promised to deliver federal grants to help build the system, if the voters voted to tax themselves to provide the local match.

The referenda in 1971 was defeated in Clayton and Gwinnett but passed in DeKalb and by a few votes in Fulton. Moving quickly as the public transit agency for the two counties, MARTA negotiated to purchase the ATS bus system, and the deal was closed in February 1972. Expansion of the system began with the placement of orders for new buses. By early 1972, ARC had replaced the ARMPC and other planning organizations as the comprehensive regional planning agency for the metropolitan area, and I had left Fulton County to join the new operation. Around the same time, MARTA announced that Alan Kiepper would be returning to Atlanta to become the organization's new general manager. These unrelated actions reunited a professional and personal relationship that had developed in the mid-1960s. When Kiepper was the Fulton County manager, he appointed me as his assistant in 1964, a relationship that lasted until his departure in 1967 to become the city manager of Richmond, Virginia.

As previously mentioned, a positive relationship between ARC and MARTA had existed for several years, but the ties grew even stronger with the two relatively new organizations being headed by individuals with established favorable working experience (I became Executive Director of ARC in March 1963). The two organizations began regular monthly meetings of senior staff to facilitate communication, coordinate work programs, and enhance individual working relationships. Both MARTA and ARC had acquired new responsibilities through the referenda and legislation and needed to establish good working relationships with GDOT.

One of the first accomplishments was the negotiation of what was then known as the Tri-Party Agreement. Signed by all three organizations, the agreement provided for annual planning work programs to be endorsed and funded and identified how they would work together. This agreement, the first of its kind in the U.S., so impressed the USDOT that it became the basis for a federal requirement across the country for a Unified Planning Work Program. MARTA was one of the first all-new rail transit systems to be funded by the

Urban Mass Transportation Administration), later the Federal Transit Administration (FTA). Some have said that the federal dollars coming to MARTA had been intended for Portland while others say the funds were for Miami. In any event, the dollars were happily received in Atlanta.

As a result of the combined circumstances, all parties involved were to some extent learning "on the go" and becoming increasingly innovative. For example, the entire MARTA referendum system was considered and approved in a single environmental impact statement, something that had not been previously done and, to my knowledge, has not been done since. These were heady times; it seemed MARTA could do no wrong.

One ARC action seemed relatively innocuous at the time, but it ultimately saved MARTA many millions of dollars. The state law that created ARC gave the agency the authority to declare certain proposals with area-wide impact to be "area plans" and it required any activity within those designated areas to be reviewed by ARC. With this authority, ARC declared all land within 200 feet on either side of the referendum system rail lines and 200 feet around the taking area of station sites to be "area plans." This resulted in the review of many private and some public developments to determine their impact on the future MARTA construction. In some cases, after having been notified by ARC, MARTA was able to negotiate with the developer to rearrange building sites to avoid future conflict and possible condemnation; in other cases, MARTA proceeded with acquisition for future use. In most cases, the developer had no idea their proposals would have been in conflict with MARTA plans, and they were willing to seek accommodation.

In our work, we anticipated that transit stations would attract future development; little did we know that this concept would later be called transit-oriented development (TOD) and would become the darling of new urbanists. With the affected local governments and the other planning partners at the table, a program called Transit Station Development Studies (TSADS) was developed. This process began including residents and businesses around the stations' development plans, reflecting their desire for the future station areas. The City of Atlanta adopted its TSADS as a part of their official development plan, DeKalb County used them as guides, and the City of Decatur had been consistent in their support of the plan for the area around the MARTA station in downtown. In many (if not most) cases, the specific plans may have been forgotten, but many of the concepts have remained.

We know today that MARTA extensions into Clayton (with the exception of Hartsfield-Jackson Atlanta International Airport), Cobb, and Gwinnett Counties did not happen, nor did the proposed freeways. The regional population at that time was around 1.5 million. The 4 million people who have arrived since sprawled out, using the surface streets and freeways that were available with improvements added. Had the 1975 plan of transit improvements been implemented, Atlanta would have developed very differently. By the early 1980s, political attitudes had changed to the extent that some county commission chairs demanded that the projected MARTA lines be removed from their county. It would be almost 20 years before a comprehensive system of rail transit would again be part of the official Regional Transportation Plan. Unfortunately, as evidenced by the continued limitations of MARTA to Fulton and DeKalb Counties, very little of that plan has been implemented, and the Atlanta region has been able to stay within air quality requirements primarily through the improved vehicle emission standards imposed on manufacturers.

With existing attitudes regarding MARTA's expansion into counties other than DeKalb and Fulton, the agency stayed in communication with representatives of the other counties and applied itself to completing the referendum system, including some changes and additions.

One of the changes that happened is important enough to justify a bit of explanation here. As mentioned earlier, I-485 was removed from the plan in 1975. Along with the removal of the Stone Mountain Freeway extension, that action made surplus many acres of land where the interchange of the two highways would have been located. Most of that area now is the location of the Jimmy Carter Library and Museum and the Freedom Parkway. For purposes of this discussion, however, it needs to be understood that I-485 as planned would have been the connection from I-85 to I-20 on the east side of downtown Atlanta, where it would have continued south by another name to I-285 and what is now I-675. Northerly I-485 would have intersected with the southerly extension of Georgia 400 (GA 400). From a transit perspective, the abovementioned roads would have included a busway, answering the previous question about transit service to Atlanta Stadium. The section from I-20 to I-285 was removed from the plan, along with an extension of what is now the Langford Parkway that would have intersected with this section and continued eastward to merge with I-20 well east of the city.

GDOT wanted to proceed with constructing the southerly extension of GA 400 from its termination at Interstate 285 to Interstate 85. The proposal was strongly opposed by the City of Atlanta. Politically, this opposition was as strident as such issues can get. Arguments on both sides that anyone could imagine were used to advance respective positions. Concerns ranging from the environment to neighborhood disruption were bandied about and countered by concerns for needed mobility and economic development. Public meetings and hearings were conducted, with as many as 2,000 people attending a meeting one evening in the Lenox Square parking garage. Unfortunately, resolution of the issue was not to be easily forthcoming. As public debate and disrespect were obviously not accomplishing anything, we decided to try a more sedate discussion. Representatives of the City of Atlanta, GDOT, MARTA and ARC met in a conference room next door to my office.

To suggest that this process was quick or easy would be misleading. Tempers were controlled, but the strength or depth of the positions was not in question.

Could GDOT have constructed the road over the city's objection? Fortunately that question did not need to be answered definitively, as examples of possible precedents were available to support both yes and no conclusions. Could MARTA have developed its busway without the road? The cost would have probably been prohibitive. The longer the discussion continued, personal attitudes seemed to soften and the meetings took on a more informal feeling even to the point where the Richard Guthman, city council representative for the area, spreading a large map on the floor and getting down on his knees to illustrate a point. We finally determined that the city was opposed not only to the road but also to the busway. Would the city be willing to withdraw its objection to the road (notice I did not say "support") if a transit rail line were in the roadway instead of the busway? As is well known by now, this was the compromise plan which removed a great hurdle, but many more hours would be expended to work out the funding arrangements. Incidentally, this project may have been the first to combine Federal Highway Administration and FTA funds, toll proceeds, and sales tax monies to fund construction.

Another policy issue with long-range implications for MARTA was the question of competing local bus service. MARTA is the federally designated recipient of FTA funds, including operating bus systems with the funds programmed through ARC's annual Transportation Improvement Program. The FTA provided the funds based on a formula using the system's route miles. As long as MARTA was the only provider of bus service, the question never arose about managing these funds. In the late 1980s, Cobb County proposed to establish its own bus service with both local and express service to Atlanta.

Keep in mind that ARC had previously included Cobb County in its plan for future transit, but then at the insistence of the DeKalb and Fulton Counties it confined transit service to those counties. An important point is that the plan had not specified the provider of bus service, just that the service was needed. While the policy makers may have thought they were removing MARTA from their counties, they actually removed all transit.

With regard to the Cobb proposal, ARC had previously stated that service was needed, but service was not in the current plan. There were legitimate questions: If bus service was needed, why not use MARTA since they obviously know how to operate buses? MARTA could not operate without a positive referendum that would assess the 1 percent sales tax, producing more money than needed for buses in Cobb. Effectively, Cobb County would then be subsidizing Atlanta. Why could Cobb not contract with MARTA to provide the service? Did it really matter if the buses are white or gray as long as the service is provided? All of the arguments of 1965 (plus some others) were raised—with maybe the most important, race, under the surface—but not discussed. Ultimately the independent Cobb Community Transit was approved and began operations in 1989. This set a precedent that was emulated just over a decade later when Gwinnett County Transit began operations in 2001. Not long afterwards the Georgia Regional Transportation Authority began operating express buses to downtown as well. With some organized vanpools and intercity buses using MARTA rail stations as interfaces, one of the goals of the MARTA rail system had been achieved: to get the polluting, smelly buses off the streets of downtown Atlanta.

Inadequate funding to expand, improve, maintain, and operate the system has been a major problem for six of MARTA's seven general managers. Only Kiepper in his decade at MARTA seemed to be able to fund the immediate tasks. Although some additions to the referendum system have been constructed—that is, the north line with stations at Buckhead, Medical Center, Perimeter, Sandy Springs and North Springs—most of the time the executives have not been able to grow the system and have reduced bus service and raised fares. They have also had to deal with an inconsistent board of directors that during many years provided little leadership as well as an oversight committee of the Georgia legislature that was intended to be the agency's support group within the state but has instead at times been counterproductive. MARTA remains the only major city transit system that receives no support from the state budget.

One can only hope that Atlanta can overcome our tendency to create competitors when we disagree with or dislike something. As many former leaders recognized very early on in the city's development, viable transit is necessary for the development and functionality of the city's core and by extension the region. At some point we must as a community and a state develop the intestinal fortitude to fix the transit mess that we have created or drastically reshuffle our development patterns.

BOOKER T·WASHINGTON
1856   1915

HE LIFTED THE VEIL OF IGNORANCE
FROM HIS PEOPLE·AND POINTED
THE WAY TO PROGRESS THROUGH
EDUCATION AND INDUSTRY·

PART 2

Diversity and Development

Zoning came to Atlanta in the 1920s. Robert Whitten prepared the city's first code based on his work on the New York City Zoning Ordinance of 1916. Whitten's concept of "stabilizing populations" took an abrupt turn when he advocated separating apartment and commercial uses from single-family neighborhoods. His 1922 Atlanta Zone Plan went much further than that of other communities by mapping blocks by race and class; it was subsequently overturned by the Georgia Supreme Court in 1926 in Smith v. Atlanta. But the damage was done. Black communities north of downtown were displaced to the southern portion of the city and segregationists began developing deed-restricted planned neighborhoods throughout the city. From the 1930s to 1950s, the Veterans Administration and Federal Housing Administration reinforced the segregated blocks with continued redlining throughout the city (Lands 2009).

Racial issues and redlining prevailed. Planning was controlled by business leaders. The primary distinguishing factor between the city's separate leadership structures was that white leaders tended to be men of commerce and industry while black leaders largely were professionals or ministers who were politically oriented (Pomeranz 1996). Everything changed when Maynard Jackson, Atlanta's first African American mayor, was elected in 1974.

Leon Eplan, former commissioner of planning, describes planning issues in his first person account of enacting community input through the Neighborhood Planning Unit (NPU) process in "The Genesis of Citizen Participation in

Figure C.1. Booker T. Washington statue, "Lifting the Veil of Ignorance"

Atlanta." Eplan describes working closely with Jackson to engage the community with the newly organized NPU system. Throughout the 1970s, they worked together to engage the entire community and their legacy remains the basis of planning in Atlanta.

"Freedom Park; A Modern Day Battle" describes the most litigated roadway in the southeast, known as the Stone Mountain Tollway in the 1970s, the Presidential Parkway in the 1980s, and the Freedom Parkway in the 1990s. Barbara Faga describes the 40-year battle between engineers, the city, the state, and the neighborhoods to stop an expressway that ultimately resulted in a parkway and park. The battle ended in 1994—in time to construct the first phase prior to the arrival of media and tourists for the 1996 Centennial Olympics.

"Race and Class in Atlanta-Style Development: Promoting Inclusion and Justice" by Michael Dobbins discusses how race, class and location informed the city's development ethic leading up to the Olympic Games in 1996. In the years since, this ethic has persisted and evolved and must now often meet the demands of communities empowered by community benefits agreements.

Charles Palmer and his good friend President Franklin Roosevelt replaced the Atlanta slums in the 1930s by building several public housing projects (Palmer 1955). In 1994 the city became known for innovative subsidized housing when the Atlanta Housing Authority demolished public housing and replaced it with mixed income housing and Section 8 vouchers. Thomas D. Boston, in "Public Housing Demolition and Neighborhood Revitalization," looks at the displacement of hundreds of families from Grady Homes. Constructed in 1942, it had devolved into slums and was demolished in 2005. Boston discusses the implementation of public housing policies to provide families with better housing and quality of life.

Maria Saporta describes the big ideas and projects of Atlanta's developers, designers, and builders in "The Evolution of the Business Leaders Who Built Modern Atlanta." Drawing from interviews with business and political leaders—including developers Egbert Perry, Tom Cousins, and former mayor Shirley Franklin, Saporta discusses issues from white flight to sprawl and from inequality to walkable centers

In "Neighborhood Quality of Life and Health in Atlanta", Nisha Botchwey, Susannah Lee, Audrey Leous, and Subhro Guhathakurta describe how planning and design affect the lives of Atlanta's residents. By controlling for socioeconomic characteristics in neighborhoods across the city, they show both overlaps and disparities in the geographic distribution of quality of life and health measures. They also identify the features common in areas that rank high in these measures, such as access to green spaces, walkable environments, and healthy foods.

As these chapters illustrate the city's civic and political leadership has differed from its counterparts in other cities by striving to grow beyond the city's past and legacy of racial tensions. Those efforts were often collaborative and crossed racial and political lines that assisted the city and its diverse population in flourishing economically, politically and socially. They also laid the groundwork for some of the city's most sterling moments such as the Centennial Olympic Games in 1996. Despite the city's progress, much work remains to done to eliminate socioeconomic and health disparities between racial groups. However, with the past as prologue, Atlanta stands poised to do this better than most.

CHAPTER 8

The Genesis of Citizen of Participation in Atlanta

Leon S. Eplan, FAICP

When Atlanta's newly elected mayor, Maynard Jackson, entered his office for the first time in January 1974, he found a city that few would have recognized just a few decades earlier. Building on an excellent railroad and highway network, Atlanta in the previous decades had evolved into the major center of economic and political activity of the southeastern region. Military operations in and around the city during World War II had strengthened that primacy, and at the end of the conflict, an important portion of this war-related activity settled in and remained. Strong economic activities followed, responding not only to the wartime growth but also to pent-up consumer demands that had gone unsatisfied during the 16 long years of depression and war. The region's population exploded, and by 1950 almost a million people were residing in the Atlanta area, with one-third of them living within the city.

Transformation in City and Region

Throughout the the 1950s, the future of the region seemed highly favorable and assured. The Atlanta region covered five counties, and it was attracting tens of thousands of newcomers, a large number of employment opportunities, and considerable investments and wealth. Construction on three interstate highways was underway, expansions were made at the international airport, and large federal grants were flowing in to underwrite new infrastructure, roads, schools, and housing. Favorable local and federal lending practices also helped underwrite new development.

Nevertheless, a sharp change had begun to take place in the region's traditional trends. While more than 313,000 people were added during the decade of the1950s, the city's growth began to take a different and slower path. Census figures for that decade showed that Atlanta had gained 156,000 residents, and it was widely assumed that the city would continue these considerable population gains. Actually, that expectation proved to be illusionary. Overlooked was the huge annexation which had been approved in 1952, which had tripled the city's size and added 130,000 persons who were living in that adjacent area. Without that annexation, the city's population would have actually increased by only about 26,000 people, fewer than had been added in the previous decade.

Nonetheless, the region's population continued to increase at a galloping pace. During the 1960s, another 450,000 people were added into the Atlanta region, bringing the total population to over 1.3 million inhabitants. By contrast, the city's shrinking growth continued, with only 10,000 more residents gained. Even with so few added, the city's population still reached almost a half million residents in 1970.[1] Unfortunately, that was to be its historical high mark, a total that has never been reached again since. An era of abandonment had set in. Atlanta's population would drop sharply, by 71,000 people during the 1970s and still another 30,000 in the 1980s. Those 20 years were catastrophic for the city in many vital ways in addition to its diminished population.

Stirrings

Few issues have been more central to the shaping of Atlanta throughout its history than that of race. The proportion of African Americans and whites came into balance in Atlanta in the early 1950s, and throughout the 1960s, the races were almost totally equal in number. Segregation was then the universal law, firmly held and rigidly enforced. Signs of a limited integration were occurring, but slowly, in small increments, and sometimes forced. Yet the walls that had long existed between parallel worlds were being pierced. This transformation was taking place even as the city, with its strong black leadership, was emerging as a national center for the civil rights movement. The Southern Christian Leadership Conference, under its president, Dr. Martin Luther King Jr., set up its headquarters in downtown Atlanta, coordinating the efforts of dozens of black churches throughout the South on strategies for local boycotts and marches (Morris 1984).

Amid this era of change, the number of perceived threats due to changes in the distribution of housing was beginning to increase. At the time, the main area where African Americans lived was confined primarily to a tightly drawn part of central downtown Atlanta, plus some fringe housing around it. The rapid growth of Atlanta's African American population in the 1950s, however, had led to severe shortages of housing for African American families. Bolstered by the discriminatory actions of real estate companies, African Americans were beginning to exert pressure to buy into white neighborhoods to the west and south, and the phenomenon of so-called "blockbusting" began. Political efforts to halt the movement of African Americans into traditionally white neighborhoods were undertaken, to no avail. Then, in April 1960, bombings took place in Adamsville and other neighborhoods (Meridan Record 1960). In October 1960, students from historically black colleges at nearby Atlanta University Center launched a number of sit-ins at Rich's, one of the two leading department stores in downtown Atlanta. That action received the immediate and full attention of the business community, whose members had always sought to portray a positive and progressive image of the city. The pressure for change was sweeping into the city, and the Downtown stores became integrated in 1961, three years before the adoption of the Civil Rights Act of 1964, which had mandated fair access to public accommodations (Allen 1996).

On August 30, 1961, nine students became the first African American students to attend several all-white Atlanta public high schools. Nine days later, on September 8, 1961, Time magazine reported: "Last week the moral siege of Atlanta (pop. 487,455) ended in spectacular fashion with the smoothest token school integration ever seen in the Deep South. Into four high schools marched nine Negro students without so much as a white catcall" (Time 1961).

Meanwhile, soon after World War II, construction was underway on Atlanta's Central Artery (later Interstate 75/85). A huge corridor was created on land formerly occupied by dilapidated, blighted rental housing units that were demolished, thereby displacing thousands of families, mostly black and very low income. The highway engineers, in fact, referred to the construction as a "slum clearance" project. During the 1960s, the city also embarked on a comprehensive urban renewal program, funded primarily by the federal government. Three projects were undertaken that almost totally cleared the land. Similar to the downtown highway project, these projects also removed thousands of low-rent, primarily substandard housing units, formerly occupied by both black and white residents (Allen 1971). Together, these two local and federal initiatives dislocated some 57,000 white and black individuals and families over a 10-year period. Regrettably, little funding was made available to assist displaced people who needed to be relocated.

A New Charter
The turbulence Atlanta faced after the end of World War II made governing the city under its existing city charter increasingly difficult. Elected and appointed officials were unable to deal adequately with the changes that confronted them, and the public was unable to assess responsibility for performance. In order to adjust

to its major managerial problems, the City of Atlanta, together with its political and business leadership, petitioned the Georgia General Assembly in 1972 to grant the city a new charter. The new charter that was issued substantially altered the city's historical manner of governance. Administrative oversight of departments was shifted from the city council to the mayor, thereby replacing a so-called "weak mayor" form of government with a "strong mayor" government. For the first time, the mayor would manage the city's daily administrative functions. Most important, the new charter gave the mayor the opportunity to lead, coordinate, and direct all executive activities in a common direction.

Following the 1973 Election

A watershed moment arrived in Atlanta history with the city-wide election of 1973. It pitted the white incumbent mayor, Sam Massell, against Maynard H. Jackson, an African American who was at the time the vice mayor of the Board of Aldermen (a position later known as the president of the City Council). Following a highly contested campaign, Jackson was handily elected as the city's first African American mayor, and Atlanta became the first large metropolis in the South to come under African American leadership.

Entering office in January 1974, Jackson was to govern over a city that was steadily growing smaller. Atlanta had a new populace, one more diverse and exhibiting wider mixtures of interests and expectations. Atlanta had started the previous decade as a majority white, middle-class, and segregated community. Now, 14 years later, thousands had moved away, taking with them not only their economic capacity but also their contribution to the social fabric of the city. Those who remained bore witness to an evolving and different culture (Kruse 2005).

Young college graduates intent on starting their careers were arriving, as were empty nesters and retirees. But by far, the largest category of newcomers arrived from farms and small towns, in search of economic opportunities. The new arrivals included thousands of individuals who were poor and dispossessed, many with little experience with urban living and its particular requirements leading some business leaders began to question Atlanta's economic future.

Early on, Jackson was confronted with the reality that the changes of the 1950s and 1960s required immediate attention. At the outset of Jackson's administration, the city had first to deal with matters which were negatively impacting the city's tax base. The considerable loss of people, especially the white middle class, was affecting the consumer markets upon which businesses depended. A serious challenge was also posed by the large increase the number of households with lower incomes, as well as the obligation to address the problems of the tens of thousands of mostly lower-income people who had been displaced by public construction projects. As a result of these changes, cuts had to be made regularly in the maintenance of infrastructure, schools, parks, and public buildings. Along with this was the related challenge of trying to retain the needed workforce, including police personnel.

In addition to these internal management issues confronting Jackson, an unexpected national economic downturn also impacted businesses already feeling the effects of the loss of their middle-class customers. Competition was felt from new shopping centers being built in the close-by suburbs. Finally, and not to be overlooked or understated, was the difficulty experienced by many white residents in adapting to the new reality of their city under African American leadership.

Reaching Out

With a new city to govern and its shifting demographics, Jackson recognized both the need and the obligation to provide a better means for connectivity between citizens and the city's public and social institutions. He spoke of providing a structured and permanent way to increase communications, not only between residents and his administration but also between newcomers and those who were long-time residents. The intent of this framework was also to carry out the charter's requirement for continuous citizen involvement in its comprehensive planning and development (CDP) process. Finally, he sought to launch such a program quickly, with a goal to put it in place in 1975, a year after he took office.

Planning under the New Charter

For the most part, Atlanta's 1972 charter was written in rather general terms. It described, for example, the duties and expectations of the mayor's office in typical general terms, leaving to the mayor the task of developing organizational guidelines. In regard to city planning, however, the charter, and its accompanying Reorganization Ordinance, was quite specific. In addition to the routine roles undertaken by most city planning components (zoning, subdivisions, research, maintenance of maps and records, and public hearings), the charter charged Atlanta's planning department to perform its current and long-term planning functions by means of an annual CDP, a unique approach among American cities. It called for the plan to cover three time periods—1, 5, and 15 years—each of which would emphasize the importance of citizen input. It was intended that the 1-year plan would indicate those city projects to be undertaken in the upcoming year, while the 5-year plan would lay out goals to be accomplished during that longer span of time. The 15-year plan was to be aspirational, intended to show how the city planned to implement the long-range goals adopted by the plan.

To strengthen the ability to implement the CDP, the Reorganization Ordinance tied comprehensive planning to the city's annual budget. To accomplish this, a new Budget Policy Bureau was created and placed with planning within in the Department of Budget and Planning. This would permit the operations and actions of the two bureaus to be linked, so that the city's plans for their implementation would be strengthened.

Finally, the charter directed that the annual CDP be presented by the mayor each year to the city council. Following possible additional citizen hearings, the council, after discussions and any amendments, would then adopt the plan by ordinance. By law, the council would have to adopt a CDP by no later than the middle of June. The ordinance would thus give the plan firm legal status, an especially valuable tool when city actions were challenged in court.

At the outset of the new planning and citizen participation process, the Bureau of Planning prepared a city-wide map showing 177 so-called "neighborhoods" in Atlanta. These areas were predominantly residential clusters, or sometimes small commercial nodes, with clearly defined boundaries and names. Some were quite large in size, while others were very small. Public housing projects, for example, qualified as neighborhoods, and even a small, organized business community was included.

With only a limited planning staff for the planning and participation program, and with so many neighborhoods to service, it became necessary to bundle the neighborhoods into larger units. Neighborhoods were placed together when they were physically close and appeared to have similar interests or characteristics. The combined clusters of neighborhoods were called neighborhood planning units, or NPUs. Generally six to eight neighborhoods would make up an NPU. In all, 24 NPUs were created, each given a letter of the alphabet (omitting J and U). NPUs would be required to elect a board annually, comprising individuals chosen by each neighborhood in the NPU to serve as its representatives for the year.

Identifying the appropriate name for each neighborhood was deemed essential. Establishing and maintaining neighborhood identity was central to the NPU process, to ensure that residents would identify with their communities and derive a sense of place and pride from living there. Once all neighborhoods had been defined, any community name that was already in widespread use locally was chosen to identify that cluster. Whenever a neighborhood lacked a widely recognized name, local interviews were conducted and, taking into account the input of the residents, a name was suggested, often referencing the name of a main street, park, or school.

Citizen Involvement

The basic structure of the NPU system put in place in the mid-1970s is still in use today. Each NPU has a monthly meeting that is open to the public. Citizens can become involved at such meetings by participating in issues or by putting forth issues that they would like to see discussed. At such meetings, opinions are sought on all proposals received by the Bureau of Planning (such as a rezoning request, a proposed public or private project, or the like), especially those that would directly impact the NPU. Following such discussion, votes may be taken on whether to approve or deny the proposal, or to not take a position. In cases when a change in that year's adopted CDP might also be required if the project is approved, the NPU can vote on whether or not it would favor the approval of a plan change. In some cases, one of the member neighborhoods may also want to discuss a proposed rezoning or a CDP change, or express the neighborhood's position at the board meeting. In many cases, the individual or company seeking the request will give a presentation at one of the meetings, or even to an affected neighborhood. In response to community input, a rezoning request may be altered to gain support for the proposal.

Whenever proposals requiring zoning change come before the Zoning Review Board (ZRB), members of the public, the NPU, and the Bureau of Planning are given the opportunity to express their opinions. Decisions of the NPU—as well as those of the ZRB—are advisory only. From these hearings, all opinions of the NPU are passed on to the zoning committee of the city council. There are no hearings at zoning committee meetings, although the opinion of the Bureau of Planning is presented. Once the committee's opinion of a proposal is determined, the matter is then forwarded to the full city council for its review and a final vote.

Most staff members of the Bureau of Planning staff are assigned to work with one or two NPUs. Planners attend monthly meetings and collaborate with NPU leadership to draw up agendas on a full range of issues to be considered at each monthly meeting. Two educational guides for citizen use were published in the 1970's: The Value of Neighborhoods and How To Do Neighborhood Planning.

As earlier indicated, the two bureaus within the Department of Planning and Development—Planning and the new Budget Policy Bureau—are continuingly involved in putting together the annual CDP. All executive department staffs are also continuously involved to get input on projects they are seeking to implement. The bureau has the responsibility of examining the city's traditional budget, put together by the Department of Finance, in order to provide links between the budget and the CDP's goals. Also reviewed by the Budget Policy Bureau is how well the proposed traditional budget relates to the mayor's priorities, reflects larger administrative considerations, makes full use of grant funds, incorporates intergovernmental recommendations, and provides for the continuation and implementation of multiyear projects (Shelby 2013).

Lessons Learned

All Georgia cities now produce comprehensive plans and also have processes that allow citizens to become engaged in urban planning and other major issues in their communities. Sometimes the initiatives of planning and citizen participation are linked, although none as closely as they have become in Atlanta.

Efforts elsewhere in Georgia to link planning and citizen participation tend to differ from Atlanta's processes in important ways, especially the following three:

- First, in a dynamic economy, plans can soon become obsolete unless a structured and permanent means is adopted for keeping both the plans and the involvement apparatus current. If it is not current, then when a comprehensive plan begins anew after a multi-year gap, most of the previously assembled information and data must be collected again, often from scratch.

- Second, even where cities require that a zoning change must conform to its plan, most places readily and quickly change their plans to comply with the zoning, giving short shrift to the long and arduous plan review process. Constantly changing a city's plan undermines the citizen participation efforts. Atlanta's process, which makes plan changes only quarterly, places considerable dependence on the agreed plan and serves as the statement of what citizens say they want their city to become. As a result, hearings in Atlanta are often very well attended, and the issues are sharply critiqued. Since the annual plan is put together with citizen input, citizens take an ownership position in preserving the plan.

- Third, all cities have developed varied means for bringing citizens into the planning process. Large hearings which usually are held ad hoc, however, have proven to be a poor way to assure meaningful citizen input, particularly when citizens do not know the background of an issue and have had little experience in how to respond to a proposal.

Conclusions

Atlanta's comprehensive planning and citizen participation processes were developed in 1975, two years after the Georgia General Assembly give the city a new charter. In each of the past 38 years, Atlanta produced its CDPs in accordance with the process described here. One major change in the original process is that now a review of the entire city plan occurs every five years rather than annually. Whenever a proposal is introduced that might require a change in the current CDP, hearings on those matters are held at the quarterly meetings throughout the year. Such discussions are also reviewed by the affected NPUs to obtain their opinions, and, when expressed, this feedback is integrated into the remainder of the city review process. The CDP, therefore, has remained central to the city's decision process, and proposed actions are not undertaken unless they first obtain a favorable recommendation to amend the CDP. Citywide plans, such as for parks or transportation or for projects to be undertaken during the year by city departments, are also reviewed by the NPUs and included in the final plan.

Throughout almost four decades, the activities of the NPUs have increased in importance at the local level. At monthly NPU meetings, proposals made to the Bureau of Planning, together with parochial matters, are discussed, often with a fair amount of preparation and passion. Localized problems are also identified and brought to the attention of city council representatives and city agencies, such as streets that need to be repaired or parks that require attention.

At the required annual NPU elections for officers, persons seeking to be selected as one of the NPU officers sometimes actively engage in campaign efforts. Though the NPU leadership positions are unpaid, their impacts on the communities are substantial, and interested persons in a neighborhood may vie to become its representative on the NPU board.

Today, the planning and participation process has resulted in a generation of Atlanta citizens who have become better informed as to how their government operates and how well. It has also encouraged residents to become better prepared to articulate their ideas and concerns. Several members of the current city council were formerly active in their NPUs

CHAPTER 9

Freedom Park: A Modern Day Battle

Barbara Faga

THERE IS LITERALLY NO PARK IN THE UNITED STATES LIKE FREE-
DOM PARK. THERE ARE PARKS DECKED OVER FREEWAYS, THERE
ARE PARKS WHERE AUTOMOBILES HAVE BEEN BANNED, THERE ARE
PARKS WHERE PARKING LOTS HAVE BEEN REMOVED, BUT FREEDOM IS
THE ONLY PLACE THAT HAS BEEN CREATED AS A LIVING MEMORIAL, IN
EFFECT, TO THE PEOPLE WHO DEFEATED A HIGHWAY.
—PETER HARNIK, DIRECTOR OF THE CENTER FOR
CITY PARK EXCELLENCE, TRUST FOR PUBLIC LAND

"Build a great park" was the direction from President Jimmy Carter in 1983
when he envisioned the design of the 20-acre site of his presidential library,
situated in the middle of a 273-acre kudzu forest (Carter 1983). The resulting
Freedom Park and Freedom Parkway evolved over four decades as a protracted series of hopes, plans, and visions set forth by a procession of mayors,
governors, city council members, university presidents, National Park Service
representatives, U.S. congress people, a U.S. President, and the true stars in
this urban drama, the neighbors. The project started in 1950 when the Georgia Highway Department (GHD) planned a state road as the new link in a
chain of expressways to join the Stone Mountain Parkway east of the city to the
Interstate 75/85 connector. The route, known as "The Tollway," was planned
in the days when road planning was accomplished swiftly by state engineers
with no "interference" from the public (Figure 9.1).

Figure 9.1. Freedom Park boundaries and the Carter Center

Fighting the Tollway

Neighbors began filing lawsuits to stop the tollway in 1965 when the state began acquiring land. Fighting the State of Georgia was a full-time job for activists from the historic Morningside, Virginia-Highland, Poncey-Highland, Druid Hills, Lenox Park, Old Fourth Ward, and Inman Park neighborhoods. Developed from the 1890s through the 1950s, the seven intown neighborhoods mounted an opposition to what ultimately became the most litigated public project in the state's history. Representatives of Neighborhood Planning Units (NPUs) and numerous neighborhood associations exerted their considerable influence to stop the road entirely, investing 40 years in a knockdown fight. In a 1970 show of strength, the GHD acquired and demolished—sometimes through the use of eminent domain—over a thousand homes that lay in the path of the proposed road. The center of the swath of destruction was historic Copenhill, the 1864 Union Army encampment for the Civil War Battle of Atlanta (Davis 2013). Ironically, again the battle lines were drawn.

Atlanta has a strong foundation of community participation in planning decisions. Passage of the National Environmental Policy Act (NEPA) was the outgrowth of a series of environmental injustices, including the construction of roadways and dams, and it was bolstered by the 1962 publication of Rachel Carson's revolutionary book *Silent Spring* (Carson 1962). NEPA established a game-changing public process requiring extensive community consultation, and the NEPA legislation included a public scoping process for review of the draft environmental impact statement (EIS) (Shepherd and Bowler 1997). Community activists, accustomed to a charade of meetings where officials only informed them of actions, were doubtful initially, but the public soon learned that working with a government agency ensured responses to their comments. The 1970 Clean Air Act, the 1972 Clean Water Act, and the 1972 Coastal Zone Management Act followed, and the public came to understand that citizen participation was their right.

Atlanta was already there. In March 1973, emboldened by NEPA, the neighborhoods persuaded then governor Jimmy Carter to stop the proposed highway. The Rome News-Tribune in Georgia reported that Carter's study committee "apparently end[ed] a ten-year controversy over building a road linking downtown Atlanta with the Stone Mountain Freeway" (Rome News Tribune 1972). Maynard Jackson, then mayor of Atlanta, also condemned the tollway. The federal government rejected the EIS, stating the NEPA conditions were not taking into account the negative neighborhood impact. "Virtue has triumphed" proclaimed Michael Padnos, Morningside's lawyer in the Spartanburg Herald (1971). With the tollway removed from Georgia's long-term highway plan, the fight appeared over; nonetheless, the new Georgia Department of Transportation (GDOT) did not relinquish title to the 273 acres.

Plans Never Die

As planners know, plans seldom die. They lay in wait for reincarnation. So it happened with the Stone Mountain Tollway. Several attempts to revive the tollway surfaced over the next decade, only to be quelled each time. Everything changed in 1981, when former president Jimmy Carter returned to Georgia in search of a location for his presidential library. Historic Copenhill was identified as the prime location, vacant and situated at the crossroads of the overgrown kudzu and trash-covered acreage previously earmarked for the tollway. Within weeks the tollway was back on the table with a new moniker, the Presidential Parkway. The city and state spun into action, this time marketing a parkway in lieu of the failed tollway. In a public relations attempt, GDOT negotiated the resale of excess parcels to their previous owners. Over 83 percent of owners repurchased their properties and, having moved on, quickly flipped them to new owners, often on the same day (Howard 1982).

Proposed as a four-lane road, the GDOT-designated Presidential Parkway was the roadway portion of a newly conceived Great Park, envisioned to be Atlanta's Rock Creek Park. Mayor Andrew Young, the Atlanta city council, and Atlanta's business community—buoyed by Governor George Busbee—all became supporters of the Presidential Parkway and the proposed surrounding Great Park (Wormer 1995). By comparison, residents of the affected neighborhoods saw the "new" project as the return of the dreaded tollway, and the old battle was reborn. The Carter Center broke ground in 1984 (Figure 9.2). Jova/Daniels/

Figure 9.2. The Carter Center within Freedom Park, circa 1997

Busby, Lawton, Umemura & Yamamoto, and EDAW made up the design team, designing four pods surrounded by 20 acres of landscape, lakes, and parking, with a commanding view of the Atlanta skyline (Carter Center 2013). I was one of the EDAW designers working on the Carter Library.

Enter CAUTION

Founded in the early 1980s, Citizens against Unnecessary Thoroughfares in Older Neighborhoods (CAUTION) was a coordinated effort by the intown neighborhoods that had one goal: stop the road. CAUTION became the legal and fundraising arm of the opposition neighborhoods. A sister group, Road-busters, was the road fight protest group. Together these organizations galvanized the neighborhoods and elected 44 of their supporters to public offices, including council and commissions in Atlanta and DeKalb and Fulton County. They raised money, chained themselves to trees, fought the road, filed lawsuits, and ultimately stopped the Presidential Parkway when the Druid Hills Civic Association and The National Trust for Historic Preservation took on the Federal Highway Administration and won (Druid Hills1985).

Even as the Carter Center was under construction, CAUTION did not skip a beat filing lawsuits. In the 1970s, young lawyers, professors, and professionals had staked their claims to the surrounding neighborhoods, revitalizing historic but long-neglected Victorian and Craftsman homes. These were neighborhoods with long histories and impressive pedigrees. Druid

Hills opened in 1895, designed as a major southern subdivision by New York's Central Park landscape architect Frederick Law Olmsted (Rybczynski 2000). Four years later Inman Park opened, completed by Atlanta developer Joel Hurt. These neighborhoods provided grand intown housing in the late nineteenth century for business owners and influential citizens, including early Coca-Cola millionaires, but had declined by the mid-twentieth century into areas of boarding houses and subdivided apartments. The young homeowners who had been drawn to the neighborhoods in the 1970s were smart and politically astute, and they were not about to lose the battle to preserve their investment in the 1980s. They had grown accustomed to the kudzu and acres of vacant land; some had built pop-up gardens and impromptu play areas on the state's property. The initiatives were grassroots: "We were young, we were professionals and we were true believers waging a crusade," explained community resident and Freedom Park Conservancy activist Cathy Bradshaw (Freedom Park Conservancy 2013). Despite the opposition, the Carter Center opened in 1987 with a temporary road as the only access.

Political Winds Change

On September 18, 1990, the city celebrated the announcement from Tokyo: Atlanta was selected as the host of the 1996 Summer Olympics, beating out the favorite, Athens, along with Belgrade, Manchester, Melbourne, and Toronto. In 1990 Maynard Jackson returned for his third term as mayor, following Andrew Young's two-term limit. No one, including then governor Zell Miller, wanted to expose the road controversy to the early media coverage of the Olympic Games. Under pressure from elected officials and local Olympic organizations, a DeKalb County judge ordered mediation to solve the problem. In 1992—led by Leon Eplan, Atlanta's planning commissioner—representatives of the neighborhoods; local, city and county governments; and GDOT locked themselves in a motel room and negotiated daily until the road issues were resolved. The resulting agreement gave GDOT its road, and CAUTION agreed the road could be built if reduced to a one-lane, limited-access parkway with a speed limit of 35 miles per hour. Tentative peace had been reached, with the promise that the Carter Center would have a landscaped parkway to bring distinguished visitors to its front door.

Everything's Negotiable

As often occurs with tentative negotiation, it does not solve issues but merely sets the stage for further negotiation. EDAW (now AECOM) was selected to design the park, and the Corporation for Olympic Development in Atlanta (CODA) led the implementation. Eplan, respecting the connection to the Martin Luther King Jr. National Historic Site and the Carter Center, proposed the names Freedom

Park and Freedom Parkway. Eplan organized the design around Frederick Law Olmsted's five themes: using open space to build a sense of community, preserving the topography, using indigenous landscape, creating wide paths and drives to avoid crowding, and sensitively integrating pedestrian bridges and all built elements into the overall plan (Faga 2006).

The neighborhoods, design team, National Park Service, city officials, Carter Center representatives, and business community members worked through weekly meetings at the Martin Luther King Jr. National Historic Site. Everything was negotiable, and everything involved discussion. One sticking point was the sidewalk width; even a 12-foot-wide sidewalk can look like a future road to a community suspicious of planning motives. Photos of comparable walks in New York, Paris, and Vienna had little effect on the neighbors. Instead the community advocated for three-foot-wide sidewalks, anticipating that limiting the width would provide no future opportunities to expand the walks into roads. Negotiation resulted in eight-foot-wide sidewalks.

Seven pedestrian bridges over existing roads were removed from the plan after exhausting discussion; today bikes and baby strollers wait patiently to cross five lanes of traffic at Moreland Avenue. After 40 years of fighting, the neighbors could not be persuaded to approve anything that vaguely resembled a road. After more than 50 neighborhood meetings in community facilities and backyards and on front porches, the neighbors approved a plan for a "passive park" that is a park for lawn and trees; no ball fields, playgrounds, attractions and absolutely no active sports facilities. In retrospect, the sidewalk issue looks mundane; however, at the time the neighbors saw any flat concrete as a probable future road.

Design Legacy

The first of five construction phases was complete by the opening of the 1996 Summer Games. CODA, the Olympic agencies, city officials, and the neighbors were relieved to have portions of the park in place. The passive park has become a cultural venue for sculpture, including legacy and temporary installations, and it is considered a success by park users and neighbors. Yet residents have a few wishes for the park says Janet Keith, owner of the King-Keith House, a bed-and-breakfast in Inman Park:

> My wish is we had planned for more houses so we could knit back the neighborhood. We had no idea that the demand for housing in Inman Park would be so great. When you look at the "steps to nowhere" from the demolished houses, you can see how great it would have been with more original old homes. [But] we've been fortunate to have quality infill housing built on much of the vacant land. (Keith 2013)

CAUTION evolved into the Freedom Park Conservancy in 1996. CAUTION's mission wisely changed from confrontation to endowment so the park could fund future projects and maintenance. A master plan update is scheduled for the park as new residents and board members consider the possibility of widening roads and sidewalks, adding pedestrian bridges, and promoting active park uses. Newcomers to the neighborhoods curse the one-lane pileups of rush-hour traffic and wonder why road planners could not have done a better job planning in a city with legendary traffic congestion. The park is considered a big win for Atlanta's park advocates, but neighbors embroiled in their own park controversies have some constructive recommendations, including transportation planner Adelee LeGrand:

> In retrospect, having the community dictate the vehicular mobility caused subadequate access from Atlanta to Decatur. I understand why the city was forced into this position at that time, but the vehicular connections on the east side will forever be stressed by this action. That said, Freedom Park is a great place to take the family for a bike ride, just as long as you don't plan to drive through the park in a vehicle at rush hour. (LeGrand 2013)

In its 2012 ParkScore, the Trust for Public Land ranked Atlanta 31st out of 50 cities, awarding it two and one-half park benches out of a possible five, with park land at 5.6 percent of city area. A 2011 study by the Centers for Disease Control, the Healthy Community Design Initiative, and the Georgia Institute of Technology's Center for GIS compared access and service areas for each park in the City of Atlanta system (Dills 2012). The study noted that Freedom Park serves the largest population, with 95 entrances; it is also Atlanta's most pedestrian-accessible city park, ironically, due to its extended perimeter in the shape of a tollway interchange.

According to George Dusenbury, commissioner of Atlanta Parks Recreation, and Cultural Affairs, Freedom Park is the legacy of activists who saved Atlanta's intown neighborhoods from dismemberment by highway construction. Twenty years later, the PATH Foundation, the non-profit dedicated to building trails throughout the region, partnered with the city and the Freedom Park Conservancy to build trails that connect west Atlanta to Stone Mountain, a distance of over 40 miles. Popular with cyclists and joggers, the trails are used for recreation and commuting (Dusenbury 2013).

Today the conservancy holds monthly meetings and has frequent fundraisers for programs to enhance and maintain the park. Twenty years ago neighbors started out vowing never to enter into negotiations, period; now the seven adjacent neighborhoods are prospering. "CAUTION protected Atlanta's most important assets. The conservancy's goal is to provide the community with a deeper understanding of how neighbors took themselves to the mat to protect the community and build the park," says Billy Davis, secretary of the Freedom Park Conservancy (Davis 2013).

CHAPTER 10

Race and Class in Atlanta-Style Development: Promoting Inclusion and Justice

Michael Dobbins, FAICP

There is perhaps no feature of the Atlanta metropolitan area more conspicuous than the politics and geography of race. A closely related feature is that of class. On the one hand, Atlanta is known for its dynamic economy, growing population, and role as home to some of the most important corporations in the nation—Delta Airlines, United Parcel Service, Coca-Cola, Home Depot, and others. And a part of that narrative is the link between the region's economic profile and its reputation as a magnet for a talented and diverse workforce. Between 1970 and 2010, the metropolitan Atlanta area's African American population grew an astronomical 452 percent. If metropolitan Atlanta's African American population were an urban region of its own, it would be one of the 40 largest in the United States and be substantially larger than some notable city-regions, such as Nashville, Milwaukee, Memphis, New Orleans, and Salt Lake City (U.S. Census Bureau 2010).

What should be known is that despite the population figures mentioned above, metropolitan Atlanta is not predominantly African American. In fact, the city's population is only predominantly African American by a very slim margin (54 percent). What is more important is how different the lived experience of the estimated 227,000 African Americans within the city differs from that of the 1.5 million who live outside of it in the greater Atlanta region (U.S. Census Bureau 2010). The rising economic tide that has made Atlanta a global city has only lifted the boats of a class of African Americans and other people of color, and not necessarily those who are native to the city.

This chapter will provide a description of the race and class divides in the Atlanta metropolitan area and how efforts through planning to mitigate them with project-driven growth have either improved relations between groups or reinforced social inequality. Furthermore, race and class are not simply unfortunate contradictions in the larger narrative about Atlanta but are "inconvenient truths" that often meet with hostile resistance from city leaders and planners who have pushed Atlanta onto the global stage, often at the expense of low-income families and neighborhoods. As this chapter will also discuss, the challenges of balancing transformative projects against the need to manage inclusive development that did not unfairly displace incumbent communities has not always been possible nor a priority. As neighborhood revitalization and gentrification change the demographics and dynamics of central Atlanta communities, inclusion and balance may become even more elusive.

What is most often understood about Atlanta is its high rates of poverty and property abandonment. Within the city limits, the poverty rate among African Americans was 34.3 percent in 2012—higher than the poverty rate for African Americans in Baltimore (27.2 percent) and comparable to Detroit (37.7 percent) and Cleveland (41.4 percent). The African American unemployment rate was a staggering 20 percent in the city of Atlanta, higher than Baltimore (17.9 percent) and again comparable to Detroit (28.9 percent) and Cleveland (25.7 percent). Approximately 20.3 percent, or 45,611 units, of the city's housing stock are vacant. Of those, 54.9 percent can be considered abandoned (i.e., not for sale or rent). In some areas of the city's core adjacent to the headquarters of the Coca-Cola Company, vacancy rates range from 34 percent (Tract 118) to as high as 56.53 percent (Tract 23) (American Community Survey 2012a).

While much of this can be tied to the economic downturn that started in 2007, much of it cannot be. In a recent series of papers about economic mobility in the United States, the commuting zone of Atlanta ranked 49th out of the 50 largest metropolitan areas for intergenerational mobility (Chetty et al. 2013). All of this begs the question: how can Atlanta be both the economic and cultural capital of the "New South" and harbor such strikingly different narratives of economic success and opportunity?

Planning for the most significant eras in the city's history have always highlighted or exacerbated Atlanta's underlying racial tensions. To build the Interstate 75/85 Connector in the 1960s, substantial sections of the predominantly African American communities of Summerhill and Mechanicsville were destroyed. The highway also served as a barrier between the central business district and surrounding low-income and predominantly African American neighborhoods (Keating 2001a). To build and expand the Georgia World Congress Center (GWCC) and Georgia Dome stadium, the predominantly African American community of Lightning, was completely displaced (Dorsey 2013).

Atlanta is not unique among American cities in demonstrating patterns of residential segregation or unequal access to labor markets and opportunity. However, where Atlanta stands out is in the range of economic classes within racial groups and with how planners attempt to engage the issues that the metropolitan region's economic and racial landscape creates and perpetuates. It is important to note here that this chapter's frame is not the city alone. To be clear, there are vast differences between the economic landscape of the city's northern neighborhoods, such as Buckhead, Ansley Park, and Virginia Highlands, and its more distressed southern parts such as Bankhead, English Avenue, Vine City, Lakewood, and Joyland. However, to clearly understand race and class in Atlanta, readers must consider the larger 10-county area that includes the counties of Fulton, DeKalb, Cobb, Gwinnett, Clayton, Henry, Douglas, Cherokee, Fayette, and Rockdale. The migration of African Americans from all parts of the South and Rust Belt states of the Midwest and northeastern U.S. has had an enormous impact on not just the city but the suburbs as well.

The Centennial Olympic Games: The Effort to Create Equity and Inclusion

Against all odds, one of the pinnacle achievements of the City of Atlanta was hosting the 1996 Centennial Olympic Games. This was but one more point of proof that Atlanta is a "can-do" city. Central contributing factors to Atlanta winning its bid to host the Olympics were mayor and former United Nations ambassador Andrew Young's international profile and his ability to showcase the city and region as a place where people of color were thriving (Weisman 1990). African delegates to the International Olympic Committee openly expressed this as being critical to their choice of Atlanta.

On the ground, there was a somewhat different reality. To make room for the then newly opened Georgia Dome, which was critically important to Atlanta's winning bid, the historically African American community of Lightning was completely displaced. To create the junction of Interstates 75/85 and 20, the Summerhill and Mechanicsville communities were also almost entirely decimated. In both cases, community groups fought vigorously for the preservation of these communities (Lenskyj 2000, 137). Where this was not possible, groups won guarantees from the City of Atlanta that the displaced would be compensated for their losses and relocations and that the city would invest in and revitalize what remained of these communities.

The gap between the public image and narrative of Atlanta as a place where African Americans possess great political capital and where they are economically strong is wide. Or, perhaps the second image, the one of displaced communities and economic hardship was and has been conveniently hidden from the view of the global public. Some progressive groups and communities, such as Atlanta's Partnership for Working Families affiliate, Georgia STAND-UP, have made it their mission to unite community, labor, and faith-based organizations committed to social equity as a locus for promoting and negotiating community benefits agreements (CBAs) on behalf of neighborhoods where major development initiatives are afoot. The fight is not to edit the narrative but to gain ground in the face of a development paradigm that prioritizes support for development in Buckhead, Downtown, Midtown, and other affluent, mainly white areas over neighborhoods with real needs.

The CBAs are aimed at lifting the voice, relevance, participation, and positive outcomes of communities in the decisions that affect their lives and futures. They represent enforceable agreements that bind the developer, public or private, to deliver on promises that will benefit the impacted community and that bind the community to support the development through and beyond the approval process. The principle threatens business-as-usual practices and calls for a more thoughtful, inclusive, and comprehensive approach for development projects. (Cummings 2007; Gross, LeRoy, and Janis-Aparacio 2005; Salkin and Lavine 2008a, 2008b Wolf-Powers 2010). These agreements have become lightning rods, sending chills down the spines of the development-as-usual players, much as Equal Employment Opportunities Commission (EEOC) and Disadvantaged Business Enterprise (DBE) provisions did in earlier eras (Sanchez, Stolz, and Ma 2003).

The concept has been applied with some success in other cities, aided by both advocacy and technical support from other affiliates of the Partnership for Working Families. Big project developers in Los Angeles, Oakland, Portland, and Denver have modified their original proposals to reflect community perspectives and needs, and where citizen guidance and approval support have actually improved projects for all involved.

Before they were called CBAs, their use in planning for Atlanta's 1996 Olympic Games was particularly notable given the numerous instances when community interests were subverted to developer-driven plans in Atlanta. Atlanta's development ethic has always been very project- and profit-oriented and over time much more focused on development in the Downtown, Midtown, and Buckhead areas at the expense of outlying neighborhoods, particularly the predominantly African American ones to the south and west.

Faced with a growing restiveness on the part of the low-wealth neighborhoods that surrounded the Olympic venues and from organized labor, including direct, non-violent actions, the Atlanta Committee for the Olympic Games (ACOG) was induced into accepting a labor agreement. ACOG, responsible for constructing the venues, then established the Community Employment Program. The grounds for the agreement, steered by AFL-CIO and Atlanta Planning Advisory Board (APAB) leaders, were the acceptance of the reality that Atlanta had persistent and systemic poverty with associated unemployment, lack of job skills, and low educational attainment, especially in the impacted, predominantly African American neighborhoods.

The agreement called for 250 Olympics construction-related jobs to go to residents of low-wealth neighborhoods. Additionally, 100 of these jobs would go to jobless people deemed nominally "unqualified" due to their criminal records or substance abuse histories. The AFL-CIO prepared the prospective workers through remedial education and pre-apprenticeship and apprenticeship training. In parallel, ACOG contracted with a number of local small and disadvantaged businesses to support its catering, media, logistical, and other needs, some of which used the Olympic jump-start to grow businesses that continue to perform today.

ACOG spent over $2 billion over six years, and while its model was not perfect, it fulfilled its end of the bargain by employing the called for numbers of people. Community and labor leaders ratcheted down their resistance to the Olympics. This was not a sea change in the relationship between Atlanta's deprived and its elites, but it was a step in the direction of equity by showing current development leadership that it could be done.

As a more recent example of the concept, in the run-up to the London 2012 Olympics, the six boroughs impacted by the Olympic Games—all areas with low wealth and high unemployment—were able to negotiate and enforce workforce, small business, and education compacts; they achieved this in consultation with the AFL-CIO leader who led the Atlanta effort. These compacts resulted in more than 20 percent of the jobs and more than 20 percent of the business activity going to "locals" living in or doing business in the boroughs. Children in the boroughs, who had been performing academically at the lowest levels in London, came to perform at the city-wide average in the six years after the Olympics award (UK Government and Mayor of London 2013).

The principles now embodied in the CBA rubric have become the subject of greater public debate for the megaprojects such as the proposed Multimodal Passenger Terminal described here. Communities have gone through planning processes to come up with listings of benefits that would show a clear, enforceable commitment to share the benefits of public investment in places where it is needed most. At this writing, a thin majority of city council members are open to the principles and are looking for ways to translate them into actionable provisions in future approvals. The affected communities that have greater access to relevant information, Georgia STAND-UP, and students at Georgia Tech are working with the communities involved in all the projects to listen to, catalog, and represent the communities' conditions, needs, and priorities. These efforts identify the benefits and suggest action options to implement them. A fundamental key to success from the community perspective is collaboration across the range of community interests leading toward the kind of unity necessary to affect the city council's approval votes and to withstand the tendency among big scale developers to pick off neighborhood people and thus erode solidarity.

As the dialogue unfolds, it becomes apparent that questions like who agrees with whom and how to craft provisions that can be monitored and enforced join the problem of overcoming developer inertia as problems to be solved. For example, an agreement approved by the city council for releasing funds could require each contract so funded to include specific jobs and job training requirements, the setting of urban design standards, mixed income housing support, use of facilities for community needs, local business procurement, the design of ongoing community involvement in the project, and other such considerations. These can be thought of in the same way that EEOC and DBE provisions are routinely part of most publicly funded contracts awarded to various consultants, vendors, developers, and contractors.

But with the Olympics limited success a fading memory, Atlanta's deprived neighborhoods face daunting challenges in leveling the playing field where this private developer-driven city measures success solely by the bottom line. And racism, while easing, underlies both the facts of Atlanta's social immobility and its business leadership's disinterest in dealing with the problem. So how do citizens and their planners committed to trying to achieve comprehensive and equitable outcomes gain influence? There are mechanisms that show promise for gaining some level of positive results. Beginning with mayor Maynard Jackson's first term in office (from 1974), Atlanta established a formalized citizen input process based on Neighborhood Planning Units (NPUs), and the 24 NPUs make up APAB, the aforementioned citywide body.

This structure is now greatly enhanced by internet-driven access to the information essential for understanding and assessing public and private initiatives. The spread and gradual improvement in the capacity and effectiveness of community-based organizations can complement the NPU structure.

Every planning and development project involves the interaction of three spheres of interest:

- The developer with the resources and the profit motive, whether private and/or public
- The government at all levels with the approval power and sources of subsidy
- The community where it happens, which most often draws the short end of the stick, whether neighborhood or business center, where the impacts will be judged for better or worse

Since the close of the Olympic Games in 1996, Atlanta has reversed the three-decades-long trend of population decline, disinvestment, sprawl development patterns, and environmental degradation. The core city has been growing as fast as any older larger core city in the country. It is rebounding from the Great Recession as evidenced by several new residential and business investments that are reinvigorating and expanding many of its traditional centers. In the context of this turnaround, the four megascale development projects now in the works by virtue of their magnitude and locations offer the opportunity for this "can-do" city to begin to erase its structural inequity. Can the city ratchet up its aspirations for greatness by lifting people into the mainstream economy? Yes, with $5 billion in projects, all with significant public investment, they can be transformational. Or the public-private ventures could proceed under the business-as-usual model, blowing the opportunity and leaving their neighborhood environs worse off than before, sumps of poverty and joblessness. All these projects are public-private partnerships, all require a crucial commitment of public funds and other public resources to proceed, and all accordingly require approval in different ways by the Atlanta City Council.

The Atlanta BeltLine

The Atlanta BeltLine, a concept for building a 22-mile loop beyond the core of the city along a series of discontinuous rail corridors, is underway, and four parks and three trail segments have been built so far. Georgia STAND-UP and its allies were able to persuade a slim majority of city council members to insert CBA language into the ordinance establishing tax-increment-financing provisions, (called a tax allocation district, or TAD in Georgia), with a reluctant mayor signing on. The ordinance called for the establishment of a TAD Advisory Committee to help guide the project. The same ordinance, again through the efforts of Georgia STAND-UP and other affordable housing advocates, committed to set aside 15 percent of the tax increment funding for an affordable housing trust fund, which also resulted in the establishment of the BeltLine Affordable Housing Advisory Board (Invest Atlanta 2014). This group was formed to guide Atlanta BeltLine, Inc. (ABI) with implementation of a comprehensive affordable housing strategy.

Currently, eight years after the TAD was approved, about $360 million has been spent, mostly in property acquisition, park and trail development, and lavish consultant contracts. About 65 percent of those funds have been expended in affluent east and north side neighborhoods. Parks and trails have been built, creating generally popular amenities, again with most of the money spent in affluent neighborhoods, which has added to their market attractiveness. Yet there has been no documentation produced to show whether any of the jobs generated by the several construction projects have employed people from low-wealth neighborhoods or NPUs. There have been at best halfhearted efforts to prepare those citizens through training or pre-apprenticeship programs to address that goal. There have been no employment provisions put into any of requirements for general contracts or subcontract on recruiting, training, or employing people from low-wealth neighborhoods. Consistent with Atlanta's typical development practices, the CBA—whose purpose was to at least make a dent in Atlanta's persistent poverty and unemployment affliction—has been at best symbolic.

New Falcons Stadium

Presently, the city has completed negotiations for the construction of a new $1.2 billion stadium for the Atlanta Falcons football team to be financed privately and publicly, including $200 million in construction costs and some $500 million in operating and maintenance expenses over 25 years, and underwritten by a hotel-motel tax (Saporta and Wenk 2013). The Falcons, the city, Invest Atlanta, the Georgia World Congress Center Authority, and the Blank Family Foundation have committed funds and established a timetable to replace the Georgia Dome with the new facility by 2017. Thus, there is real urgency to discover a planning, design, and development path that gets the project done. The issues of whether, why, and how much it will take to replace the existing facility appear to have been settled the Atlanta way: take down a perfectly good stadium and put a new "iconic" one next door for a billion dollars.

As with all large projects, the interacting spheres of developer (the Falcons), the government (city and state), and the community (the myriad affected neighborhoods) are pushing their positions. The Falcons are singularly focused on their "iconic" building and their high end patrons, which further exacerbates the divide with the neighborhoods and the Atlanta University Center campuses to the west. The city government is caught in the crosshairs between competing interests. Atlanta Mayor Kasim Reed is an all-in champion for the project and sees it as defining his legacy. The impacted communities, whose resources cannot compete with the big money interests, fear a further darkening of their prospects for reversing their downward slide. The mayor has tapped Invest Atlanta (formerly the Atlanta Development Authority), the city's development arm that Reed chairs, to manage the publicly funded aspects of the project.

In December 2013, enough pressure was mounted to induce the Atlanta City Council to adopt a community benefits plan that will invest $30 million into Castleberry Hill, English Avenue, and Vine City, while at the same time clearing the way for the issuance of the $200 million, that has now grown to $275 million in bonds needed to support the stadium's construction (Blau 2013). These neighborhoods have historically found uniting behind a single vision or leadership structure to assert their visions and priorities effectively a challenge. Some leaders are more committed to achieving locked in benefits for everyone, while others are angling for narrower gains. This reflects a profile that mirrors other community organizing efforts, especially where the gulf between needs and resources is great.

All parties nominally give lip service, though, to the idea that the opportunities afforded by the more than $1 billion expenditure of funds should result in a positive transformation of the immediate area, its neighborhoods, and the city as a whole. The problem, aside from business-as-usual inertia, is how to do it. The community-led effort is to establish clear linkages between the money and the impact, with the highest priorities placed on reconnecting the presently cut-off neighborhoods with Downtown, and on jobs, with all the recruitment, training, monitoring, and enforcement required to be effective.

Atlanta's best hope for adapting the London model to apply to the Falcons' stadium, as well as other large scale developments, lies in a collaboration among all who have stepped up to make equity in the outcome an imperative. Thus, community-based organizations, the NPUs, representatives from the Atlanta faith-based community, Georgia STAND-UP, "anchor institutions" like the Atlanta University Center Consortium and Georgia Tech, and the Westside Community Alliance are all working to coalesce around both principles and actions that would be effective in gaining needed benefits from the anticipated public expenditures. The groups are reaching consensus on a menu of community-identified benefits and actions that could advance that purpose. These latter focus on:

- job training and placement;
- transportation connectivity to transit and Downtown; storm water design and management as the neighborhoods have been afflicted for 30 years with flooding exacerbated by the hardscape of the GWCC and Georgia Dome;
- housing stabilization, conservation, and affordability aimed at resisting displacement;
- land development and urban design measures that connect the neighborhood both physically and programmatically with the existing and new facilities and downtown jobs and amenities;
- preservation and celebration of the neighborhoods' heritage, including its centrality in the civil rights movement; and
- community and educational investment to prepare the existing residents, young and old, to grasp opportunities not presently available to raise their incomes and to improve their quality of life. (Invest Atlanta 2014)

The funds so far committed to meeting neighborhood interests represent a drop in the bucket of what' is needed, and they are a tiny portion of the funds obligated to the Falcons. Invest Atlanta is conducting its own studies to identify redevelopment strategies and capital projects that could benefit from funds dedicated for neighborhood use. The extent to which its effort will respond to the community's priorities is presently unclear. At the same time, the Arthur M. Blank Family Foundation, established by Arthur Blank, the Falcons' owner and cofounder of Home Depot, is trying to figure out how it might spread its $15 million commitment to best build social capital and empowerment in the affected neighborhoods.

Projects on the Horizon

In a space known as "the Gulch," trains carry industrial freight under viaducts that hold up much of downtown Atlanta. Up until 1980, the Terminal Station sat near the space and carried passengers from all over the United States, southeastern United States, and the Atlanta metropolitan area. The demolition of the station represented the demise of commuter passenger rail in metropolitan Atlanta, and the Gulch is currently used primarily by homeless in search of shelter, for commuter parking, and for tailgating Falcon football fans (Figure 10.1).

To better utilize this vast, forlorn space, the current proposal is to create the Georgia Multi-Modal Passenger Terminal (MMPT), an estimated $1 billion investment with the potential for leveraging an additional $1 billion in private investment in the vicinity. The project is sponsored by the Georgia Department of Transportation along with the city, Invest Atlanta, Central Atlanta Progress (the downtown business association and improvement district authority), and a private-sector design and development team.

With much work yet to be done, the MMPT would serve as the hub for local, regional, and national bus lines, commuter rail, and heavy rail, and would provide greatly enhanced access to downtown offices, residential areas, universities, and event venues. Along the way, and maybe even more important, it would cover over the historic Gulch and would help heal the divide between the downtown and neighborhoods to the south.

Various public and private development alternatives have been put forward for this site for decades, none of them progressing very far. Yet the current alignment of public and private forces driving the project seems to have the combination of creativity and resources to actually move the project forward. At this juncture, an environmental impact statement to evaluate alternative site configurations is in the preparation stages.

Given the MMPT's more complicated program, the principal issues for communities are just coming into focus. Clearly, with the expenditure of another $1 billion somewhere on the horizon, the kinds of community supportive benefits under discussion in the Falcons negotiations all apply, since the same neighborhoods are nearby. That conversation, however, is not yet in the forefront of community concern—except for the Castleberry Hill neighborhood, which is closest to the facility. Its isolation from Downtown could be bridged with a properly designed and phased project. Issues of transit connectivity—indeed all connectivity with Downtown, Northside Drive, and the west side

Figure 10.1: "The Gulch," site of the proposed Georgia Multi-Modal Passenger Terminal

neighborhoods—are emerging as prime concerns. It is reasonable to assume that the same coalition-building that the community is seeking in dealing with the stadium's opportunities and threats will carry into similar dialogues with the evolving planning and design for the MMPT.

A mile and a half to the south, the impending move of the Atlanta Braves out of Turner Field in 2017 threatens to leave a gaping hole in an area that never quite found its footing after the close of the Olympic Games. The census tracts immediately adjacent to the stadium contain vacancy rates that rival some of the emptiest parts of the city and where acres of asphalt cover almost all of the land directly adjacent to the stadium property. The devastation after the displacement of part of the Summerhill neighborhood for construction of Turner Field may make it difficult, if not impossible, to find the capacity to construct a comprehensive redevelopment approach that actually benefits the nearby residents and businesses.

Prospects and Possibilities for a Brighter, Fairer, and More Inclusive Future

Another way to envision a prospective new role for the development-driven leadership in each of these projects is to study the activities related to the Cleveland Institute of Music. There, the idea of anchor institutions has emerged, in which the primary players, the sources of both jobs and procurement activities, have come to see value in adopting a proactive and community-building approach that involves surrounding neighborhoods in the University Circle area in need of fundamental transformation (Cleveland Foundation 2013). Thus the BeltLine, the Falcons stadium, the MMPT, and the redevelopment of the Braves stadium site could be projects where the funds and resources improve the long-term prospects, incomes, and quality of life of residents in low-income neighborhoods.

Progress in securing community benefits thus far is disappointing but not surprising. The moves among low-wealth neighborhoods to redirect large development initiatives to address critical community needs may still be tenuous and unconsolidated. Yet the neighborhoods have stepped up and asserted their positions in the interactions between the government and developers. They are organizing, gaining legitimacy, empowering themselves, and collaborating with a number of other groups in the immediate areas and around the city and the country.

The city is at a pivot point. Can Atlanta's business and political leaders step forward to engage the disenfranchised in models that offer people the ability to advance themselves with jobs and hope? If so, they can step forward on the national stage and describe how a big city can make a dent in its most important problems: poverty and unemployment. They can put forth initiatives that begin to address pervasive poverty and inequality. This will require a great deal of creativity and a sustained course of hard work, but if this is a can-do city it should be able to make progress in tackling its biggest problem.

CHAPTER 11

Public Housing Demolition and Neighborhood Revitalization

Thomas D. Boston

Over the last two decades, the City of Atlanta has undertaken the most far-reaching demolition and transformation of public housing projects in the nation. This process began in 1994, at a time when two-thirds of low-income housing-assisted families lived in 44 conventional public housing projects operated by the Atlanta Housing Authority (AHA). Many of the projects were large, densely populated developments that suffered from severe management neglect. Furthermore, the social and physical environments generally surrounding these rental units were not conducive to normal human development or a reasonable quality of life.

In the mid-1990s, three major factors coalesced to create the catalyst for public housing transformation. The first factor was the increasingly uninhabitable conditions of the rental units. In many developments, a quarter of the units were either abandoned or unlivable. Furthermore, a majority of all rental units were sub-standard. Children play areas were dilapidated and dangerous, crime victimization rates were several times the city's average (and Atlanta had the highest violent crime rate in the nation during the mid-1990s), buildings and units lacked security and lighting, while porches, doors, and windows were in disrepair (U.S. Department of Housing and Urban Development 1994).

Second, the socioeconomic environment was severely distressed. For example, poverty was severe as 91 percent of residents lived below the official poverty line. Also in 1995, only 14 percent of work-eligible adults were employed at some point during the year. This meant that 50.6 percent of households subsisted on a yearly income of less than $10,000 while 83.5 percent received less than $15,000. Most distressing, within these conditions, 85 percent of households were headed by single women with young children. These women were not the perpetrators of crime and social malaise. Instead, they were unfortunate victims, wedged between drug lords who headquartered their operations in the vulnerable neighborhoods but did not live there, and public housing managers who were so inefficient and incompetent that US Department of Housing and Urban Development (US HUD) threatened to take control of AHA. The third and most determining factor was the frantic desire on the part of city leaders to spruce up the face of poverty in Atlanta, because visitors and media from around the world would be converging on the City for the 1996 Olympic Games.

Driven by these factors, public housing transformation officially began in Atlanta in 1994, and it continues to this day. At the start of transformation, 7,722 families lived in public housing projects. By 2010, the transformation was so thoroughgoing that only 90 families remained in public housing. The rest had relocated with housing choice vouchers to project-based rental units or units in mixed income communities. Despite the enormous housing transformation that occurred in Atlanta, there are very few empirical studies of its socioeconomic impact on low-income families. While there is an abundance of conjectures, assumptions, and strongly held views, these are largely uninformed by empirical research and rigorous analyses.

The transformation raises numerous questions about the impact on residents and specifically, whether or not AHA achieved its intended objectives. This chapter addresses two of the most fundamental questions:

1. Did displaced families lose housing assistance because of the demolition?
2. Did families experience upward socioeconomic mobility as a result of relocating to better housing and higher-quality neighborhoods (as measured by the change in employment)?

As a case study, this chapter traces the transformation of Grady Homes into a mixed income development, now called Auburn Pointe. The transformation of Grady was also accompanied by the demolition and conversion of University Homes. The chapter evaluates the impact of this process on residents who were forced, as a result of the demolition, to relocate to other neighborhoods, receive other forms of housing assistance, and/or move into mixed income developments.

Historically, social observers have long maintained that environment matters. More specifically, it is widely believed that a fundamental key to socioeconomic mobility is access to quality housing and decent living conditions. This was a fundamental premise of the well-documented landmark study by Frederick Engels (1845), *The Conditions of the Working Class in England.*

A half century later, W.E.B Du Bois provided an equally vivid depiction of the miserable housing and living conditions of blacks, who were at the time becoming increasingly concentrated in urban ghettos of the North, in *The Philadelphia Negro* (1899). More recently, William Julius Wilson refocused researchers' attention on the adverse impact of concentrated poverty on the social and economic mobility of the poor. Wilson's most influential book in this regard is *The Truly Disadvantaged: the Inner-City, Underclass, and Public Policy* (1987). He continued this theme in his most recent book, *More Than Just Race: Being Black and Poor in the Inner-City* (2009). Based on studies of poor neighborhoods in Chicago, he argued persuasively that the adverse human and social consequences of poverty were more a consequence of the extreme spatial concentration of the poor than of poverty itself. His research changed the methodological paradigm and public policies designed to mitigate poverty (Wilson 1985, 1991a, 1991b).

Starting in the 1990s, national studies of the deteriorating conditions of public housing developments in the United States appeared to support Wilson's fundamental conclusion (National Commission on Severely Distressed Public Housing 1992). That is concentrating extremely poor families in densely populated public housing projects hindered socioeconomic mobility. Thus, deconcentrating poverty was believed to be fundamental to improving the socioeconomic mobility of the poor.

Influenced by this research, the U.S. Department of Housing and Urban Development (HUD) implemented the HOPE VI program in 1992 (Salama 1999). This program gave local housing authorities great latitude to experiment with new ways of providing public housing assistance, up to and including demolishing traditional public housing developments and replacing them with mixed income communities. The spatial aspects of this new approach to public housing found its philosophical grounding in the concepts of New Urbanism and "defensible space."

The implementation of mixed income developments through the HOPE VI program was the most sweeping change to public housing assistance since the introduction of Section 8 housing vouchers, which provided families the choice of living in the private housing market with a voucher subsidy, rather than living in public housing developments. Between 1992 and 2005, approximately $6 billion was appropriated for various HOPE VI revitalization projects across the country. Starting in 2008, federal budgetary appropriations for HOPE VI declined significantly and fiscal year 2011 was the last year in which funds were appropriated for the HOPE VI program ($100 million, although $65 million of that amount was transferred to the Choice Neighborhood Initiative).[1]

Ironically, despite this monumental change in housing assistance brought on by the HOPE VI Program, a relatively small number of empirical studies have examined the impact of this program. In recent years, the number of studies has increased, but the volume of research still remains far below what would be expected for a program that had such a landmark impact on housing assistance to low income families (Anil et al. 2010; Boston 2005; Buron et al. 2002; Chaskin et al. 2012; Cove et al. 2008; Hartley 2010; Holmes et al. 2003; Popkin et al. 2004).

Surprisingly, HUD did not mandate that public housing authorities (PHAs) track the impact of the HOPE VI program until 1998. Furthermore, it did not require grant recipients to report the location of displaced residents until 2000. The failure on the part of HUD to mandate that grant recipients monitor and evaluate the impact of HOPE VI left a rift between opponents and proponents of the program. For example, the National Housing Law Project was critical of the program and claimed HOPE VI advocates painted an unfairly negative picture of public housing conditions and exaggerated the sense of crisis so as "to justify a drastic model of large scale family displacement and housing redevelopment" (National Housing Law Project 2002, ii). The response to this harsh criticism from the Coalition of Large Public Housing Authorities, primary advocates of the program, was that that through HOPE VI "entire communities [had] experienced improved property values, increased safety and security, reinvestment by local businesses, and an enhanced quality of life for all residents" (CLPHA 2013).

Atlanta's Experience at Transforming Public Housing

Anyone traveling to Atlanta in 1994 did not have to look far to find one of the city's low-income public housing projects because they were blanketed across the poorest neighborhoods in the city. Geographically, this area stretched from the southeast corner of the city to the northwest boundary. Relative to the size of its population at that time, Atlanta had one of the nation's highest concentrations of families living in public housing developments. Techwood Homes, one of the most severely distressed public housing projects in the country and the first to be demolished in Atlanta, was tangent to Interstate 75/85, adjacent to the Georgia Institute of Technology (Georgia Tech) campus, and less than a mile north of the center of the downtown central business district.

Of the 16,349 low-income families who received housing assistance from AHA in 1995, 47.2 percent lived in the 25 low-income public housing projects (LIPH) that were reserved for non-elderly household-headed families, 20.0 percent lived in the 19 LIPH projects reserved for elderly householders and 32.8 percent received Section 8 Housing Vouchers (later replaced by the Housing Choice Voucher Program). By 2010, AHA had demolished all but two of the original 25 LIPH family housing projects, and the 2 still standing housed just 90 families. Likewise, only 12 of the original 19 LIPH elderly developments remained by 2010.[3]

TABLE 11.1.	The Transformation of Public Housing Assistance in Atlanta			
	1995	1995	2010	2010
	Households	Percent	Households	Percent
Low-Income Public Housing, Family	7,722	47.2	90	0.5
Tenant Vouchers	5,364	32.8	10,498	59.5
Project-Based Vouchers	0	0	950	5.4
Mixed-Income	0	0	2,286	13.0
Low-Income Public Housing, Senior	3,263	20.0	3,805	21.6
Total	16,349	100.0	17,629	100.0%

Source: Data compiled by author from Atlanta Housing Authority public housing, housing choice voucher, and mixed income housing administrative records.

Atlanta's public housing transformation was thoroughgoing and extensive. Reflecting on this monumental change in 2010, the housing authority's executive director Renee Glover took pride in the fact that AHA built the nation's first public housing developments and would be the first housing authority to demolish them all (Brown 2009). The demolished units were replaced with a combination of low-income rental units in 16 newly constructed mixed-income developments, project based vouchers, and housing choice vouchers. Additionally, before they were all demolished, residents could choose to relocate to other traditional public housing developments.

The change in the form of AHA's housing assistance is illustrated in Table 11.1. Between 1995 and 2010, the number of families provided assistance by AHA increased from 16,345 to 17,629. During the same timeframe, the predominant type of housing assistance experienced a massive change. In 2007, 47.2 percent of families lived in conventional public housing developments reserved for non-elderly families. By 2010, only 90 families did. Similarly, while 32.8 percent of families used vouchers in 1995, by 2010, 64.9 percent used vouchers and 13.0 percent lived in mixed income developments.

Questions Raised by the Transformation

AHA chose this approach deliberately. The authority argued a thoroughgoing transformation was the only way to achieve its fundamental housing objectives that were: 1) to end the concentration of poor families in distressed and isolated neighborhoods; 2) to create more healthy and sustainable communities by constructing high quality mixed-income developments that contained affordable housing for low-income families; 3) to create within mixed-income developments a seamless integration of public housing rental units alongside market rate rental units; 4) to ensure the delivery of high-quality housing services

Figure 11.1. Typical slum homes, on Gilmer Street looking west, demolished to construct Grady Homes, circa 1940

by off-loading the management of properties to private property managers and grounding the sustainability of the transformation within the framework of market forces; and, 5) to assist families in achieving a higher degree of self-sufficiency.[4]

While there is still no general consensus among researchers as to whether the outcomes of such efforts have been more positive or negative, this specific case study sheds more empirical light on the search for an answer. We use AHA's administrative data organized longitudinally and ranging from 2004 to 2010. While the findings of the administrative data analysis were supplemented by 30 focus group interviews, conducted between 2007 and 2009.[5]

Historical Background on Public Housing in Atlanta

By 1933, the nation had reached the depth of the Great Depression and the official unemployment rate was 25 percent. Programs evolving from the New Deal were aimed at sustaining a minimum level of spending in the economy and providing a means of subsistence for the segment of the population hardest hit by the Depression. In 1934, the United States appropriated land to build public housing projects for unemployed workers, and the nation's first construction site was Techwood Homes in Atlanta. Built in 1936 for whites only, Techwood Homes is generally recognized as the country's first public housing development. Techwood was also part of a slum clearance initiative promoted by prominent Atlanta business persons. The housing project included unemployed white families and students who attended Georgia Tech. The public

Figure 11.2. Slum property east of downtown Atlanta cleared to construct Grady Homes, circa 1940

housing project was located immediately across North Avenue, and adjacent to the institute. In fact, the housing project derived its name from Techwood Drive, which began on Georgia Tech's campus and intersected the heart of the housing project. Techwood was not racially integrated until 1968.

The aims and objectives of the government were not completely altruistic. While public housing construction provided temporary housing for low-income unemployed workers, it was also used to clear away some of the nation's worst slums and facilitate the construction of racially segregated housing communities in urban areas. Grady Homes, the housing development which is the focus of this case study, was built in 1942 exclusively for low-income black families. Grady was located immediately east of the heart of downtown Atlanta at 100 Bell Street. It was originally constructed on 22.8 acres of land in three contiguous parcels.

Figure 11.2 depicts houses that were demolished to clear the way for the construction of Grady Homes, and Figure 3 illustrates the land that was cleared for its construction. Once completed, Grady contained 52 barracks style buildings and 495 units. Each building had one or two floors and the exterior walls were made of brick on concrete block and stucco on masonry.

How Grady Homes became Socially Distressed

Grady Homes was demolished at the beginning of 2005. Using three successive annual waves of focus group interviews (2007, 2008, and 2009) the researcher gathered information on the perceptions of persons who lived at Grady Homes prior to its demolition. Likewise, 2004 administrative records on families at Grady Homes were also examined. This triangulated approach provided a broader context to understand the changes that occurred. The focus groups were restricted to heads of households who lived at the development before the demolition and relocation process started. Each yearly wave consisted of 10 different focus groups, and each group contained approximately 10 participants. The focus group participants also completed survey instruments and provided oral and anecdotal information and discussions. Based on an analysis of administrative data and review a focus group responses we can draw the following picture of Grady prior to its demolition.

Grady was once a vibrant and friendly community that sponsored many adult- and youth-oriented groups and activities, such as the Boy Scouts, on a regular basis. People who lived at Grady loved the neighborly atmosphere and maintained that residents there were more upwardly mobile than those at most AHA properties. The residents also noted that children especially enjoyed participating in the many social events that were organized jointly by AHA managers and the tenants association (Boston 2011).

Using administrative records dating back to 1995 and reviewing the economic and demographic characteristics of Grady families, we were able to confirm that adults who lived there were more upwardly mobile than were adults at most of AHA's large public housing developments. In particular, families at Grady had higher than average household incomes, rates of labor force participation, and employment.

By the late 1980s, the quality of life at Grady (and AHA's other housing developments) began deteriorating rapidly. The residents of these developments attributed this decline to a number of factors. One of the most significant was the escalation in crime associated with the influx of crack cocaine. In Atlanta and in many other urban areas, social distress associated with the trade of crack cocaine was particularly concentrated in densely populated public housing projects. The crack epidemic had a devastating impact in Atlanta because the city had such a high concentration of poor families in public housing. In fact, by 1992 Atlanta ranked number one in the nation in the rate of violent crimes, a rate which was five times the national average.

Twenty percent of the city of Atlanta's violent crimes and 28 percent of its aggravated assaults occurred within the geographic footprint of AHA's 25 public housing projects. By 1994 the average crime rate at these 25 public housing projects was 15 times the national average, and at Techwood Homes and Clark Howell Homes (which adjoined Techwood) the violent crime rate was 37 times the national average. This escalating crime wave also affected Grady Homes. In 1992 the Atlanta Police Department (APD) reported that 276 violent crimes (defined as homicides, rapes, robberies, and aggravated assaults) occurred at Grady Homes. In 2001 the APD reported 375 violent crimes at Grady, which represented an increase of 36 percent, while the size of the resident population remained constant over this period.

The problems at Grady resulting from the escalation of drug-related crime were compounded by the growing neglect of public housing properties by AHA administrators. AHA's housing stock was deteriorating with age and was poorly maintained. The neglect made the properties a convenient safe haven for criminals who frequently operated at the housing developments but rarely lived there.

Broken hallway doors, blown-out streetlights, inoperable elevators, and poor security were commonplace throughout the developments. Playgrounds were unsafe and unsanitary, apartments were infested with rodents, heating and plumbing systems were in disrepair, and hundreds of maintenance work orders were backlogged. Additionally, the physical structures themselves lacked accommodations for persons with disabilities or physical challenges, even though a large percentage of the residents were elderly. These properties were in such poor condition that a June 1994 federal audit scored the agency's operations at 37 percent out of a possible score of 100 percent. It further indicated that unless drastic changes were made, the housing authority would be placed in federal receivership (U.S. Department of Housing and Urban Development 1994).

Focus group participants indicated that the socioeconomic decline of Grady Homes was further accelerated when families from other distressed public housing properties scheduled for demolition relocated to Grady. They particularly noted a spike in crime that followed the influx of residents from the first housing projects that AHA demolished: Techwood Homes, Clark Howell Homes, East Lake Meadows, and Capital Homes. These projects were demolished first because they were more severely distressed than other AHA properties.

An unfortunate trend associated with public housing demolition occurred. Specifically, the most upwardly mobile families requested housing choice vouchers to relocate, or they moved to newly constructed mixed-income communities. In contrast, the least upwardly mobile adults usually relocated to a different public housing project, and the relocation lowered the average socioeconomic status of the receiving development. This was certainly the case at Grady Homes.

Grady Revitalization

In Atlanta, public housing revitalization began in 1994, under the direction of the newly appointed public housing CEO, Renee Glover (Figure 11.3). That year AHA began relocating 2,170 families from Techwood Homes and Clark Howell Homes in preparation for demolition. However, the first demolition of

Figure 11.3. Veranda at Auburn Pointe replaced Grady Homes and University Homes.

public housing in Atlanta was not a smooth process. Instead, AHA officials encountered strong resistance from tenant association members and housing advocates. On the opposite side of the fence, the initiative was being pushed fervently by city leaders who were wary of the huge potential for embarrassment should visitors to the 1996 Olympics witness the deplorable state of Atlanta's public housing. Through long and protracted negotiations, the AHA reached a compromise with the tenant association.

The compromise guaranteed housing assistance to anyone displaced by the revitalization efforts. It also stipulated that families forced to relocate would be provided housing vouchers upon request, and if a voucher were not immediately available, the family would be placed at the top of the voucher waiting list. Families who elected to move into another public housing project would be accommodated immediately or placed ahead of all families on the waiting list. Finally, families who elected to move into the mixed-income community once it was completed would be given first priority.

Prior to 2005, conditions for moving into a mixed income community were more stringent than those associated with living in a public housing project or receiving a housing choice voucher. To be eligible to move into a mixed-income community, families had to comply with a work requirement which stipulated that all able-bodied adults in the household (18 to 61 years of age) who were not enrolled in school full-time must work 30 hours each week or participate in a management-approved training or economic self-sufficiency program for an equivalent amount of time. Also, as part of the lease conditions, school age children in public housing families in mixed-income communities could not have unexcused absences, and parents were required to attend a minimum number of parent-teacher counseling sessions.

The demolition of Grady was also accompanied by a "re-occupancy policy," which stated that any householder who had a valid lease at Grady Homes on June 17, 2004, was eligible to return to the community after it was constructed. This right was subject to the resident's adherence to the re-occupancy policy including a criminal history check, acceptable rental and credit histories, and income verification.

During the demolition and relocation, each family was assigned to a Family Support Specialist who assisted in the relocation process, provided counseling regarding the requirements to remain lease compliant, and advocated on the families' behalf with property owners in the private rental market. Residents were given a date by which they had to indicate their interest in exercising their right to return to the mixed income development.

Baseline Characteristics at Grady Homes
Prior to its demolition in 2005, Grady provided rental assistance to 457 householders and 1,050 individuals. The average age of the head of household was 47.1 years, and youth (ages 17 and under) made up 46 percent of the housing-assisted population. The work-eligible population (often referred to as the "target population") was defined as employment-eligible adults 18 to 61 years of age and not disabled. By these criteria, 372, or 35.6 percent, of all persons at Grady were work eligible, and 37.1 percent of this group was employed. Elderly persons and disabled persons represented 9.5 percent and 10.2 percent respectively of Grady's total population, and 84.7 percent of all households were headed by women.

The average earned income of employed persons was $13,347. Median household income was $9,155, which placed 78.3 percent of families below the poverty line. The average household income deficit, or the difference between average household incomes and the poverty line (or stated differently, the average amount it would have taken to raise families out of poverty) was $7,361. The average monthly rent paid by householders in 2004 was $193.

Demolition and Relocation Process
The 457 householders who lived at Grady Homes in 2004 were all relocated in 2005. Using administrative data, we tracked the residence of those families through 2010. Table 11.2 depicts this redistribution and shows the results five years after demolition. Of the original 457 families at Grady in 2004, only 270, or 41 percent, remained active with the AHA in 2010.

Some researchers have used the absolute decline in the original population as evidence that demolition created the family displacement (Keating 2000;

TABLE 11.2.	Change in Assistance for Families Who Lived in Grady Homes in 2004				
	2004		**2010**		
	Households	Percent	Households	Percent	
Mixed Income, Family	0	0	24	8.9	
Project-Based Vouchers, Family	0	0	26	9.6	
Public Housing, Family	457	100	0	0	
Tenant-Based Vouchers	0	0	204	75.6	
Mixed Income, Elderly	0	0	6	2.2	
Project-Based Vouchers, Elderly	0	0	8	3.0	
Public Housing, Elderly	0	0	1	0.4	
Special Needs Properties	0	0	1	0.4	
Total	**457**	**100.0**	**270**	**100.0**	

Source: Data compiled by author from Atlanta Housing Authority public housing, housing choice voucher, and mixed income housing administrative records.

Keating and Flores 2000). However, no such conclusion can be drawn by simply looking at the absolute change in the number of families receiving housing assistance. This is because each year under normal circumstances, about 10.5 percent of families exit housing assistance for a variety of reasons. Therefore, it is important to control for the normal rate of attrition before one can examine this issue rigorously. Of the remaining original population, 75.6 percent relocated with tenant-based vouchers, 9.6 percent lived in project-based rental assistance (PBRA) family developments and 8.9 percent lived in mixed income developments. Additionally, 3.0 percent lived in PBRA elderly developments, and 2.2 percent lived in mixed income elderly developments.

Explaining Exits from Housing Assistance

The research also collected information on the precise reasons why families left housing assistance. An examination of the reasons given in administrative records indicates the largest number of terminations occurred because of evictions; these evictions constituted 31.6 percent of the total number of households terminated over the six-year interval from 2004 to 2010. Because our analysis is longitudinal in nature, we were also able to examine families who continued to reside in public housing projects until they were demolished. The evictions occurred to a greater extent among families living in public housing than among families who received other forms of housing assistance. In fact, evictions were a relatively common occurrence even in public housing developments that were not scheduled for demolition. This is because residents of public housing developments usually experienced a higher occurance of evictions, property abandonments, and administrative loss of eligibility for failing to pay rent or for engaging in non-lease compliant acts. In contrast, families in mixed-income developments and those who used vouchers were more likely to exit because they secured housing in the private market.

Another large category of terminations (19.7 percent) was related to transfers to Section 8 housing. Presumably, this included families who were awarded a housing voucher and put on a waiting list because housing was not immediately available. Unfortunately, it is impossible to know more details about this status because no additional information is provided in the administrative record.

Exits from public housing because private housing was secured represented the next largest category of terminations at 12.6 percent. This suggests that some exits were also driven by more upwardly mobile families. Other causes of terminations from public housing assistance included administrative loss of eligibility (11.9 percent), illness (6.5 percent), residents abandoning units without notice (5.8 percent), voluntary exits without a reason given (5.7 percent), and death (4.5 percent).

In short, the varied reasons why families exited suggests it is impossible to draw a definitive conclusion that demolition caused the loss of housing assistance. This certainly cannot be concluded by counting the number of families assisted in one year and comparing that number to those still receiving housing assistance in a later year.

Looking at this issue in more detail we found that families who were not forced to relocate from public housing projects because of demolition were more likely to be terminated, in comparison to those who were forced to relocate. The bad conditions and socioeconomic environment surrounding distressed public housing developments were more powerful forces propelling involuntary exits from housing assistance than were mandatory relocations caused by demolition. We also found that as time passed, families who moved into mixed income housing and those who relocated using vouchers were more likely to exit housing assistance than were those who lived in public housing projects. This is because families in mixed-income developments and those using vouchers became employed and self-sufficient at a higher rate. As a result, they were more likely to leave for housing in the private rental market.

Relocation and Employment

A persistent question in public housing research asks whether revitalization and relocation improved upward mobility. The primary yardstick by which mobility is measured is employment. Conclusions regarding the impact of relocation on employment are difficult. Specifically, one must determine whether relocation caused the improvement in employment or whether individuals who relocated were more likely to be employed in the first place, thus exhibiting a selectivity effect.

Measuring the employment impact of the AHA's revitalization efforts is even more complicated because the AHA implemented a mandatory work requirement policy in 2005 and because the agency eventually demolished all public housing developments. The new work requirement policy stipulated that at least one adult in each household (18 to 61 years of age and not disabled) be employed for 30 hours or more each week. The work requirement excluded elderly persons aged 62 or older and persons with disabilities. All other adults in the household had to either be employed for 30 hours each week or devote an equivalent amount of time to a combination of school attendance, job training, or part-time employment. Under certain conditions, hardship waivers were granted.

To examine the employment outcome we used generalized estimating equations with repeated observations. Figure 4 records employment rates longitudinally for Grady household heads in 2004, 2007, and 2010. In 2004, prior to revitalization and the implementation of the work requirement policy, 44.1 percent of household heads were employed. The AHA's work compliance policy was implemented in 2005 and that same year Grady was demolished. By 2007, employment among household heads reached 61.8 percent. In 2010 the employment rate had decreased to 47.5 percent, presumably as a result of the severe recession. A similar employment pattern occurred for all families who received housing assistance from the AHA over

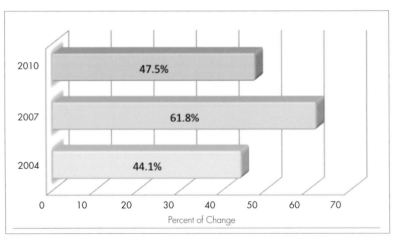

Figure 11.4. Employment rates of householders displaced by Grady Homes revitalization. (Source: Data compiled by author from Atlanta Housing Authority public housing, housing choice voucher, and mixed income housing administrative records.)

the same period of time: overall employment rate for all families was 51.2 percent in 2004, increased to 63.6 percent in 2007, and then declined to 55.6 percent in 2010.

A generalized estimation equations model was used to examine the relationship between employment and the type of housing assistance received by families who relocated from Grady Homes and other public housing developments in Atlanta. This model examined all householders in the work eligible population between 2004 and 2010. Repeated observations were taken on the same householder population in 2004, 2007, and 2010. This allowed the model to control for selectivity effects. Conducting repeated observations also allowed the analysis to control for the effect of implementing the mandatory work requirement policy in 2005.

In total, there were 33,051 observations included in the analysis, and 4.8 percent were excluded because of missing data. The attributes controlled for included the type of housing assistance received by the householder (i.e., LIPH, mixed income vouches, tenant-based vouchers, or project-based vouchers), the age and gender of the householder, the number of bedrooms in the rental unit, and the implementation of the work compliance policy in 2007 and 2010 (but not in 2004).

The results show that relocating to mixed income developments and receiving vouchers significantly increased the odds of working when compared to persons who remained in conventional public housing developments. Specifically, the results show the following:

a. Persons who lived in mixed-income developments experienced 4.7 times greater odds of working in comparison to persons who lived in conventional public housing projects.
b. Persons who received project-based vouchers experienced 4.6 times greater odds of working in comparison to persons who lived in in conventional public housing projects.
c. Persons who used tenant-based vouchers experienced 1.6 times greater odds of working in comparison to persons who lived in conventional public housing projects.
d. Persons with two-bedroom units experienced 1.5 greater odds of working than persons who lived in an efficiency or one-bedroom unit; similarly, persons with three bedrooms as well as those with four or more bedrooms were also more likely to work.
e. Women experienced 1.8 times greater odds of working in comparison to men.
f. Persons who participated in a self-sufficiency and work training program experienced 2.1 times greater odds of working than persons who did not participate.

g. Persons who were 30 to 39 years of age had greater odds of working than persons 18 to 29 years. Additionally, persons 40 years and older were less likely to work than persons 18 to 29 years of age.

h. Finally, the AHA implemented a mandatory work program in 2005. The work compliance program increased the odds of being employed by 8 percent.

Conclusion

This research focused on two important questions: (1) Did displaced families lose housing assistance because of the demolition? And (2) Did families experience upward socioeconomic mobility (measured by a change in employment status) as a result of relocating to better housing and higher-quality neighborhoods?

We found the answer to the displacement issue is more complex than researchers have yet considered. In particular, families who were not forced to relocate from public housing projects because of demolition were more likely to exit housing assistance, in comparison to those who were forced to relocate. The bad conditions and socioeconomic environment surrounding distressed public housing developments were more powerful forces propelling involuntary exits from housing assistance than were mandatory relocations caused by demolition. As time passed, families who moved into mixed income housing and those who relocated using vouchers were more likely to exit housing assistance than were those who lived in public housing projects. This is because families in mixed-income developments and those using vouchers became employed and self-sufficient at a higher rate. As a result, they were more likely to exit for housing in the private rental market.

In general, our findings suggest that if public housing transformation policies are applied correctly, low-income families can have access to higher quality housing and as a result become more economically self-sufficient. Hence, public housing revitalization can improve the self-sufficiency of low-income families without causing a loss of housing assistance, to a greater extent than what would have occurred under normal circumstances.

CHAPTER 12

The Evolution of the Business Leaders Who Built Modern Atlanta

Maria Saporta

Atlanta's destiny—for better and for worse—has always rested in the hands of its business community. In the past 60 years, the building of modern Atlanta can be traced to an impressive group of business leaders—people who have evolved over the past six decades as the city has grown and Atlanta's power base has diversified. The builders of modern Atlanta are legendary, many of whom were interviewed specifically for this chapter.

There is internationally renowned architect and developer John Portman, a Georgia Tech alumnus who broke the mold by designing atrium hotels and developing his own projects. Portman designed projects in locations all over the world, including San Francisco, New York, Detroit, China, Singapore, South Korea, and Warsaw as well as 17 blocks in downtown Atlanta. There also is Tom Cousins, often seen as a rival of Portman, who developed the Omni Coliseum and what is now the CNN Center as well as numerous suburban and urban office developments. Cousins became a developer philanthropist, working with partners to transform the decaying East Lake community. Other developers— such as Wayne Mason in Gwinnett County and John Williams, founder of Post Properties—took advantage of Atlanta's sprawling metropolis. They leveraged the growth of the suburbs by building subdivisions, apartment complexes, and suburban office and retail developments—all served by metro Atlanta's highway investments. Today those very same developers are moving away from suburban automobile-oriented developments to more urban and pedestrian-oriented ones.

Different players have emerged on the scene over the years. After desegregation, a few black business leaders—once frozen out of the power structure—

found key allies. Herman J. Russell eventually built the largest minority-owned construction firm in the United States; along the way, he started developing projects of his own. His firm served as an incubator for a host of minority developers who have become major players in today's Atlanta, including Egbert Perry of the Integral Group. The Atlanta development community continues to be dominated by men, but several women have played important roles. Renee Glover served as president and CEO of the Atlanta Housing Authority (AHA) for a transformative 19 years. Former Atlanta mayor Shirley Franklin worked for Cousins before and after her time in office and is now CEO of Purpose Built Communities, a nonprofit founded by Cousins, which is trying to replicate the East Lake model in other cities. There have been other women players, such as Susan Mendheim, former CEO of the Midtown Alliance and an influential leader in the planned resurgence of the business, residential, retail, and cultural district along Peachtree Street. But historically, Atlanta has been a city that has been developed primarily by white men.

Back in the 1950s, Atlanta was just a medium-sized Southern town with big dreams. Architect and developer John Portman recalled former Atlanta mayor William Hartsfield saying, "We would have the biggest airport in the world"—a dream that actually became true decades later. "Hartsfield said you had to stake out where you wanted to go and work like hell so they don't call you a liar," Portman recalled. "We had a great *esprit de corps* in Atlanta" (Cousins 2013).

Atlanta developer Tom Cousins also witnessed the power of "the big mules," the business leaders who helped set the tone of racial tolerance in Atlanta. "The biggest thing was civil rights," Cousins said. "Atlanta was just an island in the South. When images of Birmingham were shown around the world with Bull Conner and the fire hoses, that's when Atlanta really took off. That was the end of the competition." Cousins, one of the youngest business leaders at Atlanta's power table in the 1960s, credited Coca-Cola magnate Robert Woodruff for being open to racial integration and helping guide the city through those sensitive times. Woodruff worked with then mayor Ivan Allen Jr., a well-respected businessman who gained national notoriety for being the only elected official from the South to testify in 1963 in favor of what would become the 1964 Civil Rights Act. "When I grew up, Atlanta, Birmingham, Chattanooga, Nashville, and Jacksonville were all about the same size," said John Williams, who became a leading suburban apartment developer with the founding of Post Properties. "One of the great things about Atlanta was that Atlanta figured out how to have better race relations than the other cities" (Williams 2013).

A Changing Power Structure

Portman said an important group in the early 1970s was the Atlanta Action Forum, a group of white and black business leaders who would meet on Saturday mornings once a month to discuss Atlanta's problems. "People really wanted to make things better," Portman said. "We were creating a force for the good. You could not keep from being excited about the city" (Portman 2013). One great example is how the group worked to get the Metropolitan Atlanta Rapid Transit Authority (MARTA) referendum passed in 1971. Although it failed in the suburban counties, it passed in the city of Atlanta, Fulton County and DeKalb County (Hornsby 2004). "When MARTA won, we felt like doing cartwheels," Portman said.

But the city was changing from one in which there was little difference between its business and political power structure to one in which blacks were gaining political influence at city hall (Stone 1989). That led to the election of Atlanta mayor Maynard Jackson in 1973, a young African American leader who began changing the city's power structure. "Maynard introduced community engagement on the neighborhood level, and that was a major innovation at the time," said former Atlanta mayor Shirley Franklin, who worked in Jackson's administration. "It was a brand new approach. People who had a lot less money, or no money at all, now had a voice. It created friction for the business leadership because they weren't accustomed to it. There was a lot of grousing by the time Andy Young became mayor" (Franklin 2013).

Suburban Flight
Partly because of the changing political and racial dynamics, Franklin said that "a lot of investment left Atlanta and the city." It was not only white flight but black middle class flight—families that wanted better schools for their children. Two developers who benefited from the flight to the suburbs were John Williams, who eventually made his base in Cobb County, and Wayne Mason, who was the leading power broker and developer in Gwinnett County.

"Gwinnett was rural and agricultural," Mason said. "We put in a water-sewer authority. We changed the form of government. We adopted a 100-year flood plan and a comprehensive land use plan. We paved or resurfaced 800 miles of road in eight years. We had a plan, there's no question about that." But Mason said that "all these people were piling out of DeKalb" and Gwinnett had to keep up with the residential growth ("we were building houses that were selling like popcorn"), so the goal was to attract commercial and industrial development. "We wouldn't tell people we were from Gwinnett. We told them we were from Atlanta," Mason said. "Atlanta was such a magnet for jobs. We always rode the back of Atlanta. We took advantage of that, no question about it" (Mason 2013).

Meanwhile, Williams was finding great success in developing beautifully landscaped apartment projects in the suburbs. "Atlanta didn't have natural boundaries. Atlanta was unique. It was always zoning friendly and lender friendly. It was a developers' town," Williams said. "I rode that wave from the 1970s to the late 1980s" (Williams 2013).

John Portman, who had grown up in the center of the city, opted to remain based downtown while he watched other developers spread their wings out to the suburbs. "Atlanta has had so much land available that was so inexpensive," Portman said. "At the end of World War II everything started becoming unzipped in the United States because we had the highway system. There was the rush to the suburbs. Most American cities had to go through this. I always felt Atlanta could be a great city. I didn't go to the suburbs until very, very late in my career. I went out to North Park to try to understand the suburbs, but my heart really belonged Downtown. I believe that no city is a great city unless it has a great heart. I think Atlanta has the beginning of a great heart" (Portman 2013).

Portman Versus Cousins

During their decades downtown, Portman and Cousins always seemed to be caught in a competitive tug of war about how the central business district would grow. The competition became most pronounced in the early 1970s when both developers had competing plans to build the state's major convention center in downtown Atlanta. Portman wanted to locate the convention center just northeast of his Peachtree Center development—close to AmericasMart and the hotels that he had designed in an area near the city's new Civic Center complex along Piedmont Avenue. Cousins wanted to locate the convention center on the western edge of downtown next to the Omni Coliseum near a major railroad corridor. Several economic development impact studies were done. There was an intense political lobbying effort that took place between both developers. Finally, Cousins agreed to donate the property for what is now the Georgia World Congress Center and to guarantee the cost of constructing, and even to managing, the complex.

Today, Portman graciously acknowledges that the convention center is in the right place. "It's better where it is now than where I wanted it to be," Portman said. "We lost that one, and I'm glad to say today that I'm glad we didn't win. It's better for the city where it is" (Portman 2013).

Cost of Sprawl

During the 1980s and 1990s, the Atlanta region had become nationally known for its suburban sprawl and apparent lack of regional planning. "Much of it was opportunistic," Cousins said. "Could there have been more and better planning? Yes, but I could say that about any city in America" (Cousins 2013). Cousins went on to say that there were planning attempts by city and county governments, but metro Atlanta has so many local governments that planning can be a challenge.

The region was beginning to pay the price in terms of traffic congestion, air quality, and water resources. "Atlanta was like a laboratory on urban sprawl," Williams said. "You could tell we were gobbling up a huge number of acres and developing way past the capability of our infrastructure of water and sewer and roads. We could not continue to go further and further out." It was in the late 1980s when Williams said he "got religion" and joined the new urbanism movement. He started developing "live, work, and play" developments in the city. "I certainly went through an evolution," Williams said (2013). During those decades, the power of developers also began to change as other groups were given opportunities to weigh in on decisions. Developers could no longer dictate what they would build, and they often had to go through a much more collaborative process with people in the community.

Planning at its Best

One of the best examples of a collaborative planning process in Atlanta was Blueprint Midtown. In 1997 the Midtown Alliance—an organization of business and civic leaders—received a $300,000 grant from the Robert W. Woodruff Foundation to undergo an extensive planning process for the area (Midtown Alliance 2013). "Midtown, like a number of urban centers, had been allowed to atrophy and decay," said Susan Mendheim, who served as president of the Midtown Alliance from 1982 to 2012. "We came together as a whole community. It was grassroots. And we had an inclusive rather than exclusive business group" (Mendheim 2013). Mendheim had attended a Georgia Conservancy program and heard a presentation from New Jersey urban planner Anton Nelessen, who she felt had "one of the most brilliant ways to include all the people in a community in a meaningful way" in the planning process (Saporta 1998). "Tony's outrageousness and ability to say anything freed us up tremendously," Mendheim said. "He emboldened us."

Nelessen had thousands of people in Midtown—office worker, visitors, residents and even symphony musicians—take a visual preferences survey to identify which images they wanted Midtown to become. "It was so good to use images instead of words," Mendheim said. That was followed up with a community charette and a plan that became Blueprint Midtown, which the Midtown Alliance worked with the city to have "codified into law" and made into a special zoning district. "At the end of the day, when people came into our office, they still brought all the crappy stuff, and we had to gently show them the Blueprint plan," Mendheim said. "You have to stay on top of it" (Mendheim 2013). A major test of Blueprint Midtown came early on in January 1998 when First Union proposed razing a key block at 10th and Peachtree Streets for an employee parking lot, totally contrary to the community's vision. The community was so outraged that the bank withdrew its plans within 10 days (Saporta 1998).

Today Mendheim could not be more pleased with how Blueprint Midtown turned out. "I just look at Midtown everyday and think it's the most beautiful place," she said. "It's because we had a plan, and we stuck with that plan. Then we were able to amplify that plan and make it more beautiful. All the pieces just came together" (Mendheim 2013).

All Growth is Not Equal

What Midtown accomplished was special, but Midtown also had several advantages that many other lower-income communities in Atlanta do not have, according to Egbert Perry, CEO of the Integral Group—a development company specializing in urban revitalization (Perry 2013). Perry, a native of the Caribbean island of Antigua, moved to Atlanta in 1980 to work for the powerful H.J. Russell & Company and was promoted to president within a year. During Perry's 13 years at Russell, the company went from having revenues of about $11 million to $200 million, becoming the third largest black-owned business in the United States. That is when Perry decided to venture out on his own to revitalize urban America. Perry and a business partner drew up a white paper about what it would take to transform poor neighborhoods into thriving communities. In 1994 they got their opportunity to team up with Renee Glover with the AHA to demolish Techwood Homes, the oldest public housing project in the nation, and replace it with a mixed income development featuring a reinvigorated elementary school and YMCA. All of it was to be done in conjunction with the 1996 Summer Olympic Games (Tubov and Piper 2005). A new development model was born—the HOPE VI program—a model that has been replicated throughout Atlanta and other cities. Today, none of Atlanta's traditional public housing developments remain.

Perry, however, is less starry-eyed about Atlanta's ability to address its societal issues over the decades. "There was a small group of white and a small group of black businessmen who had an unholy or holy alliance grounded in keeping the peace and moving the city forward," Perry said. "But later I realized they were not dealing with the tough issues. It was intentional neglect. Things were booming. People were at the table. But there was not necessarily the kind of community-based leadership being cultivated to ensure that the communities around the city were going to be healthy. The lack of balanced growth is and has been Atlanta's biggest problems" (Perry 2013).

To Perry, that growing disparity of opportunity and wealth threatens to divide the region. In addition, according to Perry, there is the political divide. "The city of Atlanta has 10 percent of the region's population. Ninety percent of the population of the region is not associated with the heart of the region," Perry said. "The end result is that you have a leadership vacuum in the making. A significant proportion of the 90 percent of the people who live outside the city have no affinity to the city of Atlanta. "There's more balkanization. That to me is the single biggest threat long term. If you cannot create a single vision for the region—a feeling that everyone is under one tent—we don't have a chance in hell. Wise investments have to be done on a regional basis. What are shooting for? We need the right vision" (Perry 2013).

Instead, Perry said he sees "a whole lot of sub stories going on" in the Atlanta region. "There is very little leadership saying how do we become the region that is the strongest region or the best region in the United States," Perry said. "Greater Charlotte is talking like a region when it comes to education and transportation. We don't have that happening at the scale we need to have that happen. Our trend lines are not good, and we have got to work quickly to change them. If we don't, we are not going to be the jewel anymore" (Perry 2013).

Former mayor Shirley Franklin said the Atlanta region has suffered because the state has not been a true economic partner. "There's essentially one Georgia that drives the Georgia economy, and that's metro Atlanta. It's in the state's best interest to be closer to Atlanta," Franklin said. "There's been a lack of investment in an integrated transportation system—bikes, rail transit. . . .Connectivity has been an issue for the past 50 years. When we started, we had the right model, but it got stalled. The state has had the authority to solve the transportation problem. It gains a lot more in a healthy Atlanta but the investment has not followed" (Franklin 2013).

A City of Big Ideas

Fortunately, Atlanta has benefitted by having business leaders who have become great philanthropists, who have been willing to invest in the city. Take Tom Cousins and the partnership created in East Lake. "Over 50 plus years I had been giving to this program and that program and not seeing the result," Cousins said. "We had been putting band-aids on things but we had not been curing the disease. I knew there was a way out of poverty. You have to get to the children. I know there's an answer to poverty, and it's been proven at East Lake" (Cousins 2013).

Cousins teamed up with AHA's Renee Glover and a host of community partners to transform East Lake Meadows, one of the worst public housing projects in the city, into a mixed-income development with a charter school, a YMCA, a public golf course, and other amenities. After initial acrimonious dealings and criticism about the displacement of poor residents, the public housing tenants of East Lake and the redevelopment partners were able to work together and even create lasting friendships.

Franklin, who worked with Cousins on East Lake, is now CEO of his national nonprofit—Purpose Built Communities—that is trying to replicate that comprehensive redevelopment approach in cities across the country. In Franklin's mind, it is all part of Atlanta being a city of people with "big ideas." From William Hartsfield and the airport to Ivan Allen and Robert Woodruff on integration. Former Atlanta mayor Sam Massell and MARTA. Former Atlanta mayor Andrew Young and the globalization of Atlanta. Ted Turner and CNN. Bernie Marcus and Arthur Blank and Home Depot (Franklin 2013).

The Atlanta BeltLine

Franklin also had her share of big ideas, including supporting development of the Atlanta BeltLine, a 22-mile corridor encircling the central city that is being turned into multi-use trails, parks, new developments, and eventually, a possible transit line.

Gwinnett developer Wayne Mason became enamored with the Atlanta BeltLine. He was able to buy 4.6 miles of the prime northeast rail corridor from Norfolk-Southern for $25 million in 2004. "I knew everything was going back to the core because of traffic," Mason said. "People had wanted our big-sized lots, good schools, and safe streets. But lifestyles change. They don't want the big lots anymore. It's a different mindset. They don't want to be in the suburbs. They want to be downtown." Mason quickly proposed developing two high-rise towers, nearly 40 stories high, on the eastern edge of Piedmont Park along his BeltLine property. To sweeten the deal, he offered to donate much of the rest of his holdings to the city. But the nearby neighborhoods strongly objected to his plans, which had been drafted with little to no community input. When he realized his plans would not fly, Mason ended up selling his BeltLine property to the city, netting a profit of about $50 million. "It hurt my feelings," Mason said. "But it was the best thing that happened to me" (Mason 2013).

Desire to Live in Walkable Centers

Today, there is amazing consensus among the developers about the demographic trends favoring walkable urban communities rather than autocentric suburban communities. Portman said it all can be traced back to demographics—young people are getting married later and having children later, if at all, the elderly are living longer, and people are wanting to live in places where they can walk. "People are moving back in to cities," Portman said. "You can't walk anywhere in the suburbs. All the young people are moving back into the city" (Portman 2013).

Over the span of his career, Portman, however, has been criticized for designing downtown buildings that are not friendly to the street. He connected his buildings with a series of sky bridges that took pedestrians off the street. And often his buildings meet the sidewalk with concrete walls rather than street-level retail. "That whole line of conversation is bogus. You want all the streets to be energized," Portman said. "With MARTA going in, it made a lot more sense to take all these blocks and tie them altogether with bridges like Venice. We were master planning all of it. If the weather is great, everyone is on the sidewalks. They're not on bridges. All the streets here are vehicular rivers. There are certain places where sidewalks are alive. Every side street cannot support every activity. What we were trying to do was create spaces. We were trying to expand spaces in the city. We opened up buildings with interior open spaces" (Portman 2013).

Over the years, Portman's urban design has evolved. One of his later developments in downtown Atlanta—SunTrust Plaza—was designed with welcoming entrances from every vista. Franklin, who has been spending time in Austin, Texas, recently decided to walk Atlanta's streets as though she were a tourist seeing it for the first time. "I walked up Peachtree Street to SunTrust Plaza," Franklin said. "It's just spectacular. The sculpture. The way it meets the street. It's wonderful to have John Portman investing in that kind of creativity in Atlanta. It is exquisite" (Franklin 2013).

Hope for the Future

In the end, Atlanta's business leaders interviewed for this chapter are still filled with the buoyant spirit that has defined the city for decades. Portman, who turned 89 in December 2013, said, "Better times are ahead, not behind us." Cousins said, "Atlanta has so much going for it. We have the airport. We have got the climate. It's just the best. It's home." Mason said that Atlanta is well-positioned. "The market is coming back. The airport is the biggest thing we have going for us." And Williams said, "The future? It's very bright. The brightest yet."

CHAPTER 13

Neighborhood Quality of Life and Health in Atlanta

Nisha Botchwey, Susannah Lee, Audrey Leous, Subhro Guhathakurta

An Atlanta Planning Legacy

Flying into Atlanta, passengers see the infamous curvilinear street network of narrow feeder streets connected to high traffic thoroughfares. This pattern is the result of the 1954 plan called *Now...for Tomorrow: A Master Planning Program for the DeKalb-Fulton Metropolitan Area* that directed future development to "correct" the gridded street pattern laid out and built throughout the core of the city (Metropolitan Planning Commission 1954). This plan resulted in the sprawling and dendritic street network that dominates the areas outside of this core. It is, in large part, this infrastructure design that has since influenced the pattern of life in Atlanta (Figure 13.1).

The plan was created to guide decision making providing adequate living space and services as the population grew, making economical use of land, and addressing efficient movement of goods and people. The plan emphasized the importance of quality communities by protecting residential areas from traffic, pollution, and unsafe conditions of industry. It recommended expressways and limited-access boulevards to quickly accommodate heavy traffic volume. Sixty years later, we reflect on these recommendations with criticism; we now value street connectivity and walkability. The 1954 plan discouraged the type of development that is now found in some of the most desirable neighborhoods in Atlanta.

A focus at this smaller neighborhood scale is needed to understand the health and quality of life in Atlanta. This chapter evaluates the mix of public safety, economy, transportation, amenities, and housing that affect the qual-

Today: Traffic on Residential Streets

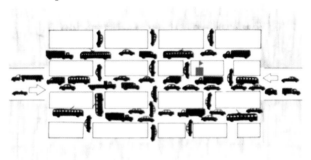

Tomorrow: New Trafficways—Quiet Homes

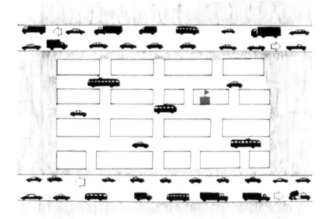

Figure 13.1. Now...for Tomorrow recommended expressways and limited access boulevards.(Source: Metropolitan Planning Commission 1954.)

ity of life, and the variation in walkability and food access that shape health outcomes in Atlanta today. These factors can aid in forecasting the future of quality of life and health in Atlanta and strategic planning and investments for targeted need areas.

Neighborhood Quality of Life and Health Indexes

Quality of Life
Quality of life is a broad concept that has been variously measured to evaluate individual or community wellbeing. Planners are interested in understanding

the quality of life at the neighborhood or local scale and the built environment features that contribute to the wellbeing of residents (Myers 1988). A place-based quality-of-life measurement is thus useful in that it enables comparisons, guides understanding of geographic patterns and longitudinal trends, and informs policy setting at the local and regional levels.

Health

Health, as defined by the World Health Organization, is "a state of complete physical, mental and social well-being and not merely the absence of disease or infirmity" (World Health Organization 1948). Population health is increasingly recognized to be influenced by the social determinants of health: where you were born, where you were raised, and the type of job you have. Today the diseases that dominate the list of concern include chronic and noncommunicable ones rather than acute and infectious ones. At the top of the list for the United States are heart disease, cancer, asthma, and stroke—all but one being an obesity-related disease (Murphy, Xu, and Kochanek 2013). Planners can influence levels of obesity and obesity-related diseases through the design of built environments that promote higher levels of physical activity and improved access to healthy food (Botchwey and Trowbridge 2011; Morris 2006; Raja, Ma, and Yadav 2008).

Quality of life and community health studies have mostly used data from one point in time. Such analyses are limited in determining causality and suffer from self-selection bias. These cross-sectional designs are unable to adequately address the question of whether positive features of a neighborhood —such as better access to green space and public transportation, access to healthy food, or low pollution levels—lead to better community health. The research reported here circumvents the problems of cross-sectional design by correlating two indicators after controlling for the socioeconomic status of neighborhoods within the city of Atlanta. More importantly, the study seeks to identify the attributes of those neighborhoods in which both quality-of-life and health indicators are high so that these neighborhoods can be studied and subsequently replicated. If the socioeconomic status of these neighborhoods varies, then the feasibility of planning high quality neighborhoods may not depend on the class or income levels of an area's residents.

The Neighborhood Planning Unit

The Neighborhood Planning Unit (NPU) was chosen as the unit of analysis to assess quality of life and health in Atlanta. NPUs are city-designated boundaries that are widely used within Atlanta and easily recognizable by residents, more so than other commonly used neighborhood units of analysis, such as block groups or census tracts. The NPU system originated in the 1970s as a formal vehicle for grassroots organizing and civic involvement and remains the dominant level at which planning decisions are made today. There are 25 NPUs in Atlanta, named by the letters of the alphabet from A to Z, omitting a single letter, U. Each NPU contains a cluster of contiguous neighborhoods. For example, NPU M is composed of Downtown, as well as three surrounding historic neighborhoods: Castleberry Hill, Sweet Auburn, and the Old Fourth Ward.

Controlling for Community Socioeconomic Conditions

While the built environment is the focus of this chapter, the social and economic aspects of a community are also widely acknowledged contributors to both community health and other quality-of-life attributes. Disparities in health outcomes among different socioeconomic groups have been well documented (Adler et al., 1994; Adler et al. 1999; Anderson at al. 1997; Braveman et al. 2005; Pickett and Pearl 2001; Robert 1998, 1999). In addition, socioeconomic status is well known to play a significant role in household location choice (Boone-Heinonen et al. 2011a; Boone-Heinonen et al. 2011b; Braubauch and Fairburn 2010; Coffee et al. 2013a, 2013b; Fussell, Sastry, and VanLandingham 2010; Han et al. 2010; Harvard et al. 2009; Pickett and Pearl 2001; Robert 1998; Sang, O'Kelly, and Kwan2011). Therefore, strong predictors of neighborhoods with high quality-of-life and health measures tend to be those that also reflect high socioeconomic status (e.g., in terms of race/ethnicity and income levels) (Collins, Hayes, and Oliver 2009).

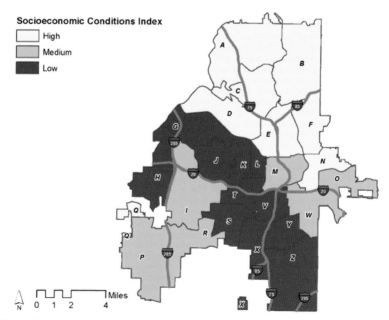

Figure 13.2. Socioeconomic Conditions Index. (Source: Map by authors.)

The Atlanta Quality of Life and Neighborhood Health Index controls for socioeconomic characteristics of a population by constructing a Socioeconomic Conditions (SEC) Index that evaluates social and economic neighborhood conditions with four indicators: unemployment, education, poverty, and income. The indicators are combined with standardized scores and the resulting values are sorted by standard deviation. High SEC status represents values that are equal to or greater than a 0.5 standard deviation; medium SEC includes the middle range of NPUs that fall within -0.5 and 0.5 standard deviations; and low SEC captures those that fall below -0.5 standard deviations. The results exhibit a geographic pattern of higher SEC measures in the northern NPUs and lower SEC ones in western and southern Atlanta, as shown in Figure 13.2.

Neighborhood Quality of Life Index

Objective measures of quality of life are not free of subjective choices and interpretations. Individuals have diverse tastes and opinions about the types of places that are desirable. Regardless, most will agree that places with a high quality of life tend to have good educational opportunities, low rates of crime, good access to parks and open space, and good transportation access. The indicators selected for this Atlanta study are well represented in prior studies of quality of life. Neighborhood quality-of-life measures are based on responses to the following questions (adapted from Guhathakurta and Cao 2010):

- Is there a program or means of collecting periodically updated data for the indicator?
- Is the indicator relevant to residents' quality of life at the neighborhood scale?
- Can the indicator be impacted by planning policy or regulation?

For this study, the five indicators that were chosen for developing the Neighborhood Quality of Life (NQoL) Index are public safety, economy, transportation, neighborhood amenities, and housing. Each indicator comprises multiple measures that are combined using standard scores to create a set of rankings for each, as shown in Table 13.1. The rankings format simplifies a comprehensive set of statistics into a universally understood measurement system. These five indicator rankings were then weighted by residents' preferences and aggregated into a single set of quality-of-life rankings. The resident preference information from which the weights were derived is drawn from a survey conducted in 2011 by the City of Atlanta for its Comprehensive Development Plan update, in which citizens provided their opinions on priorities, issues, and opportunities for Atlanta.

TABLE 13.1.	Neighborhood Quality of Life Index Indicators and Measures	
NQoL Indicators	Measures	Data Sources
Public Safety	Violent crime rates Property crime rates Traffic-related injuries and fatalities	City of Atlanta, Atlanta Police Department Georgia Department of Transportation
Economy	Jobs to labor force ratio	U.S. Census Bureau
Transportation	Commute travel times Transit access	U.S. Census Bureau Metropolitan Atlanta Rapid Transit Authority transit locations shapefile
Amenities	Parks and recreation access Retail access	Atlanta parks shapefile Reference USA business database
Housing	Home affordability Rent affordability Vacancy rates	U.S. Census Bureau

Source: Compiled by authors

The NQoL Index final results can be seen in Figure 13.3. The NPUs were broken into 8 high, 6 medium and 11 low social economic status groups based on natural breaks in the index calculation. The number 1 represents the NPUs with the highest quality of life and the higher numbers in each SEC represents those with the lowest quality of life. NPU F ranks first overall in the high socioeconomic conditions category, with particularly good amenities, public safety, and transportation. NPU M ranks highest in the medium category because of its amenities, transportation and local economy. For the low group, good transportation, and amenities make NPU T the highest ranked in that category.

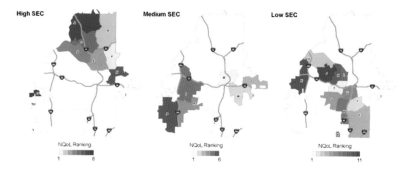

Figure 13.3. Neighborhood Quality of Life Index rankings by socioeconomic conditions status. (Source: Map by authors.)

TABLE 13.2.	Neighborhood Health Index Indicators and Measures	
Neighborhood Health Indicators	Measures	Data Source
Nutrition	Food Access	U.S. Census Bureau, Reference USA database
Physical activity	Walkability	Walk Score
Mortality	Years of potential life lost before 75 location quotient	Georgia Department of Public Health
Morbidity	Diabetes location quotient Hypertensive heart disease location quotient Esophageal cancer location quotient Uterine cancer location quotient Kidney cancer location quotient	Georgia Department of Public Health

Source: Compiled by authors

The Atlanta Neighborhood Health Index

The Neighborhood Health (NH) Index considers four key dimensions in assessing the capacity of populations to effectively prevent and decrease the prevalence of obesity: nutrition, physical activity, mortality, and morbidity, as shown in Table 13.2. Whereas healthy food access (a proxy for nutrition) and walkability (a proxy for physical activity) are measures of the built environment, mortality and morbidity assess outcomes at the neighborhood scale. Social and economic factors, which have been proven to affect health status, are controlled through the SEC Index that categorizes the NPUs.

The Neighborhood Health Index results (for which measures were aggregated with equal weights) are shown in Figure 13.4. NPU E ranks

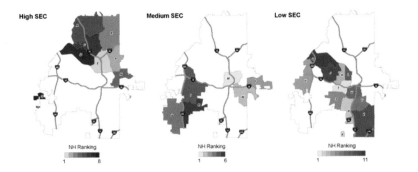

Figure 13.4. Neighborhood Health Index rankings by socioeconomic conditions status. (Source: Map by authors.)

first in neighborhood health for the high SEC category, with particularly good walkability and low concentrations of hypertensive heart disease and diabetes. NPU M of the medium group and NPU T of the low group rank highest in their respective categories because of strong food access and walkable environments.

Appraisal and Comparative Analysis

A primary objective of this study is to understand the relationships among attributes of the built environment that contribute to community health and those that affect residents' quality of life. Our results suggest that the overlap is significant and strong, but this relationship is pronounced in the neighborhoods characterized by high and medium socioeconomic conditions (Figure 13.5). The overall Spearman's Rank correlation index, a measure of how closely two sets of ranked attributes match, is 0.66 (significant at .01), indicating a reasonably high correlation between neighborhood health and neighborhood quality-of-life measures. However, when the correlations within the categories are tested, the same statistic for the low socioeconomic conditions tracts is small and not significant, while the relationship remains strong for the other two categories of neighborhoods.

Examination of the correlations between neighborhood health and the individual attributes of NQoL Index provides additional insights into NPU rankings. This analysis led to a sobering finding: the unemployment rate, on its own, could explain almost 85 percent of the variation in the NH Index.

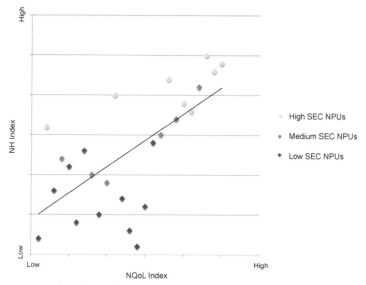

Figure 13.5. Correlation between health and quality of life rankings. (Source: Compiled by authors.)

TABLE 13.3.	Overlap of Neighborhood Quality of Life and Neighborhood Health Indexes		
Socioeconomic Conditions Status	High Quality of Life	High Health	Overlap
High	B, E, F	B, E, F	B, E, F
Med	M, W, O	M, W, O	M, W, O
Low	T, Y, G	T, X, K	T

Source: Compiled by authors

In contrast, the same indicator is able to explain a little over 30 percent of the variation in the NQoL Index, suggesting that neighborhoods with high unemployment rates would be more sensitive to the NH Index than to the NQoL Index. Two particular NPUs in the low socioeconomic conditions category, NPU G and NPU Z, emerge as "outliers" as may be observed in Figure 13.5. Both NPUs are on the periphery of the city, one on the western edge and the other on the southeastern edge. These NPUs are characterized by high levels of poverty and unemployment, although other factors, such as high affordability of homes, place them in the middle of NQoL Index rankings.

Table 13.3 illustrates the NPUs in Atlanta that rank highly on both the quality of life and the health indices. The NPUs that ranked highest for quality of life also ranked highest in health in both the high and medium socio-

Figure 13.6. NPU F, Virginia Highland Center

economic conditions categories; in the low category, only one NPU ranked highly for both quality of life and health.

To examine the qualities that cause neighborhoods to rank highly on the quality-of-life or health scales, the three neighborhoods ranked highest in each socioeconomic conditions group (NPUs F, M, and T) are described below. They vary in terms of land use, urban design, amenities, and other neighborhood characteristics, yet a number of similarities emerge. These three NPUs share the following characteristics: access to green spaces, good retail mixes, low-to average-travel times, access to healthy food, and high walkability.

Neighborhood Planning Unit F

NPU F is located in northeast Atlanta and is composed of four neighborhoods: Linridge/Martin Manor, Piedmont Heights, Morningside/Lenox Park, and Virginia-Highland. These neighborhoods are primarily residential, with middle- to upper-class residents. Major non-residential destinations include Ansley Mall, an outdoor strip mall; several Atlanta public schools; and several small, walkable commercial centers. It also includes the Morningside Nature Preserve and borders Piedmont Park, the largest park in the city of Atlanta. NPU F ranks highly on the NQoL Index because its residents have good access to green space, excellent retail amenities, low vacancy rates, low levels of crime, and short travel times. It ranks highly on the NH Index because of good access to healthy food, high walkability, and strong health outcomes (Figure 13.6).

Figure 13.7. NPU M transit

Neighborhood Planning Unit M

NPU M is located in the city center and includes four neighborhoods: Downtown, Old Fourth Ward, Castleberry Hill, and Sweet Auburn. These neighborhoods contain a variety of land uses. Downtown includes the downtown business district, government offices (city, county, and federal), Georgia State University, and a number of tourist attractions, such as sporting arenas and the Georgia Aquarium. This NPU also includes residential areas with small, older homes; the Martin Luther King, Jr. Center and other historical buildings; former industrial areas that are being revitalized and converted into residential and artist spaces; and several major roadways (Interstate 75/85 and Freedom Parkway). Emory University Hospital, the Atlanta Medical Center, and Grady Memorial Hospital are located in this NPU. NPU M ranks highly on the NQoL Index due to an extremely high ratio of jobs to labor force, excellent access to parks and retail amenities, good transit access, and short commute times. Its major NQoL Index drawback is public safety concerns due to high property crime and vehicle crashes. It ranks highly on the NH Index because it is the most walkable NPU in Atlanta and has good food access and relatively low premature mortality (Figure 13.7).

Neighborhood Planning Unit T

NPU T, located just southwest of the city center, includes the following neighborhoods: Ashview Heights, Atlanta University Center, CollegeTown (formerly Harris Chiles), Just Us Neighbors, the Villages at Castleberry Hill, West End, and Westview. It is located close to Interstate 75/85, and Interstate 20, a major state highway passes through it. This NPU is home to the Atlanta Univer-

Figure 13.8. NPU T housing

sity Center, a consortium of historically black educational institutions, including Clark Atlanta University, Morehouse College, Morehouse School of Medicine, and Spelman College. This NPU ranks highly on the NQoL Index because of an excellent retail mix, moderate green space access, above- average housing affordability for both renting and owning, and very extensive transit access. Although NPU T has fairly high levels of obesity-related chronic disease conditions, it has a high NH Index ranking for its socioeconomic conditions category due to built environment measures for good food access and high walkability (Figure 13.8).

Conclusions

In conclusion, a large number of studies show a strong relationship between human social and psychological conditions and physical health. For example, studies have shown that high levels of stress and social exclusion lead to a range of chronic conditions, including cardiovascular and heart diseases. We ask whether places that offer a high quality of life also promote better health for their inhabitants. The results of this study, based on the study of Atlanta NPUs, provide ample evidence to support our hypothesis. We find the overlaps between NPUs having high quality-of-life and health indices are significant, especially in the high and medium socioeconomic status areas. In areas with high socioeconomic conditions, two of three NPUs with high NQoL Index measures also score high on the NH Index. For the medium socioeconomic conditions areas, the three NPUs with the highest NQoL Index also have the highest NH Index measures. This overlap is somewhat weaker in the low socioeconomic conditions areas, where just one of the top three NPUs appears in both.

Another important finding is that, despite the well-documented suburbanization of amenities across the U.S., neighborhood areas such as Midtown and Downtown can support a high quality of life and healthy lifestyle opportunities for residents. Given that urban core areas provide access to jobs and amenities, this finding aligns well with responses to the 2011 resident survey. Residents indicated they like access to jobs, shopping, services, and recreation and green spaces. However, these residents also wanted their neighborhoods to be safe and clean with low vacancy levels. To the extent that urban core areas can be free from crime and squalor, they are potentially the most desirable areas in terms of quality-of-life features. In addition, this study confirms that such areas also promote healthy choices among the residents, resulting in better community health statistics.

PART 3

Travel, Traffic, and Transit Define a Region

Atlantans are bombarded with a myriad of transportation jargon daily. We know what "code red" smog, nonattainment, traffic tie-ups, congestion, road closings due to construction, the perimeter,[1] the spaghetti junction[2], the northern arc[3], and OTP and ITP ("outside the perimeter" and "inside the perimeter") refer to—and we know that none of it is good. Our TV meteorologists remind us to keep children and the elderly indoors to avoid polluted air and smog on more days than we care to admit.

Labeled the poster child for sprawl and congestion, Atlanta is cursed with a double-edged crisis. The future of the region requires building fewer roads and more rail transit, but transportation planners, elected officials, and the public do not agree. These chapters are an overview of the issues Atlantans face.

Catherine Ross gives a clear assessment of local issues in "Regional Growth, Transportation, and Congestion: The Atlanta Problem." Ross describes the history, planning, problems, and solutions in a review of our opportunities, constraints, and more importantly our competition in the southeast. As a former state transportation official, recognized expert, and sought after speaker on regional transportation, Ross looks to future issues such as moving freight from the Port of Savannah and building logistics with intelligent transport systems.

In "From Transit as a Social Service to Transit as Congestion Relief: The Failure of Transit Planning in Atlanta," Laurel Paget-Seekins relates how the

Figure D.1. The I-75/85 Connector

Metropolitan Atlanta Rapid Transit Authority (MARTA) does not meet the needs of its riders by relating the routes of two very different users. In an of the overview of the failed 2012 Transportation Investment Act referendum, Paget-Seekins describes the debacle that brought together an unlikely combination of groups—the Sierra Club, the Georgia Tea Party, and the National Association for the Advancement of Colored People— to oppose the proposed special tax, which subsequently lost by a 68 percent vote.

Atlanta is home to the busiest airport in the world. Benjamin R. DeCosta, the city's former commissioner of aviation, discusses the positive effects of planning in "Hartsfield-Jackson Atlanta International Airport: A City of Its Own." DeCosta relates the planning and building of the fifth runway, the $1.25 billion construction project that was considered necessary to meet traffic projections. Planning included extensive community consultation for approvals, and DeCosta describes what it was like to come up against community and political opposition and to build the constituency for the airport expansion and new runway.

When the last tracks were removed from Five Points in 1973 for the construction of Woodruff Park, Atlantans considered the streetcar gone forever. Jennifer Ball, the Central Atlanta Progress planner in charge of the new streetcar project, describes the path to implementation in "Modern Streetcars Return to Atlanta." Ball recounts the planning, visioning, defeats, and funding involved in taking the streetcar from idea to construction.

Atlantans love the BeltLine. They love the trails, bridges, paths, landscape, art and just about everything to do with the 22 miles of planned redevelopment along abandoned rail lines. Alexander Garvin describes the making of this iconic project in "Atlanta's BeltLine: The Emerald Necklace Shaping the City's Future." Garvin led the planning effort to establish the blueprint for land acquisition, parks, and redevelopment. Even with the development slowdown due to the Great Recession, new paths and parks are connecting infrastructure to new housing and retail development. Garvin describes how Atlantans are embracing their future with the BeltLine.

Atlanta was founded as a railroad town and the transportation legacy is manifested today in a city characterized by substantial transportation assets and liabilities. From streetcars to MARTA to the BeltLine to the busiest airport in the world, Atlanta has established its reputation as a transportation magnet. Issues remain and not everyone is in agreement whether to build roads or transit and how to improve access. Many agree the priority should be rail, but local residents will tell you that people in South do not ride trains—those are for the Northerners.

CHAPTER 14

Regional Growth, Transportation, and Congestion: The Atlanta Problem

Catherine Ross

"IT ONLY TAKES A GENERATION-PLUS OF YINNING WHEN YOU SHOULD HAVE YANGED TO WAKE UP AND SAY, 'OH MY GOD! HOW DID IT HAPPEN?'" SAYS OUTGOING MARTA GENERAL MANAGER BEVERLY A. SCOTT, WHO WATCHED FROM AFAR THE DECLINE OF HER HOMETOWN, CLEVELAND. ATLANTA'S FAILURE TO BUILD OUT MARTA LOOKS EVEN MORE SHAMEFUL WHEN COMPARED WITH WHAT HAPPENED WITH SIMILAR TRANSIT SYSTEMS IN SAN FRANCISCO AND WASHINGTON, D.C., WHICH STARTED AT THE SAME TIME AS MARTA, SHE SAYS. "THE REALITY IS, THIS REGION GOT STUCK. WE HAVE ABOUT HALF THE BUILD-OUT OF WHAT IT WAS PLANNED TO BE." BUT SAN FRANCISCO AND WASHINGTON "KEPT BUILDING AND MOVING . . . THEY HAD PLANS REGARDLESS OF WHETHER FOLKS WERE RED OR BLUE. THEY HAD A VISION AND THE FORTITUDE TO MAKE PURPLE AND KEEP MOVING. WE JUST GOT STUCK."
(MONROE 2012)

Atlanta's Dilemma

Atlanta has rebuilt and recast itself a number of times. Destroyed during the Civil War, the city began immediately to reconstruct itself as the capital of the South. This is evidenced in the petition for the corporate charter of the Atlanta Street Railroad Company, which was approved by the Georgia Assembly on February 23, 1866. The charter was approved even before Atlanta paved its streets (Martin 1975). From the very early days to current times, mobility has been at the center of the city's past and future. Transportation is synonymous with Atlanta and it is the characteristic by which the city is most often referenced—from its simple beginnings as "Terminus," the end of the railroad line, to serving as home of one of the world's busiest airports and a central place for air travel. Not surprisingly, the growth and contraction of the city has been fueled and continues to be driven by its transportation system. Neither the city of Atlanta nor the Atlanta region has continued to invest in these transportation infrastructures in keeping with the expansive growth they have experienced. While this is not unlike the fate of many American cities, the pattern is particularly crippling for the city of Atlanta and the region. This situation exists primarily as a result of the region's refusal to expand the transit network and as a result, it can offer few solutions to combat crippling congestion. The city is confronted with a number of significant challenges, including congestion, the large number of jurisdictions, local home rule, land costs, workforce housing and transportation, and the transit system. Accordingly, transportation is among the most critical issues confronting Atlanta and presents the greatest threat to its continued prosperity.

The Atlanta region embraced the construction of its highway and interstate systems yet failed to balance investments in alternative forms of transportation to support the increasingly dense and diverse city it has become. During the twentieth century, the construction of roadways provided the mobility necessary to fuel suburban expansion and the construction of suburbia to the detriment of other modes of travel. This biased investment strategy resulted in a lack of investment in the mobility system for close-in places and denser communities that are now becoming more characteristic of the city and region. Highway construction was considered to be the critical ingredient in fueling economic growth. As a result, the city and the region entered into an expansive construction of its roadway system and continued to add capacity through new construction in order to solve emerging and continuing congestion. The Atlanta region embraced this development strategy, which fueled one of the fastest growth rates of any American city. This mobility system empowered suburbia but also served as a racial barrier and resulted in the inability of those without a car to have access to employment opportunities (Konrad 2009).

A primary outcome of the highway construction activity of the twentieth century and rising suburban populations was an accompanying emptying out and decreasing populations in many American cities. Not until the latter 1970s, however, did the city of Atlanta begin to lose population (Table 13.1). In the first half of the twentieth century, the city of Atlanta was alive, bustling and denser than it was to be in subsequent years.

The impact of the lack of investment in alternative modes of travel became clear when the Olympics arrived in Atlanta in 1996. The Olympics overwhelmed the region's public transportation systems, and "this was evidenced in 1996 when Atlanta attempted to move its guests on the two-line Metropolitan Atlanta Regional Transit Authority (MARTA) rail system and on

TABLE 14.1.	**City of Atlanta Population, 1970–2010**			
1970	1980	1990	2000	2010
496,973	425,022	394,017	416,474	420,003

Source: Data from Social Explorer and U.S. Census Bureau 2013

thousands of school buses; the city had been forced to expand its network from the tenth largest in the country to something closer to the third, and the temporary growth was hard to handle. To put it nicely, the crowds weren't pleased by the network's performance, complaining about frequent delays and breakdowns" (Freemark 2009). As might be anticipated, the lack of investment in other transportation modes has contributed to Atlanta's congestion, earning it the reputation as one of the most congested cities in the United States. The average metropolitan Atlanta driver annually wastes 20 gallons of gas, making Atlanta's average commute the nation's twelfth most wasteful and seventh in terms of annual hours of delay per commuter (Texas A&M Transportation Institute 2011).

The Atlanta Regional Commission (ARC) is the official planning agency for the 10-county Atlanta region, which includes Cherokee, Clayton, Cobb, DeKalb, Douglas, Fayette, Fulton, Gwinnett, Henry, and Rockdale counties as well as the City of Atlanta and 67 other cities. Although the region added 120,023 people per year throughout the 1990s, ARC predicts somewhat slower growth in the future (Atlanta Regional Commission 2010a). The Atlanta region will continue to attract employers, adding approximately 60,500 jobs each year from 2010 to 2020, 53,000 annually from 2020 to 2030, and 64,000 each year from 2030 to 2040. The increase in jobs is expected to occur in high-paying sectors, placing even more travel on the region's transportation system (Atlanta Regional Commission 2010a). Lastly, Atlanta is sometimes jokingly called "Atlanta port," with more than one-fifth of the port of Savannah's total trade coming from Fulton County in the Atlanta region. The deepening of the port of Savannah and the Panama Canal will increase the amount of goods coming to and passing through the Atlanta region. The expansion of the canal will allow it to accommodate super tankers in 2014 (Ross, forthcoming).

The Evolution of Atlanta

Atlanta was founded in 1830 on the meeting site of several different railroad lines, establishing it as a primary center for trade. The city relied initially on streetcars but demand dwindled as automobiles became more readily available and prevalent on city streets. The city constructed a system of viaducts to maneuver north-south downtown streets over the railroads. A number of city streets were converted to one-way traffic to reduce congestion, and the era of the primacy of the automobile was ushered in, leading to the construction of high-capacity roadway systems. Approximately 3,300 lane-miles of freeway have been created since construction of the freeway system began in Atlanta in the 1950s. While the expansion of the freeway system delivered great mobility to suburban areas, it created an inability to be responsive to changing demography, travel alternatives, shorter trips, aging residents, and an aging infrastructure. Little or no infrastructure has been constructed to relieve congestion within the inner and outer rings of suburbs around major cities, including the city of Atlanta.

The expressways and the expansiveness and checkerboard design of suburbia largely reshaped the Atlanta metropolitan region. The roadway system was designed to bring people downtown but also facilitated the movement of downtown functions to the suburbs. The notions of space, relative quiet, and general privacy were defined by a development community that employed cul-de-sac streets, large blocks, and limited points of neighborhood access to reduce local traffic and limit access. The large number of disconnected streets and roadways contributed to a large increase in congestion and traffic bottlenecks; today the Atlanta region is characterized by a large number of congested corridors serving relatively low density suburban communities. Created in 1965, the Metropolitan Atlanta Rapid Transit Authority (MARTA) started operations in 1972 and began construction and expansion of the rail system during the 1980s and 1990s. Many in the business community considered the construction of a heavy rail system to be a positive way to continue to enhance and support the reputation and stature of the city and downtown. In 1971, the suburban counties, however, refused to support MARTA and would not approve a one-penny sales tax, thereby sealing the fate and limiting growth of the transit system to this day (Konrad 2009).

The legislature created the statewide Georgia Regional Transportation Authority (GRTA) in 1999 to develop transportation choices, improve land use, improve air quality, enhance the quality of life, and promote sustainable development for Georgia and particularly Atlanta's citizens. The authority was created when the administrator of the U.S. Environmental Protection Agency imposed sanctions on the Atlanta region because it did not implement adequate plans to attain air quality standards. The sanctions included restrictions on the allocation of highway funds to capacity-expanding projects. The overwhelming reliance on single-occupancy vehicles and little or no transit infrastructure are often cited among the primary causes contributing to the imposition of federal sanctions and the creation of GRTA. GRTA was created to promote Georgia's mobility, air quality, and land use practices.

Existing Plans

ARC has developed the region's regular long-range transportation budget, funded by federal, state, local, and private transportation spending. The most recent one is a 30-year plan with significant financial constraints (Atlanta Regional Commission 2011a). In order to adjust to the limited resources available, ARC is reducing the number of listed projects. One project, which would add optional toll lanes alongside Interstates 75 and 575 in Cobb and Cherokee Counties, dropped $2 billion in cost as planners realized the project was too expensive and the Georgia Department of Transportation removed a component that would carry only tractor-trailer trucks (Atlanta Regional Commission 2010a). Monies for the construction of high-occupancy toll lanes on I-75 and I-575, the relocation of State Route 92, and additional projects—such as an east-west streetcar line in Midtown possibly along North Avenue—remain in the plan. The current transportation plan for the region gives preference to high-occupancy toll lanes over high-occupancy vehicle lanes, as well as a connected regional transit plan, but a funding shortfall exists. The plan also assumes that a restriction on how MARTA spends its revenue will be lifted permanently. The federal deep pocket for transportation funding is the gas tax, which was last raised in 1993. The gas tax is charged as 18.4 cents per gallon, not cents per dollar, and so does not rise with inflation. With better gas mileage, everyone is using less gas.

The Atlanta streetcar project is a collaborative public-private partnership between the City of Atlanta, the Atlanta Downtown Improvement District (ADID), and MARTA. It will provide an integrated multi-modal, high-quality transit network that links communities, improves mobility by enhancing transit access and options, supports projected growth, promotes economic development and encourages strategies to develop livable communities. The City of Atlanta was notified in 2010 of the federal funding award of approximately $47.6 million to fund the east-west route of the Atlanta Streetcar. The total budget for the project is $92.6 million which includes $21.6 million in capital match contributions from the City of Atlanta ($15.6 million) and from the Atlanta Downtown Improvement District ($6 million). The first phase of the Atlanta Streetcar will extend three miles north-south on Peachtree and 1.5 miles east-west between downtown and the Martin Luther King Jr. Center for Nonviolent Social Change, with 12,000 to 17,700 projected daily trips. The streetcar project is the first major transit expansion within the Atlanta city limits since the Bankhead Station on the MARTA Proctor Creek Line, known more popularly as the Bankhead line, opened in 1992 (CAP 2013e).

Among the other prominent transportation projects is the Atlanta BeltLine, a $2.8 billion project consisting of 22 miles of light rail operating along miles of (mostly) inactive railroad lines circling the city's core. Its primary objective is to leverage brownfields adjacent to the improved line for new development (including 5,600 units of affordable housing) by improving public transportation, building 30 miles of trails, and creating 1,200 acres of new green space. The project is one of the most innovative plans for using transit as a redevelopment tool in the country (Atlanta Regional Commission 2011a).

Solutions

The City of Atlanta completed the Connect Atlanta Plan in 2008 which offered solutions for Atlanta and other fast growing cities throughout the United States. Most importantly, the plan was the first of its kind and its focus was the city of Atlanta. It treated the problem of high growth regional congestion as the dominant issue. And developers of the plan placed a high priority on the obvious imbalance between the roadway systems and the transit system in Atlanta.

Rejecting the traditional travel demand method, the Connect Atlanta Plan embraced more of a market-based approach and attempted to identify those areas, projects, and policies that would reduce congestion, create growth opportunities, and identify the required transport investment. These areas should be connected by transit or other transportation modes (Atlanta 2008). A primary recommendation was to build a transit terminal for commuter and passenger rail. This multimodal passenger transit terminal will include commercial and retail development, housing, open space, and civic functions. Another key recommendation was the improvement and modernization of the MARTA system with a thorough review of its route system and the attractiveness and utility of the transit system for both choice and captive riders (Atlanta 2008). In order to maximize these investments, the city's sidewalks program needs to be upgraded and provide for better maintenance.

The city and region should provide additional modes of travel (e.g., bus rapid transit and light rail) and deploy new modes and technologies, particularly in congested areas. In order to effectively utilize these investments strategies, a wide-ranging program focused on changing travel behavior is needed. The provision of bike facilities, pedestrian ways, parks, and trails will contribute to the attractiveness of the city as a place of choice.

Increasing the redundancy of the street system in different areas of the city where travel demand is increasing would provide the opportunity for travelers to make trips along different routes and serve to reduce travel on heavily used streets and arterials. The creation of new streets and routes would allow the city to respond to recent demographic changes in preferences for travel. This also presents an opportunity to support targeted development and redevelopment in areas and neighborhoods in accordance with the City of Atlanta's Comprehensive Development Plan. More importantly, Atlanta and cities throughout America need to confront the reality that not every element of our existing transportation system needs or should be repaired or maintained. Specific corridors, streets, and collectors no longer meet the travel demands of citizens currently, as entire sections of cities and communities have new residents with different travel preferences and logistics continually create more efficient networks.

Atlanta is a primary destination for goods and freight shipments, and the city will need to seek solutions to accommodate a rise in goods movement.

A multifaceted solution offers the best promise of easing the burden of this increase on the transportation network of the city and region (Atlanta 2008). The opportunity to expand rail use requires communication and planning with other cities, including Charlotte, Jacksonville, Birmingham, and other cities in the southeastern area known as the Piedmont Atlantic megaregion (Ross 2009). Currently, these cities develop and make investment decisions without information and better data about connecting cities—for example, data collected through the use of global positioning system (GPS) technology on truck activity and commodity and traffic flows. What is the future role of the Atlanta region and what joint planning can be undertaken to maximize economic competitiveness while underwriting a continuing high quality of life? Will the Atlanta region remain the central hub of the southeastern United States? With changing logistics and increasing competition, a need exists for a more strategic focus and greater coordination and joint planning.

Opportunities for Change

The Obama Administration has identified 10 future high-speed rail corridors, and one, the Southeast Corridor will link Washington, D.C., Richmond, Raleigh, Charlotte, Atlanta, Macon, Columbia, and Savannah (U.S. Department of Transportation 2009). This represents an opening to become better aligned with the national rail plan, and it also acknowledges the importance of the southeast region. This may represent an opportunity to enhance the modal diversity and efficiency of Atlanta's transportation system and that of the southeast. The Town and Country Planning Association (Blowers 1993) sees the solutions for creating a more sustainable transportation environment falling into the following broad classes:

- regulatory mechanisms to control emissions
- tax increases that would favor energy-efficient transport modes
- support for new technologies and alternative fuels
- planning approaches that would lessen the need for automobile travel

Florida and Oregon have undertaken statewide growth management while other states, including Georgia, have largely taken a hands-off policy toward managing growth. The opportunities for reuse and greater sustainability afforded by growth management, with significant benefits for the transportation system, make the strategy worthy of consideration in many places, including the city of Atlanta. In many ways, the problems and challenges confronting Atlanta are the same for a number of cities throughout the country. The challenge of reducing congestion, enhancing the transportation network to handle increasing levels of freight, increasing transit , reconnecting neighborhoods, increasing pedestrian and bicycle facilities, funding and maintaining transportation infrastructure, assuring economic competitiveness and operating the city so it remains a place of choice are both the opportunities and the challenges confronting the city of Atlanta. Few doubt mobility must continue to be at the center of Atlanta's future.

CHAPTER 15

From Transit as a Social Service to Transit as Congestion Relief: The Failure of Transit Planning in Atlanta

Laurel Paget-Seekins

As Atlanta opens it first 2.7 track miles of a modern streetcar system, it is worth remembering that over 200 track miles of streetcar and interurban rail once connected Atlanta and its first suburbs. Ironically, Atlanta's city government in 1943 adopted a resolution calling for conversion of the remaining streetcars to trackless trolleys and buses to reduce congestion and modernize the system (Carson 1981; Martin 1975). This story of the elimination of a dense streetcar network in the name of progress is in no way unique to Atlanta. However, Atlanta has managed to continue a history of public transit planning that is marked more by its failures than its successes.

Transit has always been a contested issue in Atlanta. The conflicts over transit predate the creation of the Metropolitan Atlanta Rapid Transit Authority (MARTA) in 1965. Georgia passed its first transit segregation law in 1891, which would eventually be struck down by the Supreme Court in 1959. In part, this deep-rooted conflict in Atlanta arises from the fact that public transit is more than a mode of transportation; it is public space that allows for the potential mixing of races and classes. In addition, as transit became publicly owned and operated, it became part of the struggle over the role of government and tax financing. Since much of the conflict over transit does not directly relate to its utilitarian value as transportation or a source of mobility, the context and narratives around public transit in Atlanta are necessary to understand its planning.

This chapter is framed around the story of two transit trips in the Atlanta region as they exist today: a trip to the Atlanta Public Safety Annex using

MARTA and a commute on an express bus from a park-and-ride lot near the City of Canton to downtown Atlanta. Both of these trips are outliers on the transit spectrum but serve as illustrations of two different narratives and experiences of transit riders in the Atlanta region. The lessons of these trips will be used to contextualize the 2012 failure of the Transportation Investment Act (TIA) at the ballot box, which would have been the biggest investment in public transit in Atlanta since the creation of MARTA. Finally, an alternative narrative for transit in Atlanta is suggested.

Transit as a Social Service

A person living in the city of Atlanta who needs to retrieve a vehicle that has been impounded, or fill out the paperwork to get a criminal record expunged,

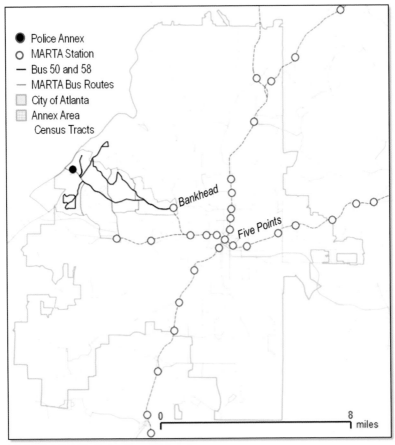

Figure 15.1. Transit service options to Atlanta Public Safety Annex in northwest Atlanta. (Source: Map by author.)

or get fingerprinted for a job, must go to the Atlanta Police Department's Public Safety Annex. For members of the approximately 40,000 households in the city without a car or for someone whose only car has been impounded, this is not an easy task (Puentes and Tomer, 2011). The annex is on the far west side of Atlanta, almost at the city limits. From the Five Points MARTA station in downtown Atlanta, a trip to the annex must begin with the train to Bankhead, a spur line off the east-west MARTA rail line that runs every 15 minutes. From the Bankhead station, the next essential step is to take a bus (Figure 15.1).

For passengers traveling via bus route 58, the closest stop to the Public Safety Annex requires a half-mile walk. Bus route 58 only runs every 35 minutes, so a bus on route 50 might arrive first. Bus route 50 also delivers riders just over a half-mile from the annex and runs roughly every 30 minutes. Both buses travel along Donald Lee Hollowell Parkway, State Route 278, a state highway lined with abandoned buildings, car repair shops, dollar stores, and modest houses. By the time this route emerges from the west side of the city and continues eastward through the handsome Druid Hills neighborhood, it has been reborn as Ponce de Leon Avenue, a historic parkway with a section designed by Frederick Law Olmsted Sr. as a linear park.

Waiting at the MARTA station in Bankhead (not to be confused with the MARTA station in the wealthy area of Buckhead), riders are already in a downtrodden part of the city that the majority of middle class Atlantans or visitors to the city have never seen. From here the bus routes pass through census tracts that are all over 90 percent black (U.S. Census Bureau 2010). Thirty-two percent of families have been on food stamps within a calendar year compared to nine percent for the Atlanta metropolitan statistical area (MSA) and 14 percent for the city of Atlanta. Almost half of the households in the area have incomes under $25,000, compared to 31 percent of the city and 20 percent of the region (U.S. Census Bureau 2012).

Buses entering and exiting the Bankhead MARTA station will likely be full, even in the middle of the day, with young families, shift workers, teenagers, and seniors. Over 20 percent of the working residents of this area rely on public transit to commute, double the 11 percent of city of Atlanta residents who commute by transit (U.S. Census Bureau 2012). MARTA is often the transportation mode of last resort; half of MARTA riders report they use MARTA because no car is available for their car trips and another 12 percent cite financial reasons, such as the high price of gas (MARTA 2008).

Outbound buses from the Bankhead MARTA station eventually cross Interstate 285 at the point where freight trucks exit the highway to reach the Atlanta Industrial Park. At this point, the surrounding environs are hardly recognizable as part of the city of Atlanta. Once on foot, travelers en route to the Public Safety Annex pass the empty lot that was Bankhead Courts. Demolished in 2012, Bankhead Courts was one of Atlanta's last public housing projects; a closed-down branch of the Atlanta public library and a shuttered elementary school are all that remain of the project.

Along the route, the buses pass the former Bowen Homes, another demolished public housing project, and the site of the former Perry Homes, one of the broken promises of Atlanta's history. Though few people today remember, MARTA funding did not pass when it was first placed on the ballot in Fulton and DeKalb Counties in 1968, a result blamed on a lack of support from black voters. African American leaders pressured the downtown business interests pushing MARTA to make sure the system would serve low-income residents of the city and not just suburban commuters. They were promised several stipulations: the east-west line would be rail, not a proposed busway; improvements would be made to the previously private bus system; the fare would be 15 cents; minorities would be hired; and a rail line to Perry Homes would be created as a spur off the east-west rail line. With the support of the black community, the second referendum one-cent tax passed in Fulton and DeKalb Counties in 1971, but it failed in suburban counties due to both a lack of planned rail service and racially motivated fears that transit would provide black residents with access to the suburbs (Altshuler and Luberoff 2003; Keating 2001a).

However, MARTA officials exhibited little enthusiasm for actually building the line to Perry Homes as promised; instead, they prioritized extending the north line into the primarily white suburbs. Community activists kept up the pressure, and the first part of the line to the Bankhead station was finally built in 1992. After the Atlanta Housing Authority demolished Perry Homes in 2001, MARTA's extension of the line—never a priority to begin with—was abandoned altogether (Altshuler and Luberoff 2003).

As a result of so many missteps in transit planning and construction over the decades, the trip to the annex is a slow and tedious one. With some luck, and depending on the starting location, the one-way trip there might only take just over an hour. More likely, though, the trip is closer to 90 minutes, despite the fact that the transit traveler does not leave the city of Atlanta in the process. What should be a relatively easy task—and one that is often required for low-income job seekers—is now a half-day ordeal simply due to the lack of access. For the low-income and black residents still residing in neighborhoods gutted by the demolition of public housing projects and ill-served by MARTA, accessing the rest of the city and region by transit is a daunting task indeed.

The long-standing dominant narrative treated MARTA as a social service, not a $6.4 billion investment in transportation infrastructure. In a common but offensive local joke, the acronym is said to stand for "Moving Africans Rapidly Through Atlanta"; by the statistics, "rapidly" is the least accurate part of that statement. In 2008, 76 percent of MARTA's riders were black, while 13 percent were white, 4 percent identified as another race, and 8 percent were Hispanic (MARTA 2008).

The perception that MARTA is for poor (read black) people without cars is a reinforcing cycle. Since its riders are not politically powerful and decisions continue to be made through a racial lens, MARTA does not receive the investment it needs to provide either the service needed by the transit dependent or to attract other riders. The perception continues to be that MARTA is the mode of last resort. This message is reinforced by the common sight of ads for used car dealers in MARTA trains and on buses.

MARTA is the largest transit system in the country that does not receive operating funds from the state government. MARTA relies on the one-cent sales tax passed in 1971 in Fulton and DeKalb Counties and on federal funds, which as of 1998 cannot be used for operations. Despite not providing funding, the state continues to impose financial oversight and refuses to lift the original law that requires MARTA to spend half of its local sales tax revenue on its capital budget. This constraint makes it even harder for MARTA to maintain a basic level of operations. In 2010 the system was forced to cut 10 percent of bus service and 14 percent of rail service. Its buses run on average every 30 minutes during peak periods and 45 minutes off-peak.

The narrative that sees transit as a social service is based on the premise that cars are a necessity for transportation in Atlanta. With this as a given, Atlanta's transportation problem is then identified as one of congestion. In response to concerns about congestion in 2004, then governor Sonny Perdue set up a Congestion Mitigation Taskforce. In 2005 the Taskforce recommended three major measures, including increasing the weighting of congestion relief from an equal weight with other factors to 70 percent of the weighting in transportation funding decisions at the regional level. This recommendation was adopted by the Atlanta Regional Commission, the region's metropolitan planning organization (MPO), in 2006.

This step codified the dominant discourse that Atlanta's transportation problem is congestion by prioritizing resources to address it. Alas, the emphasis on congestion relief did nothing to help Atlanta residents needing to get to the annex or the low-income black communities on the west side of Atlanta. Instead, it placed the focus on transit as one of congestion relief.

Transit as Congestion Relief

In contrast to the experience of riders on MARTA, transit riders can spend a very different 90 minutes in the Atlanta region by boarding express bus 490 outside of the city of Canton in Cherokee County, a northern suburb. This transit ride is a 40-mile trip that begins in a park-and-ride lot in Canton and ends in downtown Atlanta. Used by commuters attempting to avoid congestion on Atlanta's interstates, the service is operated by the Georgia Regional Transportation Authority (GRTA), a state agency. This section examines the response to Atlanta's noncompliance with the Clean Air Act and the creation of transit for congestion relief.

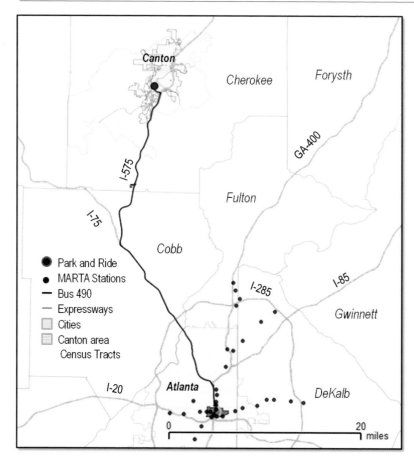

Figure 15.2. Express bus route 490 from Canton to Atlanta. (Source: Map by author.)

Route 490 has four buses running each weekday morning and four in the afternoon. The route starts in Canton and stops once in Woodstock, another northern suburb, before continuing directly to the heart of Atlanta's business district (Figure 15.2). Its origin is Boling Park, one of the region's 36 park-and-ride lots, which has 173 parking spots with a utilization rate of 50 percent (Atlanta Regional Commission 2012c).

Ninety-seven percent of all express bus passengers start their trips by driving or being dropped off. In a 2008 survey, no rider on the route 490 walked or bicycled to access the bus. The average driving distance to the Canton park-and-ride lot is approximately 5.75 miles (Georgia State University 2008; Zuehlke 2009). This means that the census tracts that surround the city of Canton are the likely catchment area for this park-and-ride facility.

TABLE 15.1		MARTA and Express Riders' Household Incomes, 2008				
MARTA (own scale)		MARTA (common scale)	EXPRESS (common scale)		EXPRESS (own scale)	
Under $10,000	17.9%			1.7%	Under $15,000	
$10,000-$19,999	24.6%	63%	8%	5.9%	$15,000-$29,999	
$20,000-$29,999	20.4%					
$30,000-$39,999	14.9%			13.3%	$30,000-$44,999	
$40,000-$49,999	7.2%	30%	44%	14.3%	$45,000-$59,999	
$50,000-$74,999	7.8%			16.2%	$60,000-$74,999	
Over $75,000	7.2%	7%	49%	32.7%	$75,000-$119,999	
				15.9%	Over $120,000	

Source: Data from MARTA 2008; Georgia State University Public Performance and Management Group 2008

Canton has two local bus routes that run every hour during the day with average weekday boarding of 110 people (Atlanta Regional Commission 2012c). However, due to the limited schedules of the buses, riders are not able to transfer to and from the express bus service. Even with this local service, less than one percent (.53 percent) of commuters in the five census tracts surrounding Canton use public transit to commute to work. This compares to just over three percent for the Atlanta MSA as a whole (U.S. Census Bureau 2012).

This area has a population that is 84 percent white; the largest minority group is Hispanic, with 13 percent of the population. The area is economically diverse, with a wide range of incomes. It matches the Atlanta region overall, with just under 20 percent of households making under $25,000 in both geographic areas. In the 2007-2011 American Communities Survey sample, six percent of families in the Canton area received food stamps assistance compared to nine percent in the MSA.

However, it is not the people living in poverty in the suburbs who use the express bus service. At $75,000 in 2008, the median household income of an express bus rider is higher than the region's median income of $57,000 between 2007 and 2011 (Georgia State University 2008; U.S. Census Bureau 2012). This income is also triple the median income of a MARTA rider, which in 2008 was approximately $25,000 (MARTA 2008). Table 15.1 shows a comparison of MARTA and express bus riders' incomes.

Express bus ridership in Atlanta is still dominated by people of color, but 45 percent are white riders compared to just 13 percent of MARTA riders. The express bus route 490 is an exception, with whites making up 80 percent of the ridership (MARTA 2008; Public Performance and Management Group 2008).

The express bus leaves Canton and travels on Interstate 575 through Cherokee County. This interstate spur was first opened in 1980 and extended up to Canton in 1985. The roadway was not built in response to current demand but, rather in anticipation of future growth. This growth materialized once the highway was built; in 1990 the city of Canton had a population of just under 5,000 people, and by 2010 it was almost 23,000.

In Cobb County, the express bus merges onto I-75 south. From I-575 to I-285, the interstate is five to seven lanes in each direction and ranks in the top 10 percent of congested freeway segments in Atlanta (Atlanta Regional Commission 2012c). The bus continues on I-75, past the point at which I-75 merges with I-85 to form the Downtown Connector, and exits on the southern edge of midtown Atlanta. The bus stops first at the MARTA Civic Center station, allowing passengers to transfer to MARTA for jobs located in Midtown. The bus then winds its way through downtown Atlanta, making stops near major employment centers such as Peachtree Center, Georgia State University, and government office buildings.

The Cobb Community Transit express bus service is almost exclusively used for work commutes. Over 96 percent of riders report using the service for work trips. In addition, almost all of the riders have employers who pay at least part of their transit fares. In 2008 almost 70 percent of riders reported that their employer paid 100 percent of their fares and only three percent reported that less than 10 percent of their fare was paid by their employer (Public Performance and Management Group 2008). Employer-subsidized transit passes are in fact not common; only eight percent of residents of the region responded in a 2011 travel survey that their employer-subsidized transit passes (PTV NuStats 2011).

Since MARTA did not become a true regional transit agency, transit in the Atlanta region has been balkanized. MARTA started operations in Fulton and DeKalb Counties in 1972. Changing demographics led the three counties that originally voted out of MARTA to start their own local bus services. Cobb County started a county bus service in 1989 and Gwinnett County followed in 2000 with local and express service to Atlanta. Clayton County, to the south of Atlanta, started a local bus service that connected to MARTA at the Atlanta airport in 2001 but shut the service down in 2010, leaving thousands of transit-dependent passengers stranded.

The next possible attempt at regional transit for Atlanta came in 1999, when GRTA was established in response to the federal government's declaration in 1998 that Atlanta was not conforming with the Clean Air Act. The crisis of losing federal transportation funds prompted then governor Roy Barnes to propose a new agency with wide ranging powers over both transportation and land use. These powers include the ability to design, construct, and operate mass transportation and to coordinate between the existing operators. In addition, GRTA has the power to plan and request modification of regional transportation plans.

GRTA has jurisdiction over counties not in compliance with the federal Clean Air Act, which amounted to 13 counties at the time of the agency's creation. GRTA has not used many of its powers but in the early 2000s did decide to start a regional express bus system. Service started in 2004 and has expanded to include service to 12 counties.

The express bus service was originally funded by agreements between counties and GRTA; in exchange for funding the bus service, counties received money for arterial road projects. In addition, GRTA received start-up money from the federal Congestion Mitigation and Air Quality Improvement fund. The new service promoted the idea of transit as a means of congestion relief and a way to improve air quality.

However, express bus riders are a very small percentage of transit riders in the Atlanta region. In 2010, GRTA-operated express buses had average weekday boardings of 7,676 people compared to 460,945 for MARTA. GRTA ridership is even smaller than the ridership on the shuttles operated for the Georgia Institute of Technology (18,180) and Emory University (12,082), despite the fact that these shuttles are free. GRTA's boardings do not include the number of passengers who use express buses operated by Cobb and Gwinnett Counties, where local and express daily boardings combined are 17,229 and 7,814, respectively (Atlanta Regional Commission 2012c).

The relatively small numbers of express bus riders suggest that this transit option alone is not likely to address Atlanta's problem with traffic congestion or air quality. Not only are express buses used by a relatively small number of people, but the vast majority of riders live in locations where a car is necessary for just about every other trip, including the trip to the transit stop. In addition, work trips in the United States themselves account for less than 30 percent of vehicle miles traveled and 20 percent of person trips (McGuckin and Srinivasan 2005).

It is possible that express bus service actually encourages or at least facilitates sprawl by allowing people to live miles away from their jobs and take advantage of a transit service that for the most part is paid for by their employers. At the same time, transit designed for congestion relief does not serve the transportation needs of low-income, transit-dependent communities. Because of infrequent schedules with a focus on peak-hour trips, limited destinations, and origins in park-and-ride lots, express bus service often does not even serve work trips for transit-dependent riders. The city of Canton happens to have local bus service, which is very rare for exurban Atlanta, but the service is not coordinated with the express bus service and therefore does not provide access.

Even though GRTA can operate transit through the Atlanta region, politically the entity is not accepted as a regional transit agency. This has to do with the issue of governance: the board of GRTA is appointed by the governor of Georgia, with no power given to local jurisdictions. Given the history and political and demographic differences between the Atlanta region and the rest of the state, local leaders will not accept full state control, but any changes to GRTA board or new regional agency requires action by the state legislature. Currently attempts at regional transit decision-making are occurring through a committee of the Atlanta Regional Commission, but this committee has no official authority.

The lack of a true functioning regional transit body was one of the factors limiting Atlanta's most recent attempt to pass a sales tax to fund transportation projects. More importantly, the failure of the transportation referendum is partially due to the limitations of the two narratives identified here: transit as a social service and transit as a means of congestion relief.

Conflicting Narratives and Why the Transportation Investment Act Failed

This section helps to explain the failure of the TIA as a result of these two narratives. The project list included half transit projects, but the campaign for the referendum was unwilling to sell transit as congestion relief within the context of the long (racialized) history of transit as a social service. Under political pressure, the Georgia State Legislature passed a bill in 2010 that allowed the 12 regions of the state to put a one-cent sales tax on the ballot to fund transportation projects. The process was two-fold: first, a panel of local elected officials chose the projects to be funded with the 10-year tax revenue, and then the measure went to the voters for approval in July 2012. For the purposes of the referendum, the Atlanta region consisted of 10 counties, an area smaller than the MSA or MPO.

The roundtable of elected officials had to allocate 85 percent of the projected tax revenues to transportation projects. The remaining 15 percent was set aside for local governments to use for projects of their own choosing. Local governments submitted over $22.9 billion worth of transportation projects for a project list that was constrained at $6.2 billion.

The 21-member panel met between February and October of 2010. In the end, they approved a project list that dedicated just over half the funds to transit-related projects. About 11 percent of the total was allocated to maintain or restore existing local transit service, 2.5 percent was for express-bus-type service, and 38.6 percent was dedicated to new rail and rapid bus projects. Putting aside concerns from transit advocacy groups that the money allocated for transit was inadequate and that the transit projects were not equitable, this was a remarkable step for a region that has not seen an additional dedicated source of transit funding since the MARTA sales tax in 1971.

Transit advocates of all types united in a Fair Share for Transit campaign and pushed the roundtable for transit funds. This coalition included groups advocating for transit as congestion relief, environmental organizations organized around improving air quality, organizations representing choice transit riders, and transit equity organizations pushing to improve transport for low-income riders.

Their success in convincing the roundtable to support transit projects is also attributable to a shift within Atlanta's elite. Around the time that the federal government ruled Atlanta out of compliance with the Clean Air Act in 1998, a split emerged in the business community. Some leaders started to reject the premise that Atlanta could build itself out of congestion. While those allied with the road construction industry remain entrenched, another group formed to advocate for more smart growth and transit solutions for Atlanta's transportation problems (Henderson 2004). Politicians and business leaders alike had come to accept that Atlanta had to build transit to remain economically competitive.

The referendum was heavily supported by the political and business elites. The business community raised over $8 million to run a campaign to convince voters to pass the referendum (McCaffrey and Hart 2012). Other organizations raised money and ran their own campaigns, but the campaign associated with the Chamber of Commerce had the most money and significant public profile. They made the decision to use a narrative of congestion to sell the referendum.

Their campaign messaging and images identified congestion as the transportation problem in Atlanta and the referendum as the solution. Their campaign was targeted at white suburban voters and did not highlight the fact that half of the funding was for transit projects. Instead of attempting to build a case for transit investment, even as congestion relief, to counter the long-standing narrative of transit as social service, they effectively ignored the issue of transit spending.

Opponents of the referendum argued against the referendum because it included too much transit. Accepting that congestion is the problem, they claimed that transit spending would not improve it. Some opponents also still used racialized arguments, albeit in code, against transit. A Tea Party leader told the Atlanta daily newspaper, "Criminals catch that kind of transportation into our county. . . and I'm not going to support anything that works toward increasing our crime either" (Hart 2011).

Meanwhile, the Fair Share for Transit campaign effectively dissolved after the project list was decided. The campaign was unable to withstand the conflicts between proponents of transit for choice riders and proponents of improving transit for dependent riders. As discussed previously, transit designed as congestion relief or to serve choice riders with cars does not necessarily serve the transportation needs of the transit dependent.

Notwithstanding the intentions of the initial organizers, the issue of race could not be ignored. The transit campaign was started by a business-backed smart growth organization holding invitation-only meetings ("transit stakeholders meetings"). This approach rankled transit equity organizations, for which the issue of an inclusive process was as important as the outcome transit projects.

Despite the failings of the process, some transit equity organizations still supported the referendum as the best possible deal. As with the original MARTA referendum in 1968, however, some African American leaders opposed the referendum because they felt the transit projects did not adequately serve their communities. The DeKalb County chapter of the National Association for the Advancement of Colored People opposed the referendum because it did not include rail service to the primarily black south DeKalb County, where residents have been paying the MARTA tax for 40 years and still lacked adequate transit service. In addition, some environmental groups opposed the referendum because they felt it included too much spending on roadway projects.

At the ballot box fewer than 40 percent of the voters in the Atlanta region supported the one-cent sales tax; the referendum failed to pass in any of the 10 counties. The initiative received the least support in the outer and white suburban regions but also failed to pass in majority black communities.

The overwhelming loss can be attributed to a number of factors, but one conclusion is clear. While 90 percent of Atlantans agree that transportation is a problem (Atlanta Journal-Constitution 2012), they are split on how to identify the problem and, therefore, which solutions are the best ones. Note that victory was not impossible; the referendum did pass in three other regions in tax-averse Georgia. The political elites accepted that transit should be part of the referendum, but the business community that led the campaign refused to attempt to sell the transit projects as part of the solution to the problem they had identified: congestion. This approach was very likely rooted in the longstanding negative (and racialized) perceptions of transit as social service. This left organizations opposed to transit and taxation plenty of room to oppose the referendum on the very grounds offered by the business community.

Clearly, the perception of transit as a social service has not allowed transit to meet the transportation needs of the poor in Atlanta. Instead, it has starved the system of resources and left transit as a means of last resort. The failure of the 2012 transportation referendum suggests that the lingering perceptions of transit also contributes to an inability to obtain more transit funding, even if it is for congestion relief or transit for choice riders.

Framing transit as a means of congestion relief is very unlikely to solve the congestion problem because it does not address the underlying causes of the congestion, such as sprawling land use patterns. This approach provides a temporary solution for the smaller number riders who use the express bus service but preserves car-based transport as Atlanta's main building block.

A more holistic narrative that views transit in terms of regional accessibility is needed to plan transit that meets real transportation needs. The problem for both the express bus rider on route 490 from Canton and the MARTA rider trying to reach the Public Safety Annex is a lack of access. The problem is not congestion or that the region needs to provide something for citizens who are too poor to have a car.

In a sense, this situation is an argument for rationality in the planning process. Alas, all of the layers of symbolism and politics around public transit in Atlanta must be stripped away before transit—and by extension transportation—planning can be rational in any sense of the word. Achieving this goal will be impossible without addressing how transit is racialized; instead of attempting to pave over Atlanta's past, the region must face it head-on.

CHAPTER 16

Hartsfield-Jackson Atlanta International Airport: A City of Its Own

Benjamin R. DeCosta

Life has risks. Major airport infrastructure investments have more than most if you do not do smart things. Add complexity and you have challenges that make success a real gamble. This is the short story of lessons learned, combined with luck and smart actions by a cohesive, forward-looking Atlanta team that built the impossible fifth runway at the world's busiest airport. The story illustrates how "the most important runway in America"[1] was planned, approved, designed and built at a cost of more than $1.2 billion (Hartsfield-Jackson 2013). We, the airport's senior leadership team, learned that stakeholder management, smart negotiations, and execution under conditions of uncertainty are essential tools for those who would undertake huge public project challenges.

In most cities, airports are an economic and transportation necessity. They meet the needs of the traveling public and contribute to the regional economy, yet they sit mostly beyond view. They are thought about only when they grow, change, or experience difficulty. Aircraft noise and emissions make being a good neighbor to communities in the flight path difficult. Nonetheless, being a good neighbor is a necessary critical part of effective airport management. The Hartsfield-Jackson Atlanta International Airport defines that bedrock standard. With over 7.8 million passengers per month in 2013, it is the busiest airport in the world (Hetter 2013). With an Atlanta-based work force of almost 60,000 employees and an average of over 250,000 passengers daily, the airport is comparable to a small city. Atlanta also ranks highest in aircraft operations—that is, takeoffs and landings . In 2013 Atlanta had 930,000 takeoffs and landings compared to 878,000 in Chicago and

639,000 in Los Angeles (Airports Council International 2013). The 4,700-acre facility is a major economic engine for the Atlanta region, delivering a $34 billion economic impact while providing transit access across the U.S. and to every corner of the world (Fulton County 2011). From the Atlanta airport, travelers can reach 80 percent of the population of the United States in two hours. Atlanta serves Delta Air Lines (merged with Northwest Airlines), the merged Southwest and AirTran airlines, and a full complement of domestic and international carriers. With more than 930,000 total flights in 2012, the airport provides nonstop flights to 156 U.S. cities and nearly 80 international cities in 50 countries (AirportTechnology.com 2013).

With 4,700 acres (7.4 square miles), the airport is easily two times larger than downtown Atlanta.[2] Thus this small city—with its huge impact on the economy and 400,000 jobs generated directly and indirectly—needed to plan for the future, much like many cities, to remain competitive and to grow without artificial constraints. The airport's plans were and are a practical affair that reflects the city's needs and aspirations, and in some ways even leads them. The airport master plan must take into account the economic forces within the region, the airlines' plans for growing profitable global businesses, the competitive nature of the aviation industry, changes in technology, and the impact of economic forces on competing regions and their airports across the nation and around the world. The plan must be realistic, affordable, and feasible. Most important is this last point, which requires that the master plan is acceptable to public officials and to the voters who elected them.

History

Today, Hartsfield-Jackson is the latest of many iterations in Atlanta's history as an airport hub. The city's political leadership is chiefly responsible for Atlanta becoming the world's busiest airport. Atlanta has been blessed with visionary leaders who empowered aviation professionals to produce one of the nation's finest airports. Mayor William Hartsfield had the first vision, realizing that aviation was the path to Atlanta's future. Among other things, Mayor Maynard Jackson convinced the federal government to move a U.S. highway to make room for the new airport in the 1970s. Mayor Bill Campbell empowered the airport leadership to prepare the airport for the 1996 Centennial Olympic Games and to complete a master plan for the airport's future operations. Mayor Shirley Franklin, a natural and engaged problem solver, supported and led her empowered airport leadership to execute one of the most complex large-scale airport expansions in its history, at a cost of over $5.4 billion (Airport 2000).

Atlanta's first airport was the Candler Air Field, which hosted its first flight in 1926. By 1930 the airfield was quickly growing and competing with airports in New York and Chicago. In the 1940s, Candler Air Field became the Atlanta Municipal Airport (Pritchett 2013). Two significant developments contributed to the demand for a sophisticated and sprawling airport. Macon-based Delta Airlines expanded and grew, and both Delta Airlines and Eastern Airlines (originally headquartered in Miami) made the decision to locate their hubs in Atlanta. These simultaneous developments forced Atlanta to grow its airport to accommodate additional passenger traffic and to consider fully how the airport could be used to expand the region's economy.

Hartsfield-Jackson Planning in the Contemporary Era

Of course, technical professionals can undertake the master planning effort without the input, participation, and collaboration of laypeople, citizens, community activists, and key aviation and business stakeholders. But without stakeholders, those plans have no credibility and are therefore not feasible. Our experience proves that the master plan for a large hub airport (and for most large-scale projects) requires many midwives in order to be successful. The last major planning effort was in 1997 when Angela Gittens, chief operating officer from 1993 to 1998, formed a Master Plan Coordinating Committee (MPCC) to work on the planning and future development of Atlanta's airport. Under the direction of Mayor Maynard Jackson (in his third non-consecutive term as mayor) and later Mayor Bill Campbell, Gittens convened the city's political and business leaders along with community members to prepare a master plan with a vision to enter the twenty-first century.

Stakeholder engagement was incorporated as a critical feature of the plan to obtain the ideas, consensus, and commitment of the major stakeholders and, more importantly, create the constituency to support future development. Gittens led the very diverse committee in the development of the vision themes for the planning effort, a process that: 1) engaged the stakeholders, 2) obtained buy-in from the broader public, and 3) determined executable, sustainable projects. The 44 members of the MPCC represented the local and regional community. Five cities (East Point, College Park, Riverdale, Jonesboro, and Forest Park) along with Clayton and Fulton Counties were represented. Key members of the committee included representatives of the Federal Aviation Administration (FAA); the domestic and international airlines; the hub carrier, Delta Air Lines; and members from the local chambers of commerce. Of course, Delta was critical to the completion and success of the plan, and its commitment facilitated the complex funding and lease negotiations. Angela Gittens, aided by her professional staff and consultant of national and local experts, developed a process for the development of a consensus on the vision themes for the planning process (Table 16.1).

Public engagement was the key to the success and implementation of this plan, as Gittens and her team recognized the master plan would be successful only if it could be implemented. Agreements between the committee members turned out to be the glue that held the plan together and enabled the later

TABLE 16.1. **Master Plan Coordinating Committee Vision Themes**

Vision Themes

Safe and Efficient Operations	Hartsfield International Airport is identifiable as the safest, most efficient, and most accessible facility for flight, ground, passenger, and freight operations and for both daily operations and special events.
Environmental Sensitivity	Hartsfield International Airport is the best in its class for effective management and leadership on noise and other environmental issues.
Vision-Driven Planning	Hartsfield International Airport undertakes cost-effective, flexible, and bold planning that is driven by a vision.
Community Relations	Hartsfield International Airport has a functional and cooperative relationship with local, state, national, and international communities.
Technology and Innovation	Hartsfield International Airport has a commitment to innovation.
Financial integrity	Hartsfield International Airport maintains financial integrity and strength.
International Role	Hartsfield International Airport is the preeminent gateway to the world for commerce, people, and ideas.
Customer Friendly Environment	Hartsfield International Airport is the airport all passengers look forward to using, no matter what their language or physical condition may be.
Economic Engine	Hartsfield International Airport generates business and economic opportunities locally and throughout the southeast.

Source: Atlanta 1999

problem-solving that was required to implement it. To enhance their effectiveness, the MPCC members worked in professionally facilitated subcommittees.

Serious negotiations involving the airlines and local political leaders led to support by local communities. Bickering among stakeholders would have poisoned the atmosphere and sapped the energy needed to get the key projects underway. The vision themes and the process used to develop them created a fertile common ground of understanding and personal relationships that made conflict resolution easier. These multilayered discussions and negotiations established a balance of interests between key decision making parties (Hartsfield Atlanta International Airport 2000). The results included speedy completion of the needed environmental impact statement (EIS) for the fifth runway; an agreement with the airlines to take the risk to start the runway design before the EIS was completed and before a record of decision approving the runway was in hand; efficient and effective negotiations for the funding, financing, and decision-making process for executing a $5.4 billion, multiyear program; agreements with College Park and Clayton County for needed condemnation authority for land acquisition; and the creation of an "aerotropolis" hotel and office complex opportunity by anchoring the land development with a new $600 million Consolidated Rental Car Facility in College Park (Hartsfield Atlanta International Airport 2000).

The airport's priority was to grow traffic while reducing congestion delay. An ongoing major obstacle since the early days of Atlanta's airport was the lack of land; more elbow room would be needed. By 1998 the Atlanta airport was also handling more traffic than any U.S. airport and was experiencing costly congestion delays, estimated at $5 million per week. Master plan forecasts for 2015 estimated 121 million passengers going through Atlanta; more airport airfield and terminal capacity would be required (Hartsfield Atlanta International Airport 2000).

We know that forecasts are not always reality and we use them as a guide; investments are triggered when the traffic materializes. Due to the terrorist attacks of September 11, 2001, and the recent Great Recession, coupled with the huge rise in global jet fuel prices, the numbers forecasted did not materialize and some of the plan investments had to be delayed as a result. In 2012 passenger traffic at Hartsfield-Jackson was 95 million and forecasts for 2013 were about 100 million. Beijing in 2012 had 81.9 million passengers and London handled 70 million passengers. Chicago and Los Angeles, ranked number two and three in the United States, serving 66.6 and 63.7 million passengers, respectively. Passenger and air traffic were growing, but the airport needed expansion of the original airport facilities, specifically a new international terminal, a new rental car facility, more runways, and a new air traffic control tower.

Airports are categorized by two types of traffic. Origin and destination airports are located where most passengers live, travel, or visits; connecting airports are ones at which passengers pass through but generally do not stop. As the only major airport in the Atlanta region, Atlanta has a catchment area population of almost 6 million. Connecting passengers make up 65 percent of the Hartsfield-Jackson traffic and 35 percent are origin-and-destination passengers. Airport traffic forecasts are notably tough to predict. It was impossible to know that Delta would file for bankruptcy in 2005, or go on to merge with Northwest in 2009. The attacks of September 11, 2001, caused an immediate decline in travel and the recent Great Recession caused another decline in passengers and traffic.

Without a crystal ball, key members of the master plan coordinating committee supported the final $5.4 billion infrastructure investment plan which team members had negotiated with the airlines. The Hartsfield-Jackson Atlanta International Airport Competition Plan was recommended, and it was approved by Mayor Bill Campbell and the Atlanta City Council on January 3, 2000. Notably, the major Atlanta airport master plan projects were executed with openings

Figure 16.1. Maynard H. Jackson International Terminal

of the tallest air traffic control tower in the U.S., the $1.25 billion fifth runway in 2006, the $600 million consolidated rental car facility in 2009, and the $1.4 billion Maynard H. Jackson Jr. International Terminal in 2012.

The Fifth Runway: Centerpiece of Improvement

Without airfield capacity at a large hub airport, nothing else matters. My position as aviation general manager began in 1998. Recruited from the Newark International Airport, where I had led, as general manager, New Jersey airports for the Port Authority of New York and New Jersey, I was selected to implement the master plan by then mayor Bill Campbell. Having succeeded Angela Gittens, I finished the master plan, selected the final alternative for the airport's expansion, and reached an agreement with all key stakeholders for approval and execution of the major projects within the plan. The problems and challenges involved in complex programs managed by the airport and its various interested parties could never really be accurately anticipated (Hendricks 1999). We were also fortunate in having an interested newspaper reporter who provided excellent information to the public through well written articles. Early broad-range engagement produced connections and relationships between the parties that allowed solutions to be effectively formulated. The local business community believed the fifth runway was the key to future economic development in the region. But not everyone was ready to go. The recommendation for building the runway needed approval from two major governmental entities, Clayton County and the City of College Park. Both

Figure 16.2. The Atlanta airport fifth runway, the most important runway in America at the world's busiest airport

were vocal in their opposition, with one very influential county commissioner telling me that the runway would be built "over his dead body." It is one thing to enter negotiations with opposing concerns—but it is quite another circumstance when the public opposition accompanies an uncompromising and show-stopping position.

The $1.25 million fifth runway was necessary for the airport to function successfully to meet the origin-and-destination and connecting traffic projections. The land for the runway was part of Clayton County and the city of College Park. Almost one thousand acres needed to be acquired in order for the runway to be built. Without condemnation authority, acquisition would have been impossible as owners would demand prices for their properties that would have been impossible to pay. Elected officials are primarily motivated to provide for the good of their communities. They balance the benefits and potential disadvantages of the airport's expansion. Stakeholder engagement was the single most important aspect of obtaining elected officials' approval for this runway (Hartsfield-Jackson 2013) .

Under Georgia law, the consent of local jurisdictions must be obtained before condemnation can be made, meaning that another governmental jurisdiction had to be involved. So before the City of Atlanta could condemn property in College Park and Clayton County for the construction of the fifth runway, we needed to get the consent of their jurisdictions. Not only did we have to satisfy their local constituencies, but we had to provide economic and financial value so that they would approve our rights of condemnation. Showing sincere respect for the opinions of stakeholders created a durable relationship and knowledge and understanding of pluses for the regional economy and the prosperity of their constituents (Hartsfield 1998). We stressed the job-generating capacity of an expanded airport and explained its contribution to the economy. We also negotiated arrangements with College Park and Clayton County for real estate purchases and tax payments totaling $110 million—$82 million to College Park and $28 million to Clayton County—to compensate for the burden that these neighboring communities bore with construction of the fifth runway and the expansion of traffic to and from the world's busiest airport (Hirshman 2006). We also reached an agreement with the FAA regarding the scope of these agreements. The FAA was well represented on the MPCC (Hendicks 1998).

Master Plan Requirements
Successful master plans should include at least these three basic elements:

1. realistic estimates of time and money required to obtain the desired infrastructure investment benefits;
2. broad stakeholder agreement tailored to the needs of all who have significant interests; and
3. negotiable agreements that resolve issues for implementable plans.

After the extensive review of the technical work by the MPCC and its involvement in the details of the various elements of the master plan development, our public focus shifted to small group meetings. We met with public officials, sometimes with residents in attendance and sometimes one-on-one, and we conducted town hall meetings to engage the residents in the surrounding communities and cities. I conducted separate meetings with city council members, mayors, and other elected state officials representing these residents as well as state transportation officials at the Georgia Department of Transportation.

Late in this engagement process, I conducted a standing room only town hall meeting in a Clayton County school gymnasium. In my view, we broke through the political opposition in that one last forum. In my opening remarks at 6:00 p.m., my first statement was that I planned to be the last person to leave the building that night. I said I would stay until all the questions were answered. Once the attendees understood I would be there to turn out the lights, the groups became more engaged in a detailed discussion. Their elected officials stood around the edges of the crowd located in the rear of the auditorium; I wondered if some of them had prepared to make a quick get way should the tide turn ugly and against the plan. The local sheriff offered me a back-door route to the parking area, noting what seemed at first to be an unfriendly crowd. However, directly engaging the community helped turn the tide as the questions continued. People were emotional, but the more questions they asked the more they developed an understanding of why we believed we needed the land for this runway and why the investment was in the best long-term interests of everyone.

Regional planning is among the most difficult, and often plans are shelved because elected officials are not engaged enough to take a risk for a plan that does not adequately engage a supportive constituency. Airport planning is at the top of the list when it comes to engaging the public with topics that are an anathema to its interests. Finding a constituency among the public to engage in discussions about noise, land acquisition, traffic congestion, and environmental issues led us to engage interested parties in the most effective sequence, given our knowledge of their expressed interests and positions. The best way to engage the community is to first, listen to leaders who are decision makers; second, identify key stakeholders who can make the program viable; and third, address the interests of each key stakeholder including the broadest community interests. By following this path, we were ready for the implementation of the airport master plan. Successfully implemented plans, I can assure you, incorporate the interests of the important stakeholders.

In summary, do not go it alone. The longer, uncertain journey of major, complicated infrastructure investments requires a community of interests pulling together. Go together. Large programs take many years to effectuate, and surprises along the way are a certainty. Only through consensus and general agreements can you progress as we did in the face of terrorist attacks on September 11th, the largest recession since the Great Depression, changes in political leadership (locally and nationally), the rise of worldwide oil prices, the bankruptcy of airlines and their mergers, the growth of global airline alliances, and the huge changes in airline fleets—to name just some of the challenges we endured during the execution of the airport's master plan. Hartsfield-Jackson will grow and continue to sustain the Atlanta regional economy because of wise master planning and execution approaches established over the last 20 years.[3]

CHAPTER 17

Modern Streetcars Return to Atlanta

Jennifer Ball

The fact that modern streetcars are returning to the streets of Atlanta can be traced back to neighborhood-oriented land-use and transportation planning processes in Downtown and Midtown that resulted in recommendations that the core of the city needed "last-mile" transit connections. The *Blueprint Midtown* (1997) and *Imagine Downtown* (2004) plans both focused on the future growth and redevelopment of dense, mixed use activity centers along with the infrastructure investments that would be necessary to support this vision (Central Atlanta Progress 2009; Midtown Alliance 2013). In this context, each district was focused on the need to improve walkability through the addition of pedestrian amenities and safety features. However, the real key to supporting the desired density of activity and a walkable character that would serve as the thriving heart of a growing region would be the utilization and expansion of a world-class transit system.

Since the Metropolitan Atlanta Rapid Transit Authority (MARTA) heavy-rail network was planned and built in the 1970s and 1980s, both Downtown and Midtown were well served by the core of the network, albeit in a predominately north-south linear fashion. Since the 1980s, higher-density office, institutional, and residential building construction has located along this north-south path, which is also the Peachtree ridge. Following the 1996 Centennial Olympic Games and benefiting from a strong regional economy and urbanization trends, newer construction in both districts continued to expand to available and affordable land to the east and west, farther away than a close five-minute walk from MARTA rail stations.

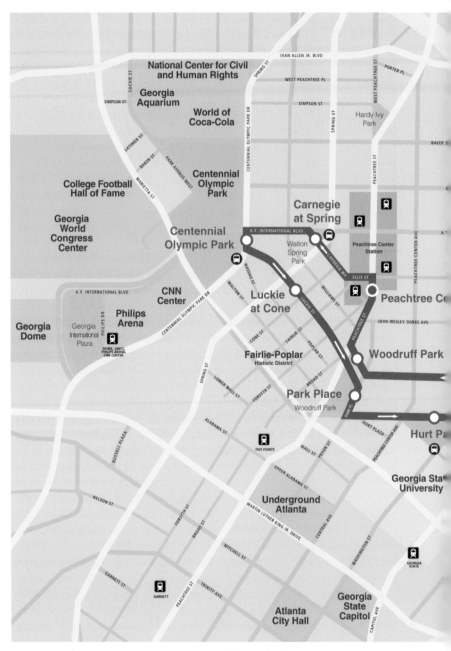

Figure 17.1. Atlanta Streetcar map, 2013. (Source: Map by Central Atlanta Progress.)

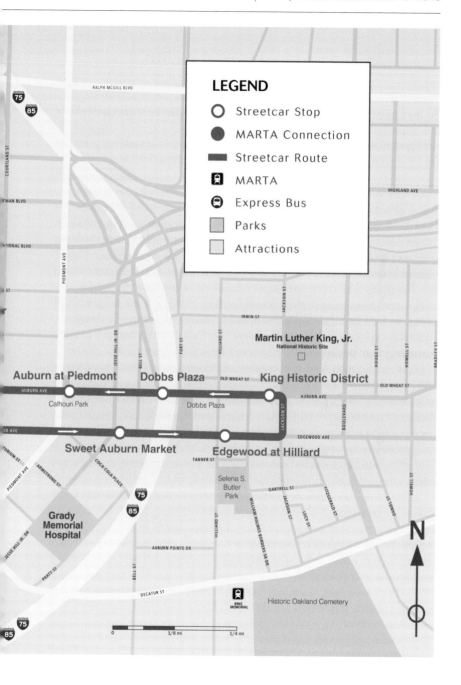

In Downtown, the creation of Centennial Olympic Park and the transformation of concentrated areas of the Atlanta Housing Authority's public housing into modern mixed income communities resulted in new visitor attractions, more jobs, and more residences—sprawling away from the Peachtree ridge and growing the footprint of the walkable city center. This increased activity—and city planners' desire to see the trend continue—led to the need to find a way to better connect the larger district with transit service that in turn fostered additional investment in an urban mixed use built environment.

European cities that have invested in trolley and tram systems, as well as American cities like Portland and Seattle that were inventing the "modern streetcar" movement, helped Atlanta planners recognized the opportunity for a streetcar network that would take the city "back to the future." A streetcar network as illustrated in Figure 17.1 could help connect job centers in Downtown and Midtown both to one another and to surrounding neighborhoods and destinations north, south, east, and west. Concurrently, U.S. federal government funding policies—like the Federal Transit Administration New Starts and Small Advances programs—were also becoming more programmatically supportive, while the technology associated with electric, in-street transit modes was also advancing. The seeds were being planted for a modern streetcar system in Atlanta.

Funding the Vision

The City of Atlanta's adoption of the *Imagine Downtown* and *Blueprint Midtown* plans and their recommendations for streetcar routes did not mean that the projects were a *fait accompli*. Like many milestone events in the history of Atlanta's growth, a unique partnership between elected municipal leadership and community corporate leadership emerged to ensure that a transformational—yet at times, seemingly unattainable—vision was given a chance to thrive.

This partnership initially took the form of a series of specific organized initiatives, many named for and focused on the original priority corridor for streetcar implementation, Peachtree Street. The following initiatives were involved in advancing a streetcar project in Atlanta.

Atlanta Streetcar, Inc. (2003–2004)

Atlanta Streetcar, Inc. was a privately-funded initiative led by Lanier Parking Company's chief operating officer, Michael Robison, and Atlanta city councilperson, H. Lamar Willis, with a board of directors of influential corporate and nonprofit leaders. This organization was the first to take a planning document recommendation to the next level of design and engineering analysis.

Peachtree Corridor Taskforce (2005–2006)

Mayor Shirley Franklin appointed the Peachtree Corridor Taskforce, and it was co-chaired by Tom Bell, formerly the chief operating officer of Cousins Properties, Inc., and Egbert Perry, president of The Integral Group., The taskforce—comprising a who's who of Atlanta's business leadership—analyzed the core components for the transformation of the Peachtree corridor into a "great street." These elements included land use and zoning, finance, mobility, housing, architecture, and design for the corridor between Fort McPherson on the south to the city limits on the north in Buckhead.

Peachtree Corridor Partnership (2007–2008)
Following the report of the taskforce, the Peachtree Corridor Partnership was charged with executing the associated recommendations. The partnership was supported by the Atlanta Committee for Progress; the Atlanta Development Authority (now Invest Atlanta); and the Downtown, Midtown, and Buckhead community improvement districts. Eventually, the efforts of the partnership were assumed by the three improvement district organizations.

Beyond the individual accomplishments of each organization, the overarching outcome of this work was the building of a coalition of supporters and committed advocates who understood the benefits of the Atlanta Streetcar and who were focused on its fruition. This coalition was built through many large public, small group, and individual meetings and presentations. The meetings were supported by a marketing and communications effort that focused on educating and bringing awareness to a diverse group of community stakeholders, including Midtown and Downtown property and business owners, institutional leaders, residents, and crucial elected leaders such as the mayor and city councilmembers.

As community support grew, one fundamental challenge remained—how to financially support the construction and operation of the system. One key funding-related recommendation of the Peachtree Corridor Taskforce was the creation of a special property tax assessment district along the transit route to raise local

Schematic of the Atlanta Streetcar in operation along Edgewood Avenue

funding to support the project. Despite concerted efforts to develop a supportable solution for the district, opposition to the funding proposal ultimately overwhelmed the effort and the plans for a property tax district were abandoned.

This local defeat occurred on the cusp of the recession that hit Atlanta and the nation beginning in late 2008. This downturn in the economy led to a heretofore unimagined funding opportunity. Seeking to jumpstart the economy by generating economic activity and creating jobs, the U.S. Department of Transportation created a stimulus program, the Transportation Investment Generating Economic Return (TIGER) program (U.S. Environmental Protection Agency 2013b). The TIGER program sought to quickly invest federal funding in "shovel-ready" transportation infrastructure projects that would also support economic competitiveness, sustainability, and liability, and it did so in an innovative way. The Atlanta Streetcar project seemed ready-made for the TIGER program. Working with the City of Atlanta, the Atlanta Downtown Improvement District and the Midtown Alliance (which has been advancing the planning work for the proposed Peachtree Streetcar following the work of the Peachtree Corridor Partnership) by 2009 had engaged MARTA in providing technical support and exploring cost-saving opportunities through coordination with the existing heavy-rail transit system.

A TIGER application was completed and submitted by the City of Atlanta that envisioned a streetcar route along Peachtree Street between Marietta Street and 17th Street, as well as an east-west downtown loop. This aggressive investment was projected to cost over $300 million. The TIGER application was unsuccessful and critics believed the proposed project was too large and lacked sufficient local funding.

Learning from the first application experience, the City of Atlanta re-scaled the project by reducing the route of the downtown loop and worked to find additional local funding support. In 2010 the city made another application for the second round of TIGER funding. By this time, the project planning partners—the city, MARTA, the Atlanta Downtown Improvement District, and the Midtown Alliance—were also close to completing the National Environmental Policy Act planning process and securing a categorical exclusion for the project, which helped with the competitiveness of the TIGER II application. In October 2010, the City of Atlanta was notified by the U.S. Department of Transportation (US-DOT) that its application for the Atlanta Streetcar would be awarded $47.6 million in TIGER funding to support the construction of the project.

The Atlanta Streetcar Characteristics

The initial downtown loop route connects the Centennial Olympic Park area—home to the Georgia Aquarium, the World of Coca-Cola, the Georgia World Congress Center, CNN, and the future National Center for Civil and Human Rights—to the Martin Luther King Jr. National Historic Site. Along the 2.6 track

TABLE 17.1	Summary of Atlanta Streetcar System
Route	2.6 track miles with 12 stops
Vehicle	Modern electric streetcar made by Siemens with an overhead power system (single trolley wire) that operates on-street in lanes shared with other traffic
Frequency	Service operating with a 15-minute frequency (average) and 10-minute one-way running time
Hours	Service operating 7 days a week; 5:00 a.m. to 11:00 p.m. weekdays, 8:30 a.m. to 11:00 p.m. Saturdays, and 9:00 a.m. to 10:30 p.m. Sundays
Fares	Will be consistent with MARTA fares and will use the Breeze smart-card technology
Ridership	Projected ridership of 2,600 per weekday and 13,000 per week
Maintenance	Vehicle maintenance facility, a "trolley barn," to be built along the route under the Interstate 75/85 bridge at Auburn and Edgewood Avenues
Enhancements	System capital investment to include conversion of Luckie Street to two-way traffic, the addition of one-way paired bike lanes on Auburn and Edgewood Avenues, sidewalk improvements at stop locations, and the upgrade of water lines in the corridor associated with the Clean Water Atlanta program
Capital Funding	Total $99 million capital cost to deliver the Atlanta Streetcar includes: • $47.6 million in TIGER II Federal Transit Administration grant funds • $32.6 million from the City of Atlanta via bond funding and the Department of Watershed Management • $6 million from the Atlanta Downtown Improvement District • $11.34 million from the Atlanta Regional Commission Livable Centers Initiative Program through three separate grants for related roadway, bicycle, and sidewalk enhancement projects • $1.2 million from the Westside and Eastside Tax Allocation Districts
Annual Operations	Operational funds committed for 20 years and will be covered by fare box revenue, advertising, federal grant funds, Atlanta Downtown Improvement District contributions and City of Atlanta car rental and hotel motel tax proceeds.[1]

Figures from Central Atlanta Progress

miles and 12 stops, the route passes various destinations, including the Fairlie-Poplar and Sweet Auburn historic districts, Peachtree Street, and Georgia State University's campus. The Atlanta Streetcar connects to MARTA at the Peachtree Center rail station. Table 17.1 provides details of the streetcar system.

A Unique Partnership

The Atlanta Streetcar is a collaborative public-private partnership. Its design and construction has been guided by a tri-party intergovernmental agreement between the City of Atlanta, the Atlanta Downtown Improvement District (ADID), and MARTA. Along the implementation path, numerous other partners have engaged with the core partners to ensure the successful construction, operation and long-term benefit to the community.

The City of Atlanta has led the effort to build the Atlanta Streetcar and will own the assets of the system. As the applicant to the federal government for the TIGER II funding, the city has been the grantee—the prime signatory of a grant agreement with the FTA—and the recipient of those funds. The city also initiated and is the prime signatory of an intergovernmental agreement with MARTA and ADID.

Following its role in the initial land-use and transportation planning that generated the idea of a modern streetcar system, the Atlanta Downtown Improvement District has remained an implementation partner. ADID has provided financial support, both for construction and future operations, and it serves as a liaison for the project with Downtown property owners and stakeholders.

MARTA is the Atlanta region's FTA funding designee. As such, MARTA plays an important role as a signatory, with the City of Atlanta, on the TIGER grant agreement and oversees the federal grant funds dedicated to the project. MARTA has also served as a technical resource through the planning, grant application, and construction processes, most critically as a procurement manager. As the streetcar construction finishes, MARTA will remain involved to ensure—either with internal or, more likely, contracted resources—the operation of the system.

The Atlanta Streetcar partners desire to build a streetcar system in a street environment that supports multimodal activity, including vehicles, transit, walking, and cycling. ARC, through its Livable Communities Initiative planning and transportation infrastructure program, has been a key funding partner for the Atlanta Streetcar. ARC has supported infrastructure costs related to vehicular, pedestrian, and cycling access in the streetcar alignment corridors. It has also supported studies and consultant work to foster redevelopment of the streetcar neighborhoods.

The Atlanta Streetcar could not have made the implementation progress it has without the USDOT and specifically the FTA. Federal policy supporting smaller, start-up transit service—such as streetcar systems—and the creation of TIGER funding have benefited the Atlanta Streetcar. FTA oversees the expenditure of grant funding consistent with the grant agreement executed by the city and MARTA. It is anticipated that USDOT will also provide operational funding support to the system in the future through the Congestion Mitigation and Air Quality program.

Concurrent with planning for the Atlanta Streetcar, the Atlanta BeltLine, Inc. had also been planning for light rail or streetcar service. The Atlanta BeltLine is the 22-mile-long former railroad right-of-way that encircles downtown Atlanta and is also home to new parks, trails, and neighborhood investment. Since funding was identified for the Atlanta Streetcar, Atlanta BeltLine, Inc., as an affiliate of the City of Atlanta, has taken the lead in planning and analyzing expansions of the city's streetcar network between the Atlanta BeltLine corridor and the Atlanta Streetcar alignment. The stated goals of the Atlanta Streetcar project include attracting investment to and revitalizing the neighborhoods along the streetcar alignment. As identified through initial planning and documented in the TIGER funding application, over 80 acres of land and 30 buildings and structures within two blocks of the proposed route are considered underutilized. Central Atlanta Progress, in partnership with Invest Atlanta, aims to leverage the federal and municipal investment in the Atlanta Streetcar by encouraging redevelopment along the route. Invest Atlanta, Atlanta's development authority, plays an integral role in this effort by managing development finance tools like tax increment financing, new markets tax credits, and tax exempt bonds to support development.

Project Goals: Walkable, Livable, and Sustainable

The Atlanta Streetcar will provide an integrated multimodal, high-quality transit network that links communities, improves mobility by enhancing transit access and options, supports projected growth, promotes economic development, and encourages strategies to develop livable communities.

First and foremost, the Atlanta Streetcar is a transit system that fills in missing circulation links and provides direct connectivity to existing transit services in Downtown, as well as future commuter rail and regional light rail, including the Atlanta Beltline. By providing these connections, the streetcar enhances mobility as the "last mile" connection to destinations for transit-dependent populations while also making transit work for choice riders including residents, tourists, and students. Streetcar service provides this mobility in a more sustainable way than buses with less noise and fewer emissions.

The streetcar does not cause development to happen, but rather sets the stage—along with other supportive land use policy and public investment—to attract and shape development that is compact, walkable, high density, mixed use, and sustainable. Characterized by high-quality streetscapes—including parks, plaza, and public art—the result is animated neighborhoods that are a visually interesting mix of historic and modern buildings. The investment in the Atlanta Streetcar is an integral place-making tool because it is consistent with the guiding principles essential to the redevelopment of streetcar corridor neighborhoods, including:

- *Housing flexibility:* the presence of a dense, diverse, and quality housing stock to meet the needs of a range of demographics that desire an urban lifestyle
- *Retail character:* vibrant shopping and dining uses that activate the street and provide communal gathering spaces
- *History and culture:* authentic experiences for visitors and residents alike that strengthen and enrich the living legacy of Sweet Auburn and Fairlie-Poplar

The improved accessibility that the streetcar will provide with its attendant lifestyle options appeal to both young and urbane populations, as well as smaller older households who value easy, quality transit access to goods and services. This mixture of residents and households is a hallmark of sustainable communities. Attractive, convenient service increases transit ridership, foot traffic, and customers for businesses served by the streetcar. For the Atlanta Streetcar, this will benefit the existing residents, businesses, and destinations along the corridor as well as create an opportunity to attract new residents, businesses, and destinations.

Challenges

Despite the progress to bring the Atlanta Streetcar to fruition, the implementation team has had to overcome many challenges in order to ensure the long-term success of the project. From its inception and particularly following the commitment of project funding, the Atlanta Streetcar has been criticized for its investment in transportation infrastructure that will not significantly reduce vehicular congestion (Hart 2010). As a metropolitan region that suffers from congestion, pressure is strong from across the region to direct limited transportation funding resources primarily into roadway and highway projects. However, within the city of Atlanta, citizens and elected and appointed leaders are more supportive of investments in transit, walking, and cycling as a means to building a multimodal transportation network that reduces vehicular congestion through alternative modes. The Atlanta Streetcar is part of the city's effort to build communities that are less auto-oriented and dependent. An exclusive focus on the mobility aspects of the streetcar also ignores the stated and desired economic development benefits.

In an environment of scarce transportation resources and an atmosphere of suspicion of government funding, the streetcar project has had to be vigilant about adhering to the project's original budget, which has proven challenging. As the city and region's first modern streetcar project, the learning curve for both construction and operational expertise has been significant. Managing projected costs with construction techniques and actual field conditions in the oldest parts of the city has necessitated difficult budget decisions related to utility relocations, the corridor alignment, and adjacent sidewalk enhancements.

Another criticism of the Atlanta Streetcar relates to its route and a perception that it does not go anywhere (Barr 2010). While the initial downtown loop is short—2.6 track miles—and only serves an area that is one mile from end to end, the old adage applies—you have to start somewhere. As the initial segment of an envisioned citywide network, the downtown loop will serve a corridor with 71,800 jobs, 2,700 housing units, 6.5 million square feet of office space, 800,000 square feet of retail space, 8,500 hotel rooms, and

5 million annual visitors. As planning for the future expansion of the system has progressed, this critique has been subsiding.

As the project construction is completed and decisions are made about operations, additional challenges remain. Chief among them are operating hours and headways. Project planners remain optimistic that an optimal balance between the budget and convenient, attractive transit service can be found. Another task that remains for the streetcar team is educating the public about safety issues related to the streetcar. The prime public outreach message that will be directed at motorists, cyclists, and pedestrians is how to safely share the road with the streetcar.

The Future

The Atlanta Streetcar is on track to open for revenue service in spring 2014, but planning and engineering is already well underway to expand the streetcar network beyond the initial downtown loop. This work is guided by the Connect Atlanta Plan from 2008, the City of Atlanta's first citywide transportation plan designed to direct the next 25 years of transportation policy and investment. Connect Atlanta set forth a citywide vision for connecting neighborhoods and destinations with streetcar technology that would advance Atlanta's larger vision of creating a more modern, vibrant, and sustainable city. Because a significant portion of this envisioned network is planned along the Atlanta BeltLine alignment, BeltLine staff is directing route planning and corridor evaluation for future extensions of the Atlanta Streetcar to connect with the Atlanta BeltLine.

CHAPTER 18

Atlanta's BeltLine: The Emerald Necklace Shaping the City's Future

Alexander Garvin

At the start of the twenty-first century, residents of many American cities, including Atlanta, spent increasing amounts of time on longer and longer stretches of clogged highways traveling to and from sprawling agglomerations of single-family houses. Atlanta is unique among the nation's large cities, however, in deciding to create an alternative lifestyle around a very different public realm framework. In 2005, Mayor Shirley Franklin created the BeltLine Partnership to promote a combination of park, trail, and transit to replace the ring of railroad lines that encircled the city about a mile and a half to three miles from the center of the city. The city council followed by approving the BeltLine Redevelopment Plan and a tax allocation district to pay for it. The following year Atlanta BeltLine Inc. (ABI) was established to implement the project.

The new BeltLine will consist of more than 20 new or expanded parks occupying 1,300 acres connected by 33 miles of multiuse trails and 22 miles of new transit lines (Figure 18.1). The project is already having a huge impact on Atlanta. As of January 2013, more than $360 million from both public and private sources has been spent on the entire Atlanta BeltLine program, including five new open parks, 200 additional acres of new park land, and seven miles of new permanent public trails. This huge public investment has already resulted in 8,908 new privately financed residential units and 870,700 square feet of new commercial property completed within the BeltLine corridor, representing more than $1 billion in privately financed development (Atlanta BeltLine Inc. 2010, 2013). More importantly, upon completion the BeltLine will have supplanted the city's interstate highways as a focus of the daily life for hundreds of thousands of Atlantans.

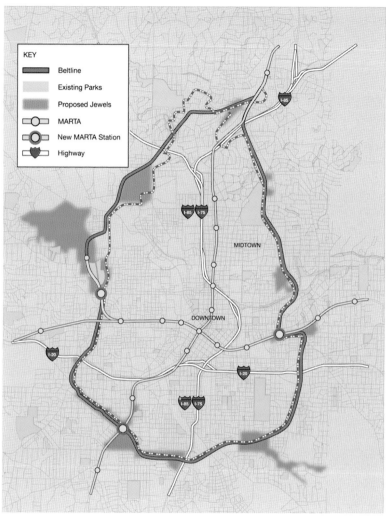

Figure 18.1. Combining major new, expanded, and existing parks with the BeltLine trail and anchoring the combination at intersecting MARTA stations were first proposed by Alexander Garvin in a 2004 Trust for Public Land study. (Source: Garvin 2004.)

Converting unused rail lines into recreational trails had been gaining traction in the United States since 1986, when the Rails-to-Trails Conservancy began operation. At that time, there were only 200 rail-trails in the United States. By 2013 there were eight times as many, covering more than 20,000 miles (Rails to Trails Conservancy 2013). Some have become major recreational resources; the 3.5-mile-long Katy Trail in Dallas serves more than 300,000 residents who live less than a mile away. Others have become major tourist destinations; the 1.5-mile-long elevated High Line in Manhattan attracted 3.7 million visitors during 2011 (Friends of the High Line 2013).

The Atlanta BeltLine, however, was not conceived primarily as a recreational facility or tourist destination. In the project's first incarnation, in a 1999 Georgia Tech master's thesis by Ryan Gravel, the rail lines that would become the BeltLine were reimagined as a transit corridor tying together 45 communities encircling downtown Atlanta.

Where most people saw separate rights-of-way owned by the Norfolk Southern Railroad, the CSX Railroad, and the Georgia Department of Transportation, Gravel perceived an opportunity for a continuous public realm. At first, people questioned the idea. Rights-of-way ranged in width from as little as 45 feet in some places to as much as 200 feet in others. Many sections would require extensive regrading and retaining walls in order to accommodate a trail and transit system. Other sections were crossed by creeks and low-lying floodplains or sewer and storm-sewer infrastructure. At five different locations, the rail lines did not even connect with one another (Figure 18.2) (Garvin 2004).

Despite the physical and engineering obstacles, however, the idea gained traction because the concept was so appealing and its potential to transform Atlanta was so beguiling. The more people heard about the BeltLine, the more they liked the idea. It gained vital support from then city council president Cathy Woolard and then mayor Shirley Franklin. James Langford, Georgia state director for the Trust for Public Land (TPL), however, was the player who advanced the BeltLine beyond its status as an appealing idea.

The Trust for Public Land had been established as a nonprofit foundation in 1972 "to protect land in and around cities and to pioneer land conservation techniques" (Trust for Public Land 2013). To date, TPL has been involved in more than 5,200 projects nationwide—everything from salvaging abandoned city lots and transforming them into small, urban community gardens to preserving large stretches of wilderness (Garvin 2004). In 2003, TPL published a study of the 50 largest American cities. Atlanta was identified as among the lowest ranking in terms of territory devoted to public park land: 3.8 percent (Sherer 2003).

Langford perceived the BeltLine as an opportunity to provide Atlanta with much-needed additional public park land. He persuaded a distinguished group of leaders from government, nonprofit organizations, and the business community to become members of a TPL BeltLine Greenspace Steering Committee, tasked with reviewing opportunities for adding to the city's meager parks inventory along the transit corridor Gravel had identified. Langford raised funds from the Arthur M. Blank Family Foundation, the Kendeda Fund, and the Morgens West Foundation to pay for the committee's efforts and to commission Alex

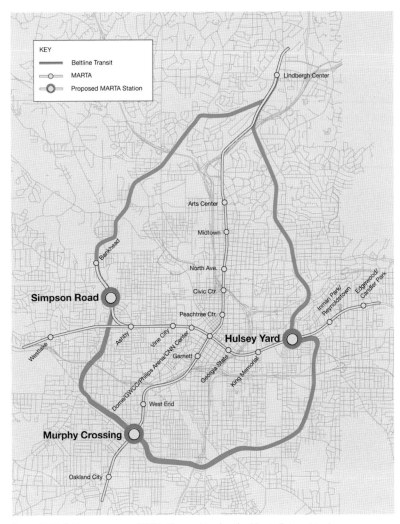

Figure 18.2. BeltLine transit map, 2004. (Source: Map by Alex Garvin & Associates.)

Garvin & Associates to analyze Atlanta's green space challenges and opportunities.[1] The firm (now known as AGA Public Realm Strategists) grew out of my individual practice of more than 35 years in planning, architecture, real estate development, and public service. Our firm appealed to Langford because we took an interdisciplinary, market-based approach to planning.

Our team members began by searching for properties that could be reused as parks. We scoured maps, aerial photographs, property records, and geographic information systems data to determine ownership and land

Figure 18.3. Aerial view of Bellwood Quarry site

values. We also searched for the best real estate development opportunities along the BeltLine to be sure that, once developed, projects would generate the taxes needed to pay for maintaining the entire system. Members of the team hiked, climbed, and even crawled along the entire BeltLine right-of-way and took several helicopter flights to get a deeper understanding of the relationship between the rail corridor and surrounding communities. On the first of those helicopter rides, I identified the still-functioning, 100-year-old Bellwood Quarry as a great potential site for a large new park. Two years later, the City of Atlanta acquired the site for what will become the Westside Reservoir Park, the largest park in Atlanta (Figure 18.3).

In December 2004, TPL published our firm's report: a 141-page proposal called The BeltLine Emerald Necklace: Atlanta's New Public Realm. We confirmed TPL's conclusion that whether BeltLine transit happened in the distant future or never happened at all, the BeltLine would be a great success by using pedestrian and bicycle paths to connect city park land and to create a public realm framework for infill development that could accommodate Atlanta's population growth. Much more importantly, we identified major opportunities for new park land, for expanding existing public parks, and for private development that could become prime residential or commercial destinations. Our report pointed out that each of these potential sites could provide recreational facilities that were appropriate at that location but could not be duplicated in other communities. Thus, the paths (and the transit lines, when they emerged) would allow residents to get to and use every type of recreational facility. This would produce a park system that eventually would become the envy of cities with many times the amount of park land.

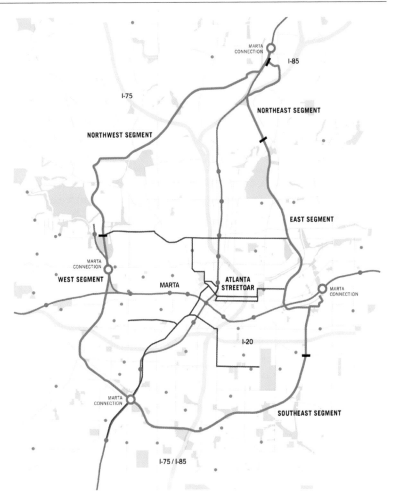

Figure 18.4. Beltline transit map, 2013. (Source: Atlanta Beltline Inc. 2013.)

Several of the proposed parks—in particular Boulevard Crossing, Murphy Crossing, and the parks in the Old Fourth Ward—would have green fingers that extend fairly far into surrounding neighborhoods, thereby tying the BeltLine into surrounding community life. Thus, they would play a vital role as social mixing valves for an ever-changing variety of park users.

The BeltLine's potential for improving mass transit remains one of the least understood components of the BeltLine plan. The Metropolitan Atlanta Rapid Transit Authority (MARTA) already provides service to and from the city's major destinations: Hartsfield-Jackson Atlanta International Airport, Downtown, Midtown, and Buckhead. However, it does not provide service to a great many of the city's residential neighborhoods. The BeltLine plan proposed modification of the three MARTA rail lines that cross the BeltLine corridor so that residents of the 45 residential communities along the BeltLine could transfer to MARTA to reach the major destinations it serves (and vice versa), in the process making MARTA more appealing for many Atlantans (Figure 18.4).

Five years after approving the BeltLine, the city initiated the Atlanta Streetcar Expansion Strategy (ASES). When the initial 2.7-mile Atlanta Streetcar Project begins operation in 2014, it will service the core of downtown Atlanta. Upon completion, ASES will provide supplementary east-west connections across the city and tie the BeltLine directly into downtown Atlanta. Once the entire ASES system is in operation and transfer stations are built where MARTA crosses the BeltLine, getting around Atlanta by mass transit will be easier for many city residents, who currently spend far too much time in endless rush-hour traffic.

Since the 1990s, an increasing number of the nation's young people have been choosing to live in urban areas, rather than in the suburbs. All of us who participated in the TPL study thought the BeltLine's combination of recreational opportunities would attract them to BeltLine neighborhoods and that the resultant increase in demand would, in turn, motivate developers to acquire and build along the BeltLine. This role as a public realm framework for private development has turned out to be the BeltLine's single most important impact on Atlanta.

However laudable these goals may have been, they would never be achieved without huge amounts of money and community support. While my firm was creating the plan for the BeltLine, the Atlanta Development Authority hired EDAW Inc. (now AECOM), to prepare a study of the feasibility of tax increment financing and to manage a process of community engagement. EDAW, a landscape architecture and planning firm led by Barbara Faga, had considerable experience in Atlanta, having been previously responsible for the city's Centennial Olympic Park and Freedom Parkway, which connected downtown Atlanta with the Jimmy Carter Presidential Library and Museum.[2]

In order to build support when the BeltLine came up for a vote at the city council in late 2005, Faga led an elaborate public participation process. More than 120 public meetings were held in every community along the route of the BeltLine. The Saturday workshops included presentations, outside speakers, videos, and even simulated fly-throughs. As she later vividly explained, "The fact is that if we'd had to go door to door, we would. Public process is not for the faint of heart" (Faga 2006). This reliance on public participation has been continued by the ABI and is the reason that the BeltLine retains such widespread public support.

The BeltLine is an expensive project. The 2005 estimates commissioned for EDAW's feasibility study concluded that the total project development cost in 2005 dollars would be between $1.5 and $2.2 billion, including right-of-way acquisition, trail development, transit development, open space development, infrastructure, and workforce housing. The ABI's 2013 estimate is approximately $4.8 billion, indexed to inflation and to estimated dates of delivery (Atlanta Beltline Inc. 2013). As with any major municipal capital investment, the project would have to be financed by issuing long-term bonds, rather than out of annual revenues. Project proponents thought that the income stream to cover debt service payments on the bonds should come from the properties that received the benefit of the BeltLine. But the city government depended on revenues from those taxes to pay for police protection, sanitation services, and other government services. The solution was a tax allocation district (TAD) in which any increase in property taxes (ostensibly the result of capital investment) would go to pay debt service on BeltLine bonds, while the city would continue to collect the existing taxes that it previously received in order to continue to provide the usual government services.

From the beginning, the ABI had to contend with three lawsuits challenging the legality of the use of tax increment financing from the TAD. In the first case, Woodham v. City of Atlanta, the Georgia Supreme Court ruled in 2008 that the City of Atlanta did not have the right to divert educational tax money from the school system for non-educational redevelopment purposes. As a result, the Georgia Constitution was amended to allow such diversion of tax dollars in the future and the City of Atlanta adjusted its intergovernmental agreements to reflect the change. The other two cases were dismissed in 2013 by the Georgia Supreme Court, which found that constitutional amendments were "expressly made retroactive with respect to the county, city, and local board of education approvals" (Wheatley 2012; Cardinale 2012, 2013)." Despite the lawsuits and loss of revenue while litigation was underway, the first seven years of existence the ABI leveraged $150 million from the TAD, $144 from City of Atlanta funds, $41 million in private donations, and $26 million in federal funding, for a total investment of roughly $362 million (Atlanta BeltLine Inc. 2013).

Not willing to rely on congressional appropriations, supporters of mass transit had proposed financing transit from a new local sales tax. A successful model to follow already existed in Denver. In 2004 voters in the Denver metropolitan region had approved a similar tax for its FasTracks system, which will eventually fund more than 119 miles of new light and commuter rail, 57 new transit stations, and 18 miles of bus rapid transit. Georgia supporters of mass transit had expected a similar result. However, a funding setback occurred in Atlanta in 2012 when metro Atlanta voters rejected the Transportation Special Purpose Local Option Sales Tax (T-SPLOST). This regional one-cent sales tax had been expected to raise a total of $7.2 billion over 10 years, $600 million of which was to pay for portions the Atlanta BeltLine and Atlanta Streetcar transit system (Kissel 2012). As a result of the failure of T-SPLOST,

New housing near Historic Fourth Ward Park and Ponce City Market

BeltLine transit, streetcar service from the BeltLine, and passenger transfer stations between the BeltLine and MARTA remain dependent on federal funding and other sources.

The ABI has been particularly creative in making major investments by collaborating with nonprofit organizations whose interests coincide with its development program, particularly the Path Foundation, Trees Atlanta, and TPL. Working in tandem with the Path Foundation beginning in 2007, the ABI was able to obtain and spend $11.6 million from a variety of sources (including private contributions, federal programs, and TAD proceeds) to create 4.3 miles of the Beltline trail system (Tanyard Creek Trail in the northern quadrant of the BeltLine, Southwest Connector Trail, and West End Trail) (Atlanta Beltline Inc. 2010). In cooperation with Trees Atlanta, the ABI has spent more than $1.3 million creating a linear arboretum that will display trees native to the Atlanta region along its trail system (Davidson 2013).

The collaboration with the Trust for Public Land began at the creation of the BeltLine. Not only did the TPL commission the initial plan for the Beltline and advocate its development throughout the city, it purchased nearly 50 acres of land on an interim basis and transferred it to the City of Atlanta or ABI at cost.[3] As a result, the ABI could develop the Historic Fourth Ward Park, complete Phase 1 of Boulevard Crossing Park, and begin to expand Enota Park (Harrop 2013).

EDAW's 2005 Atlanta BeltLine Redevelopment Plan estimated that the project would generate between $20 and $30 billion in private development on properties affected by the BeltLine. This investment, in turn, would produce between $2 billion and $3 billion in new property taxes (ABI's 2013 estimate is $1.45 billion), which would be enough to pay for BeltLine projects that would not be paid for by the federal and state governments or by individual donors. The City of Atlanta, Fulton County, and Atlanta Public Schools (all of whom depend on real-estate tax revenue) accepted the estimate and approved a 6,500-acre TAD with a 25-year life. Starting in 2030, they would get the usual taxes plus the taxes generated by the TAD.

During the extensive public review process leading up to approval of the BeltLine and the equally extensive continuing public participation process led by the ABI, considerable demand was expressed for both "affordable" and "workforce" housing. The result has been the addition of a subsidized housing component to the BeltLine. As of August 2013, 15 percent of total net bond proceeds, or $8.8 million, has been raised for the

TABLE 18.1. **Total BeltLine Sources and Uses of Funds**

Sources of Funds	Amount ($)	Percent of Total
Tax increment	1.545 billion	33
Federal funds (estimated)	1.272 billion	29
Federal, state, regional or local funding for streetscapes (estimated)	343 million	8
Local funding for parks (est.)	157 million	4
Private funds (est.)	157 million	6
Unidentified	157 million	20
TOTAL	4.393 billion	100
Uses of Funds		
Parks	553 million	13
Trails	246 million	6
Transit	2.298 billion	52
Streetscapes	343 million	8
Affordable housing	302 million	7
PILT (Payments in Lieu of Taxes) payments	211 million	5
Repayment of existing debt	164 million	4
Economic development incentive fund	100 million	2
ABI operating costs	176 million	4
TOTAL	4.393 billion	100

Source: Atlanta BeltLine Inc. 2013

Artwork in Historic Fourth Ward Park

Atlanta BeltLine Affordable Housing Trust Fund. These funds have been used to create 263 units of housing either through home ownership assistance to low-income persons, developer subsidies for affordable housing, or the purchase of land that has been leased to developers of assisted housing (Atlanta Beltline Inc. 2013).

In mid-2013, when Paul Morris became the ABI's third president and CEO, the organization evaluated its progress to date and took a fresh look at the BeltLine's capital requirements and the resources that would need to be available to complete the BeltLine. For the first time, these estimates were based on an assessment of the probable date of each project's construction and the probable cost at that time, after considering probable rates of inflation. The ABI projected the total remaining cost of the BeltLine to be $4.393 billion (Table 18.1) (Atlanta Beltline Inc. 2013).

The quality of life is already changing for people who live along developed sections of the BeltLine. It is becoming the place where residents of every ethnicity, income level, and social class encounter one another, skate, jog, sit on benches reading books, picnic, or just wander. The parks and trails that are already open have greatly augmented the opportunities for recreational activities and increased the amount of time that nearby residents devote to exercise. As stores open onto the BeltLine and children in the schools along the BeltLine get used to cycling home along the BeltLine, Atlanta residents will also come here to dine, shop, and even do business.

Among the reasons that personal health and wellbeing are on the rise among those who live or work along the open sections of the BeltLine is that the

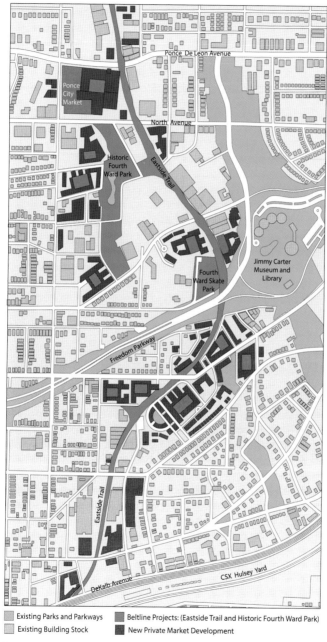

Figure 18.5. Recently opened projects on the BeltLine's Eastside Trail in 2013 triggered widespread and sustained private market investment. (Source: Map by Owen Howlett and Alexander Garvin.)

amount of contaminated land in the area is decreasing. More than 73 acres of brownfields have been remediated, including portions of the Eastside Trail and 17 acres at the Historic Fourth Ward Park (Figure 18.5). Moreover, the trails and parks have replaced dozens of acres of impervious surfaces with grass, playgrounds, and other permeable materials, allowing for more rain water percolation and reducing stormwater runoff. This improvement in water quality has been accompanied by improvement in air quality and a reduction in the ambient temperature as a result of thousands of newly planted trees.

Improving quality of life and providing a healthier environment for the people who live and work along the five new BeltLine parks and the seven miles of new BeltLine trails are certainly great accomplishments. The project's major achievement, however, is the extraordinary private market reaction to what is a very small part of what will emerge in 2030 when the Beltline will be complete. Since 2005, within a half-mile of the Eastside Trail alone, private real estate development that is completed or underway represents an investment of approximately $775 million (Atlanta Beltline Inc. 2013).

The largest of these projects is Ponce City Market, the conversion of an old two-million-square-foot Sears Roebuck building, which was being used for municipal offices and called "City Hall East" at the time of the TPL study. When the complex opens in 2014, it will include 300,000 square feet of stores and restaurants, 450,000 square feet of office space, and 260 residential units, all directly accessible from the BeltLine. This development will be among the first of many others that will open over the next 17 years. Consequently, the new mixed use public realm that will emerge on the Atlanta BeltLine will be very different from New York City's High Line or any of the many other single-function trails that have replaced railroad rights-of-way.

Most of the $775 million private development along the Eastside Trail, however, is residential. What is astounding about this amount of housing investment is that much of it started during an economic downturn; other projects have started during 2013, when more than 29 percent of the mortgages in metropolitan Atlanta were still in arrears, three times the national average (Cougherty 2013). These residential and commercial projects are indicative of the growing national return to urban living. More importantly, they are the harbinger of massive, widespread, and sustained private investment that can be expected during the life of the TAD. In the years ahead, as the BeltLine's implementation continues with new residences, stores and restaurants, community facilities, trails, parks, and transit, the project will have the potential to supplant the city's interstate highways as the focus of the daily life for hundreds of thousands of Atlantans.

PART 4

Boom and Bust

Atlanta's wealth was created by its institutions. CNN, UPS, DELTA, Georgia Pacific and many other business owners make this city what it is today; a busy twenty-first-century conglomeration of people and projects. The backbone of the boom is widely attributed to a few iconic leaders; a carbonated beverage concocted in the 19th century, a cable news trailblazer, and the international airport. Coca-Cola, CNN and Hartsfield-Jackson Atlanta International Airport are certainly not the only leading entities in the city but they are the organizations that set the stage for notoriety and successful economic development.

The business community has a long tradition of supporting elected officials with projects and in times of crises. Through bad times and good the city's political and business leaders traditionally work together to heal the city or make a big venture a successful. Whether Atlanta is named the 1984 "Best City in America" by Rand McNally or host of the 1996 Centennial Summer Olympic Games it is a well known fact that it is all due to the coalitions and network of business leaders with elected officials and civic groups that are the backbone of this city (Stone 1993). These authors discuss a few of the projects and programs that "boom and bust" the city.

Perhaps without credential and with a touch of boosterism Atlanta has always promoted itself as an international city. Everything changed when the city was awarded the 1996 Olympic Games. Randal Roark, in "The Legacy of the Centennial Olympic Games," discusses how business leaders raised

Figure E.1. Centennial Olympic Park at night

private funds to put together the Games with little support from federal, state, or local government. With a small investment by today's standards leaders of ACOG, MAOGA, and many other organizations brought international recognition to the city. While the Olympics are credited with bringing back a failing downtown and building university housing, many wish that more could have been done for the intown neighborhoods and infrastructure. Lasting legacies are tough to plan for when you are preparing to host the world. Roark presents the opportunities, constraints, and outcomes of this monumental event.

Jennifer Clark states a resounding case for "growing smart" in "Rethinking Atlanta's Regional Resilience in an Age of Uncertainty: Still the Economic Engine of the South?" Clark's comparisons and conclusions are valuable to Atlanta and other cities as they struggle to adapt to the new norms with a lack of central governance and underemployment. While the city concentrates on new stadiums and public projects, the region should instead invest more on educating the work force for the jobs of this century. Clark addresses how Atlanta should readjust immediately to overcome the label of Southern boomtown with a touch of Rustbelt fragmentation. As an expert on regional economies, Clark is well published on manufacturing, development policy, and innovation.

In "Economic Development: From Porsche to Tyler Perry" Elisabeth Kulinski describes the incentives that drive corporations to the region. New development includes the U.S. headquarters of Porsche which recently announced plans to relocate adjacent to the Hartsfield-Jackson Atlanta International Airport. Attracting manufacturing, businesses, and the film industry to the state is a full-time job for public and private officials. Kulinski's first-hand account is a result of her work with the State of Georgia Senate Budget Office and the private development group that attracted Porsche to Georgia.

Michael Carnathan describes the boom and bust of housing in "After the Crash: Foreclosures, Neighborhood Stability and Change." In this chapter he recounts Atlanta as the fastest growing metro region and the national leader of job creation in the 1990s. Often described as "sprawl city," the Great Recession and liberal lending policies transformed the Atlanta region from a homeowner's paradise into the fourth worst location for home foreclosure.

Frank S. Alexander, in "Building the Land Bank," traces the creation and evolution of the Fulton County/City of Atlanta Land Bank from its authorization in 1991 through its emergence as one of the most creative and innovative land banks in the country by 2011. Alexander describes the initial organizational structure and challenges, its foray into operational policies and procedures, its primary areas of success, and the challenges it confronted less successfully. Alexander also describes the pivotal restructuring and transformation during the period from 2007–2009, and the role of the land bank in the creation of the most advanced state land bank legislation in 2012.

These chapters give an overview of the highs and lows of regional accomplishments. These authors give a brief and practical look at what really shapes this economy. While boosterism and bravado are the reputation of the politicians and business leaders who run this region, the facts are the facts. These chapters give the reader an accurate and up-to-date view of what shapes politics, manufacturing, tourism, relocation, housing, and neighborhood stability—the foundations of the economy and planning in the Atlanta region.

CHAPTER 19

The Legacy of the Centennial Olympic Games

Randal Roark

Between the 1990 announcement of Atlanta winning its bid to host the 1996 Centennial Olympic Games and the onset of the recession in 2007, the Atlanta metropolitan area saw a larger growth rate than most other American metropolitan areas of similar size and an increase in the population of Atlanta's central core. Some of this growth can be attributed to changing demographics and a growing demand for urban amenities in an area that was still affordable to the middle class. However, much also can be attributed to the impact of the 1996 Centennial Olympic Games, as construction and events were staged in the same central area.

The literature shows that there are several kinds of legacies that can be achieved by and for cities hosting the Olympics (Andranovich, Burbank, and Heying 2001; Engle 1999). In addition to quantifiable legacy investments, the following questions help to assess the less quantifiable long-term legacy of the Olympic Games in Atlanta:

- Did the Olympics leave behind buildings, monuments, or public spaces that have ongoing functional or iconic value?
- Did it result in traditional forms of economic impact in the near and long term?
- Did it raise the international visibility and business opportunities for the city of Atlanta and the region?

- Did it incent or influence investments to raise social capital to improve the quality of life of the city's residents?
- Did it change in the way we think about and invest in the central city?

The intent here is to analyze the actual investments in the Olympics, direct and indirect, for both the short and long term. The indirect impacts include those intended to catalyze other investments, those previously planned but accelerated by the Olympics, and those that were unforeseen.

The Run-Up to the Olympics (1990–1996)

If Atlanta won its bid to host the Olympics today rather than in 1990, the look of the games would be very close to what was actually implemented, with several improvements. The options going forward were based on both assets and challenges framing implementation choices. Atlanta's assets as a host city candidate were obvious from the start. The city was almost unmatched in accessibility: an international airport that was then the second busiest in the world, a relatively young and modern rapid rail transit system, and local freeways in good condition. The city was home to three major league teams, several colleges and universities with large facilities in the central core, and the 72,000-seat Georgia Dome that opened in 1990; much of what was needed for the Olympics was already in place. In addition, the city had already developed a robust convention and tourism infrastructure that included, at the time of its bid, several facilities able to accommodate large events and exhibitions and 1,200 hotel rooms in the downtown area.

In spite of the transformative potential of the Olympic Games, there were formidable challenges to overcome. With steady depopulation of the downtown and midtown areas during the 1970s and 1980s, many areas experienced blight. This led to the substantial demolition of buildings, many of which were vacant or converted into surface parking lots. New office and hotel complexes in Downtown created enclaves that faced inward with a full complement of amenities. The long-term result of this was the slow but steady abandonment of the pedestrian function of the street and the physical deterioration of the public environment.

In 1990 Atlanta proper had a relatively small population of 394,017 (U.S. Census Bureau 1990). Its central core was surrounded by several low-income and largely African American neighborhoods, ones that struggled with poverty, deteriorating housing stock, and a lack of public amenities. The downtown area was surrounded by a thriving metropolitan region experiencing the opposite trends of population and economic growth. By 1990 middle income and mostly white neighborhoods such as Edgewood and Candler Park saw rehabilitation efforts while the poor and mostly African American neighborhoods had yet to experience any such developments. Even more troubling was the close association with the neighborhoods surrounding Downtown that were struggling with poverty, deteriorating housing stock, and a lack of public amenities. Its central core was surrounded by several low-income neighborhoods, and all of this was surrounded by a thriving region 12 times its size, which exhibited the opposite trends of population and economic growth.

The Twin Peaks of Mount Olympus: Two Plans for the Olympic Games

In 1992 Mayor Maynard L. Jackson put forth a dual agenda for the Olympics. He described the challenge as scaling the "twin peaks of Mount Olympus": one peak was to stage a spectacular Olympics and the other was to use the Olympics to revitalize inner city Atlanta (Roughton 1991). Andrew Young, his predecessor and a pivotal agent in securing the Olympics, saw the role of host city as focusing much more on hosting a successful event (Newman 1999a). Jackson's more expansive view raised expectations for what could and should be done during the Olympic preparations and broadened the debate over what hosting the Olympic Games should mean for the city's residents (Andraovich, Burbank, and Heying 2002).

The Olympics was privately funded, and it remains the Olympic event of the past 18 years with the smallest budget. The sanctioned organization for preparing and hosting the event, the Atlanta Committee for the Olympic Games (ACOG) focused its attention and funding on the Olympic Games themselves but left public improvements needed to support it to others. The management of this dual agenda fell to two distinct entities.

The Atlanta Committee for the Olympic Games Plan: Inside the Fence

ACOG's task was to develop venues, the Olympic Village, and Centennial Olympic Park. The organization would also engage in outreach through the Cultural Olympiad. ACOG also undertook an ambitious community outreach initiative, which included neighborhood job training, employment, and youth programs related to various preparations for the Olympics. Though laudable, ACOG's goals were perhaps most striking for what they did not include. There were no significant plans to construct new facilities or to rehabilitate existing ones, structures that would become permanent parts of Atlanta and the city's tapestry of cultural amenities (Lomax 1997).

The primary sports events would be located in Downtown Atlanta and use existing sports arenas, several universities, and some new facilities. Most Olympic events were dispersed within the downtown area with transit facilities and pedestrian corridors connecting the venues. This urban area was known as the "Olympic Ring," a circle with a three-mile diameter. The plan to house the more than 9,600 athletes involved occupying the Georgia Tech campus and creating one of the largest Olympic villages by capacity, to that date. After 1996 the new housing remained to serve Georgia Tech and Georgia State University students. The Olympic Village required $241 million in new construction, jointly funded by ACOG ($47 million) and state university system revenue bonds ($194 million) paid off by future student rents.

In late 1993, ACOG proposed the construction of what would become the primary icon of the Centennial Games, Centennial Olympic Park. This park became the principal social and gathering space for visitors. The State of Georgia, through the Georgia World Congress Center, built, managed, and owned the park. Phase I of construction was completed in July 1996 at a cost of $28 million. The park contains 21 acres and supported 5.5 million visitors during the Olympics, with the peak daily attendance reaching 75,000. Phase II construction took place shortly after the Olympics and was completed in 1998 at a cost of $15 million.

As is standard, the International Olympic Committee requires that all host cities sponsor a cultural festival showcasing the local culture and arts to parallel the sporting events (Terrazas 1996). Starting in 1993, ACOG sponsored the Cultural Olympiad which culminated in the Olympic Arts Festival. This nine-week festival held all over the city but centered at the Olympic Village showcased the work of over 3,000 artists in over 200 shows, numerous exhibitions, and 19 public art displays (Terrazas 1996). In that time, over 250,000 tickets were sold to over 2.6 million attendees.

The City/Corporation for Olympic Development in Atlanta Plan: Outside the Fence

The other side of Mayor Jackson's "dual agenda" had three main components: (1) implement the six primary pedestrian corridors connecting the Metropolitan Atlanta Rapid Transit Authority (MARTA) system to the main Olympic venues; (2) supplement the Olympic agenda with needed permanent public improvements; and (3) pursue improvements to the 15 neighborhoods surrounding downtown Atlanta. To facilitate this, the city created the Corporation for Olympic Development in Atlanta (CODA) in 1993. This nonprofit corporation would be led by the co-chairs of the board, the mayor, then Maynard Jackson, and an appointed business leader. Neighborhoods affected by the construction of Olympic venues would have two seats on the board (Newman 1999a). In the fall of 1993, the CODA Master Plan was adopted and incorporated the mayor's dual agenda (Table 19.1).

The CODA Public Spaces Program included pedestrian corridors, which expanded to include 11 corridors; 8 parks and open spaces; a public arts initiative resulting in the installation of 55 works of art on 24 separate sites throughout the city; the creation of pedestrian-friendly amenities through enhanced public spaces and walkable corridors; and over

250 interpretive historical markers inside the Olympic Ring (French and Disher 1997). The CODA Neighborhood Revitalization Program involved a detailed physical survey of the nine square miles making up the 15 ring neighborhoods and the adoption of community redevelopment plans for the five innermost neighborhoods, with implementation of community initiatives as time and funding permitted.

A common assumption is that the U.S. federal government does not directly provide funds to American cities hosting the Olympics. A federal audit done by the Government Accounting Office (GAO) in 2006 for the most recent Olympic Games hosted in the U.S. showed that numerous federal agencies provided considerable support. For the Atlanta Games, the GAO identified funding across 24 federal departments totaling over $608 million, 30 percent of which was allocated to staffing and security and 70 percent to permanent capital improvements, mostly for transportation projects.

The $75 million CODA raised to implement all the projects by 1996 came primarily from the Federal Transportation Enhancement Program, the passage of a local bond referendum in 1994, and private funding of $6 million. Neighborhood improvement in the areas within and adjacent to the Olympic Ring received half of the infrastructure investment along with a modest-scale housing development totaling 1,317 new and rehabilitated units. Table 19.2 shows CODA's budget for public spaces and Table 19.3 outlines costs for the 1996 Olympics by sources of funds across major contributing entities. This includes both Olympic venues and capital improvements to prepare the city for the Olympics.

The Event and Its Immediate Impacts (1996–1998)

To maximize the benefits the city would enjoy from pre-Olympic investments and development and for metropolitan Atlanta to continue to grow as it had before the games, significant investments would have to continue. And continue they did, helping to create a solid footing for ongoing investments in the Downtown area. While investments in neighborhood revitalization were not as significant after the games, there were some gains made beyond the Olympic Ring. The clearest examples of short- and long-term investments made beyond Downtown are in the legacy sports facilities, many of which are still in use today (French and Disher 1997).

Economic Development and *Operation Legacy*

One year after the Olympic Games, a public-private partnership called Operation Legacy had generated more than 2,000 new jobs, and it had exceeded its goal of 6,000 new jobs by the end of the third year. This partnership was created by the for-profit power utility Georgia Power Company, NationsBank (now merged with Bank of America), the State of Georgia Department of Eco-

TABLE 19.1	Corporation for Olympic Development in Atlanta (CODA) Programs, Master Development Program Plan, 1993
CODA Program	
Pedestrian corridors	11.7
Neighborhood sidewalks	20.4
Parks	8
Public artworks	55
Street trees added*	2400
Street lights added	1736

*When combined with trees planted by Trees Atlanta, Inc., over10,000 street trees were added to the Olympic Ring by 1996.

Source: Data from Atlanta Committee for the Olympic Games archives

nomic Development, the Governor's Economic Development Council, and the Georgia and Atlanta Chambers of Commerce to utilize the Olympics as a marketing tool for economic development (Engle 1999).

Direct Olympic Legacy Investments

Nearly all of the Olympic venues inside the Olympic Ring were permanent investments and significantly contributed to the legacy of the Olympics (Table 19.4). The Georgia Tech campus received the $24 million Aquatic Center, a $12 million renovation of its coliseum, and substantial communications infrastructure (including 1,700 miles of fiber optic cable) in order to fulfill its role as the Olympic Village. The Atlanta University Center on the west side of the Olympic Ring is a consortium of historically African American colleges and universities (Morehouse College, Spelman College, Morris Brown College, Clark-Atlanta University, the Morehouse School of Medicine, and the Interdenominational Theological Center). ACOG made $49 million of improvements to basketball and field hockey venues on those campuses.

Long before anyone could have conceived of Atlanta as host to any major event such as the Olympics, it was endowed with a significant system of parks. The city's two most beloved parks are Piedmont Park and Grant Park, both master planned by the Olmstead Brothers in 1904 and 1912, respectively). The Olympics provided an opportunity to expand the number of parks considerably. In addition to Centennial Olympic Park's 20 acres in the center of Downtown Atlanta, Freedom Park—the largest new urban park built in the U.S. in the second half of the last century—was built in advance of the Olympics using the rights-of-way of two proposed freeways. CODA managed both the master planning process and the first phase of construc-

TABLE 19.2	CODA Public Spaces Projects		
	Funding Source (Millions of Dollars)		
Projects	Local and federal public sources	Private and foundation funds	Total budget
Pedestrian corridors	$48.845	$7,819	$ 56,664
Woodruff Park	48	5,887	5,935
Freedom Park	50	730	780
Summerhill Park and Streets	835	29	864
Neighborhood streets and sidewalks	7,167	0	7,167
Soft costs: design, management, etc.	493	3,785	4,278
TOTAL	$57,438	$17,520	$ 74,958

Source: Data from Atlanta Committee for the Olympic Games archives

TABLE 19.3	Summary of Direct Costs for the 1996 Atlanta Centennial Olympic Games (millions of dollars)			
Funding source	Federal	Local/state (including 1994 city bond referendum*)	Private (Sponsors, TV rights, tickets, corporate, foundations)	Total
ACOG (direct)				
Sports venues	$33,650		$499,080	$532.730
Other	151,350		1,021,180	1,172.470
Subtotal	$85,000		$1,520,200	$1,705,200
CODA/city				
Public spaces	$24,750	$ 32,688	$ 17,520	$74,958
Neighborhoods	15,000	42,916	29,864	87,780
Subtotal	$39,750	$75,604	$47,384	$162,738
Other (Indirect)				
GA DOT	$214,753			$213,753
MARTA	114,000			114,000
Airport		$600,000		600,000
GA Power		67,000		67,000
MAOGA		100,000		100,000
Other public	55,000			55,000
Subtotal	$383,753	$767,000		$1,150,753
TOTAL	$ 608,503	$ 842,604	$ 1,567,584	$3,018,691

Souce: Data from Atlanta Committee for the Olympic Games archives

tion, at a cost of $1 million. Woodruff Park is a small four-acre park in a very prominent location. Built in 1973 at the historic Five Points intersection, the park was completely rebuilt before the start of the Olympic Games for $6 million. Other new smaller urban parks in Downtown Atlanta developed before the Olympics include Hardy Ivy Park, Spring Walton Park, and John Wesley Dobbs Plaza in the historic Sweet Auburn district.

Downtown and Neighborhood Development

There were numerous investments, both direct and indirect, that were made in Downtown Atlanta and the neighborhoods surrounding the Olympic Ring. The Atlanta Housing Authority was awarded a HOPE VI grant in 1993 to redevelop Techwood Homes and Clark Howell Homes, located adjacent to Centennial Park and the Olympic Village. The redevelopment program was greatly expanded after the Olympics and ended in 2010. Before the Olympics, more than 3,400 sub-standard houses were demolished, 200 vacant lots were cleaned, and volunteers refurbished nearby playgrounds and painted 280 homes. Two important fundamental changes were the establishment of community development corporations in several low-income neighborhoods and the establishment of the legal and institutional infrastructure necessary to foster development in these areas.

After World War II and before 1990 very little residential development took place in downtown Atlanta. An exception was the Bedford Pine Urban Renewal Area on 78 acres adjacent to the downtown area. With the Olympics, downtown residential development began to experience a revitalization. Perhaps the greatest and most dramatic Olympic legacy is the new housing created in the central city. This often stated goal was actually made possible by the boost from the Olympics. In brief, the rental leases developers executed before the Olympics period provided equity that enabled financing to convert vacant offices into apartments. More than 500 units of housing were leveraged in time for initial occupancy during the Olympics (Patton 1999).

Other areas benefited as well but perhaps not as much as Downtown nor over the long term. The Metropolitan Atlanta Olympic Games Authority (MAOGA) was established in 1991 to represent public interests in preparation for the Olympics. MAOGA also coordinated over $18 million of projects in Summerhill, an area adjacent to the then standing Atlanta-Fulton County Stadium and future home of the Olympic Stadium (now Turner Field). These projects included permanent track and field practice fields, revitalization of 10 commercial storefronts, two primary pedestrian corridors, and Greenlea Commons, a mixed income development with 76 units.

The construction of Centennial Olympic Park helped foster development that has continually created benefits for the Downtown Atlanta area in the 18 years that have passed since the Olympic Games. The impact of the park itself is difficult to separate from the associated amenities, which included new hotels, housing, restaurants, and visitor attractions. Almost as important are some of the signature projects that might have been unthinkable before the Olympics and construction of the park, including the Georgia Aquarium, the National Center for Civil and Human Rights, and the various commercial developments connecting the city's core with its west side along Ivan Allen Boulevard. The 180-foot Skyview Atlanta Ferris Wheel opened in 2013; it faces the park and offers 15-minute rides in air-conditioned gondolas.

Permanent Supporting Investments

Many investments were made in the overall infrastructure of the region to support the Olympic Games and also to contribute to permanent long-term improvement of the city. Three of these investments together totaled nearly $1 billion. MARTA added three stations, seven miles of track, and 1,290 buses to meet the travel demand of the Olympics. During the Olympic Games, the system operated 24 hours a day, and travel was free to anyone with an event ticket. Managing this complex system required over 15,000 paid staff and 6,000 volunteers. The Georgia State Department of Transportation used federal funds to create an intelligent transportation system to manage and monitor the existing and anticipated traffic demand.

To accommodate a surge of tourists and visitors at Hartsfield Atlanta International Airport, during and after the Olympic Games, the city issued $350 million in bonds to build a dedicated international concourse that opened in 1994. This expanded capacity established Atlanta as an international transportation hub. The city also undertook a $250 million program of airport passenger improvements, including a new atrium that opened in time for the Olympics. Atlanta's airport became the world's busiest in 1998 after the Olympics and experienced 103 percent growth in international passengers, totaling 6 million annually. This created demand for an independent international terminal that opened in 2012.

The city's power infrastructure was less visible, but also needed improvements before the Olympic Games. To that end, Georgia Power invested $67 million to bring the downtown electrical grid to full capacity. Georgia Power also made direct contributions to the Olympics, such as street and venue lighting, temporary power supplies, and the initiation of the Operation Legacy economic development partnership between the company and some of the region's largest employers. Georgia Power's overall contribution in capital investments to the region was over $250 million (Vaeth 1998).

The Long-Term Legacy (1998–Present)

Long-term direct impacts generally run their course in 5 to 10 years and can be calculated by recognized formulas employing multipliers for secondary and tertiary impacts. For Atlanta, several sources have shown the overall fiscal impact to be up to $5 billion with 80,000 jobs created in the short-term and $176 million in state tax revenues (Engle 1999). These broader and longer impacts are perhaps the most important measures of the legacy of the Olympics.

To be sure, Atlanta's reputation as a magnet for talent, phenomenal population and economic growth, and a high standard of living are tied to its Olympic legacy. Much of its most impressive growth occurred immediately following the Olympic Games. In the years after the Olympics, many of the higher education institutions benefitting from direct investments on the campuses have grown in size and stature. Specifically, the construction of the dormitories that were later used by Georgia State University facilitated that institution's transition from a largely commuter school to an increasingly residential one. The university has made substantial contributions to the redevelopment of areas of downtown Atlanta immediately adjacent to its campus, including the historic Auburn Avenue area. In 2010 Georgia State University opened several new dormitories closer to its campus, which has allowed it to further develop the campus and to serve as an anchor to eastern downtown Atlanta.

The long-term legacy can be seen in many other places. Nearly all of the physical projects remain in use and many have catalyzed additional places and programs. Some of the more important include the various stadiums that were built on different college and university campuses and the Olympic Stadium, converted into Turner Field and home of the Atlanta Braves major league baseball team. In some cases, the renovations and reuse of the former Olympic venues created new life for their former hosts. The Aquatic Center of the Games was renovated in 2001 to become the Georgia Tech Campus Recreation Center, one of the most celebrated campus centers of its kind in the nation. Morehouse College's Forbes Arena served as the official venue for basketball and Spelman College served as the practice facility for tennis.

In some other cases, the venues went underutilized and now sit fallow. Morris Brown College hosted field hockey and gained a new football stadium for its part. When the college lost its accreditation in 2002, for reasons completely unrelated to its stadium or the Olympics, it lost much of its student body, closed its athletics program, and subsequently had no need, nor the resources, to maintain this large facility. The stadium was briefly used by Georgia State University for its football program, but the program since relocated to the Georgia Dome a few blocks away.

There is also lingering skepticism on how various neighborhoods in the central city were included in the gains brought by the games (Lohr 2011; Newman 1999a). Sadly, predictions that the Olympic Stadium would fall into disrepair if not paid for by ACOG or its future tenant, the Atlanta Braves baseball franchise, are being used 18 years later to justify the team's relocation from that site in 2017. On the west side of downtown in the Vine City and English Avenue communities, trust funds established to construct new housing, rehabilitate existing housing and make other community investments have failed to revitalize those areas (Dorsey 2013).

Development Reorganization

With the mandated dissolution of CODA in 1997, its mission was assumed by a "superagency," the Atlanta Development Authority (ADA, now Invest Atlanta), which consolidated five existing agencies into a single multi-purpose authority. The ADA had the capacity to take advantage of the public-private development opportunities that were part of many Olympics projects. This included the 1994 $100 million empowerment zone designation, which added 15 more neighborhoods to those under CODA. The Renaissance Policy Group, made up of public and private individuals engaged in redevelopment, made housing in the city center a priority, with a goal of building 25,000 new middle-income units in 10 years—an ambitious goal that was actually attained in 5 years.

Immediately after the Olympics, through the leadership of Central Atlanta Progress, the COPA district was established to manage development in the Centennial Olympic Park area, including Centennial Place, a high-rise residential tower near the park, and the construction of 300 residential units by 2012. CAP attributes most downtown growth to Centennial Olympic Park, the anchor for more than $1.8 billion in hotels, office buildings, and high-rise apartments. One of the most important developments since the opening of the park was the Georgia Aquarium, the world's largest aquarium at the time of its opening in 2005. The World of Coca-Cola relocated to the park from a site near the Five Points transit station and the Georgia State Capitol. These new additions to the area paved the way for the National Center for Civil and Human Rights, which will house the papers of Martin Luther King Jr. and other exhibits and events tied to human rights efforts around the world.

Conclusions

The Atlanta Olympics proved to be an event for the average American. Over 8.5 million tickets were sold, still the most for any Olympics, and unlike other Olympics where many tickets were bought but not used, Atlanta played to a near full house. Atlanta was more accessible to Americans in many ways in that the games were within a two-day drive by over half of the American population. Atlanta also stands alone in both the number of tickets sold and used. Overall, the Atlanta Olympics cost considerably less than any other in the last 50 years. Atlanta's total cost of $2.3 billion compares to $46 billion for Beijing, or 20 times the cost for Atlanta (in constant U.S. dollars).

For the Olympics, one saw the event in terms of business opportunities, and the other saw a chance to correct the socioeconomic problems accrued over many years. Thus, many stakeholders—business, civic, institutional, and community leaders—all wanted to see some version of the "dual-agenda" fulfilled. That is, have Atlanta host a very successful international event and make substantial investments and improvements to the city that were long overdue and would last well beyond the games themselves. Perhaps, many were guilty of overreaching in their expectations of what the Olympics could realistically do. The Olympics usually makes visible what realities constitute the heart and soul of a city over the long run. There is no real way to hide flaws or change a century of layered social, cultural, and architectural attitudes in six years. The Olympics is therefore more of a mirror than a window on the future.

Maybe one of the most important features of the Atlanta Olympic legacy is what each subsequent host city replicated and avoided. The London Olympics provide a good model for the process. There, the six Host Boroughs where the Olympics were staged were able to oblige the London Committee for the Olympic Games and their delivery authority to set goals for hiring local residents and for procuring local businesses to provide services. They started with a "Creating Wealth and Reducing Poverty" action plan. They followed up with a collaboration between the delivery team, their contractors, job training providers, and community representatives to broker the process and implement the plan. Over 20 percent of the Olympics construction and operations workforce were "locals," over 20 percent of procurement went to local businesses, and the process continues into the post-Games era.

The Atlanta Olympics, staged primarily on a private shoestring, cost only 13 percent of what the 2012 London Olympics did, and the city walked away with, among other things, a new baseball stadium, over 200 acres of new park land downtown, and no municipal debt. However, the most enduring Olympic legacy perhaps is that, after 15 years, all the improvements are still there. Thanks in part to the legacy of the Olympics, Downtown Atlanta is once again brimming with life.

CHAPTER 20

Rethinking Atlanta's Regional Resilience in an Age of Uncertainty: Still the Economic Engine of the South?

Jennifer Clark

Atlanta: Global City in a World Economy

One of the great challenges facing large, diverse metropolitan economies is how to build and maintain sustainable and resilient cities. For several years now, people have recognized the critical and expanding role of "global cities." Although Sassen's initial conceptualization focused on leading financial centers—London, New York, and Tokyo—the notion has developed to encompass broader ideas about how diverse metropolitan economies serve as regional nodes in a global network (Sassen 2001). These global cities serve as the engines behind national and regional economic growth. Increasingly, academics and policy advocates have argued that global cities constitute the most important interconnected network of economic, cultural, and social ties and relationships—a network far more critical to understanding and engaging the economic challenges of the twenty-first century than the national boundaries that set the stage in the nineteenth and twentieth centuries (Christopherson and Clark 2007; Storper 1997).

Cities, however, are inherently complex and unique. And in that complexity lies much of their resilience. In fact, Atlanta itself holds onto the formal Latin motto, *resurgens*, meaning "rising again." Amid the renewed interest among planners, policy makers, and academics in modeling the resilience of urban and regional economies, both as environmental systems and as economic entities, Atlanta is a case of some interest. Indeed, Atlanta is a city with experience adapting and responding to economic transformation and social change. Atlanta is a dynamic place with diverse communities; the regional economy has become more demographically diverse over the last several decades. The simultaneity of Atlanta's economic and social transformation recalls its informal motto, "a city too busy too hate." In other words, growth or "rising again" trumps everything else.

Any discussion of economic development in Atlanta carries with it a question about distributional equity. The city has a long history of spatial segregation (Bayor 1996; Keating 2001a). Historically, the urban growth machine approach documented by political scientists and urban economists dominated strategy in Atlanta as elsewhere (Dreier, Mollenkopf, and Swanstrom 2001; Mollenkopf 1983). However, that emphasis on growing the pie and postponing the question of how it is divided has left a legacy of uneven development in Atlanta's neighborhoods just as it has elsewhere. Recent economic development polices and projects send mix signals about the whether the Atlanta region has become a leader in best practices or one of the last major metropolitan areas to successfully shift to a sustainable approach to regional economic development that integrates both community and economic development priorities (Clark and Christopherson 2009).

Dual Identity: Atlanta's Legacy as Regional Growth Machine

In many ways, Atlanta remains a tale of two economic development models: the twentieth century urban growth machine and the twenty-first century high-road, high-tech strategic approach to regional innovation and development. At present, both models exist in tandem, with the first dominating implementation and the second dominating the rhetoric.

Since 1960 Atlanta served as the economic growth engine for the metropolitan area and for the greater southeast. Much has been said about the growth of Atlanta from a regional hub competing with places like Birmingham, Alabama, for business and prestige to its present status as ninth largest metropolitan area in the U.S. From Mayor Ivan Allen's leadership through the 1960s to the successful bid for and later hosting of the 1996 Olympics, the civic and business communities have maintained a focus on economic development (Allen and Hemphill 1971; Keating 2001a).

The confluence of population growth and real estate development fueled an economic model based on expansion and consumption and resulted in the emergent global city that Atlanta is today. In this period, there was little focus on "smart growth" from either an environmental or economic perspective. Simply put, there is no need to grow smart when you can just grow big. This singular focus on growing the pie overshadowed efforts by neighborhood and community advocates to rethink how to divide it. In the wake of the global recession, however, the cracks in this growth model are beginning to show in Atlanta as they are in cities with a similar approach.

For example, the state of Georgia's per capita personal income ranked 40th of 50 states in 2012 at $36,869 compared to the U.S. average of

$42,693.[1] In February of 2013, Georgia's unemployment rate remained at 8.6 percent, higher than the national average of 7.7 percent.[2] In the Atlanta region, the unemployment rate of 8.7 percent in January 2013 ranked it 219th among 372 metropolitan statistical areas.[3] However, the region's gross domestic product ranked it 10th among metropolitan statistical areas, with a 2011 growth rate of 2.2 percent.[4]

In addition, Georgia and the Atlanta region have struggled with K-12 educational attainment, which is a crucial factor in workforce development and up-skilling the labor market. The decade of the 2000s appeared to produce steady gains in high school graduation rates. However, in 2012 the required adoption of a more rigorous federal standard for measuring a "graduate" dropped the state's graduation rate from 80.9 percent to 67.4 percent. School districts in the Atlanta region reported dramatic declines in actual graduation rates after the adoption of the federal formula. For example, suburban Clayton County's graduation rate fell from over 80 percent to 51.5 percent. The Atlanta Public Schools were also forced to report a 52 percent graduation rate rather than the 69.5 percent previously reported.[5]

The *Atlanta Journal Constitution* reported on the story: "'They spent more time trying to fix the numbers, than they did trying to fix the problem,' said Cathy Henson, an advocate for education reform and former state Board of Education chair. 'My frustration is that if you're giving people phony data, then they don't understand the magnitude, the urgency of the problem'"(Badertscher and Guckian 2012).

These sobering statistics are a stark juxtaposition when compared to the news highlighted by the civic and business community. Invest Atlanta, the city's economic development agency, and the Metro Atlanta Chamber routinely tout Atlanta's high rankings in publications like *Forbes.com*, *Kiplinger's*, and *Site Selection* magazine for categories such as "Top State Business Climate Rankings" and "Best States for Business."[6] And indeed, the region has significant economic assets. The Atlanta airport ranks number one in passenger volume in the United States. The region features a large college and university student population, estimated at 175,000 full-time students, with flagship institutions such as the Georgia Institute of Technology, Emory University, Georgia State University, Morehouse and Spelman Colleges, and Clark Atlanta University, establishing a core of universities with an international reputation for research and teaching.[7] The Atlanta region is also a magnet for new immigrants.

Despite the presence of these assets, observers have begun to question whether Atlanta has built the resilient economic base required to plot a more sustainable and equitable path towards prosperity. The stubborn unemployment rates, low per capita personal income rankings, high poverty rates, and persistently low high school graduation rate all point to uneven development rather than a sustainable economy. Although such unevenness in global cities is certainly not unique to Atlanta, the region does provide an unusually instructive example of the challenges of economic development practice in the new service-based, "knowledge" economy (Clark 2013; Mollenkopf and Castells 1991).

Defining a Diversified Metropolitan Economy: Industries and Occupations

Describing the regional economy in Atlanta can be a challenge. Unlike some regions of similar size with distinct specializations, such as Detroit and the auto industry or Houston and the energy industry, Atlanta is highly diversified. As a consequence, Atlanta lacks an industrial branding narrative and instead attempts to define itself in cultural and economic terms that are self-consciously dehistoricized. Civic leaders and economic development professionals struggle to define established and emerging clusters of specialization by identifying dominant industries or occupational groups. This uncertainty about the region's defining economic characteristics opens the door for uncertain and nonspecific branding narratives around current hot topics like the "creative class" or amorous advantages such as "business friendly."

In fact, Atlanta fits the model of a large, diversified metropolitan service economy rather than that of a specialized production region with clear export-oriented industry clusters. As one of the largest metropolitan areas in the United States, data on the economy of the Atlanta area are readily available.[8] These data indicate that emerging from the global recession has not been a straightforward process for the region. Total nonfarm employment stood at more than 2.3 million in November 2012,[9] but the unemployment rate remains more than half a percentage point higher than the national average. In November of 2012, the U.S. Bureau of Labor Statistics reported a year-over-year 1.5 percent increase in jobs for the region, placing Atlanta one tenth of a percentage point ahead of the U.S. as a whole but squarely in the middle of its peer group of the 12 largest metropolitan areas. In-migration, both domestic and international, are key elements of Atlanta's growth over the past two decades. The recession and high unemployment have discouraged in-migration since 2010. Whether that drop will dramatically affect the trend lines going forward is a matter of some debate among experts.

The current occupational profile of Atlanta reflects its unusually diversified economy (BLS Southeast Regional Office 2012). Recent employment trends during the 2011–2012 period underscore this reality. The industry supersectors recording the largest employment gains during that period included professional and business services; trade, transportation, and utilities; leisure and hospitality; and education and health services. Declines in employment continued in the government sector, and this was in line with the direction of national trends in public sector employment, although Atlanta's declines were almost a full percentage point higher. Notably, manufacturing in the region

TABLE 20.1.	Atlanta-Sandy Springs-Marietta, Georgia Metropolitan Statistical Area Occupational Employment and Wage Estimates, May 2012[10]			
Occupation code	Occupation title	Employment	Location quotient	Median hourly wage
25-2023	Career/Technical Education Teachers, Middle School	4,090	12.74	NA
53-2011	Airline Pilots, Copilots, and Flight Engineers	7,150	6.21	NA
53-2031	Flight Attendants	8,310	5.63	NA
43-9111	Statistical Assistants	930	3.61	$11.90
29-1199	Health Diagnosing and Treating Practitioners, All Other	1,830	3.45	$46.59
27-1026	Merchandise Displayers and Window Trimmers	4,390	3.44	$12.11
53-2022	Airfield Operations Specialists	350	2.88	$25.30
13-1032	Insurance Appraisers, Auto Damage	570	2.77	$32.10
41-9021	Real Estate Brokers	1,730	2.68	$31.78
53-6051	Transportation Inspectors	1,120	2.66	$31.43
27-1019	Artists and Related Workers, All Other	310	2.64	$42.47
51-6064	Textile Winding, Twisting, and Drawing Out Machine Setters, Operators, and Tenders	1,170	2.46	$15.45
51-9083	Ophthalmic Laboratory Technicians	1,250	2.45	$12.25
49-3011	Aircraft Mechanics and Service Technicians	5,000	2.42	NA
21-1091	Health Educators	2,260	2.35	$38.02
17-2021	Agricultural Engineers	100	2.35	$50.38
43-9011	Computer Operators	2,910	2.34	$16.63
13-1111	Management Analysts	21,540	2.3	$37.71
53-2021	Air Traffic Controllers	880	2.19	$69.43
41-9022	Real Estate Sales Agents	6,000	2.13	$20.69
51-6091	Extruding and Forming Machine Setters, Operators, and Tenders, Synthetic and Glass Fibers	640	2.09	$18.28
13-2053	Insurance Underwriters	3,340	2.09	$30.53
43-5041	Meter Readers, Utilities	1,390	2.03	$14.57
49-2021	Radio, Cellular, and Tower Equipment Installers and Repairers	530	1.92	$14.04
27-1027	Set and Exhibit Designers	280	1.89	$18.37
27-1025	Interior Designers	1,330	1.88	$21.83
13-2041	Credit Analysts	2,000	1.88	$28.53
49-9052	Telecommunications Line Installers and Repairers	4,320	1.87	$16.22
51-6061	Textile Bleaching and Dyeing Machine Operators and Tenders	360	1.85	$15.70

TABLE 20.1.	Atlanta-Sandy Springs-Marietta, Georgia Metropolitan Statistical Area Occupational Employment and Wage Estimates, May 2012[10]			
Occupation code	Occupation title	Employment	Location quotient	Median hourly wage
19-1022	Microbiologists	600	1.85	$39.17
17-3025	Environmental Engineering Technicians	600	1.84	$18.01
43-4199	Information and Record Clerks, All Other	5,670	1.83	$16.76
11-3011	Administrative Services Managers	8,250	1.8	$39.94
41-3011	Advertising Sales Agents	4,520	1.79	$22.24
51-6063	Textile Knitting and Weaving Machine Setters, Operators, and Tenders	650	1.78	$15.39
13-2061	Financial Examiners	870	1.78	$40.32
39-4011	Embalmers	150	1.76	$20.17
33-3011	Bailiffs	500	1.76	$9.81
53-1011	Aircraft Cargo Handling Supervisors	200	1.74	$25.63
15-1131	Computer Programmers	9,520	1.73	$37.94
49-2022	Telecommunications Equipment Installers and Repairers, Except Line Installers	6,230	1.72	$27.47
29-2012	Medical and Clinical Laboratory Technicians	4,680	1.71	$16.75
27-4011	Audio and Video Equipment Technicians	1,600	1.69	$19.30
49-2091	Avionics Technicians	490	1.68	$28.07
49-2011	Computer, Automated Teller, and Office Machine Repairers	3,280	1.67	$19.27
47-3013	Helpers–Electricians	1,720	1.67	$12.78
23-1021	Administrative Law Judges, Adjudicators, and Hearing Officers	410	1.67	$22.41
11-1011	Chief Executives	7,390	1.66	NA
25-2053	Special Education Teachers, Middle School	2,760	1.65	NA
41-4012	Sales Representatives, Wholesale and Manufacturing, Except Technical and Scientific Products	40,200	1.64	$26.13
13-2082	Tax Preparers	1,730	1.63	$22.13
29-2054	Respiratory Therapy Technicians	380	1.62	$21.94
15-1151	Computer User Support Specialists	14,740	1.62	$22.24
37-2021	Pest Control Workers	1,710	1.61	$12.53
15-1141	Database Administrators	3,130	1.61	$40.84
13-2081	Tax Examiners and Collectors, and Revenue Agents	1,830	1.61	$22.73
51-9195	Molders, Shapers, and Casters, Except Metal and Plastic	850	1.58	$11.56
43-4051	Customer Service Representatives	62,910	1.58	$16.25
17-2111	Health and Safety Engineers, Except Mining Safety Engineers and Inspectors	640	1.57	$35.01

TABLE 20.1.	Atlanta-Sandy Springs-Marietta, Georgia Metropolitan Statistical Area Occupational Employment and Wage Estimates, May 2012[10]			
Occupation code	Occupation title	Employment	Location quotient	Median hourly wage
44-9919	Training and Development Managers	750	1.57	$47.27
42-8005	Transportation, Storage, and Distribution Managers	2,690	1.57	$38.17
44-866	Sales Managers	9,400	1.57	$56.44
35-2015	Cooks, Short Order	4,400	1.56	$8.90
27-1014	Multimedia Artists and Animators	790	1.55	$25.22
40-9743	Computer and Information Systems Managers	8,330	1.55	$57.85
47-3016	Helpers–Roofers	330	1.54	$11.33
25-3021	Self-Enrichment Education Teachers	4,780	1.53	$15.59
23-2011	Paralegals and Legal Assistants	7,010	1.51	$23.45
19-3091	Anthropologists and Archeologists	160	1.5	$38.26
00-0000	All Occupations	2,261,690	1	$17.02

Source: Data from U.S. Bureau of Labor Statistics 2012

grew at an anemic 0.1 percent deviating from the recent resurgence in this sector nationally (at 1.1 percent for the period) after a period of steady declines (BLS Southeast Information Office 2013a).

A closer look at the occupational concentrations in the region highlights the importance of both professional services and other services (health, leisure, and hospitality) to the overall employment profile. The Bureau of Labor Statistics reports unusually high concentrations of employment in a series of professional service occupations and transportation occupations. Table 20.1 includes all the occupations reporting location quotients over 1.5 for the region, indicating a potential specialization in these areas. Many of the transportation occupations listed involve the airport and air traffic system (pilots, flight attendants, aircraft repair). This is consistent with the presence of Hartsfield-Jackson Atlanta International Airport.

Also notable among the highly concentrated occupations is the high number of employees in categories such as "customer service representatives" (62,000 employees at $16.25 an hour) and "sales representatives" (40,000 employees at $26.13 an hour). In fact, many of these occupations appear to be related to customer service, computers, telecommunications, and general office services. This is consistent with the growing emphasis in the region on professional and administrative services as an occupational category rather than a specialized export sector.

This diversified, service-based economy complicates efforts by regional stakeholders to characterize the Atlanta regional economy and target export-oriented economic development. The growing recognition of this reality has motivated some civic leaders to take a closer look at the employment dynamics in the region and where best to focus economic development investments. One recent effort to recognize the role and the contributions of workers who fall outside of the high-tech story about innovation and exports is the research of The Essential Economy Council. The first report issued by the group in February 2013 demonstrated that the occupational cluster—represented by the workers in Georgia's tourism industry in urban areas and agricultural industry in rural areas—constitutes 25 percent of Georgia's total employment. This proportion stays fairly consistent from county to county, underscoring the argument that this workforce is an essential part of the labor market (Essential Economy Council 2013). In the metro Atlanta area, the core urban county of Fulton counted 21.9 percent of its workforce in the essential economy whereas the suburban county of Forsyth counted 27.1 percent of its workers in this category.[11]

Uneven Transformations:
Twenty-First Century Urban Entrepreneurialism

In Atlanta, as elsewhere, real estate development is a core function of economic development planning and practice. In many ways, Atlanta and its surrounding jurisdictions continue to use a real-estate-based approach to economic development rather than production-based one. In the wake of the global recession, however, the city of Atlanta has begun to carve out alternative approaches to this practice that fit in line with the best practices seen in other global cities. Consequently, economic development strategies in the region simultaneously reflect an entrenched path of dependency alongside an emerging capacity for urban innovation. Recent projects that serve to illustrate these contrasts: 1) the Atlanta BeltLine project; 2) the redevelopment of a former Sears distribution center into a municipal facility, City Hall East, and now into Ponce City Market; 3) the new stadium for the Atlanta Falcons National Football League (NFL) team; and 4) the role of major institutional actors (Georgia Institute of Technology, Georgia State University, and the Midtown Alliance) in the development and redevelopment of midtown and downtown neighborhoods, notably the Tech Square and "innovation district" partnerships.

The collapse of real estate prices during the recession hit Atlanta's residential and commercial markets particularly hard. In fact, Atlanta has often ranked at the top of lists of home foreclosures and outstanding mortgages that exceed the current value of homes ("underwater" homes). The housing collapse came at a time when Atlanta's intown neighborhoods were systematically gentrifying, particularly on the east side. This process brought new property tax revenues to the city and provided a tax base able to share the burden of large and necessary infrastructure projects such as a major storm sewer and sewer project. This developing tax base presented an opportunity for new financial stability in the city after the effects of suburbanization undermined the residential tax base, thus making reinvestment projects difficult to finance. It was during the apex of this process that the city endorsed the Atlanta BeltLine plan, the first example of Atlanta's recent real estate approach to economic development (Dewan 2006).

The Atlanta BeltLine is one of a set of urban redevelopment projects—similar to the High Line in New York City—that convert unused or underused rail beds into "linear" parks (Brown 2013). In the U.S., these projects are the evolution of the "rails-to-trails" projects popularized by federal transportation funding in the 1990s. Sometimes the projects are consistent with "daylighting" stream restoration projects, such as the Cheonggyecheon River Project in Seoul, or other highway removal plans. In the case of the Atlanta BeltLine, potential has long existed for a transit component formed around a network of linked parks ringing the city and connecting neighborhoods that are currently difficult to navigate via the existing road network. Generally these projects incorporate multimodal transportation systems with increased park space in central cities and intown residential areas. They are explicitly cast as urban sustainability projects that use urban design approaches to rationalize the connections between outmoded transportation systems and emerging "live-work-play" environment promoted in "back-to-the-city" movements across the U.S.

The second example of Atlanta's current real estate approach to economic development is the development of Ponce City Market, located adjacent to the Eastside Trail of the Atlanta BeltLine. According to its developer, Ponce City Market is the largest adaptive reuse project in Atlanta's history. As in several cities, Atlanta's Sears, Roebuck & Company distribution center once occupied a superblock in a neighborhood adjacent to downtown (Severson 2012).[12] After the distribution center shut down in the 1980s, the inactivity of the block created serious urban deterioration issues. The city of Atlanta bought the building from Sears in the early 1990s and attempted to use it as City Hall East (Risley, 1991). That effort never effectively occupied the space or stabilized the area.

Many cities have faced similar issues with large commercial and industrial buildings. The City Hall East case in Atlanta parallels the situation in Minneapolis where a block on Lake Street in the Powderhorn Park and Phillips neighborhoods of southeast Minneapolis was similarly occupied by a decommissioned Sears distribution center. The redevelopment process of that Sears into Midtown Global Market skipped the intervening step as a public services building. The plan to redevelop the building was initiated by community and neighborhood groups and opened in 2006.

In the Atlanta case, the city was able to sell City Hall East to a private developer, Jamestown Properties, to develop the Ponce City Market plan only after the Atlanta BeltLine's eastern portion and connecting Historic Fourth Ward Park were well underway (Brown 2011a). In part this had to do with drainage challenges of the building that limited its commercial marketability without mitigating the negative externalities generated by factors offsite. Thankfully, the construction of the park resolved those challenges. Jamestown Properties also developed Chelsea Market in New York City as well as the White Provisions property in Atlanta on the west side near the site of what is now the Atlantic Station development, formerly a steel mill that shut down in 1998 (Chamberlain 2006).

More broadly, the distinction between the Ponce City Market and the Midtown Global Market cases is the difference between public-private partnerships in redevelopment and the public subsidization of private projects. It is the tendency in Atlanta's economic development history for private money to follow public money rather than partner with it. In cases such as the High Line in New York City or the Midtown Global Market in Minneapolis, community and neighborhood-based organizations initiated projects that developed into formal partnerships with public and private sector entities as co-investors in showcase urban redevelopment projects. In the Atlanta case, the city has made initial investments that then create a comfort zone for private investment. This limits the ability of private and public actors to work as co-investors and develop the collaborative capacities and shared returns on investments for neighborhoods and communities as seen in other regions. No project highlights this challenge in Atlanta more than the recent decision to build a new NFL stadium.

The public financing of sports stadiums housing privately owned professional franchises has been an urban development issue for decades. In 2013 Atlanta's NFL team, the Atlanta Falcons, successfully convinced the City of Atlanta to finance about a third of the costs of a new stadium (estimated at more than $200 million) in downtown Atlanta on approximately the same site as its current 22-year-old stadium, in spite of broad public opposition (Tierney 2012). The negotiations involved several public authorities, including the Georgia World Congress Center (GWCC) and Atlanta's economic development arm, Invest Atlanta. In the end, the factors that motivated the city council and Mayor Kasim Reed to accept public financing were essentially the same as in all such publicly financed stadium deals: 1) the threat of relocation of the franchise and 2) the promise of increased tourism by the presence of a franchise associated with the city itself.

In the Atlanta case, the redevelopment of the new site for a new stadium is complicated by the legacy of the existing site at the edge of downtown Atlanta. That site encroached on the adjacent, historically African American neighborhoods, cutting them off from access to downtown and overwhelming the area with a civic building sitting in a sea of infrastructure and parking lots that are only intermittently active on game and event days. The disinvestment in these neighborhoods over the previous period is only highlighted by the recent proposals by the new stadium developers (the GWCC and the Atlanta Falcons) to expand the site by buying out two African American churches in the neighborhood. Two of Atlanta's elite, the historically African American colleges Morehouse and Spelman, were founded in one of the churches at risk, Friendship Baptist (Severson 2013).

Finally, the role of Georgia Tech in the redevelopment of midtown Atlanta and Georgia State University in downtown Atlanta, parallels the emerging role of urban universities as real estate redevelopers as seen across the U.S. (Etienne 2012). In recent years, Georgia Tech embarked upon the development of the Tech Square area in midtown, which expanded the campus across the 5th Street Bridge and the Interstate 75/85 highway corridor, creating a commercial anchor between downtown and midtown Atlanta with office space, restaurants, a hotel, and conference center. In 2013 the Midtown Alliance and Georgia Tech announced a partnership to establish an "innovation district" emanating from the implementation of Tech Square. These expanded economic development activities challenge universities, especially public universities, in a time of public budget cuts, to take on new responsibilities and new risks with limited support from the localities that directly benefit from their strategic engagement in the built environment (Christopherson and Clark 2010; Clark 2013; O'Mara 2005).

The contrasts between these three major projects—the Atlanta BeltLine, the Ponce City Market, and the Atlanta Falcon's new stadium—highlight the choices facing Atlanta as it navigates its own, distinctive twenty-first century approach to economic development and redevelopment. The projects underscore the tendency in Atlanta to embrace simultaneously the new models of neighborhood development of global cities like New York and Seoul alongside traditional practices more reminiscent of the 1980s and 1990s. The result is a two-track public approach to urban redevelopment that mixes high-road and low-road strategies to public investment in real estate.

Conclusions: Regional Resilience through Innovation and Production

In conclusion, Atlanta faces two major challenges to its broader economic growth and regional resilience: 1) persistently fragmented governance and 2) a bifurcated labor market. In both cases, these challenges have been exacerbated by recent policy choices and a narrow approach to regional economic development and the institutional infrastructure investments required to build resilient regions: education, infrastructure, and collaborative civic institutions.

The data show a complex mix of good news and red flags for a region that has grown enormously in size and scale but remains committed to entrenched institutional models from an earlier era. In a 23-country metropolitan area with a central city spanning two core counties, people continue to perceive city-country coordination between Atlanta and Fulton County as a remarkable level of civic cooperation. Such persistent metropolitan fragmentation puts Atlanta in a class of Sunbelt boomtowns and troubled Rustbelt cities known for their inability to collectively and strategically address real estate bubbles, sprawl, and urban disinvestment. According to Atlanta's civic leaders, however, the region would rather be counted among its peer group high-tech cities associated with the creative class, such as Austin, Portland, San Francisco, Seattle, Portland, Minneapolis-St. Paul, and Boston (Bluestein 2012). Notably, these are all regions in which significant progress has been made towards regional governance and cooperation. These cities have also prioritized economic development investments that improve the quality of life for residents and not just cater to tourists and convention attendees.

Purely technical solutions to urban challenges rarely measure up to the promises of their advocates. The diffusion of urban innovations in policy and planning requires adaption to local contexts and communities. Each city has its own unique quirks and its own embedded set of norms and values—its own peculiar way of getting things done. In this sense, Atlanta is no different from its peers. Whether the challenge is developing new financial models for infrastructure investment (as in Chicago), figuring out how to deploy public transit in low-density environments (as in Denver), or finding ways to reinvest in neighborhoods and communities overlooked or underappreciated by previous generations, it takes diverse stakeholders within and across cities collaborating on innovative solutions to a wide array of interdisciplinary challenges. For Atlanta, the time has come to "grow smart"; perhaps the first step in that direction should be aimed at building dialogue, fostering relationships, and sharing knowledge about what works and—equally—what does not.

CHAPTER 21

Economic Development: From Porsche to Tyler Perry

Elisabeth Kulinski

PRACTITIONER PERSPECTIVE

Attracting Porsche

Georgia has certainly experienced a period of growth, evident from a number of major economic development "wins" over the last several years. In May 2011, Porsche Cars North America unveiled a new headquarters facility to be located near Hartsfield-Jackson Atlanta International Airport on the south side of Atlanta. The carmaker has committed to invest $100 million in the new facility, touting a high-test road track and a Porsche enthusiast museum (Karkaria 2011). In early 2012, both Caterpillar and Baxter Pharmaceuticals announced the development of new manufacturing and headquarters facilities just outside of Atlanta; each facility would provide more than 1,500 new jobs and hundreds of millions of dollars in investments (Sinderman 2013). Much of this growth and expansion can be attributed to the state's overall low tax rates, business-friendly environment, and high quality of life. However, Georgia's attractiveness has markedly increased over the last decade in response to the development of a competitive portfolio of tax credits created to directly encourage new job creation and investment.

Georgia's largest tax credit program, the Job Tax Credit Program, provides state corporate income tax credits to businesses within targeted industry sectors that create a minimum number of net new jobs within the state. Credits are valued from $750 to $3,500 net per new job, per year and are available for up to five years, as long as the jobs are maintained (Table 21.1).[1]

The amount of the tax credit is determined by a county tier system in which Georgia's 159 counties are ranked and tiered by economic vitality; Tier 1 counties are the least developed whereas Tier 4 counties are considered highly

TABLE 21.1.	State of Georgia Job Tax Credit Program, 2013		
Tier	Job Tax Credit	Joint Development Authority bonus	Job creation requirement
1	$3,500	$500	2
2	$2,500	$500	10
3	$1,250	$500	15
4	$750	$500	25
Military zone/opportunity zone	$3,500	n/a	2
Less developed census tracts	$3,500	n/a	5

Source: Data from Georgia Department of Economic Development 2013

developed. Minimum job creation requirements are also tiered. Businesses must meet a tier's minimum job creation requirement within a 12-month period to trigger the credits. Qualified businesses locating to counties that are part of a Joint Development Authority are entitled to a $500 bonus per new job.[2] Qualified businesses creating at least five net new jobs within one of the state's Less Developed Census Tracts may qualify those jobs for credits equal to locating to a Tier 1 county, regardless of which county the business is located within. Any business, including retail businesses, creating at least two net new jobs within a designated Military Zone or Opportunity Zone may also qualify those jobs under Tier 1 status.

The state categorizes its targeted industry sectors to include manufacturing, warehousing and distribution, processing, telecommunications, broadcasting, tourism, research and development industries, biomedical manufacturing, services for the elderly and persons with disabilities, and manufacturing of alternative energy products for use in solar, wind, battery, bioenergy, biofuel, and electric vehicle enterprises.[3] As an incentive for businesses to utilize a Georgia port, the state provides an additional bonus credit of $1,250 per net new job, each year for up to five years, to businesses that increase their port usage by more than 10 percent over the previous year or base year. Base year port traffic must be a least 75 net tons, five containers, or 10 twenty-foot equivalent units.[4]

Georgia offers enhanced credits to companies that create jobs paying above the stated average wage within the county in which the job is located. The Quality Jobs Tax Credit Program provides companies that create a minimum of 50 net new high-paying jobs in a 12-month period a credit that ranges from $2,500 to $5,000 per job, per year for up to five years, regardless of county tier. The jobs must pay more than 110 percent of the county average wage to qualify (Table 21.2).[5]

TABLE 21.2.	State of Georgia Quality Jobs Tax Credit Program, 2013
Average Wage (% above county average)	**Quality Job Tax Credit**
>110% and <120%	$2,500
>120% and <150%	$3,000
>150% and <175%	$4,000
>175% and <200%	$4,500
>200%	$5,000

Source: Data from Georgia Department of Economic Development 2013

Attracting Vampires and Ron Burgundy

In recent years, Georgia has become a magnet for the production of major film and television projects. The films *Gone with the Wind* and *Dukes of Hazard* seem long ago; Georgia's film industry resurgence is expanding. In 2013 Downtown Atlanta was transformed for three weeks into 1980s New York City for *Anchorman 2: The Legend Continues*, while small towns around Georgia have become tourist destinations for zombie hunters and vampire lovers (the CW Television Network's *Vampire Diaries* and AMC's *The Walking Dead* are filmed north of Atlanta in Covington and Grantville).

Not only attracting on-location filming, Georgia has also seen the growth of several large film studios in the last several years. Tyler Perry Studios, located in southwest Atlanta, has produced more than 16 movies and 5 television shows since 2008 and is expecting a huge expansion (Trubey 2013). Four additional major studio construction projects have been announced in the last year. The resurgence of both on-location and studio filming is credited to the state's temperate climate, ease of travel through Hartsfield-Jackson International Airport, and the favorable tax climate for film productions (Longwell 2013).

Enacted in 2009, Georgia's Entertainment Industry Investment Act provides a flat tax credit of 20 percent of qualified production or post-production expenditures for projects that spend more than $500,000 in the state. Productions may earn a bonus 10 percent credit for adding the Georgia promotional logo to production credits. The tax credit is available to television, film, music, gaming, and digital media productions throughout the state.[6]

The impacts of these economic development efforts are substantial. Due in part to Porsche, Baxter, and Caterpillar's projects, the state saw the creation of 29,176 new jobs and almost $6 billion in capital investment through headquarters and other targeted industry growth in 2012. And thanks to the Tyler Perrys, vampires, and Ron Burgundys of the world, in fiscal year 2012 the state saw the production of more than 333 film and television projects, employing more than 25,000 Georgia residents and generating over $3.1 billion in economic impact (Grillo 2013).[7] If the state continues to extend its strong business attraction offerings, Georgia will ride this momentum into a very strong economic future.

CHAPTER 22

After the Crash: Foreclosures, Neighborhood Stability, and Change

Michael Carnathan

Atlanta has a long history of being a pioneer in the field of housing, for better or worse. In 1935 it became home to the first public housing project in the nation, Techwood Homes, located between Georgia Tech and Downtown Atlanta. Built for low-income whites, Techwood Homes was a truly progressive project during a time when many Americans lacked basic shelter. Several decades later, Atlanta initiated one of the nation's most aggressive programs to tear down public housing projects, also considered to be a pioneering effort to combat concentrated poverty. Between 1995 and 2005, metropolitan Atlanta led the nation in the annual number of residential building permits. Later, it was one of the national leaders in mortgage fraud, foreclosure filings, and bank-owned properties. A storied history indeed.

Atlanta's eventual place in history, however, has largely been written during the past two decades. Since hosting the Olympics in 1996, Atlanta has experienced explosive growth, one of only three metropolitan areas to add more than a million new residents during the 2000s. The vast majority of this growth occurred in suburbia, earning Atlanta the epithet of "Sprawl City" (Bullard 2000). The suburban style of homes—mostly single-family dwellings on relatively large lots—dominated the building landscape, although the city of Atlanta also underwent a housing renaissance.

Atlanta attracted new residents from all over the nation, particularly from areas with overheated housing markets—coastal cities and Sun Belt boomtowns. The fact that jobs were plentiful helped the in-migration. In fact, Atlanta's home-building binge kept prices low, so Atlanta never experienced a bubble of the magnitude in other metropolitan areas. One thought among industry experts at the time was that Atlanta was immune to a housing bubble because of the relative stability of home prices. Despite avoiding the excessive appreciation seen in places like Las Vegas, Phoenix, Miami, and New York, home prices in Atlanta took a beating nonetheless; prices are 23 percent below their 2007 and, within the past year, they have risen above 2000 levels. Most other markets have been at 2000 levels for a couple of years.

In an economy that is renowned for its diverse base, Atlanta's growth was too reliant on growth itself. The construction and real estate industries represented an outsized slice of Atlanta's economic expansion. When the housing bubble popped and dragged the economy down, Atlanta's economic engine stalled. In-migration stopped because, first, people in California, Florida, New York, and other northeastern states could no longer sell their houses, and these were the main feeder states to metropolitan Atlanta. In addition, the job market dried up, further restricting migration because people had no impetus to move to the area. Thus, many recent homebuyers who bought at the height of the market were stuck with loans that had unfavorable terms in a down market, and later when jobs began disappearing at dizzying rates, people could no longer afford their homes, regardless of the loan product. Metropolitan Atlanta was also among the national leaders in bank repossessions. The Urban Institute dubbed this vexing situation of declining home prices and rising unemployment "double trouble"—Atlanta was the only metropolitan area in the Southeast, outside of Florida, to be classified as such in 2010.

The situation, however, has improved lately. Home prices have risen 15 percent since the beginning of 2013 (Standard & Poor's 2013), due in part to large investment companies buying up thousands of houses at lower-than-market rates, thus reducing the glut of housing and stabilizing prices—at least temporarily. The number of foreclosure filings also continues to drop, and employment continues to rise. More residents are eschewing suburbia and moving back into more urban, walkable environments. Atlanta still has not regained its glory, and the heady days of the decade following the Olympics seem like a fuzzy memory that is well out of sight, if not entirely out of mind.

We Built It, and They Came

The 1990s provided a confluence of events that ultimately led to Atlanta becoming the fastest-growing metropolitan area in the nation, at least for awhile. In September 1990, when the International Olympic Committee announced that Atlanta would host the 1996 Olympics, city and regional leaders began unparalleled efforts to upgrade Atlanta to an "international city," a challenge Mayor Andrew Young had put forth years earlier. At the same time, the Hope VI Program, a U.S. Department of Housing and Urban Development (HUD) plan to transform public housing projects into mixed income communities, took

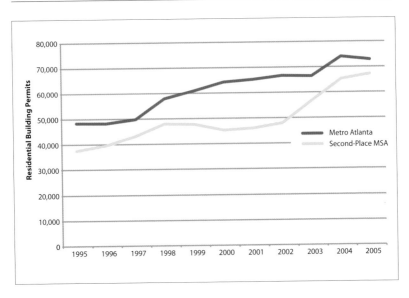

Figure 22.1. *Residential building permits, 1995–2005 for metro Atlanta and the "second place" metropolitan statistical area (MSA) (above). Figure 22.2. Residential building permits, 2006–2011 for metro Atlanta and the "first place" MSA (below). Metro Atlanta led the nation in residential building permits each year between 1995 and 2005, often by rather large margins, when compared to the second-place metropolitan area (a rank that switched among Phoenix, Houston and New York). When the housing market turned sour in 2007, the drop in permitting activity was particularly large in Atlanta. (Source: Data from U.S. Department of Housing and Urban Development 2013b.)*

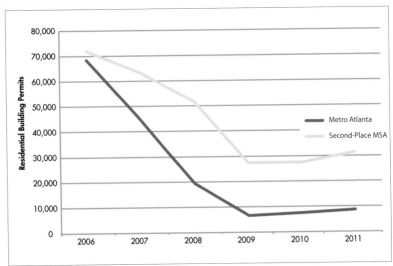

center stage in the city's revitalization efforts. There are wide-ranging debates about the efficacy and the implications of the Olympic Legacy Program that are beyond the scope of this chapter (Newman 2002). One lasting legacy, however, was that it became fashionable to build within the city again.

As regional leaders excitedly prepared to host the Olympics, the national and local economies improved dramatically, and metropolitan Atlanta was a national leader in job creation in the 1990s second only to Dallas, Texas.[1] Because of improving economic conditions and the national and international buzz Atlanta generated, new residential construction took off everywhere in the region, not just in the city of Atlanta. The city was permitting, on average, 6,000 residential units per year after the Olympics until the crash. This comes after averaging less than 1,200 permits each year between 1990 and 1996 (U.S. Department of Housing and Urban Development 2013b). Overall, the Atlanta metropolitan area led the nation in building permits each year between 1995 and 2005. In fact, between the years 1999 and 2002, 70,000 more residential units were built in metropolitan Atlanta than in its closest competitor, Phoenix—which, not coincidentally, also suffered mightily during the housing downturn (Figures 22.1 and 22.2). Despite renewed building in the city of Atlanta, the majority of these new units were in suburbia.

Beginning in 2000, the pace of permitting in Phoenix (and other metropolitan areas) began to flat line, not picking back up until 2003. In contrast, metropolitan Atlanta's pace of permitting continued to increase, even during the recession of 2001 and the aftermath. By the end of 2007, however, the pace of permitting activity in the Atlanta metropolitan area nose-dived, falling well below that of the national leaders, Houston and New York. While Atlanta is still in the top ten nationally in the number of building permits issued, it is at about a third the level of the peak building activity in 2004 and around half of the permitting activity now seen in Houston and Dallas.[2] In-migration fell dramatically as well.

With all the building—and overbuilding—in the early 2000s, metropolitan Atlanta's home prices stayed affordable. While prices certainly rose, the area never experienced the inflated bubbles observed in other hot housing markets. This phenomenon worked to Atlanta's advantage in attracting young professional workers to the area in search of a high quality of life and affordable, quality housing. Metropolitan Atlanta homes prices peaked in July 2007, which by that point represented an appreciation of 96 percent since the beginning of 1991. Meanwhile, home prices in other large metropolitan areas peaked a year earlier, in June 2006, with an appreciation of 188 percent since 1991, almost double the rate of home price change in metropolitan Atlanta (Figure 22.3) (Standard and Poor's 2013).

In many ways, metropolitan Atlanta was enjoying the best of both worlds. Home prices were rising, and homeowners, investors, real es-

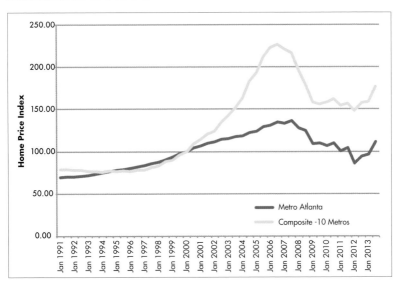

Figure 22.3. Home prices (Case-Shiller Index). While home prices certainly increased at a good pace in metro Atlanta, prices as well as the rate of change were nowhere near that of other major metro areas. (Source: Data from S&P Dow Jones Indices and CoreLogic 2013.)

tate professionals, constructions workers, and the like all benefitted, either through refinancing, selling, commissions, or seemingly unending employment opportunities. But prices never rose so high that they became a barrier to attract new growth. Thus, Atlanta entered into a virtuous cycle where growth begot growth. To put it another way, Atlanta's housing market was affordable, which helped metropolitan Atlanta attract more than 100,000 new residents each year. This created more jobs to fuel this growth, which in turn attracted new residents seeking employment, and so on. While in the throes of this cycle, it is easy, in retrospect, to see why many in the construction and real estate professions were irrationally exuberant that Atlanta's housing market was recession-proof.

Metropolitan Atlanta is revered for its balanced economic base, but during the heyday of building, construction and real estate jobs began to take on outsized importance to the regional economy. Figure 22.4 shows the percentage of employment in the construction and real estate industries[3] in both metro politan Atlanta and the nation as a whole). The numbers show that between 1995 and 2008 (but particularly 1999–2001), metropolitan Atlanta's economy was more skewed toward construction and real estate jobs than the nation as a whole, a possible indication of over-reliance. While homebuilding and overall population growth continued mostly unabated in metropolitan Atlanta, warning signs of an inflated housing market were pop-

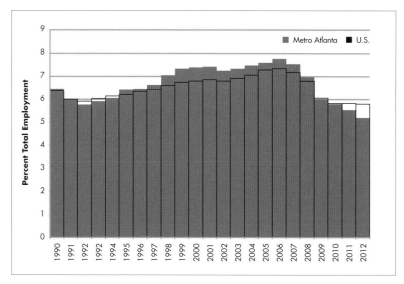

Figure 22.4. Metro Atlanta employment in the construction and real estate industries. Metro Atlanta's economy became increasingly reliant on the construction and real estate industries beginning in 1995 but particularly so between 1999 and 2001. (Source: Data from U.S. Bureau of Labor Statistics 2013b.)

ping up in other areas of the country, mostly in coastal areas of California and Florida. Again, this was mostly advantageous to metropolitan Atlanta's growth because people could sell their house in these hot markets, move to the Atlanta area where jobs were still relatively easy to find, and find a

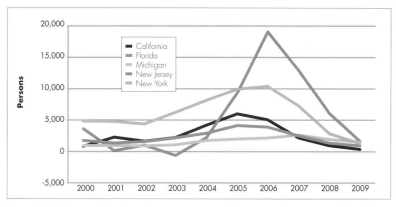

Figure 22.5. Net immigration from other states into metro Atlanta. Metro Atlanta's unprecedented growth was fueled, in part, by a hot housing market and a churning job market. When the housing bubble burst, taking the job market with it, migration into metro Atlanta virtually stopped. (Source: Data from U.S. Internal Revenue Service 2013.)

comparable house for hundreds of thousands of dollars less. At least that is a popular narrative, and the data back it up.

As mentioned earlier, beginning in 2003, net migration from Florida, California, and New York increased dramatically. This upward trend continued until 2007, when the housing bubble burst. When the housing market was still frothy, between 2003 and 2007, metropolitan Atlanta netted (taking out-migration from   the area to those states into account) more than 100,000 new residents from these three states alone, or about 20,000 annually. In the two years that followed, that influx slowed to less than 7,000 annually (Figure 22.5). Thus ended metropolitan Atlanta's unprecedented run, a run that included a million more new residents calling it home. It also ended any talk of Atlanta being recession-proof.

Requiem for a Housing Boom

The bursting of the housing bubble and the subsequent economic downturn hurt all metropolitan areas, but Atlanta was one of the harder hit areas because, in part, Atlanta's economy became too reliant on growth itself. In other words, the industries that thrived during Atlanta's boom were all industries that were needed to accommodate growth–construction, real estate, and finance, to name a few. And while the Great Recession spared

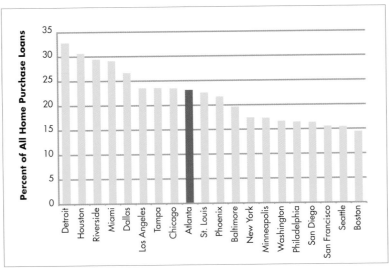

Figure 22.6. Subprime home purchase loans, 2004–2006. About 23 percent of all home purchase loans between 2004 and 2006 in metro Atlanta were considered subprime, placing Atlanta in the middle of the 20 largest metros in the nation (based on the number of total housing units in 2010). These subprime mortgages were a trigger for greater housing woes once the Great Recession began in 2007. (Source: Data from Foreclosure-Response.org.)

no sector of the economy, jobs losses in these population-serving industries were particularly brutal.

The national economic slowdown along with local struggles helped expose underlying troubles that continue to plague the Atlanta market. Unsustainable loan products and mortgage fraud led to a wave of foreclosures that caught everyone off-guard, including builders, developers, and local governments. As the Great Recession became more entrenched, heavy jobs losses added to the housing woes and people who had taken out conventional loans began to lose their homes as well. These trends flung Atlanta's housing market into a downward spiral from which it is only now recovering.

The signs of looming trouble were evident well before the Great Recession began, but hindsight provides a clarity practically no one had during the "good times." Between 2004 and 2006, some 23 percent of all home purchase loans in metropolitan Atlanta were high-cost loans, which ranked ninth among the 20 largest metropolitan areas in the nation (Figure 22.6). At the time, these subprime loans were seen as a good way to increase homeownership, and the rationale was that higher interest rate levels did not really matter as long and home values kept appreciating the way they had been (Guttentag 2007). However, as home prices started their inexorable decline, people holding these risky, high-cost loan products were in the first wave of those who lost their homes.

Initially, foreclosures were confined to mostly the urban core of the Atlanta region, where predatory lending and mortgage fraud were much more prevalent. For example, Atlanta's 30310 zip code was frequently mentioned as one of the worst-hit areas in the nation in terms of mortgage fraud (Fulmer 2010). As Figure 22.7 shows, the heaviest concentrations of foreclosure filings in 2007 were located within the urban core, particularly in the city of Atlanta, Clayton County, and south DeKalb County. In fact, of the neighborhoods with the highest foreclosure density in the 20-county Atlanta region, 66 percent were located inside the Interstate 285 perimeter, which is a rough approximation of Atlanta's metropolitan urban core.[4]

As the jobs crisis spread throughout the region, so did the concentrations of foreclosure filings. By 2012 only 43 percent of the neighborhoods with the highest foreclosure density were found inside the perimeter.[5] The more suburban area of Gwinnett County (to the northeast) surpassed its more urban counterparts in the total number of foreclosure filings. As Figure 22.8 shows, the crisis spread out of the urban core into suburban neighborhoods of Gwinnett and Cobb Counties. As the foreclosure crisis morphed from one due mostly to loan products and practices to one being driven primarily by loss of jobs and employment opportunities, the geography of foreclosures also shifted. The phenomenon was no longer an urban thing; it was a metropolitan Atlanta thing. Driven by activity in metropolitan Atlanta, Georgia ranked fourth nationally in overall foreclosure activity, and the Atlanta metropolitan region had the third

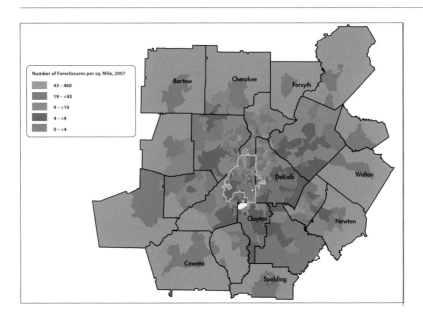

Figure 22.7. Foreclosure filings, 2007 (above). Figure 22.8. Foreclosure filing, 2012 (below). (Source: Data from Neighborhood Nexus.)

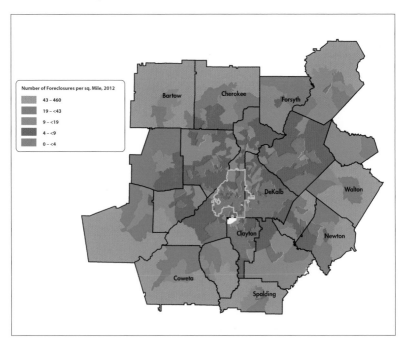

largest rate of real estate owned (REO) inventory as of September 2011,[6] behind only Detroit and Las Vegas.

National Crisis Spawns a National Response: Neighborhood Stabilization Program

While things were certainly bad in metropolitan Atlanta, they were bad all over. As more and more people began to lose their homes to foreclosures, the federal government's response was direct aid to local governments through the Neighborhood Stabilization Program (NSP). The NSP was administered by HUD and signed into law in 2008 as part of the Housing and Economic Recovery Act. The NSP unfolded in three phases, but overall, HUD administered more than $7 billion in NSP funding nationwide, with approximately $124 million coming to metropolitan Atlanta jurisdictions. The NSP allowed local governments some leeway in how they allocated the funds for different interventions, including acquisition of land and property, demolition, rehabilitation, and down-payment and closing-cost assistant for low- to moderate-income buyers

The nine jurisdictions in the Atlanta region that received funding from the NSP program used a mixture of these strategies to acquire more than 1,200 units, with the majority of these subsequently rehabbed and sold or rented (Atlanta Regional Commission and Piece by Piece 2012). Local governments, even with a fairly sizeable infusion of money, could only do so much, however, to get these foreclosed houses back on the market. In Atlanta's case, many of these properties ended up in the hands of investors after ownership reverted back to the lender. With the tightening of the credit markets making it more difficult for individuals to purchase homes, many of these properties came back on the market as rentals. As mentioned earlier, metropolitan Atlanta was among the leaders in the nation of REO inventory, which has helped spawn an investor-friendly atmosphere, especially in some distressed urban neighborhoods where properties could be had for pennies on the dollar.

A recent publication explored the role of investors in Fulton County, the center of the Atlanta metropolitan area and its largest county, and found that large investors were more likely to buy REO properties in the most distressed neighborhoods of Atlanta. These properties were less likely to subsequently sell than REO properties purchased in more affluent areas. When they did resell, it was much more likely that they were sold to another investor. This type of activity—with constant changes of ownership—has a destabilizing effect on neighborhoods, particularly ones that already are challenged with high poverty rates and low educational levels (Immergluck 2013).

Simply put, different types of neighborhoods and different populations are being affected in different ways by the foreclosure crisis in metropolitan Atlanta, making it impossible to develop a one-size-fits-all approach. In general, the high-foreclosure neighborhoods inside the Interstate 285 perimeter (ITP, as it is

TABLE 22.1.	Demographic Composition of High-Foreclosure Neighborhoods				
	% White	% Black	% Asian	% Hispanic	% Other
Inside the perimeter	33.8%	56.4%	3.2%	4.3%	2.3%
Outside the perimeter	16.2%	59.1%	5.1%	17.3%	2.3%

Source: Data from 2010 Census, through Neighborhood Nexus

known locally) have higher proportions of whites than do the high-foreclosure neighborhoods outside the perimeter (OTP), although both sets of neighborhoods have large non-white majorities. The main difference is that OTP high-foreclosure neighborhoods have higher percentages of Hispanic and Asian populations, while the ITP high-foreclosure neighborhoods are largely bi-ethnic, either white or black (Table 22.1).

Two Neighborhoods: Same Problem, Worlds Apart

As discussed previously, the 30310 zip code in the city of Atlanta was among the hardest hit areas in the entire nation, not just metropolitan Atlanta. This area was notorious for mortgage fraud and subprime lending, which led to high numbers of foreclosures. In 2007 neighborhoods including West End, Pittsburgh, Adair Park, Mechanicsville led the region in foreclosure density (foreclosures per square mile).[7] These neighborhoods are still—five years later—struggling with foreclosures. The population in these neighborhoods declined by almost 7,000 between 2000 and 2010. Around 91 percent of the residents are black, more than 11 percent of the residents are 65 years or older, and, overall, these neighborhoods have a poverty rate of around 37 percent.[8] According to Zillow, the average price of houses sold in the 30310 zip code was around $45,800 in August 2013, down from around $130,000 almost five years ago. Several houses in the area sold for less than $10,000. In sum, these are highly vulnerable populations living in distressed neighborhoods that were struggling before the Great Recession and have yet to recover even to those prerecession levels.

These ITP neighborhoods were in the first wave of the foreclosure crisis. The foreclosures that occurred here were largely due to fraudulent activity and unsustainable mortgage products. In 2007 almost 2,200 foreclosure filings occurred in these neighborhoods, which make up an area of around 11 square miles. According to the 2010 Census, there were around 22,000 units in this area, so roughly one in every 10 housing units received a foreclosure notice in 2007).[9] By 2012 the number of foreclosure filings in these ITP neighborhoods had fallen dramatically to 740, a 66 percent drop. This decline, however, is not due to fundamentally better economic conditions but rather is due largely to the fact that these areas were hit so hard initially that the housing stock is largely tapped out.

To the northwest of zip code 30310 is another cluster of neighborhoods plagued by foreclosures, but they jumped into the game later, so the housing woes here are more related to declining economic and employment opportunities rather than fraud and loan product. The 30044 zip code and surrounding areas in suburban Gwinnett County typify high-foreclosure, OTP neighborhoods—ones that look very different from the inner city neighborhoods in Atlanta proper. Foreclosure activity in this area was muted early on, but as job losses mounted, the foreclosure crisis shifted away from intown neighborhoods into the suburbs. Today, this area has among the highest foreclosure density rates in the region.

In contrast to the aforementioned inner city neighborhoods, this area in Gwinnett added almost 17,000 new residents during the 2000s, with almost all of that growth—roughly 14,000—coming from those born abroad. In fact, roughly one of every four residents is considered to be linguistically isolated, meaning that English was not their first and primary language. These Gwinnett neighborhoods are vastly more diverse than the inner city neighborhoods. Some 36 percent of residents are Hispanics, 30 percent are black, 20 percent are white, and 12 percent are Asian. They are also vastly younger, with only five percent of the population 65 and older. According to Zillow, the average price of homes sold in the 30044 zip code was $119,300 in August 2013, whereas four years ago the average price was around $163,000. Thus, home prices in this area are recovering at a much faster pace than the comparison ITP neighborhood. The poverty rate in the 30044 area is still relatively high at 19 percent, but it is almost half the poverty rate observed in the inner city neighborhoods (U.S. Census 2012a). Although completely different demographically, this OTP area shares two things in common with its inner city counterpart: high foreclosure rates and a highly vulnerable population.

The OTP neighborhoods were in the second wave of foreclosures. In 2007 there were 704 foreclosure filings in this area spanning about 22 square miles. With almost 29,000 housing units, that works out to roughly one foreclosure filing per 41 housing units. By 2012 foreclosure filings increased to almost 2,000, an increase of 180 percent, almost exactly the opposite of what occurred in the inner city neighborhoods. Although these neighborhoods share the same problem, the two places could not be any further apart. This helps explain why metropolitan Atlanta's housing market continues to struggle—it is hard to develop a comprehensive strategy to a problem so widespread and amorphous.

Atlanta: Rising from the Ashes Again?

Like General Sherman 150 years ago, the Great Recession took a scorched earth approach through metropolitan Atlanta, leaving hundreds of thousands of homeowners struggling to stay afloat. As other metropolitan areas slowly recovered, Atlanta continued to struggle. But as the old adage goes, it is always darkest before the dawn, and several major investors now see the light on the horizon.

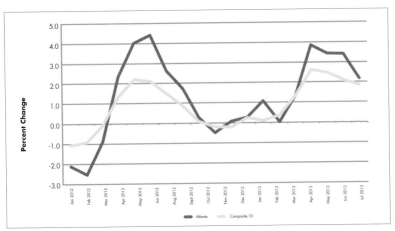

Figure 22.9. Change in home prices, 2012–2013. In looking at month-over-month percent changes in home prices, metro Atlanta actually performed better for most of 2012 than a composite of 10 similarly sized metros. (Source: Data from S&P Dow Jones Indices and CoreLogic 2013.)

Huge investment groups like Blackstone, Colony Capital, and Silver Bay Realty are buying thousands of homes in a select few markets nationwide, with Atlanta being the investors' latest darling (Gittlesohn and Perlberg 2013). This flurry of activity has helped stabilize home prices. In fact, for the first time since the crisis began, home prices in metropolitan Atlanta are better than a composite of 10 similarly sized metropolitan areas on a month-over-month basis (Figure 22.9). Overall, the last year and a half has shown improvement for metropolitan Atlanta: home prices have risen by some 30 percent, 116,000 jobs were added, and foreclosure filings are 50 percent lower in September 2013 than they were in January 2012 (Standard and Poor's 2013).[10]

Of course, this is not the first time investors have taken a shine to Atlanta's housing market. This time, however, today's investors appear to be holding onto the properties, rehabbing them, and renting them out. Most reports suggest that institutional buyers plan to adhere to this strategy for anywhere from three to seven years. In the short term, this seems to be a positive for Atlanta's housing as the glut of inventory is being slashed. In the long term, the biggest question is what is going to happen to these thousands of homes that are owned by large, out-of-town investors with little stake in the neighborhoods in which they invest. Are we just ramping up to another crash once those houses go back on the market?

CHAPTER 23

Building Atlanta's Land Bank

Frank S. Alexander

This chapter traces the creation and evolution of the Fulton County/City of Atlanta Land Bank from its authorization in 1991 through its emergence as one of the most creative and innovative land banks in the country by 2011. It describes the initial organizational structure and challenges, its foray into operational policies and procedures, its primary areas of success and the challenges it confronted less successfully. It also describes the pivotal restructuring and transformation during the period from 2007–2009, and its role in the creation of the most advanced state land bank legislation in 2012.

The Impetus for the Atlanta Land Bank

Every program or initiative that combines cultural transformation and governmental initiatives is a story with many actors, stages, plots, and twists. The drama of land banks and land banking in Georgia is a play that is still being written, with origins that trace back a mere 25 years. From the creation of the first land bank by Fulton County and the City of Atlanta in 1991 through the enactment of the revised and comprehensive Georgia Land Bank Act in 2012, land banking in Georgia is a story of trial and error, of education and experimentation, of strategic successes and systemic reforms. Each successive land bank in Georgia learned from and built upon the work of sister land banks. Each neighborhood has confronted its own challenges of vacancy and abandonment informed by the work of other communities. Each city and county utilized the tool of land banking with greater creativity and success by statutory amendments and intergovernmental collaboration.

The trigger for the creation of land banks, both here in Georgia and throughout the United States, is relatively simple and straightforward (Alexander 2011). Some parcels of property lie dying in a state of vacancy, abandonment, and deterioration. In an otherwise stable or vibrant economy, these parcels become inaccessible to open market purchases because of systemic legal barriers. In a weak or declining economy, there is simply insufficient demand or value to justify resolution of the barriers. The owners of these properties have made a strategic financial decision to abandon them, or the ownership has become so highly fractured among diverse entities that no one entity has sufficient interest to force a new use or a transfer to a new owner (Tappendorf and Denzin 2011).

By the late 1980s, inner city residential neighborhoods in the city of Atlanta had begun to emerge from two decades of relative economic stagnation. Neighborhoods began to experience substantial rehabilitation of residential structures and their conversion from subdivided rental stock back to single-family owner occupancy. New construction of single-family and multifamily residences reemerged alongside the nascent conversion of commercial and industrial spaces into residential lofts. By 1992 Atlanta's impossible dream of becoming an international Olympic city had become a firm reality (Alexander 1994).

In the midst of this reemergence, however, one could drive down residential streets less than one mile from the heart of downtown Atlanta and encounter abandoned residences, heavily deteriorated, with windows broken out, doors long gone, roofs partially collapsed, all largely hidden by a covering of kudzu. Potential private developers who might be interested in acquiring the property, as well as nonprofit developers such as Habitat for Humanity Atlanta, found acquisition of the property to be impossible. Atlanta had a growing inventory of "dead" property even in the face of rising economic investments and pressures for gentrification.

This inventory of vacant, abandoned, and substandard property had one common characteristic, a single proposition of law, which erected an impenetrable barrier to marketability. Property taxes on these properties had become delinquent not just for one year, but for five years or ten years or more. For each year of delinquency the taxes compounded at 18 percent. At the same time, appraised values (for property tax purposes) remained artificially high, when the market value declined because owners who abandoned the property abandoned all desire to contest appraised values. Property tax enforcement laws, with clear origins from a century earlier, lost all effectiveness in forcing a tax sale because the law stipulated a minimum bid at a tax sale of all delinquent taxes, penalties, and interest (Alexander 1995). The minimum bid far exceeded fair market value and the disparity only grew greater with each passing year.

The 1990 Land Bank Statute and Creation of the Atlanta Land Bank

In late 1989 and early 1990, an informal coalition of affordable housing advocates and key elected leadership in the City of Atlanta and Fulton County began looking for creative solutions to this challenge of problem properties that were inaccessible to the market. They found in Louisville, Kentucky, and Cleveland, Ohio, a potential solution. Building upon concepts embraced by the first local government land bank in the country in St. Louis in 1973, state legislation in Ohio authorized the creation of the Cleveland Land Bank in 1976 and in Louisville in 1989 (Alexander 2005). Based principally upon the Louisville statutory framework, the original land bank legislation in Georgia was passed by the General Assembly in 1990.[1] This initial legislation had two dominant characteristics, one dealing with creation and governance, and the second with the core power of addressing delinquent property taxes.

The 1990 Georgia land bank statute permitted the creation of a land bank only by agreement between a municipality and the county in which it was located. Neither a municipality acting alone, nor a county acting alone, could create a land bank. Perhaps as a reflection of the reluctant dance in the sharing of powers by the City of Atlanta and Fulton County, the legislation mandated a board of directors of just four persons, two appointed by the city and two by the county. The statute further specified that no property located within the city could be transferred by the land bank without approval by the city's board appointees, and no property located in the county outside of the city limits could transferred without the approval of the county's board appointees.

The core power for lands banks authorized in the 1990 legislation was the power to extinguish liens for delinquent property taxes on any property owned by a land bank. This power was aimed clearly and directly at the growing inventory of "dead" properties where the delinquent taxes exceeded fair market value and property tax foreclosure sales were never completed. The General Assembly authorized the creation of a land bank:

> to acquire. . . tax delinquent. . . properties in order to foster the public purpose of returning land which is in a non-revenue-generating, non-tax-producing status to an effective utilization status in order to provide housing, new industry, and jobs for the citizens of the county.[2]

The First Decade of Work

The Fulton County/City of Atlanta Land Bank Authority formally came into existence in 1991 following the approval of an intergovernmental contract by the city and the county, the filing of articles of incorporation, and the appointment of its first board members. Once again suggestive of the hesitancy to venture far into intergovernmental collaboration, for the first three years of its existence the Atlanta Land Bank had no staff of its own and no budget, with its operational functions alternating each year between the land use and planning departments of the two distinct governments in tandem with annually alternating board chairmanship. It was not until fiscal year 1995 that the Atlanta Land Bank received its first direct budget appropriations from the two local governments and hired its first full-time executive director in May 1994 (Alexander 1994).

For the next 15 years of its existence, the Atlanta Land Bank was remarkably consistent and single-minded in its operational focus, with virtually no change in either the composition of the four-member board of directors or the professional staff. The board also made a pivotal affirmative policy decision that the Atlanta Land Bank would not retain ownership of property for any length of time and would focus instead only on the exercise of its power to extinguish delinquent property taxes. Functionally this resulted in the Atlanta Lank Bank having a primary focus on a "conduit" transfer program, in which a nonprofit affordable housing entity would identify and acquire a parcel of property heavily burdened with delinquent taxes by paying a nominal amount to the owner and taking the property subject to the outstanding tax liens. Such an entity would then convey the property to the land bank, which would extinguish the delinquent taxes and immediately re-convey the property to the entity with restrictions and requirements that the property be redeveloped for affordable housing.

The Challenge of School Taxes

Between its original enactment in 1990 and the passage of the comprehensive new Georgia Land Bank Act in 2012, the original land bank legislation was amended in key aspects on three occasions. The first amendment occurred in 1992 and addressed directly the application of the power of tax extinguishment to public school property taxes. Because school taxes comprised well over 50 percent of annual property taxes in the city of Atlanta and Fulton County, the effectiveness of the power to extinguish taxes was limited if it did not apply to the school board's portion of such taxes. The legislative amendment in 1992 made clear that such school taxes could be extinguished but only with the consent of the board of education. As an operational matter, initially the Atlanta Land Bank sought such consent on each separate property. Upon becoming convinced that delinquent taxes— at least as to the target property of the land bank—yielded no revenue to the school district and that transfers from the land bank to a new owner would yield new tax revenues, the school district created a "default" position that the land bank could extinguish all delinquent property taxes unless the school district objected.

The Challenge of Tax Liens and Tax Sales

The second major amendment to the original land bank statute occurred in 1995 and addressed the connections between land bank inventory acquisition and the tax foreclosure process. This amendment created express authority for the land bank to tender a bid at a property tax foreclosure sale in an amount equal to the minimum bid, where the bid could be a "credit" bid consisting of the assumption of responsibility for the property tax lien. When coupled with the separate power of a land bank to extinguish property tax liens on property it owns, the effect of this amendment was to place land banks in a position to change the character of any and all property that had become "dead" to the market because taxes exceeded value and tax sales were not occurring. The timing of this amendment coincided with the enactment by the Georgia General Assembly of an entirely new system of property tax foreclosure (at local option), a judicial *in rem* foreclosure proceeding, and a land bank that became authorized to tender credit bids at both nonjudicial and judicial foreclosure proceedings (Alexander 1995).

During the 20 years between 1990 and 2010, the success of the Atlanta Land Bank—with its "conduit" transfer program and its overall operational productivity—encountered new forms of resistance. Despite the initial success, the Atlanta Land Bank began its second decade of work encountering growing policy differences with the Fulton County tax commissioner. Alone among the 159 tax commissioners in Georgia, the Fulton County tax commissioner elected to sell delinquent tax liens to private investors, essentially undercutting any possibility of a land bank being able to resolve the problems posed by key abandoned properties. When the tax lien is held by a private third party investor, it is no longer possible for a conduit transfer program, or donation program, to be viable as the core power in such programs lies in the ability to extinguish delinquent taxes on property owned by the land bank. Such power could not apply to privately held tax liens. By the early 2000s, the Atlanta Land Bank was also coming under increased criticism from its traditional allies in nonprofit community development corporations, affordable housing advocates, and elected officials (including the tax commissioner) for not taking action to resolve title questions, to ensure redevelopment in accordance with public priorities, or to have any clear strategic plan (Keating 2001b).

Transformation of the Atlanta Land Bank (2007–2009)

By the advent of the Great Recession in 2007, an entirely new board of directors was appointed by the City of Atlanta and Fulton County, and by 2008 new leadership and new programs began to emerge with clarity and focus. Chris Norman was initially appointed chair of the new board of directors but, by 2009, was persuaded to step down as board chair and become president and chief executive officer of the Atlanta Land Bank.

In early 2008, the Atlanta Land Bank created the first "Land Bank Depository Agreement Program" in the entire country, an initiative designed directly to deal with growing inventories of properties for which there was simply no market demand (Alexander 2011; Fitzpatrick 2010). With the federal recognition of land banking for the very first time in the Housing and Economic Recovery Act of 2008, the Atlanta Land Bank played a key role in the utilization of Neighborhood Stabilization Program funding to acquire and manage inventories of foreclosed properties (Alexander 2009).

Demonstrating its effectiveness in the conversion of abandoned and heavily tax-delinquent properties into new productive uses over the course of its first five years of work, the Atlanta Lank Bank became a model for other local governments in Georgia. The Columbus-Muscogee County Land Bank (1992), the Macon-Bibb County Land Bank Authority (1996), the Savannah-Chatham County Land Bank Authority (1997), and the Valdosta-Lowndes County Land Bank (1999) followed suit. The Augusta-Richmond County Land Bank (1998) and the Athens-Clarke County Land Bank (2009) were created once the legislation had been amended to allow for consolidated governments.

The Atlanta Land Bank of the New Georgia Land Bank Statute

The experience of the five to ten active land banks in Georgia during the first decade of this century demonstrated the value of a flexible yet highly focused tool for local governments to address the broad range of problems caused by properties that lay dead to the market. Each of the land banks emphasized a slightly different approach, using different levels of staffing and budgets, and collaborating with different sets of local partners. What these Georgia land banks also realized, however, were the limitations in existing Georgia law on their ability to address effectively their statutory mission and local priorities.

Between 1999 and 2008 a new generation of land banks and land banking programs had emerged, first in Michigan, and second in Ohio (Keating 2011; Silva 2011). This second generation of programs built upon the experiences of the first generation (St. Louis, Cleveland, Louisville, Atlanta) while addressing their deficiencies and expanding on their successes. In both Michigan and Ohio, new statutes were passed which created far more direct and efficient ties between land banking and property-tax enforcement systems. The new statutes expressly acknowledged and facilitated more expansive options for regional and intergovernmental collaboration, allowing single land banks to be formed by multiple local governments or multiple local land banks to collaborate in achieving economies of scale in operations through intergovernmental agreements. This second generation of land banking also included a far broader range of internal financing mechanisms such as a limited property tax recapture on properties conveyed from the land bank to a new private owner and placed back on the tax rolls (Alexander 2011).

Coalition Building

In late 2010, two decades after passage of the first Georgia land bank statute and in the wake of a foreclosure crisis that was ripping through neighborhoods across the country, land bank directors from nearly all of the Georgia land banks joined community development, nonprofit housing advocates, and local government officials from all over the state for a gathering in Atlanta at Emory University. The purpose of this meeting, the first of its kind in Georgia, was to begin building and connecting a statewide network of land bank leaders to share resources and best practices and to brainstorm and develop the key ingredients of a legislative agenda for Georgia land banks moving forward. In that early meeting, three key themes emerged. Land bank leaders agreed that Georgia land banks could increase their efficacy and impact with new legislation that a) authorized and encouraged regional collaboration in land banking, b) provided land banks with self-financing mechanisms and increased access to funding sources, and c) authorized and encouraged land banking responsive to locally determined priorities.

Under the strong leadership of the Atlanta, Macon, Augusta, and Valdosta-Lowndes County Land Banks, a statewide association—the Georgia Association of Lank Bank Authorities (GALBA)—was formed in 2011. Its mission is to facilitate education, collaboration, and cross-training among existing land banks in Georgia, and to provide assistance to other local governments in Georgia that are exploring the possibility of creating land banks. Most significantly, GALBA—with Chris Norman serving both as the leader of the Atlanta Land Bank and the president of the new statewide association—began to press the question of whether the existing Georgia land bank statute could be amended or replaced in a manner that incorporated the best thinking and best experiences drawn from land banks throughout the United States. Between 2011 and 2012, GALBA took the lead in the preparation of new comprehensive legislation for the State of Georgia, enacted in 2012 as the Georgia Land Bank Act.[3]

Regional Collaboration

The 1990 Georgia land bank statute provided for the creation of land banks by a single consolidated government, or by a single Georgia county and one or more cities located within that county. All of the Georgia land bank authorities created prior to 2012—including for example, the Fulton County/City of Atlanta Land Bank, the Valdosta-Lowndes County Land Bank, and the Augusta/Richmond Land Bank—reflected this legal structure. In response to the desire for increased regional collaboration expressed by Georgia land bank leaders, the 2012 Georgia Land Bank Act authorizes multiple counties and cities or consolidated governments to come together and form a single land bank (Jourdan, Van Zandt, and Adair 2010). This regional option may provide a helpful tool for rural counties, cities, and local governments to collaborate in addressing the challenges of vacant, dilapidated, and tax delinquent properties across regions. Similarly, the regional option could provide increased access for land banks to address problem parcels in cities that lie in multiple counties, such as that portion of Atlanta that lies in DeKalb County

The 2012 Georgia Land Bank Act also expressly permits land banks to contract with one another for services across jurisdictional boundaries. This key power may encourage regional collaboration in neighborhoods that span multiple jurisdictions. In addition, multijurisdictional contracts for services could encourage the development of economies of scale or specific expertise in one land bank that may be offered and utilized by other land banks as a more efficient and effective alternative to developing similar economies of scale or expertise in every land bank in the state of Georgia.

Financing Mechanisms

With the exception of providing that proceeds from the sale of land bank property could be used for land bank operations, the 1990 Georgia land bank statute offered relatively little guidance on funding resources available to Georgia land banks. Because land banks primarily acquire properties that are heavily tax delinquent and dilapidated, and because early land bank operations in Georgia emphasized disposition of property through donation or transfer for public and not-for-profit use, proceeds from the sale of land bank property provided little revenue for land bank operations. As a practical matter, most Georgia land banks have historically derived their funding from line items in local government annual budgets, from local and state grant funds including Community Development Block Grants, and in recent years from federal grants including the Neighborhood Stabilization Program. Even as the need for funds to impact vacant, abandoned, dilapidated parcels through the state increases exponentially, federal, state, and local grant programs are being diminished and extinguished in the aftermath of the Great Recession, and local government budgets throughout Georgia are experiencing drastic cuts. Georgia land bank leaders anticipated this economic shift in their early meetings in 2010 and structured the 2012 Georgia Land Bank Act to include increased funding options for Georgia land banks.

The 2012 Georgia Land Bank Act provides that land banks may receive funding from local, state, and federal government budgets and programs and from any other public or private sources. In addition, the 2012 act expressly provides that Georgia land banks may utilize revenue obtained through the sale or lease of land bank property, and through contracts for the provision of services to local governments, other land banks, and other public and private entities.

Perhaps the most distinctive feature of the 2012 Georgia Land Bank Act is the authorization of a self-financing mechanism for Georgia land banks— the optional five-year/75 percent tax recapture program. Pursuant to the 2012 act, the local governments that create a land bank may authorize up to 75 percent of the newly generated tax revenue (excluding school district taxes) on properties disposed of by the land bank to be returned to the land bank for a period of five years. This is key feature of the "third generation" of land bank statutes including those in Michigan, Ohio, Kansas City, Missouri, and New York, and provides a much-needed funding resource to land banks at minimal cost to local governments.

Georgia land banks focus on the acquisition of tax delinquent and dilapidated properties that currently generate no tax revenue for the local government and indeed impose significant public liabilities in the form of increased police and fire costs. The success of Georgia land banks in acquiring, cleaning, and responsibly conveying such properties to new owners directly benefits local governments and communities and results in newly generated tax revenues. Authorizing a land bank to recapture 75 percent of such newly generated tax revenue for a limited period of five years, and to utilize that revenue to acquire and return additional properties to a productive tax-generating status, allows a land bank to self-finance at no cost to local government budgets. In addition, during the five years of the tax recapture program, the local government receives 25 percent or more of newly generated ad valorem taxes on parcels that previously provided no revenue—25 percent of something is preferable to 100 percent of nothing.

Locally Determined Priorities

Pursuant to the focus on affordable housing in the 1990 Georgia land bank statute, and also in response to the economic realities of the 1990s and early part of the twenty-first century, Georgia land banks historically limited their mission to the creation of affordable housing. While the support and creation of affordable housing programs remains an essential policy in many communities, land bank leaders recognized many different pressing needs for real property in local communities throughout Georgia from the outset of the 2011–2012 legislative effort.

Some Georgia communities have an abundance of affordable housing but a dire need for green space, for affordable commercial or industrial spaces for local small businesses, or for space available for various public uses. Other communities experienced significant population loss or rapid changes in industry over the last two decades and must prioritize demolition over preservation of vacant and abandoned parcels. In light of this diversity of priorities for problem parcels in communities throughout Georgia, and in recognition of the fact that local communities are in the best position to define and direct local priorities, the 2012 Georgia Land Bank Act expressly provides that local land banks or their creating local governments may establish the priorities for the use of property conveyed by the land bank.

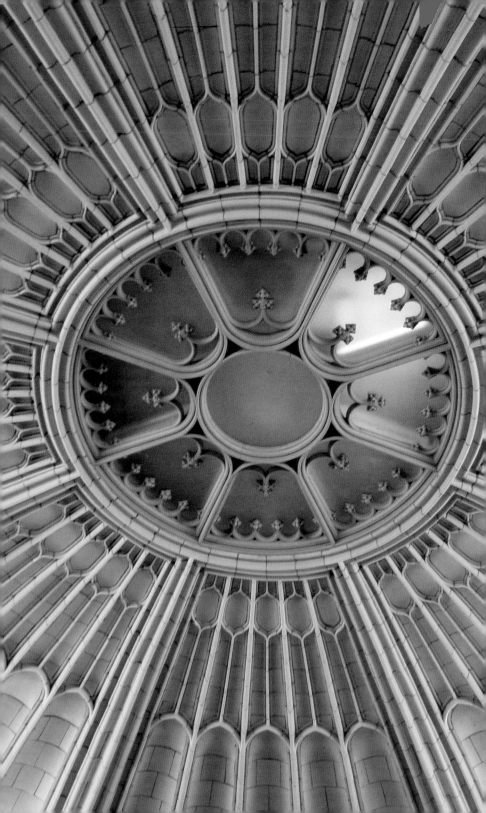

PART 5

Innovation and Challenges
Shape the Future

Atlanta is a Goldilocks kind of place: often too hot, occasionally too cold, and sometimes just right. Northerners are amazed that Atlanta's schools close if the weather drops below 10 degrees, and a forecast of sleet or snow can cause customers to empty the supermarket shelves of milk, bread, and beer. Without a doubt, summers are hot and sticky. Atlantans love to tell the story that the bid proposal for the 1996 Olympics stated the average July temperature in Atlanta is 75 degrees—in fact, the average is 89 degrees.[1] Spring dogwoods and autumn color make up for the extremes, and those are reasons why we live here. Boosterism and bravado can persuade, yet Atlantans know that all is not copacetic. Big problems face the region around the economy, housing, social justice, transportation, and quality of life issues.

Eric Hardy offers an in-depth account of water problems facing the Atlanta region in "Maelstrom: Contextualizing the Failed Privatization of the Water Supply System." Hardy recounts the problems presented by a lack of natural watershed in a city without access to a major river, lake, or ocean. At the regional level, the tri-state water war threatens Georgia, Alabama, and Florida. In a region resembling the "little old lady in the shoe," the demands are great and the shortages are real.

The abandoned Atlantic Steel Mill was the unwanted and unattractive centerpiece of Midtown Alliance's master plan. Several developers had tried to redevelop the site but the environmental issues made it a monumental task.

Figure F.1. Healey Building on Forsyth Street in downtown Atlanta

It was not until 2000, when The Jacoby Group, Mayor Maynard Jackson, and Governor Roy Barnes put together a coalition of people and agencies to address the slag and access problems of the centrally located site, that a successful redevelopment of the property was made possible. Brian Leary, with his first-hand knowledge of the site issues while working with Jacoby, outlines how the mixed use center became a reality in "Atlantic Station: Location, Location, Location." The outcome is that Atlantic Station contributes $400 million each year in local taxes—up substantially from the $300 thousand the former steel mill contributed—and makes this redevelopment a big win for the region.

In "Planning for the Forest and the Trees" Jason Vargo describes the tree canopy loss and related climate impacts the region will likely experience as more rural land is developed for low-density housing. Times have changed since the last century, and the land—rather than the trees—has become the valuable commodity. Once the city with the highest percentage of tree cover canopy in the U.S., Atlanta has lost tree cover at the rate of 50 acres per day over the last two decades. Vargo traces urban and suburban growth patterns to show that increasing density and preserving forested land are essential to the region's sustainability and desirability.

Jim Durrett in "The Buckhead Community Improvement District" discusses the changes occurring in that affluent area of the city in an effort to develop a walkable neighborhood. In the early 1990s the Buckhead Coalition, a group of business leaders, put together a master plan that explored improving the neighborhood's quality of life in the face of major development pressure. At the time, the group wanted nothing to do with any type of business improvement district or self-taxing method of funding improvements. Twenty years later, new plans and projects using a variety of funding sources are making vast improvements to the area, including an enhanced Peachtree Road, new sidewalks and parks, and multimodal accessibility enhancements.

In "Atlanta's Role in the State of Georgia," David Pendered summarizes the political and planning issues the city continues to encounter within the state of Georgia. Atlanta Regional Commission (ARC) works both inside and outside the region and prides itself on its award-winning Livable Cities Initiative, with the goal of improving the quality of life in existing housing and employment centers. Pendered explains what went wrong with the failure of a major 2012 sales tax proposal, the tensions between the city and the state, and the effects of two-party politics in a red-state/blue-city region.

The big question asked persuasively in these chapters by these authors is clear: change is needed, but is it possible? Professionals in the planning community—in all levels of governments and in all sectors are intent on continuing to improve the quality of life for the city, region, and state. Water, transportation, land use, tree cover, health, and quality of life are just a few of the issues we face, and we must make sure we will know what to do.

CHAPTER 24

Maelstrom: Contextualizing the Failed Privatization of Atlanta's Water Supply System

Eric M. Hardy

At the close of the 20th century, Atlanta mayor Bill Campbell recognized that his administration faced an acute financial dilemma. Not only would the city have to comply with a 1998 federal consent decree intended to eliminate the amount of pollution spewing from its overburdened wastewater infrastructure, but it also needed to find a way to make long-overdue improvements to its municipally owned and operated water supply system. Staring down the barrel of an estimated $1 billion in capital improvement costs and reluctant to seek higher water and sewer rates from his constituents, Mayor Campbell decided to undertake a dramatic experiment. On January 1, 1999, after a controversial review and bidding process, the City of Atlanta effectively privatized its entire water supply system, transferring its operations, maintenance, and management to United Water Services Atlanta (UWSA) for a period of 20 years.[1, 2]

Despite optimistic claims that private management of the Atlanta Water Works (AWW) would yield up to $30 million in annual savings, the city decided to dissolve its contract with UWSA after only four years. Citing evidence of lackluster customer service, fraudulent billing, and poor water quality, Campbell's successor, Mayor Shirley Franklin, pulled the plug on USWA and brought the AWW back into the municipal fold as part of a massive $4 billion infrastructure improvement campaign known as Clean Water Atlanta.

The privatization of Atlanta's water system, the largest public-private contract of its kind in the country, generated a considerable amount of national attention, even if some of it simply served as a cautionary tale against corporate profiteering and predation.[3] These assessments notwithstanding, it is beyond the scope of this essay to determine the merits of privatization per se or if local circumstances doomed Atlanta's venture. I argue, instead, that Atlanta's difficulties in stewarding its water-related infrastructure are also indicative of a broader struggle to adequately manage the region's limited water resources.

Due to geologic factors that will be explained, the Atlanta metropolitan area is almost wholly reliant on surface waters originating within Georgia. Although the region averages a healthy 48 inches of annual rainfall, only about 18 inches is available to serve as a source for stream flow after evaporation and transpiration occur. In addition, while periodic droughts have frequently reduced the total quantity of water reaching the metropolitan region, the area's numerous ridges and valleys have created a myriad of drainage basins that divert water withdrawn from its main water source, the Chattahoochee River. This flow of water away from the Chattahoochee and into different watersheds, moreover, has limited the river's ability to dilute increased amounts of effluent, which has subsequently made wastewater management a more problematic and expensive endeavor.

Haphazard regional planning and lax environmental programs have exacerbated the constraints nature has imposed. Since the 1940s, Atlanta's civic leaders have pushed for dams and reservoirs to impound the Chattahoochee's meager flows while also engaging in policies that seemingly encouraged decentralized population growth and profligate water consumption.[4] Meanwhile, Atlanta continued to dump millions of gallons of untreated municipal sewage into its local waterways because the city consistently delayed making necessary improvements to its wastewater system, negligence which eventually prompted federal and state regulatory agencies to levy nearly $20 million dollars in fines against the city and repeatedly threaten it with construction moratoriums.

This combination of aggressive water use and persistent pollution ultimately led to a dazzling array of litigation, particularly as downstream water users and environmental activists sought court action to force the city to confront the external costs of its lumbering approach to metropolitan development. In 1990 the states of Alabama and Florida, fearful that Atlanta's great thirst would severely affect their own economic well-being, initiated what would result in more than 20 years of litigation to decide whether metropolitan Atlantans have the right to withdraw increased amounts of water from the federally operated Lake Lanier reservoir, a compound which the plaintiffs argued that Congress created strictly for the purposes of hydroelectric power, flood control, and navigation. Though a recent appellate court decision determined that water supply for Atlanta is an authorized purpose of Buford Dam, the stakeholders have yet to define how much water can be allocated for supply purposes.

In a separate case, citizen activists successfully sued the City of Atlanta in 1995 for its failure to meet federal and state water pollution control standards. The resulting consent decree—signed by the City of Atlanta in 1998—

committed the city to an accelerated program of remedial activities designed to further improve water quality in metropolitan Atlanta streams and rivers. Consequently, Atlanta citizens are currently paying some of the highest water and sewage rates in the country in order to resolve more than a generation of environmental neglect.[5] Clearly, the issue is not simply the amount of rain that falls from the sky, but how that amount has been managed over time.

The Georgia terrain upon which metropolitan Atlanta sits is the product of a spectacular series of natural developments that were no less brutal in their effects than they were unhurried in their culmination. The Appalachian Mountains, Piedmont, and Coastal Plain provinces that lay within Georgia evolved through a series of accordion-like motions of the earth's crust that began about 480 million years ago. Over time, oceans opened and closed as massive lithospheric plates crashed together, were pulled apart, or sideswiped one another like cars in a demolition derby. Periodically, the future southeastern portion of North America was overtaken by shallow seas, existed as volcanic islands, and at times displayed towering peaks not unlike the present Himalayan Alps.[6] As writer John McPhee explains, "The [Appalachian] rocks not only had been compressed like a carpet shoved across the floor but in places had been squeezed and shoved until folds tumbled forward into recumbent positions. Some folds had been broken. Some entire regions had been picked up and thrust many miles northwest" (McPhee 1983, 111).

The plate collisions, faulting, and varying degrees of rock consolidation have had a profound impact on Georgia's available water resources. Surface water provides approximately 78 percent of the total freshwater used throughout the state, with most of it flowing from the Blue Ridge Mountains (situated in Georgia's northeastern corner) and upper Piedmont (U.S. Geological Survey 2006). From this area emerges the Apalachicola-Chattahoochee-Flint (ACF) River basin system, which drains 19,800 square miles into western Georgia, eastern Alabama, and the Florida panhandle. From northeastern Georgia, the ACF flows through Buford Dam and Atlanta at the Chattahoochee River before merging with the Flint River above the Georgia-Florida state border. There it becomes the Apalachicola River, which continues south through the Florida panhandle into Apalachicola Bay before discharging into the Gulf of Mexico. Indeed, metropolitan Atlanta obtains an astounding 99 percent of its water supply from the rivers, lakes and streams originating within the state and relies on the Chattahoochee River alone for over 71 percent of its total water needs (Atlanta Regional Commission 2013b).

Atlanta's natural drainage system is also unique in that the Eastern Continental Divide separates the Chattahoochee River and South River watersheds. Rain falling on the east side of the divide flows to the Atlantic Ocean via the Ocmulgee River; rain falling on the divide's west side enters the Chattahoochee and continues to the Gulf of Mexico. This fact, as well as the low flow regime of many urban streams, has made drainage and sewage disposal in Atlanta exceedingly difficult because it required the construction of numerous wastewater treatment facilities. Atlanta, moreover, is one of four major cities in the world to be perched atop a continental divide, a geographic fact which makes it vulnerable to a lack of water (Metropolitan Planning Commission 1952).

Building "Second Nature": Public Safety, Public Health, and Economic Development in Pre-WWII Atlanta

The region's earliest inhabitants obtained water from springs, wells, and cisterns. But as population densities increased in the post–Civil War era, these decentralized sources proved insufficient for what was becoming the shipping center of the southeastern United States. Local residents, chastened by the memory of Sherman's flames and fearful of being struck by the waterborne diseases plaguing other southern cities, reacted in 1870 by authorizing city leaders to finance and construct a municipal water works.

Alas, this water supply station of two million gallons per day (MGD) was a virtual stillborn. Located on the headwaters of the South River, some five miles south of downtown Atlanta, it lacked the necessary pressure to perform even its intended functions, namely fire protection and street and sewer cleansing for the downtown business district. And because the city's natural drainage courses were little more than open sewers that emptied into the water supply reservoir, the system's untreated output was considered undrinkable by the late 1870s. A similar fate befell the city's artesian well. Completed in 1886 and intended to supplement the South River station, the well was capped and abandoned in 1888 after the city chemist found that it had also been contaminated by surface drainage (Ellis and Galishoff 1977).

Convinced that public health and public safety were at stake, city officials and local businesspeople sought the assistance of noted sanitary engineer Rudolph Hering in 1889. Hering recommended abandoning the South River in favor of the pure mountain water of the Chattahoochee River, which flowed above and around the city. Following his advice, the city purchased land in 1891 and began drafting plans for Atlanta's first "modern" water works system. Completed in 1893, the new system had a 20 MGD capacity and was composed of two interconnected complexes. Water was withdrawn at the junction of the Chattahoochee River and Peachtree Creek—roughly six miles above downtown Atlanta—and thrust uphill to a 176-million-gallon reservoir at the Hemphill Water Treatment Plant. The raw water was then sent through settling basins and mechanical filters before ultimately entering the distribution system for public consumption.

Despite having both the largest reservoir in the South and the best filtering technology available at the time, the AWW's production of potable water could barely keep pace with the city's skyrocketing population and its demands for ever-cleaner water. To trap and remove suspended particle from the drinking water, engineers soon added coagulating basins and clorination was also introduced to disinfect and further enhance quality. A second reservoir was constructed in 1923, bringing total reservoir capacity to 500 million gallons and treated capacity to 62 MGD. A third major expansion was initiated in 1941 to achieve 72 Mgal/d in total treated capacity (Atlanta 1975).

The Great Thirst: Post-WWII Water Supply Issues

During the years immediately following World War II, Atlanta found itself in an unsettling position with regard to its future water supplies. Like most other large American cities in the first half of the twentieth century, Atlanta operated a municipally owned, centralized water system. This network of facilities and distribution pipes utilized improved treatment and filtration techniques to provide increased capacity for local economic development and population growth. But these technological developments were insufficient for servicing the water needs of a population rapidly spreading into unincorporated suburban periphery that enveloped the city. Unlike Houston, which was able to meet its regional water demands by supplementing its groundwater reserves with the plentiful waters of the nearby San Jacinto River, and unable to tap into distant sources as Los Angeles had done with the Owens Valley, Atlanta was forced to rely on the inconsistent flows of the Chattahoochee River for its source of water.

To Atlanta's good fortune, the federal government was intent on fostering southeastern economic development and buttressing national defense in the post-war decades through the construction of multipurpose dams along the ACF River basin. Indeed, with military and economic preparedness still a concern after 1945, Congress looked favorably upon the construction of multipurpose dams as an important investment that could provide seemingly limitless power on demand as well as other benefits like navigation. Recognizing opportunity when it knocked at their door, Atlanta's metropolitan leaders and planners urged that a dam be constructed to the north of the city, arguing that the region's future economic growth—and its contribution to the nation— would be jeopardized unless regulation of the Chattahoochee's erratic flows was achieved. After Army Corps of Engineers Brigadier General James B. Newman suggested combining several hydroelectric sites into one large reservoir at Buford, Georgia, approximately 40 miles north of Atlanta, Congress decided to authorize and fully fund the construction of the multipurpose Buford Dam in 1946 (Hardy 2011).

Confident that the Lake Lanier reservoir system would meet the region's water resource needs for the foreseeable future, the City of Atlanta engaged in a two-pronged plan of attack to mitigate the deleterious effects of ongoing suburban sprawl (i.e., the loss of population, tax revenue, and white political control due to decentralized metropolitan growth). First, city officials tripled Atlanta's corporate boundaries and acquired 100,000 new tax-paying citizens through the annexation of portions of unincorporated northern Fulton County under the so-called "Plan of Improvement."[7] Second, the City of Atlanta collaborated with its regional planning agency, the Metropolitan Planning Commission, to bolster the area's network of highways, streets, and attendant urban services to ensure that the city remained the economic and cultural anchor for the four-county metropolitan area (Metropolitan Planning Commission 1952).

In 1952, two years after ground was broken on the Buford Dam project, the AWW embarked on a multiyear capital improvement program geared at supplying water to the new "citizen customers" created by the 1950 annexation. Divided into two five-year periods, the program was projected to cost $1 million dollars per year and include the expansion of distribution pipes, additional storage tanks, and the construction of another treatment facility near the Chattahoochee River. Upon the completion of the Chattahoochee Water Treatment Plant in 1960, Atlanta became the only city in the nation to have two independently operating water systems. By 1965, moreover, the city had extended its distribution network to cover a service area of approximately 600 square miles and could treat up to 92 MGD (Atlanta 1975).

Don't Flush on Me: Post-WWII Pollution Control Concerns

Despite this dynamism, metropolitan Atlanta did not exist in splendid isolation, and as its water capacity expanded in the post-war years, disputes over conflicting water demands quickly emerged. Buford Dam was merely the northernmost of four federally operated dams constructed between 1957 and 1963 to regulate the flow of the ACF River basin. Support from communities south of Atlanta had been instrumental in securing congressional authorization for these projects. For most ACF water users located to the south of Atlanta, supplying the burgeoning metropolis with adequate amounts of water was merely an incidental function of Buford Dam. Far more important to them was the achievement of river regulation for purposes of power generation, flood control, and navigation (Willoughby 1999).

Water pollution became the focus of downstream angst during the 1960s, particularly after the federal government declared in 1965 that the Chattahoochee River was "grossly polluted for about 100 miles below Atlanta" (Hardy 2011). As the mistreatment of the American landscape became better understood during the 1960s, the federal government's role in environmental affairs evolved from being a passive stimulator of economic development into an active promoter of environmental quality. The Water Pollution Control Act Amendments of 1972, otherwise known as the Clean Water Act (CWA), is an excellent case in point. The CWA not only established stricter pollution abatement requirements and enforcement measures, but also boosted up the federal share of facility construction from 35 to 75 percent (Milazzo 2006).

Assured of federal largesse for wastewater treatment facility upgrades, Atlanta officials began to tackle some of their most pressing pollution control needs. Most notable was the Three Rivers Water Quality Management Program, a mammoth $200 million facility enhancement and tunneling project. Completed in 1985, the project accomplished two major goals. First, the city's five facilities were modified to remove approximately 85 percent of the biological content from effluent (up from a mere 35 percent). Second, wastewater collected and treated in the eastern side of the continental divide was diverted away from three smaller receiving rivers and then delivered—via a 7.5-mile-long tunnel—back to its point of origin, the Chattahoochee River.[8]

Despite the tremendous expense of money and labor involved in the Three Rivers Project, the city's pollution control officials were again under mounting regulatory pressure by the end of the 1980s. The CWA's grants-in-aid program assisted only in the construction of treatment facilities; sewer collection system upgrades were not included. Atlanta, in fact, had 330 miles of combined sanitary and storm sewers beneath its downtown and midtown areas that were ineligible for CWA funds. A relic of nineteenth-century engineering, this system typically operated efficiently under dry weather conditions. But during heavy storm events, the wastewater treatment facilities fed by the system became overburdened, leaving excesses of storm and sanitary waters completely untreated. This stew of chemical and biological water was instead released into nearby creeks through relief structures known as combined system overflows. The resulting unfiltered debris and wastewater, which contained bacteria and chemical levels hundreds of times higher than federal water pollution standards, flowed through Atlanta's parks and neighborhoods and to downstream communities.[9]

Constrained by past technological choices but bereft of federal munificence, the city announced a pair of design plans in 1990 that officials hoped would bring Atlanta into compliance with federal and state water quality standards as quickly and cheaply as possible. To reduce the pollution, the city floated a $20 million proposal to build "mini treatment" plants at five of the city's most troublesome overflow points. In addition, city engineers suggested boring a second underground tunnel to store and treat phosphate-laden effluent, which was regarded by ecologists as a major contributor to the extreme depletion of oxygen, or eutrophication, of water bodies.

Each plan ran headlong into a diverse but determined grassroots opposition that reflected the racial and class composition of each affected community. Arguing that the city's remedial efforts amounted to a "band aid" approach, activists demanded design alterations. Some asserted that complete sewer separation was the only responsible answer. Other activists, however, chafed at any plans to expand facilities in or around majority-black neighborhoods and denounced such measures as evidence of "environmental racism" (Hardy 2011).

Struggling with this hydra-headed opposition, Atlanta missed its mandated compliance deadlines. As a result, the city not only incurred millions of dollars in pollution control fines but also had to weather a storm of sewer moratoria. Fed up with the city's inaction, a group of citizen-activists decided to sue the city in 1995 for its continued violation of federal water quality standards, a prescient maneuver that ultimately resulted in the aforementioned 1998 consent decree and Mayor Franklin's Clean Water Atlanta initiative (Hardy 2011).

Will the Water Last?: The Spectre of the Tri-State Water Wars

Throughout the 1990s, while Atlanta's water managers struggled to address deficiencies in the city's water supply and wastewater infrastructure, a new series of legal hurdles emerged that threatened to reduce the amount of water available to the region. Though the so-called "tri-state water wars" had no direct bearing on the city's decision to privatize its waters supply system, the issue was an ambient concern that could not be ignored.

The origins of this interstate dispute are complex and diverse, but litigation largely revolved around whether Congress intended for water supply to be included among Lake Lanier's authorized uses.[10] Metropolitan Atlanta experienced rapid population in the years after Buford Dam was completed in 1957. And as the region's population increased, so did its total water needs, which heightened downstream tensions over Atlanta's perceived abuses of the ACF basin. During the early 1970s, when metro water usage was roughly 188 MGD, the Army Corps of Engineers (Corps) and the Atlanta Regional Commission (ARC) began studying alternative means for satisfying metro Atlanta's anticipated water demands. After 16 years of study, the Corps proposed the reallocation of storage in Lake Lanier from hydroelectric power to water supply use so that metro Atlanta could withdraw the 529 MGD that the ARC believed the area required (Hardy 2011).

Alabama, a downstream user, was concerned that Atlanta's ever-increasing thirst would severely limit its own use of water for power generation, fisheries, and barge traffic. It sued the Corps in June 1990, arguing that the agency did not properly assess—as required by the National Environmental Protection Act—the environmental impacts of water withdrawals from Lake Lanier before entering into contracts with water supply providers from Atlanta. Shortly thereafter, Florida, another downstream user, joined the suit, claiming that it needed enough freshwater to reach the Apalachicola Bay in order to sustain its multimillion-dollar shellfish industry. Both plaintiffs also argued that water supply was not among the intended uses of Lake Lanier. The State of Georgia, along with the ARC and the City of Atlanta, countered that not only is water supply an authorized use but that Georgia, as a sovereign state, has the right to maintain control over the allocation of water originating within the state, provided minimum state-line flows are delivered.[11]

The case was immediately "stayed" to allow for negotiations among the principal stakeholders. But in 2009, after two decades of comprehensive studies, a failed interstate compact, and no agreement on an allocation formula, the litigation was revived and argued before U.S. District Judge Paul Magnuson. Based on his interpretation of congressional action in 1946, Judge Magnuson ruled that the only authorized purposes for Lake Lanier are hydropower, flood control, and navigation. He also gave the parties three years to obtain congressional sanction for water supply purposes. Failure to gain that approval, he declared, would result in the operation of Buford Dam reverting to "base line" operations of the mid-1970s.

The State of Georgia and its supporters appealed the ruling immediately, arguing that returning metro Atlanta's water withdrawals to mid-1970s levels would present a public health and safety threat to the three million people of metro Atlanta who depend on Lake Lanier for water supply and would also wreak havoc on the economy of the southeast. Fortunately for Atlanta, the appeals court rejected Judge Magnuson's ruling and concluded on June 28, 2011 that downstream water supply is an authorized purpose of Lake Lanier (Hardy 2011). The ruling further gave the Corps one year to determine the extent of its authority, to which the Corps responded on June 12, 2012 with plans for further analysis and evaluation of proposals from the three states. Florida and Alabama, meanwhile, maintained their intent to appeal this decision to the U.S. Supreme Court, a motion the court denied on June 25, 2012 (Bluestein, Rankin, and Trubey 2012).

Conclusion

Atlanta has experienced economic and demographic dynamism on par with the most resolute of American cities. Yet Atlanta is unlike virtually every other city in at least one key respect: it was not founded upon a major river or body of water and has been unable tap into distant sources of water. This has resulted in the need to reconcile its ambitions as a regional metropolis with the limitations of a natural watershed.

Constraining as the physical environment has been, it did not determine Atlanta's course of development. Of greater importance were the ways that social values and political priorities affected the appropriation and use of available resources. All available evidence suggests that Atlanta's political and civic leaders clearly wanted to facilitate economic growth. This intent runs straight through the successful lobbying for the construction of Buford Dam as well as for the highways, skyscrapers, sports stadiums, and shopping centers that have been constructed over the past half century.

However, even as regional leaders were urging the federal government for assistance in securing water supplies, the City of Atlanta implemented annexation and regional land use plans that would later strain its water resources. The irony of these developments is striking. Atlanta leaders entered the 1950s with a clear understanding of the limitations of the Chattahoochee River watershed but exited that decade engaging in practices that undermined the best intentions of regional planners. Buford Dam certainly regulated the Chattahoochee's flows but the rapid extension of highways, lack of regulations to limit the geographic extent of suburban development, and expansion of water treatment capacity invited a kind of water consumption at odds with the coordinated regional development that Atlanta officials purportedly championed.

In 1968 journalist W. Eugene Smith wrote, "Atlanta officials might be compared to the little old lady who lived in a shoe in respect to pollution control—they have so many problems they don't know what to do." (Smith 1968). Indeed, not only did Smith's humorous assessment neatly express the difficulties Atlanta had in addressing its pressing water quality problems, but it is also suggestive of the city's "whack-a-mole" approach to addressing the broader range of water issues it faced during the twentieth century: resolve one problem and another pops up. As this chapter has tried to illuminate the costs and consequences of the city's belated attempts to properly manage its limited water resources, let us hope that Atlanta has learned from its past mistakes and opts for more comprehensive—and sustainable—environmental policies for the twenty-first century.

CHAPTER 25

Atlantic Station: Location, Location, Location

Brian Leary

PRACTITIONER PERSPECTIVE

Atlantic Station—a massive, mixed use development—is located in the middle of the largest city in a state that has a poor history of cleaning environmentally challenged sites. Opened in 2005, the community now has over 7,000 employees working in 1.5 million square feet of class-A office space. The project also includes 1.3 million square feet of retail and entertainment space, 2,600 residential units, and 10,000 parking spaces (3,000 less than original zoning required). Five thousand people now reside in the single-family homes, townhomes, low-rise apartments, and high-rise condominiums within the master planned development. The community is the subject of extensive media attention and has won numerous environmental and development awards, including the prestigious National Phoenix Award from the U. S. Environmental Protection Agency (EPA) and the Atlanta Business Chronicle Deal of the Year award.

The Atlanta region experienced unprecedented growth in the 1980s and 1990s, but that growth was exclusively suburban. At the time, Atlanta was changing into a region whose residents endured increasingly longer commutes, a degradation in air quality, and a deterioration of the perceived quality of life. TV sitcoms such as *Happy Days*, *Leave it to Beaver*, and even *Alf* reinforced the American Dream as exclusively suburban. Everything changed with the sunset of the 1980s, when TV shows such as *Sex in the City* and *Seinfeld* redefined public perceptions of city living as an attractive, lucrative, and desirable alternative. City living could fulfill the American dream, and Atlantic Station was poised to take advantage of the change in attitudes.

In 1901 the founders of the Atlanta Steel Hoop & Barrel Company saw the need for a scrap mill in the southeast. Scrap metal was shipped from the eastern U.S. to the steel site located along the southern rail line. The scrap was melted and reworked into barrel hoops, nails, wire, and chain link. A century of operations at Atlantic Steel took a toll on the property at the same time that Atlanta grew to encompass the site. Had it not been home to an active steel mill, the site would have been redeveloped years ago, given its prime proximity two miles north of downtown Atlanta and along Interstate 75/85. Fortunately, the property had been well managed by a single owner throughout its operation and had limited toxic waste. Extensive historical records provided by the owner were useful in making the site eligible for an expedited remediation process (DeSousa and D'Souza 2013).

By the mid-1990s, the Atlantic Steel property had been on the market for ten years with a list price of $100 million. Local and national developers envisioned many possibilities, including an Olympic stadium, a horse racetrack, and even a casino (illegal in the city of Atlanta and the state of Georgia). Finally, the Jacoby Group closed on the property in 1998 for $76 million. At that time, direct vehicular access to the site was nonexistent, with no exits from the adjacent Interstate 75/85, Atlanta's 21-lane downtown connector. The northern boundary of the Atlantic Steel property is the Norfolk Southern railroad and to the west is the transitional industrial West Midtown, an area developing into a mixed use neighborhood. Home Park, a rental neighborhood that was 80 percent renter occupied by Georgia Tech students during Atlantic Steel's last days, is located south of the site.

Project XL Cleanup and the Greenlight Committee

Permitting for the mixed use development required that the site to be cleaned up and that direct access be provided to the Interstate 75/85 connector. To provide access to the interstate, ramps and bridges had to be constructed. Atlanta was classified by the EPA as a nonattainment zone in 1997 due to ground-level ozone, and the region failed to deliver a conforming transportation plan per the Clean Air Act. Consequently, the EPA would not permit new transportation projects until Atlanta was in conformity, a process that could take several years to remedy. The developers convinced then governor Roy Barnes and the state legislators that the proposed mixed use community could provide a live-work-play community adjacent to Atlanta's midtown area and reduce vehicular trips generated while providing concentrated activity. Barnes established a cross-agency Green Light Committee to ensure that the project was a high priority and that the positive momentum was maintained.

The site was remediated in partnership with the Georgia Environmental Protection Division (EPD) of the Georgia Department of Natural Resources (DNR). Jacoby formed Atlantic Station LLC with AIG Global Real Estate, the entity tasked to clean up and develop the site, and the EPD monitored the remediation process called Project XL. The Jacoby Group engaged LAW Engineering (now Amec), which had over 50 years of geotechnical experience with the Atlantic Steel plant to assess the feasibility of the site (U.S. Environmental Protection Agency 2013a). Although it had been a steel mill, the fairly low-impact operation and site operations made it a manageable remediation assignment.

Atlantic Station could not go vertical until the cleanup and access issues were solved. Green Light Committee members from over 20 agencies—including representatives from the EPA, the EPD, the DNR, federal and state transportation agencies, the governor's office, the state of Georgia, Fulton County and the city of Atlanta—were required to meet each week. After two years of meetings, construction permits were finally issued for the 17th Street Bridge over the connector, and the site cleanup began. A fundamental question pertaining to the remediation plan was what to do with the inert steelmaking byproduct, slag, which was considered nontoxic but had to be removed to a permitted facility or encapsulated onsite. The gravel-like slag ranged in depth from four inches to 40 feet over the site, with a volume close to one million cubic yards. After the cost of off-site removal was estimated to be over $100 million, the engineers decided to encapsulate and balance the slag onsite (Dobbins 2013).

The Squeaky Wheel

Concerned about traffic cutting through their neighborhoods, residents of the adjacent communities of Home Park and Loring Heights refused to approve certain street connections, making it impossible to provide access by completing the street grid (Dagenhart, Leigh, and Skach 2006). This issue is singularly memorialized in Atlantic Station's convoluted rezoning, which included 26 additional conditions—a record which still stands in the city.

Residents of a third neighborhood, Ansley Park, located one mile east of the connector, were supportive during the rezoning process but later during the environmental assessment threatened legal action over potential cut-through traffic. After numerous community meetings and highly publicized threats to halt the cleanup and bridge permits, the neighborhood pressure proved effective, and developers offered $2.6 million to the Ansley Park Civic Association for pedestrian and traffic improvements. The permits were issued and construction began.

The Future

The community's master plan is approximately 45 percent complete, reflecting development slowing primarily due to the effects of the Great Recession. Downtown Atlanta no longer features major retail, making Atlantic Station the place to go for intown shopping. Shoppers can choose from over 80 national and local retailers ranging from Ann Taylor to the Z Gallerie, plus the first and very popular IKEA in the southeastern U.S. On Sundays, the Midtown Bridge Church calls the movie theatre home, and Soka Gakkai International recently built a 12,000-square-foot Buddhist cultural center—making it one of the first live-work-play and pray communities built in the twenty-first century.

What makes community living great at Atlantic Station is the diversity of its population and residential options. Student housing units rent from $450 per month; a block away, apartments lease for $3,000 a month. The town-house at the top of the Atlantic highrise tower sold in 2013 for $1.5 million. Target, Publix, and IKEA are all within walking distance. Jobs are diverse as well, with employers ranging from Wells Fargo Bank to Ogilvy & Mather to West Elm. An economic boost to the city has resulted from the 300 workers employed at the steel plant in the 1980s to the over 10,000 employees currently working onsite. In 1988, the last year of the steel mill's operation, the tax bill for the property was slightly more than $300,000. Today, close to $20 million in annual property taxes are generated, despite the fact that the build-out is currently at 45 percent. With approximately $400 million in new annual retail sales, the seven percent local tax rate delivers tens of millions of dollars to the City of Atlanta, Fulton County, and the Metropolitan Atlanta Rapid Transit Authority (MARTA). These extraordinary increases in property tax and sales tax revenues are central to the legacy of Atlantic Station, demonstrating the economic and civic value of transforming environmentally challenged sites into new uses and opportunities.

Atlantic Station has evolved into a magnet for sports, shopping, and entertainment. The project design evolved from big-box to "macro mixed use" to broken-up blocks that cater to pedestrians. Bike lanes are prominent and the wide streets will eventually accommodate a dedicated rail transit line. Shuttles run regularly to the Arts Center MARTA station less than one mile away, which links to a system that helps Atlantans make over 69 million rail trips a year. Atlantic Station is best described locally as a small town in a big city (Trubey 2013).

CHAPTER 26

Planning for the Forest and the Trees: The City in a Forest

Jason Vargo

Since Atlanta's beginnings, the city and surrounding settlements have been connected to the forest. The southeastern woods run along the Appalachian spine and cover the northern half of Georgia with old hardwoods, tall pines, and an understory of dense rhododendron. The area was once home to the Creek and Cherokee Indians. The region's first Western settlers made their livings in Atlanta's sawmills, and development proceeded in close relation to the region's natural environment. Removing trees and grading the hard red clay took time and energy. Today's modern machines and tools make building something in Atlanta much quicker and easier. Though it still involves clearing the land of trees, the connection between urban life at the center and the region's natural landscape, the forest, has been lost.

This historic natural character of the Piedmont forest earned Atlanta the nickname "the city in a forest," and helped form the city's identity. Atlanta's position as a transportation hub—first as "Terminus," a railroad hub and more recently as home to one of the world's busiest airports—has helped solidify this dominant environmental feature in the city's ethos. Many travelers flying over the Atlanta metropolitan area may have the pleasure of noticing the region's rich canopy of trees. From the air the city appears green and blossoming; however, as recent storms have taken down old trees in some of Atlanta's leafier neighborhoods, tree loss has gained attention in the region (Brown 2011; WSB-TV 2011). While recent droughts have been blamed for these losses, other evidence suggests that large-scale forest loss is an issue that deserves serious attention; Atlanta may be sacrificing its

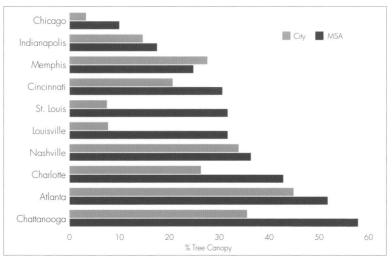

Figure 26.1. Forest coverage in Southeast/Midwest cities for both primary city and metropolitan statistical area, 2001. (Source: Data from U.S. Department of the Interior 2009.)

greatest environmental resource and an integral part of its character as a result of rapid growth.

This chapter uses the example of Atlanta's forest, as a prominent natural feature of the region, to demonstrate the effects of growth patterns on resource consumption and the 'environmental' services provided by natural landscapes. While this review focuses on a specific aspect of the environment, the myriad benefits of the forest and its connections with other environmental systems—such as air, water, and soil health—must not be overlooked. The findings from this example help solidify a role for planning activities in environmental management, one that extends beyond forest conservation or preservation to more directly address the relationship between metropolitan growth and natural systems.

A Disappearing Regional Resource

Atlanta remains one of the most forested cities in the country: among 14 major American metropolitan areas in a recent analysis (Figure 27.1), Atlanta has the greatest tree canopy density and most overall regional tree cover (Nowak et al. 2008). Surely, as homes have been built, trees have had to come down. We can assume that new, larger homes farther from the city center would take down more forests, but to what degree is this occurring? How do we evaluate tree loss and determine what needs to be done? And what is the role of planning in this process?

The first question regarding the measurement of forest decline is typically one of environmental management and science. Metrics that describe the structure and fragmentation of the forests give us a better idea of how exactly the forest is changing over time and begin to uncover the causes of these changes. Georgia's forests were once valued for the "[t]imber [as] a crop [that] can be harvested again and again" (American Forest Products Industries 1948). Today, the land on which forests stand is the commodity, rather than the trees, and the approach is to destroy forests rather than sustain them in order to achieve profits. Satellite images since the 1970s show the loss of nearly 50 percent of the region's tree canopy, and with varying rates from county to county as growth has proceeded outward (American Forests 2002). The expansion of Atlanta's urban area—an increase of more than 250 percent from 1973 to 1999—has badly fragmented the region's forests, degrading the habitat of birds, amphibians, and mammals while also increasing the susceptibility of remaining trees to pests, drought, and disease and making the restoration of original ecosystems more difficult (Kramer et al. 2003; Miller 2012).[1] So, despite Atlanta's stature as a forested city (Figure 26.1), comparisons over time yield less favorable descriptions.

Answering the question of whether forest loss merits action requires identifying and quantifying the benefits of the forest around Atlanta. The value of a stand of trees once they are turned into boards and reams is one measure. Another would be the increase in home value from large trees on properties, or the energy savings provided by the same trees as they shade homes. The habitat provision, biodiversity, air pollution reductions, water quality improvements, and flood management are other benefits of the forest. Studies have shown the additive effect of trees and forest conservation hold significant net benefits for cities (McPherson et al. 2005; Peper et al. 2007). In 2001, American Forests estimated the value of forests in the Atlanta metropolitan area to be approximately $2.5 billion, with some benefits ($86 million for storm water) accruing annually (American Forests 2001). Because the health and economic benefits of regional forests are significant, maintaining and capitalizing on this resource are important to planning, political, and development goals.

In considering the connections between environmental change and the health, financial stability, and overall sustainability of the region more comprehensively, we ask the most important question: what is Atlanta to do about this? The most effective solutions require a more nuanced understanding of the causes behind these trends. We should intuitively start by comparing environmental trends with population trends. Indeed, beginning in the 1970s and continuing through the 1990s and into the housing bubble of 2006–2007, Atlanta experienced large increases in population and developed area. In the 1990s, the Atlanta metropolitan region contained some of the fastest-growing counties in the nation. Over the course of the last 20 to 30 years, the metropolitan statistical area (MSA) has continued to expand, to include 28 counties in 2010 covering more than 8,000 square miles (Metro Atlanta Chamber 2006).

Linking Population Growth and Environmental Change

Understanding the relationships between Atlanta's recent growth, development patterns, and forest loss can help inform policy and design strategies to reduce regional forest loss. A study at Georgia Tech's Urban Climate Lab examined strategies to mitigate urban heat by estimating the land cover change per capita between 1992 and 2001 resulting from urban, suburban, and rural development patterns. The goal was to understand how much different patterns of development contributed to forest consumption and replacement with impervious surfaces like pavement and concrete (Vargo et al. 2013).

Satellite imagery showing the locations and amount of forest converted to developed land was combined with population data to link the number of people moving to an area with the amount of forest land converted. By considering environmental change with particular land uses and growth management strategies, this approach connects regional resource preservation to planning. Categorizing the region into urban, suburban, and rural areas was done to capture important differences in population density and the character of settlement throughout the Atlanta region; small blocks and a regular layout typify urban tracts, while rural areas contain many more forested and cultivated patches (Figure 26.2).

This analysis shows that much of the MSA consists of rural landscapes and the majority of the population increase in the 1990s involved suburban settlement patterns (Figure 26.3). This means that the majority of new growth (new population and homes) in the region followed a pattern similar to that seen in the suburban image in Figure 26.2. For the area shown, this pattern appears to include a fair amount of development and considerable forest cover. The region's lack of physical boundaries accommodates considerable suburban growth with lots that can still contain several trees. This puts a significant portion of the region's canopy on private property, hampering regional oversight and putting the problem of forest loss out of sight for most residents until trees fall in their neighborhoods.

A closer look at the land conversions claiming Atlanta's forest (Figure 26.4) shows changes in the suburban and rural areas. These areas constitute the ma-

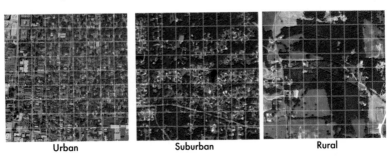

| Urban | Suburban | Rural |

Figure 26.2. Examples of urban, suburban, and rural classes around Atlanta. Each image is approximately 81 NLCD pixels (about 81 acres). (Source: Maps from Google Earth; analysis by author.)

ATLANTA METRO

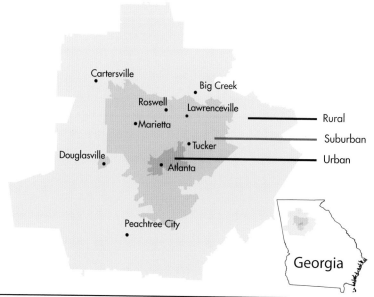

	Total	Rural	Suburban	Urban
Area (1,000 acres)	3,972	3,043	872	57
		76.6%	21.9%	1.4%
1990 (1,000 pers.)	2,960	792	1,834	334
		26.8%	62%	11.3%
2000 (1,000 pers.)	4,112	1,231	2,528	353
		29.9%	62.3%	8.6%
Population Change (1,000 pers.)	1,152	440	694	18
		38.1%	60.3%	1.6%

Figure 26.3. Population and area of the Atlanta metropolitan regional by urban-rural classification. (Source: Data from U.S. Department of the Interior 2009; U.S. Census Bureau 1990, 2000.)

jority of the region (Figure 26.3) and possess undeveloped land. About 400 square miles (about 250,000 acres) of Atlanta forest were lost between 1992 and 2001. This acreage represents about seven percent of the total metropolitan area and a loss of 12 percent of the existing forest area in 1992. If that rate of loss continued, Atlanta's forest would make up less than 15 percent of the entire region by the end of the century, a far cry from the more than 50 percent at the beginning of the study period and what would hardly constitute a "city in a forest." The trend raises important questions about the overall value of the north Georgia forests. For example, does the regional economic benefit of forest

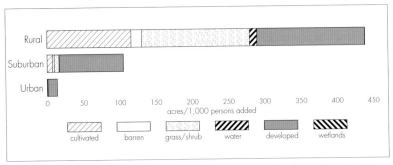

Figure 26.4. Atlanta forest conversions by urban, suburban, and rural class. (Source: Data from U.S. Department of the Interior 2009; U.S. Census Bureau 1990, 2000.)

conversion to agricultural land and chicken farms outweigh the benefits of the forest on that same land? Several have already argued that such a change to the region's ecosystem is alarming, if not also costly in terms of the environmental services sacrificed (American Forests 2001, 2002).

During the same decade, the region added about 200 square miles (about 125,000 acres) of developed land cover,[2] almost all of it coming from land that was previously forested (Vargo et al. 2013).This is an average of about 4,000 square feet of building, asphalt, and concrete per person added to the region. This additional developed land cover is not entirely from residential construction, but also includes the new construction of commercial buildings and parking lots as well as the municipal construction of new roads, libraries, police stations, and other structures. The construction and maintenance of these facilities is a substantial financial cost for the city and region to absorb in addition to the lost environmental benefits. Consider that Atlanta is now notorious for its constantly polluted waterways and expensive sewer remediation projects (Pace 1999),[3] and the region's forests become more valuable as the bills for these projects climb.

The differences across the urban-suburban-rural typology make clear the role of planning in slowing deforestation. Figure 26.4 shows that on a per capita basis more forest is lost for each rural and suburban resident than for their urban counterparts. Likewise, more developed land is added for each new resident in suburban and rural areas than for residents in urban areas. Indeed, some rural lands are transitioned from forest to other uses because of urban residents – for example, some forest on the outskirts of the MSA are converted to agricultural land to help support the increased population of the region, some of whom live in urban areas. To examine the direct land cover requirements of new residents, the forest-to-developed conversions, specifically, were considered.

There are several reasons, however, that rural and suburban patterns of development are expected to directly require more forest and developed land

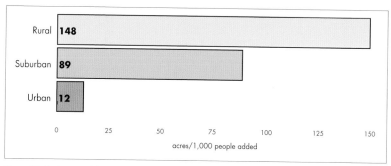

Figure 26.5. Amount of forest converted to developed land by urban-rural classification. (Source: Data from U.S. Department of the Interior 2009; U.S. Census Bureau 1990, 2000.)

for each new resident. The first and most obvious reason concerns density. The increased density of urban areas means 10 acres can accommodate 50 new residents compared to the 100 acres required in a less dense area. For a greenfield development on previously undeveloped land, this reduces the amount of forest that needs to be removed. When existing urban sites are adapted or redeveloped to accommodate increased density, forests do not necessarily need to be cleared. In fact the construction process presents an opportunity to reassess site-level tree canopy. Not only are people closer together in downtown areas, but they also live in smaller homes, on smaller lots with smaller yards, and with fewer vehicles. This results in less driveway paving, less roof space, smaller garages, and narrower roads. In addition to conserving the native forest around Atlanta, more compact development also improves the utility and cost-effectiveness of investments in public transportation and sanitation and electrical infrastructures. Concentrating people around these strategic infrastructures increases their use and efficiency. With the added benefits of conserving forest, encouraging this type of "small growth" makes sense for both environmental and fiscal reasons.

The potential impact of encouraging new urban rather than suburban development is shown through satellite data for specific locations that were forest in the beginning of the 1990s and became developed land by 2000. These conversions for new residents added through rural and suburban development patterns are 12 and 7 times, respectively, the magnitude that of urban land conversions (Figure 26.5). The lesser impact in urban areas is due in part to smaller homes that are closer together, restaurants and grocery stores with apartments above, and less land devoted to parking. If half of the suburban population growth during the study period had been added following a more urban pattern of development, over 77 square miles (about 50,000 acres) of forests may have been preserved the equivalent of 20 percent of the total forest lost during the decade.

Grow Trees, Preserve Forests

Clearly, Atlanta's forest, while impressive compared to the forest cover of other American cities, is being lost; that loss comes at a cost to the region (Nowak and Dwyer 2007). Population growth and environmental change show that the type of growth in the region matters immensely for forest preservation. This runs counter to an approach focused on the development of individual lots, which suggests that more single-family homes on larger lots provide the opportunity for increased onsite conservation by individual property owners (Mincey, Schmitt-Harsh, and Thurau 2013). While it is true that lower density will likely produce more lots where trees surround homes, this pattern of development also places more homes in the middle of wooded areas. Or rather, this development pattern breaks up the forest with new homes and relies on a supply of such lands for regional growth. The impact on the forest, particularly with respect to the fragmentation of forested land, becomes evident only when a regional perspective is taken.

Certainly, site planning and local regulation have an important role to play in preserving tree canopy. This is particularly true of urban areas. Preservation measures in areas around new construction, the replacement of lost trees, and landscaping in public rights-of-way must occur to ensure that urban areas are not completely stripped of vegetation. Properly integrating trees into the dense built environments of urban areas requires new planting techniques and better landscape design standards. The City of Toronto has pioneered the use of new infrastructure technology called Silva Cells to support its street trees and provide 1,000 square feet of soil per tree, which the city now requires (DeepRoot Canada Corportation 2013). This innovative system encourages new urban canopy as the city works to reach its goal of increasing the tree coverage from 17 to 40 percent in order to cope with climate change, manage storm water, and create a more pleasant and attractive environment for residents.

Effective tree ordinances also play an important role by identifying acceptable species for new plantings, providing stipulations for tree removal, and valuing trees as part of the urban landscape. The City of Atlanta tree ordinance is a model for surrounding communities (Atlanta 2003). Through the ordinance, the city collects funds from fees for permitted tree removals and this money is used for new plantings around the city. The metropolitan area's acting urban forest steward and leading advocacy organization for trees, Trees Atlanta, has planted an estimated 88,000 trees since 1985 (Trees Atlanta 2013; Warhop 2007). Those efforts, however, pale in comparison to the amount of forest lost around Atlanta's edges. The Natural Resources Spatial Analysis Lab at the University of Georgia estimated that over much of the last two decades, 50 acres of tree canopy disappeared each day. Assuming that the stands of trees around Atlanta's periphery being taken down were only moderately dense, Trees Atlanta's decades of plantings are equivalent to what was lost to Atlanta's growth in less than a month.

Thus, urban forestry is a necessary but insufficient part of the solution (Hill, Dorfman, and Kramer 2010). Widely different ecological trends across the urban-rural typology (Figures 26.4 and 26.5) suggest a role for environmental planning in championing regional environmental approaches while providing design and policy guidance for urban ecological integration. Regional growth management strategies for new development can help minimize costs and impacts. Urban growth boundaries are perhaps the best-known strategy for pacing the expansion of urban areas and required services, but others include capital improvement planning, tax incentives for preservation of lands, impacts fees, and zoning. Public ownership of lands, including parks and preserves, is another important piece of the preservation puzzle. These actions go beyond the forests themselves and can also help preserve water, soil, and air quality. Particularly at the exurban fringe, regional investment in lands could be an efficient and effective way to protect regional environmental services. Regional water planning boards, state and national agencies, county recreation departments, and major businesses all have stakes in preserving this aspect of Atlanta, and these entities should participate in developing solutions.

Today's Forest Is Tomorrow's Forest

By 2040, the metropolitan area population of Atlanta is expected to top more than eight million people, double the population in 2000 (Atlanta Regional Commission 2010). If the region follows the same development pattern it did in the 1990s, a quarter of the remaining forestland in the 20-county area will be converted to developed land, not including the forest that will be converted to large lawns around new homes. This is a massive change in the ecosystem of north Georgia, and only regional foresight and administration can help the metro region grow in number without subsequent negative environmental outcomes.

Research has shown that Atlanta's forest is disappearing and the costs are quantifiable; what is desperately needed now are strategies to preserve Atlanta's sylvan character in real and sustainable ways. The large-lot, low-density approach might save trees, but it hinders the preservation of the most valuable parts of the forest, large stands of contiguous forest. Planning that considers the synergy between development patterns and urban design can address environmental degradation at various levels—from landscaping on individual lots to complex regional trends and growth. Most importantly, such strategies benefit not just the environment, but also improve public health, livability, and quality of life in Atlanta.

CHAPTER 27

The Buckhead Community Improvement District

Jim Durrett

The Buckhead community on the north side of the city of Atlanta came into existence in the mid-1800s in the area around the present-day intersection of Atlanta's "Main Street"—Peachtree Road—and West Paces Ferry Road. Its evolution has been one of distinct transition: from streetcar-served "country" homes belonging to downtown Atlanta's business leaders, to an automobile-dominated suburban collection of large-lot subdivisions and the largest shopping mall (Lenox Square) in the southeastern United States, to a more walkable urban center of commerce served by several rail transit stations. Formed in 1999 by a vote of commercial property owners according to procedures and for purposes spelled out in Georgia state law, the 2.5-square-mile Buckhead Community Improvement District (BCID) has funded projects and programs addressing transportation needs and other aspects of the public realm that have set the stage for the growth of Buckhead's commercial core as a more walkable, livable urban center.

In Georgia, community improvement districts (CIDs) are created by a vote of commercial property owners that must pass two tests. First, a simple majority of owners of commercial parcels within the proposed district boundaries must vote to form the district. Second, owners of at least 75 percent of the assessed value of commercial property within the proposed district boundaries must also vote to form the district. An ad valorem tax millage rate is set that applies only to non-residential property. The local government jurisdiction within which the CID is to be established then votes to approve the district and a board of directors is selected. *Ad valorem* taxes are subsequently collected and spent by the CID to make improvements within the district as determined by the board of directors (Rainey 2013) .

The initial priority project for the BCID was figuring out how to address increasing traffic congestion on Peachtree Road, a state route, that was choking future growth prospects for the district, an extremely important job center and tax base in the city of Atlanta. A multiyear, collaborative visioning, planning, design, and construction project has now transformed 1.2 miles of Peachtree from a virtual sewer for cars into a "complete street." This project received the Grand Award from the American Council of Engineering Companies of Georgia as part of its 2008 Engineering Excellence Awards. Planning for the transformation of the remaining mile of Peachtree within the BCID boundary is now underway, with construction expected in 2014 (Livable Buckhead Community 2013; Pendered 2013c).

Three additional projects addressing multimodal accessibility are recently completed, under construction, or planned for construction in 2014. First, the pedestrian bridge over Georgia State Route 400—a collaboration with the Metropolitan Atlanta Rapid Transit Authority (MARTA), the Federal Transit Administration, and others—will create a much-needed connection between residential and commercial properties separated by a major state highway; provide an important new entrance into MARTA's Buckhead station; transform transit-challenged properties into transit-accessible properties; and stimulate additional transit-oriented development (Buckhead CID 2013). Second, PATH400—an effort involving Livable Buckhead and the PATH Foundation—will be a multiuse trail utilizing a state highway right-of-way and will extend approximately five miles from the neighborhoods north of Buckhead's commercial core to connect with the Atlanta BeltLine (Pendered 2013). Third, the renovation of streetscapes in the area surrounding the much-anticipated Buckhead Atlanta mixed use redevelopment at Peachtree Road and West Paces Ferry Road will enhance multimodal access.

Other transportation projects are in different stages of planning, but they all address current and anticipated needs based upon changing demographics and future land use changes guided by two special public interest (SPI) zoning ordinances, SPI-9 and SPI-12. These ordinances cover the majority of the BCID and were recently rewritten with funding and other support from the BCID and its community and agency partners. These two zoning ordinances were the first form-based codes adopted in the city of Atlanta (Rainey 2013).

The BCID has recently funded a study (from which PATH400 became a reality) to determine the open space needs and opportunities of the larger Buckhead community. The BCID also funds a free last-mile-connectivity shuttle, "the buc", connecting rail transit stations to places of employment during morning and evening commute times, and it provides financial support to the Buckhead Area Transportation Management Association, which provides commute options support to area businesses and employees. Finally, in 2013 the BCID worked with several other CIDs in the Atlanta region to raise local funds to match national foundation funding to conduct an analysis of the region's walkable urban places. The study was directed by Christopher Leinberger of the Brookings Institution and George Washington University (GWU), with support from the Atlanta Regional Commission and Georgia Institute of Technology's School of City and Regional Planning. The methodology, results and conclusions were published in *The WalkUP Wake-Up Call: Atlanta*, published by GWU's Center for Real Estate and Urban Analysis (Leinberger and Austin 2013).

The Buckhead CID's success and impact to date are due to several factors: a board of directors that is able to see beyond today to anticipate the needs of tomorrow; a small but highly-skilled staff with complementary strengths and the ability to work with private-sector consulting engineers and planners as well as other partners and stakeholders; a relationship of earned trust and respect with partner city, regional, and state agencies; and a commitment to plan, design, and implement projects and programs based upon a holistic and data-driven view of transportation, land use, and placemaking. At a recent meeting in Detroit, I learned of a fascinating study funded by the Knight Foundation called "Soul of the Community," which examined why people love—or become attached to—where they live, and ultimately why that matters to cities. The research confirms what many of us already know to be true: if people are attached to their communities, local economies thrive. The report found that the principle drivers of attachment are availability of social offerings, aesthetics, and openness of a place (Knight Foundation 2010). Buckhead CID is working on projects with the goal of attaching people to our community.

CHAPTER 28

Atlanta's Role in the State of Georgia

David Pendered

Georgia has never been particularly fond of its fifth capital city. Nor has Atlanta been such a good fit in Georgia, as W.E.B. Du Bois (1903) observed when he described Atlanta as "south of the North, yet north of the South"—the cradle of the civil rights movement in the United States that took the phoenix as its symbol, for Atlanta's rise from the ashes of the Civil War. The city's climb within its own deep South state has often been a battle onto itself.

The Georgia General Assembly designated Atlanta Georgia's capital in 1868. Simultaneously, the legislature implemented a county-unit system of voting intended to dilute the political strength of urbanizing areas—which happened to have significant numbers of black voters—such as Atlanta (Hill 1994). This electoral system concentrated political power in rural, white-dominated communities for a century, until a Fulton County resident filed a voting rights lawsuit that resulted in the U.S. Supreme Court overturning the practice in 1963 (Carter 1992). Atlanta's business elites further exacerbated the racial divide between city and state by adopting as Atlanta's slogan a line attributed to Mayor William Hartsfield: "A city too busy to hate" (Sjoquist 2000).

In the inflamed social conditions nationwide after the 1968 assassination of the Martin Luther King Jr., Atlanta's civic leaders sought to present a progressive image to the world by hosting an appropriate funeral for the slain Atlanta-born Nobel laureate. Robert Woodruff, the retired president of Coca-Cola Company who learned of King's assassination while imbibing with President Johnson in the White House, called Atlanta Mayor Ivan Allen and instructed him to spare no expense or effort regarding the funeral—with the understanding that Coca-Cola or Woodruff himself would reimburse the city (Pendergrast 2007). Atlanta's respectful honoring of King's funeral stood in stark contrast to the images, just three years earlier, of the attacks on civil rights marchers crossing the Edmund Pettus Bridge (National Park Service 2013).

Despite generations of rancor, these two uneasy bedfellows—Atlanta and the rest of Georgia—have fostered the world's busiest passenger airport, created one of world's major complexes for conventions and entertainment, and established the urban core of a metropolis that ranks as the 13th largest of exporters among the nation's 100 most populated cities (Hetter 2013; McDearman, Donahue, and Marchio 2013). These advances occurred while voters in both the city and the state elected Democratic leaders throughout the twentieth century.

In 2002 the GOP took control of state government, winning the governor's office for the first time since Reconstruction, and also the State Senate. The House of Representatives followed in 2004. Atlanta voters have retained mostly Democrats at Atlanta City Hall. However, Atlanta's relations with the state capitol had been strained since 1973, when Atlanta elected its first African American mayor, Maynard Jackson, who immediately implemented affirmative action programs that affected construction contracts at Atlanta's airport and other city projects (Rice 2014). While the legislature today remains overwhelmingly white, male, and now Republican, and Atlanta's legislative delegation is diverse and mostly Democratic, political power has shifted from agrarian-based south Georgia toward Atlanta and the rest of industrialized north Georgia. Consequently, despite partisan differences, Atlanta and state leaders now face the types of challenges that are shared by regions: issues defined less by politics and more by governance, such as roads, water and sewer infrastructure, job creation, and education (Beatty 2013). Current Republican Governor Nathan Deal and Democratic mayor Kasim Reed have fostered a reputation for collaborating when possible, especially on the proposed deepening of the Port of Savannah so it can handle post-Panamax cargo ships (Nellenbach 2013). Georgia's ports generate more than 350,000 jobs statewide and $2.5 billion in state and local taxes (Humphreys 2012). Deal has provided state funding for the deepening, and Reed has provided access to the Obama administration to seek federal funding (Henry 2012).

The complete record of tangible benefits exchanged between Atlanta and Georgia has not been tabulated. Plenty of anecdotal information is available to fuel a perpetual disagreement over whether the state does enough, or too much, to benefit Atlanta. Key issues include school funding, social services, and transportation, according to Alan Essig, who has helped devise many of Georgia's budgets in his various positions with both the legislative and executive branches, and who now serves as executive director of the Georgia Budget and Policy Institute (Essig 2013).

"The problem that arises when one metro area dominates a state is whether the metro area is getting its fair share," Essig said. "In Georgia, there was a recognition [in the 1970s] that Atlanta is the economic engine of the state, that if Atlanta suffers, the rest of the state suffers. Whether Atlanta deserves X percent more than it's getting is a legitimate argument, but it's not the fundamental argument. Because Atlanta has a high concentration of poverty in certain areas, its needs are so much greater, and that is an issue regarding state funding. Transportation funding is an issue, where Atlanta needs more roads and commuting alternatives, and the state is building a lot of rural highways" (Essig 2013).

Paved roads are a highly charged issue in both traffic-congested Atlanta and across road-hungry regions of Georgia. Roads are at the root of one barbed witticism Georgia legislators often share toward the end of the annual legislative sessions, when lawmakers anxious to go home will quip that the prettiest sight in the world is Atlanta's skyline in the rearview mirror. Many of these lawmakers will leave the capitol, located in downtown Atlanta at the vortex of two interstate highways, and drive on multilane highways that eventually will narrow to two-lane blacktops in counties that have miles of unpaved roads. School buses periodically slip off rain-slick dirt roads into ditches (Fox 31 News Team 2013) A full 24 percent of Georgia's 117,453 miles of public roads were unpaved in 2009. To put Atlanta's massive road system in context, paved roadways in metropolitan Atlanta's five core counties comprise 14.5 percent of the state's total paved mileage of 89,203; unpaved roads in the same five counties account for 0.007 percent of Georgia's total unpaved mileage (Georgia Department of Transportation 2009).

One example of the state's support for Atlanta, often cited by lawmakers from outside the region, is the state-owned and operated Georgia World Congress Center (GWCC). The center describes itself as, "one of the best sports and entertainment campuses in the world," and it fuels Atlanta's largest industry, convention and tourism (Georgia World Congress Center 2013). The future Falcons football stadium is to be built on land owned by the GWCC. Garnering legislative support in the 1970s for the beginnings of the facility was not easy, especially in a state just a decade removed from the county-unit system of electing lawmakers.

"We passed that through a rural-dominated General Assembly at a time they called it, 'Atlanta's World Congress Center,'" said retired state legislator and current University System of Georgia regent George Hooks. Hooks is regarded as a state historian by virtue of being a sixth-generation native of Sumter County, in southwest Georgia, with 32 years of total service in the House and Senate (Hooks 2013).

"It [the GWCC] has directly benefited the economic health of the city of Atlanta," Hooks said. "Atlanta always got its due under the rural-dominated legislature. That's because Atlanta spoke with one voice back in the old days: Mills Lane [Atlanta banker and civic leader] and Robert Woodruff [of Coca-Cola]. Even in the county unit system, people like [former House Speaker] Tom Murphy, who were the rural champions, were able to cut through that and do what was best for the state of Georgia. Believe me, what they did was brought up by their opponents in a lot of legislative campaigns" (Hooks 2013).

The discord over paucity or plenty for Atlanta stems partly from the tremendous size of Georgia, according to Tom Baxter, an Atlanta-based political journalist. In addition to struggling under the county-unit system, Atlanta—while now the core of a metropolitan area of more than five million people—was for most of its years just one of several significant cities and towns that sought state funding and support. "It's not like Maryland, where Baltimore has tremendous impact on the state, but the state doesn't impact Baltimore because the state just isn't that big," Baxter said. "This goes to the point that Atlanta's always had a difficult situation maintaining its place and getting its due" (Baxter 2013).

Planning for the public space is one area where state resources clearly pale in comparison to those of Atlanta and its metro neighbors. The Atlanta Regional Commission (ARC) is the metropolitan planning organization for Atlanta and is responsible for regional planning in a 10-county area, as well as collecting air quality data for 10 adjoining counties. Its annual budget is about $63 million, compared to the state appropriation of $59 million to the Georgia Department of Community Affairs (DCA) (Atlanta Regional Commission 2013a; Georgia Office of the Governor 2013). The DCA, in addition, manages more than $280 million in state and federal funds in its mission to promote "safe and affordable housing, community and economic development, and local government assistance." Former DCA commissioner Mike Beatty said ARC's capacity to help guide the urban challenges of Atlanta far exceeds that of DCA, though the state department does oversee a number of urban renewal and job encouragement programs that Atlanta utilizes. Atlanta civic leaders were progressive in forming the predecessors of ARC in 1947 when Atlanta, Fulton County, and DeKalb County created the nation's first publicly funded, multicounty planning agency (Atlanta Regional Commission 2010). Since that time, the organization has recommended projects that resulted in many of the Atlanta region's defining characteristics: a regional transit system; constrained growth inside a perimeter (Interstate 285); a merchandise mart and civic center; a regional nature preserves plan; and major parks, including Stone Mountain and a portion of the Chattahoochee River National Recreation Area.

More recently, ARC has created an innovative program of competitive planning grants under a program called the "Livable Centers Initiative" (LCI). LCI grants intend to promote renewal and development in existing centers and corridors throughout the region. Atlanta's three community improvement districts have received a total of $24.8 million for planning studies, design and engineering, right-of-way acquisition, and construction. The LCI grants in Buckhead total almost $3 million, which has helped restore pedestrian mobility along the signature Peachtree Road. In Midtown, $10.8 million in LCI grants has helped fund alternative transportation and a sustainability "greenprint." In downtown Atlanta, $11 million helped pay for projects, including the Atlanta Streetcar development strategy and a long-range plan for a corridor that now connects the hotel district with major attractions near Centennial Olympic Park (Goodwin 2013).

ARC was at the center of a planning effort that may well define metropolitan Atlanta for generations to come. The exercise, intended to improve mobility, painted a vivid image of modern-day politics in the Democrat-dominated city that still bills itself as "a city too busy to hate," and its Republican-dominated suburbs. On its face, the planning effort seemed basic: ARC provided operational assistance to a roundtable of elected officials from 10 metropolitan counties who were tasked with devising a project list for a proposed one percent sales tax that would fund road and transit improvements throughout the region. This sales tax proposal was the Georgia legislature's response to address the dwindling federal and state funding for roads, freight corridors, sidewalks, bikeways, and transit. Metro Atlanta was one of the 12 districts established in Georgia to prepare a project list to present on the July 31, 2012 ballot for a sales tax referendum (Georgia General Assembly 2010).

Trouble in the Atlanta district brewed from the outset, as the legislature debated the proposal and then passed it in 2010. Some Atlanta residents contended that Republican governor Sonny Perdue, a businessman from rural middle Georgia, had rigged the statewide sales tax referendum process so that Atlanta's expected request for transit funding would fail. One theory was that the governor and his allies in the legislature had placed Atlanta in the same district with suburban counties in order to enable the larger influence of Atlanta's suburbs to doom Atlanta's efforts to provide transit to millennials and poor, working African Americans. Some suburban residents claimed the process was rigged against them when a heavy rail transit line was penciled into Cobb County (Davis 2012a). Tempers of many constituencies boiled after the roundtable did not elect Atlanta's mayor to serve on the five-member executive committee that was to short-list projects. This imbroglio was resolved when former Georgia Tech band director Bucky Johnson, the mayor of Norcross in Republican Gwinnett County, agreed to abdicate his seat on the executive committee to make room for Reed, provided that Johnson be made the non-voting chair of the executive committee (Atlanta Regional Commission 2010c).

This campaign provided the first glimpse into the modern day evolution of political relationships among entrenched and emerging political groups in Atlanta and its neighbors. The DeKalb County chapter of the National Association for the Advancement of Colored People came out as an early opponent of the proposed sales tax, with chapter President John Evans saying DeKalb was being cheated out of a Metropolitan Atlanta Rapid Transit Authority's (MARTA) extension of heavy rail into the county's eastern—largely African American—neighborhoods that had been promised heavy rail decades ago (Wheatley 2012). From Atlanta's Republican suburbs, Tea Party members contended the state and local governments had enough resources, including the ability to raise the motor fuel tax, to improve transportation and transit without seeking a sales tax hike (Pendered 2012). Based in Atlanta, the Georgia chapter of the Sierra Club maintained that the transportation projects would promote sprawl to a degree that outweighed the transit funding (Kiernan 2011). The roundtable approved an $8.5 billion recommendation for the Atlanta region. The list was tilted slightly in favor of investments in transit, including some $600 million for transit projects associated with the Atlanta BeltLine, plus a bus rapid transit line to serve eastern DeKalb County (Atlanta Regional Commission 2011d).

No expense was spared in the campaign urging passage of the sales tax referendum: $7 million was raised, and spent, including a significant portion on ads delivered via direct mail and Atlanta's expensive television air waves (Georgia Government Transparency and Campaign Finance Commission 2013a). To put that spending into context, Governor Nathan Deal ran his 2010 statewide campaign on $8.3 million (Georgia Government Transparency and Campaign Finance Commission 2013b). The sales tax campaign included informational "wireside chats" between callers and elected officials, which were facilitated by ARC, while campaign ads featured caricatures and professional voice-over talent. The absence of a regional leader urging voters to support the sales tax referendum focused attention on one backer who was sharing the stump for the tax with the governor, but not in paid advertising. That backer was Atlanta Mayor Kasim Reed, a presumed regional leader, who is a black Democrat and outspoken supporter of President Obama in a state where Republican Newt Gingrich outpolled Mitt Romney by almost two to one in the March 2012 presidential primary election, and where Romney went on to carry in the November 2012 election by a seven-point margin (Georgia Secretary of State 2012).

When ballots were counted July 31, 2012, the proposed sales tax was rejected by 62 percent of voters in the 10-county area. Atlanta voters passed the sales tax referendum with 59 percent of the vote. DeKalb voters rejected the tax by more than 51 percent of the vote (Georgia Secretary of State 2013). As ARC's interpretation of the electoral outcome observed, "While it may be possible to make some observations about those precincts that voted for or against the referendum, it is difficult to make any broader claims based upon the results. Regardless of motivations, voters made it clear that they were not interested in the set of regional transportation investments as it was presented to them" (Atlanta Regional Commission 2012b) No other professional analysis of the vote has been made public.

Governor Deal has responded to metro Atlanta's mobility woes with a renewed emphasis on managed toll lanes, state funding to maintain regional bus service operated by the Georgia Regional Transportation Authority, and a hands off position—at least in public—on a GOP proposal to completely overhaul the MARTA Act of 1965 in order to "extensively revise" MARTA's governance and management. Deal never opined in public about the proposals to restructure MARTA; one possibility is that he agreed for the state to hold off in order to provide a newly installed MARTA chief operating officer time to get grounded and also to avoid clashing with Atlanta over control of MARTA at a time the state needed the city's aid to provide $200 million in construction funding to the future Falcons stadium (Pendered 2013a).

Meanwhile, the GOP-controlled legislature and two Republican governors have promoted municipalization along Atlanta's borders. The subtle force has nibbled at the perception, if not reality, of the city's influence. True motives for municipalization may never be known, concealed, it is said, in the hearts of individuals. Historian Kevin Kruse contends that the motive in Atlanta can be traced to a collective desire by those who choose to live outside the urban core to isolate "themselves from the city and all the problems they associated with it" (Kruse 2005). Dan Reuter, chief of ARC's land use division, expresses a view commonly held in some Atlanta circles that residents may simply want reliable public services that sometimes are not provided efficiently by county governments that serve more than 500,000 residents (Reuter 2013).

Municipalization runs contrary to a smaller and older movement in Georgia to consolidate city and county governments, as was done historically in Augusta, Athens, and Columbus. Sandy Springs was the first community in recent times to incorporate, in 2005 with 95 percent of the vote. Sandy Springs began its effort toward cityhood after the community thwarted Atlanta's attempt to annex the area in the 1970s. In turn, Atlanta blocked Sandy Springs' proposed incorporation through its control of the local legislative delegation and the influence of allies, including House Speaker Tom Murphy. The political calculus changed when the Republicans took control of the state government and legislative rules were altered to allow Sandy Springs to vote for incorporation (Kruse 2005). Following the Sandy Springs incorporation, only one portion of southwest Fulton County remains unincorporated, because cities were formed in 2006 in the former communities of Johns Creek and Milton and in 2007 in Chattahoochee Hills. DeKalb County communities followed suit: first Dunwoody in 2008 and then Brookhaven in 2012. At least three others are discussing the merits.

Despite the Republican gains around Atlanta, Georgia's capital city remains in the control of Democrats. The near-term future of the relationship between Atlanta and the rest of Georgia promises to be symbiotic, perhaps even openly friendly. The voter rejection of the 2012 transportation sales tax eliminates a lot of potential friction over project schedules in competing jurisdictions. Atlanta is focused on self-funding or federal funding for major urban renewal programs, including the Atlanta BeltLine and Atlanta Streetcar. Govenor Deal and Mayor Reed rarely miss an opportunity to share a stage announcing an economic development—the Porsche headquarters near the airport, for example, public funding for the future Falcons football stadium, and most significantly, the planned $600 million-plus deepening of the Port of Savannah.

Atlanta also has a goodwill ambassador embodied in Mayor Reed's political ambitions. The term-limited mayor has been talked up for a number of higher offices. Reed has already served in the state legislature, so the U.S. Senate appeared to be the next step. That was before Reed took himself out of contention for the Georgia Senate races in 2014 and 2016, leaving a potential bid for governor. The office next comes up for election in 2018, less than a year after Reed leaves office, and the term-limited Deal cannot seek reelection to a third term. Reed has called on Democrats to give Deal a pass in Deal's reelection bid in 2014, saying Deal "has done a good job as governor" (Cassidy 2013). Deal's chief of staff returned the favor, donating $250 to Reed's 2013 mayoral reelection campaign (Pendered 2013b).

One thing is certain: the future relationship between Atlanta and the rest of Georgia will grow from roots that date back to the Reconstruction era. The economic future of city and state will continue to intertwine as each side seeks tangible benefits from the other, or has ones to offer. Essig, the budget analyst, predicted that the real distribution of benefits may never be known and may never balance: "In any state with one totally dominating metro area, I'm not sure if there's ever a cost benefit that works out fairly to that metro area, which is the economic engine that funds the rest of the state. It's always going to be a political balance, a policy balance" (Essig 2013).

EPILOGUE

Shirley Franklin

Each of us has a story to tell and lessons to learn from those stories. I think cities have stories as well. The story of Atlanta has many backdrops, characters, conflicts, and themes. Atlanta's storied past has lead to imagining a city whose future is brighter and better than we could have ever dreamed. Unlike people, cities live on and for hundreds of years; their futures do not have to be stalled or stifled by intergenerational curses or complacency.

Atlanta's resiliency and ability to imagine the future is not new. In fact, it is nearly as old as the city itself. The historic past as a spirited war-torn city that rose from the ashes is a common theme in Atlanta's story. Redemptive and irrepressible, that is the Atlanta I grew to love.

Atlanta has been known as Terminus, Marthasville, the gate city of the region (1850s), the city of the "new South" (Henry Grady), a city too busy to hate (Ivan Allen), the next great international city (Maynard Jackson), and a city on a hill (Andrew Young). Atlanta promoted itself as a good place to invest, to live, and to learn, even in the 1880s and 1890s. The foundation for business and public sector partnerships was laid 150 years ago. A cursory glance at Atlanta's history teaches us many lessons. When its neighbors and sister cities retreated from self-promotion and closed themselves off to immigrants, Atlanta's leaders welcomed outsiders and rallied to sell the city to the world. When faced with near extinction from war and violence, Atlanta's leaders rallied again to resurrect the city from the ruins.

In the late nineteenth century, when the races were divided and neither women nor blacks had the right to vote, Atlanta's leaders found a way to include them in the most significant peaceful gathering of hundreds of thousands of Americans in the South—the Cotton States Exposition of 1895. Atlanta led the region's cities as sweeping federal policy upended the social traditions of the time. Atlanta's role in the civil rights movement through civic and social organizations, churches, businesses, and the Atlanta University Center set a course for the strategic development of today's African American leadership, including my election as the city's first female mayor. Accepting our differences, rallying for a cause, engaging everyone, building unlikely alliances, challenging the status quo—these became part of Atlanta's culture and tradition.

Jane Jacobs, the author of *The Death and Life of Great American Cities*, once said, "Cities have the capability of providing something for everybody, only because, and only when, they are created by everybody" (Jacobs 1992, 238). Atlanta is a city that has been created by everybody. The diverse names of those who have contributed, shaped, and changed this city's course in history are innumerable. There are many whose names we do not know and others whom we may have forgotten. I know that I stand in the shade of a tree that I did not plant. It was planted, watered, and nurtured by women like Grace Towns Hamilton, Connie Curry, Carolyn Long Banks, Elaine Alexander, Rita Samuels, Coretta Scott King, and Evelyn Lowery—just to name a few.

As mayor, the hardest work I tackled was imagining Atlanta's future, 50 years out and the ways in which my actions or inactions would influence the city. How would my efforts today affect residents in the future? For any city to be its best, it must embrace its history, learn from history's lessons, discard that which is no longer relevant, and expand its perspective. It is the combination of history and vision that will define the great cities of the future. Of course, infrastructure, water, sidewalks, world-class parks, transportation, and innovative development are necessary elements in making Atlanta's future even brighter.

But Atlanta's history and spirit is defiant, and the coming decades are likely to redefine the Atlanta we know today. We know from history that without taking risks Atlanta would likely be the insignificant city that 180 years ago some leaders predicted it would become. Knowing the challenges of our past gives us strength and fortitude in imagining a better future and a better Atlanta.

ENDNOTES

INTRODUCTION

1. "Sminings" is a phrase used to describe a combination of the towns of Smyrna and Vinings.

CHAPTER 2

1. The 2010 Census included some changes in the way income and poverty data are collected. Income and poverty data for the years 2000 and 2010 are not directly comparable because of the different sources used to collect the data (the census long form in 2000 and the American Community Survey in 2010). See the U.S. Census Bureau website for more detailed information on the difference between the data sets at www.census.gov.

2. The Atlanta Regional Commission is the state-designated regional commission for 10 counties: Cherokee, Clayton, Cobb, DeKalb, Douglas, Fayette, Fulton, Gwinnett, Henry, and Rockdale. The other 10 counties in the metropolitan statistical area are covered by other regional commissions.

CHAPTER 3

1. This refers to the maximization of profit in the marketing of real estate; the "market" approach is to get the highest price possible for a piece of property, whether improved or unimproved.

2. The HOME Investment Partnership Program is administered through the U.S. Department of Housing and Urban Development.

3. The Historic District Development Corporation did not have the option of cherry-picking projects based on profitability or ease of completion, which is generally how the for-profit real estate market functions.

4. Joseph Reid, director of the Atlanta Empowerment Zone, and Larry Wallace, COO of the City of Atlanta, were convicted of crimes related to misuse of Empowerment Zone funds.

CHAPTER 5

1. Does Crimmins and White's (1989) statement that "'Atlanta' now dominates and defines a region, harboring layers of a past that can be read in its landscape" still hold true when considering all the losses?

2. "The Historic District Development Corporation (HDDC) is a nonprofit community development corporation whose mission is to facilitate the preservation, revitalization and non-displacement of residents in the Martin Luther King, Jr. National Historic District" (Historic District Development Corporation 2013).

3. The 1971 landmark preservation case in Memphis, Tennessee, was Citizens to Preserve Overton Park v. Volpe.

4. Just a block away, the internationally recognized architect I.M. Pei's first office building, the modernist Gulf Oil Building at Juniper and Ponce, was not as fortunate, as this Atlanta landmark building was demolished in part at the beginning of 2013 to make way for a $50 million residential complex (Saporta 2013).

CHAPTER 8

1. Neither of these figures actually describes the complete story. Results of the censuses are net totals. They give the number who lived in the city in 1960 and 1970. In fact, between those years, far more people (and businesses) had left the city than indicated, while many also arrived.

CHAPTER 11

1. See U.S. Department of Housing and Urban Development (2013a).

2. Information based on the author's examination of Atlanta Housing Authority (AHA) administrative records.

3. For more information, see Atlanta Housing Authority (2013).

4. Several natural experimental research models were employed, including generalized estimation equations using repeated observations and Cox regressions with time-dependent covariance. Since this chapter is oriented toward the general reader, we do not go into details of the model construction or its stochastic properties. We simply report the results and invite those who are interested to solicit from the author more explicit details of the models' construction and analyses.

CHAPTER 16

1. This is as locally identified by Bowen (2010).

2. Central Atlanta Progress (2014) reports downtown is four square miles.

3. A new master planning process began in 2012 and is scheduled for completion in 2013 (Hartsfield-Jackson 2014).

CHAPTER 17

1. This is effective April 2013. Operational details subject to modification as project progresses.

CHAPTER 18

1. I first heard about the BeltLine in 2003 from Tim and Mary Committee, two Atlanta real estate developers, when they hired me to make a presentation to Mayor Franklin about the importance of park land. A year later, Jim Langford, another of the participants in the meeting, decided to commission my firm to examine the feasibility of adding green space to the BeltLine.

2. In 2005, EDAW was acquired by AECOM.

3. The cost includes the purchase prices plus the cost of carrying the property between purchase and conveyance to the BeltLine.

PART 3

1. The perimeter is I-285, the expressway circling the city.

2. The spaghetti junction is the I-285 and I-85 intersection.

3. The northern arc is the often discussed east-west interstate proposed for the northern counties.

CHAPTER 20

1. For more detailed data and statistics, see U.S. Bureau of Economic Analysis (2013b).

2. For more detailed data and statistics, see U.S. Bureau of Labor Statistics (2013a), Employment Situation Summary.

3. For more detailed data and statistics, see U.S. Bureau of Labor Statistics (2013a).

4. For more detailed data and statistics, see U.S. Bureau of Economic Analysis (2013a).

5. *The Atlanta Journal-Constitution* provided extensive coverage during the spring of 2013.

6. For more on the business recruitment marketing strategies in Atlanta, see Metro Atlanta Chamber (2013) and Invest Atlanta (2013b).

7. The Metro Atlanta Chamber estimates that the region's colleges and universities enroll 250,000 students annually. A report by the Atlanta Regional Council for Higher Education (2008) places full-time college enrollment at about 175,000 students.

8. The Atlanta-Sandy Springs-Marietta, Ga. Metropolitan Statistical Area (MSA) includes the counties of Barrow, Bartow, Butts, Carroll, Cherokee, Clayton, Cobb, Coweta, Dawson, DeKalb, Douglas, Fayette, Forsyth, Fulton, Gwinnett, Haralson, Heard, Henry, Jasper, Lamar, Meriwether, Newton, Paulding, Pickens, Pike, Rockdale, Spalding, and Walton in Georgia.

9. For more detailed data and statistics, see U.S. Bureau of Labor Statistics (2013b).

10. See the Occupational Employment Statistics report cited in references from the U.S. Bureau of Labor Statistics for a full listing of occupations and details on data disclosure (U.S. Bureau of Labor Statistics 2012).

11. The "essential economy" is an occupational cluster that includes restaurant kitchen staff, janitors, landscape crews, farm workers, nursing aides, stock clerks, and other non-managerial positions. The cluster spans six major economic sectors from agriculture and construction to hospitality and personal care.

12. There are 10 of these properties in the United States.

CHAPTER 21

1. See Official Code of Georgia Ann., § 48-7-40.1.

2. As of December 2013, 158 of Georgia's 159 counties qualify for the Joint Development Authority (JDA) bonus. Webster County is not within a JDA.

3. See Rules and Regulations of the State of Georgia, 110-9-1-.03.

4. See Official Code of Georgia Ann., § 48-7-40.15.

5. See Official Code of Georgia Ann., § 48-7-40.18.

6. See Official Code of Georgia Ann., § 48-7-40.26.

7. As of November 2013, the Georgia Department of Economic Development has revised its figures for fiscal year 2013 to $3.3 billion in economic impact.

CHAPTER 22

1. For more information, see the U.S. Bureau of Economic Analysis website at www.bea.gov.

2. For more information, see the National Association of Home Builders website at www.nahb.org.

3. To facilitate easy comparisons between metropolitan Atlanta and the U.S., this analysis only included employment in the construction and real estate sectors. It does not include the myriad other professions that are involved in the building, buying, and selling of homes.

4. Using data available from Neighborhood Nexus, it is possible to isolate high-foreclosure areas to perform this type of analysis. The source of the data was Equity Depot, a local firm that tracks fore-closure filings from county legal organs and deeds from courthouses. The filings were normalized by square miles to develop a foreclosure density measure. Because there are no reliable sources for small area housing unit data between decennial census years, square miles was used to provide a better "apples-to-apples" comparison of census tract trends, as the size of census tracts can vary widely. For more information, see the Neighborhood Nexus website at www.neighborhoodnexus.org.

5. For more information, see the Neighborhood Nexus website at www.neighborhoodnexus.org.

6. This is based on the number of lender-owned properties per 1,000 mortgageable properties. See the Brookings Metro Monitor available at www.brookings.edu/research/interactives/metromonitor#US-recovery-overall-nv.

7. For more information, see the Neighborhood Nexus website at www.neighborhoodnexus.org.

8. These figures are based on 2010 Census and 2007–2011 American Community Survey data from the Neighborhood Nexus website at www.neighborhoodnexus.org.

9. The 2010 unit counts were used because there is no reliable source of small area housing unit data for 2007; the "one-in-every-10" measure is a very rough estimate. For more information, see the Equity Depot website at www.equitydepot.net.

10. For more information, see the U.S. Bureau of Labor Statistics and Equity Depot websitess at www.bls.gov and www.equitydepot.net.

CHAPTER 23

1. See Official Code of Georgia Ann., § 48-4-60 to 48-4-65.

2. See Official Code of Georgia Ann., § 48-4-60 to 48-4-65.

3. See Official Code of Georgia Ann., § 48-4-100 to 48-4-112.

PART 5

1. Weather.com states that "the average warmest month is July" (The Weather Channel 2014).

CHAPTER 24

1. By the late 1990s, the city shared ownership of a new 90 MGD (million gallons per day) treatment facility with Fulton County, but its more than 2,400 miles of pipe and two older treatment plants, which had a combined capacity of 184 MGD, were beginning to show signs of old age. Moreover, reductions in water rates for out-of-city water users, contributions to the more than $17 million in pollution fines that had accrued since 1990, and 20 percent leakage losses meant that the Atlanta Water Works struggled to fund its own repairs, much less serve as a golden goose for the city's treasury as it did in the past. Cognizant that federal enforcement of water quality laws would require the city to more than double its existing water and sewer rates to pay for needed capital improvements, Mayor Bill Campbell sought politically feasible ways to minimize the city's economic burden (Labovitz 1999).

2. Privatization also seemed tailor-made for such a predicament. As Elizabeth Brubaker explains, privatized management of municipal services generated a great deal of public enthusiasm during the 1990s as financially stressed communities struggled to meet stricter environmental standards with outdated infrastructure. For aging cities searching for a way to meet these demands, privatization promised the benefits of efficiency, effectiveness, cost-savings, and competition that the free markets supposedly offered. Campbell stated that he thought the privatization of water systems would happen to cities across America because the financing of the infrastructure required would not be possible without private funding (Brubaker 2001).

3. The failed attempt at privatization generated a fair amount of coverage in the media as well as in professional publications (Jehl 2003; Powers and Rubin 2003; Public Citizen 2003).

4. According to the Metropolitan North Georgia Water Planning District, the average resident of Fulton County, for example, consumes 168 gallons per day, whereas the average American consumes less than 150 gallons per day (Metropolitan North Georgia Water Planning District 2009).

5. According to PolitiFact Georgia, the average residential customer in Atlanta has a monthly combined sewer and water bill of approximately $156. "Atlanta has the highest monthly bills in most categories. When it is not first, Atlanta is typically second" (Stirgus 2011).

6. For specific information on Georgia's geologic history, see Fisherer (1971).

7. For in-depth examinations of racial motivations and consequences of the Plan of Improvement, see Rice (1981) and Bayor (1996).

8. The Three River Water Quality Management Program was to achieve improvements in three major areas. The first set of improvements involved enhancements to the city's existing Intrenchment Creek, South River, and Flint River "water pollution control plants" to enable them to produce an effluent quality satisfactory for discharge into the Chattahoochee River. The second set consisted of the construction of two combined sewer overflow storage and treatment facilities, plus construction of separate sanitary sewers in one area to reduce the number of pollutants from combined sewers entering Intrenchment Creek and the South River. The last group included construction of force main, tunnel, and gravity sewer systems to convey the treated wastewater from the above three disposal plants to the Chattahoochee River for discharge. For more details, see Hardy (2011).

9. For more information on the design and operation of modern sewers and combined sewer overflows, see Fair, Geyer, and Okun (1966), Melosi (2011), and Tarr (1996).

10. Technically speaking, the tri-state water wars include litigation over allocation of the Alabama-Coosa-Tallapoosa River basin as well.

11. For a more detailed explanation of the litigation and points of contention, see Hardy (2011).

CHAPTER 26

1. An analysis of the 13-county Atlanta area found urban land grew by 247 percent between the years 1973 and 1999. During the same time, the population of the 13-county area increased by only 96 percent, suggesting less intensive use of land, or a greater demand for land for each additional resident to the area (Yang 2008).

2. To a satellite detecting the land cover changes, developed land is characterized as having a high percentage (greater than 30 percent) of constructed materials, including concrete, asphalt, and buildings.

3. A $3.2 million penalty assessed against Atlanta in the two-part settlement is the largest fine ever levied against a city under the Clean Water Act. Prior to the settlement, Atlanta paid more than $20 million in U.S. Environmental Protection Agency fines for delays in correcting its sewer system violations. As of May 2012, Atlanta had already completed the majority of the work required under the 1999 consent decree to address water quality violations, reducing sanitary sewer overflows by an estimated 97 percent since 2004 at a cost of $1.5 billion. A proposal in 2012 extended the deadline to complete the estimated $445 million in remaining work from July 1, 2014 to July 1, 2027. The extension reduces the financial burden on Atlanta ratepayers, who are already paying some of the highest rates in the country, and it allows the city to simultaneously address competing priorities to improve its drinking water system.

REFERENCES

Abdullahi Samir (research associate, Gwinnett Chamber of Commerce). 2013. E-mail interview with Ellen Heath, April 1.

Adler, Nancy E., Thomas Boyce, Margaret A. Chesney, Sheldon Cohen, Susan Folkman, Robert L. Kahn, and S. Leonard Syme. 1994. "Socioeconomic Status and Health." *American Psychologist* 49 (1): 15–24.

Adler, Nancy E., and Joan M. Ostrove. 1999. "Socioeconomic Status and Health: What We Know and What We Don't." *Annals of the New York Academy of Sciences* 896 (1): 3–15.

Airports Council International. 2012. "ACI Releases Its 2011 World Airport Traffic Report: Airport Passenger Traffic Remains Strong as Cargo Traffic Weakens." Available at www.aci.aero/News/Releases /Most-Recent/2012/08/27/ACI-Releases-its-2011-World-Airport-Traffic-Report-Airport-Passenger -Traffic-Remains-Strong-as-Cargo-Traffic-Weakens.

Airports Council International. 2013. "ACI Annual World Airport Traffic Report." Available at www.aci .aero/Data-Centre.

AirportTechnology.com. 2013. "Top 10 Busiest Airports in the US." Available at www.airport-technology .com/features/feature-busiest-airports-in-the-us-passengers/.

Alexander, Frank S. 1994. *The Fulton County/City of Atlanta Land Bank Authority, Inc.: Problems and Promises.* Atlanta: The Atlanta Project.

_____. 1995. "Property Tax Foreclosure Reform: A Tale of Two Stories." *Georgia Bar Journal* (December): 10–15.

_____. 2005. "Land Bank Strategies for Renewing Urban Land." *Journal of Affordable Housing & Community Development Law* 14 (2): 140–169.

_____. 2009. *Neighborhood Stabilization & Land Banking.* Boston: Federal Reserve Bank of Boston.

_____. 2011. *Land Banks and Land Banking*. Washington, D.C.: Center for Community Progress.

Allen, Frederick. 1996. *Atlanta Rising: the Invention of an International City, 1946–1996*. Atlanta: Longstreet Press.

Allen, Ivan, Jr. and Paul Hemphill. 1971. *Mayor: Notes on the Sixties*. New York: Simon and Schuster.

Altshuler, Alan A, and David E. Luberoff. 2003. *Mega-Projects: The Changing Politics of Urban Public Investment*. Washington, D.C.: Brookings Institution Press.

American Forest Products Industries. 1948. "Georgia Joins American Tree Farm Program." Available at http://foresthistory.org/ATFS/documents/Georgia-TreeFarm-1948-PR.pdf.

American Forests. 2001. *Urban Ecosystem Analysis Atlanta Metro Area: Calculating the Value of Nature*. Washington, D.C.: The Turner Foundation.

_____. 2002. *Projected Environmental Benefits of Community Tree Planting: A Multi-Site Model Urban Forest Project in Atlanta*. Washington, D.C.: USDA Forest Service and Georgia Forestry Commission.

Anderson, Roger T., Paul Sorlie, Eric Backlund, Norman Johnson, and George A. Kaplan. 1997. "Mortality Effects of Community Socioeconomic Status." *Epidemiology* 8 (1): 42–47.

Andraovich, Greg, Burbank, Michael J., and Heying, Charles H. 2001. "Olympic Cities: Lessons Learned from Mega-Event Politics." *Journal of Urban Affairs* 23 (2): 113–131.

Anil, Bulent, David L. Sjoquist, and Sally Wallace. 2010. "The Effect of a Program-Based Housing Move on Employment: Hope VI in Atlanta." *Southern Economic Journal* 77 (1): 138–60.

Applebome, Peter. 1993. "Carter Center: More than the Past." *The New York Times*, May 30. Available at www.nytimes.com/1993/05/30/travel/cartercenter-more-than-the-past.html.

Atlanta (Georgia), City of. 1975. *A Century of Progress, 1875–1975: The Story of Atlanta's Water System*. Atlanta: Department of Environment and Streets, Bureau of Water, City of Atlanta.

_____. 1999. *Working Paper #3, Vision and Policy Document, Hartsfield Atlanta Master Plan 2000–2010*. Atlanta: Department of Aviation, City of Atlanta.

_____. 2003. *Article II: Tree Protection*. Available at www.atlantaga.gov/modules/showdocument.aspx?documentid=1522.

_____. 2008. *The Connect Atlanta Plan*. Available at web.atlantaga.gov/connectatlanta/.

_____. 2011. *Comprehensive Development Plan*. Available at www.atlantaga.gov/index.aspx?page=376.

_____. 2013. "NPU by Neighborhood." Available at www.atlantaga.gov/index.aspx?page=404.

Atlanta BeltLine, Inc. 2010. *Atlanta BeltLine Annual Report*. Available at http://beltlineorg.wpengine.netdna-cdn.com/wp-content/uploads/2012/05/ABL-2010-Annual-Report.pdf.

_____. 2014. "The Atlanta Beltline: The 5 Ws and Then Some." Available at beltline.org/about/the-atlanta-beltline-project/atlanta-beltline-overview/.

Atlanta Housing Authority. 2010. *15 Year Progress Report, 1995–2010*. Available at www.atlantahousing.org/pdfs/AHA_15year_ProgressReport.pdf.

_____. 2013. *FY 2014 MTW Annual Implementation Plan*. Available at www.atlantahousing.org/pdfs/AHA%20FY%202014%20MTW%20Annual%20Plan.pdf.

Atlanta Journal-Constitution, The. 1998. "Hartsfield Can't Stay in a Holding Pattern; Growing Pains: Residents and Nearby Businesses' Concerns Must Be Heard and Addressed, but Expansion Is Inevitable." *The Atlanta Journal-Constitution*, September 20.

_____. 2012. "TSPLOST Poll Results." *The Atlanta Journal-Constitution*, July 29. Available at www.ajc .com/news/transportation/TSPLOST-poll/.

Atlanta Regional Commission. 2010a. "ARC's Population Estimates Show Region's Slow Growth Continues." Available at www.atlantaregional.com/about-us/news-press/press-releases/arcs-population-estimates-show-regions-slow-growth-continues.

_____. 2010b. *Plan 2040 Regional Assessment.* Available at http://documents.atlantaregional .com/plan2040/docs/lu_draft_ra_doc_2-1-10.pdf.

_____. 2010c. *Still Booming After All These Years: 60 Years of Regional Planning and Progress.* Available at www.atlantaregional.com/File%20Library/About%20Us/Overview/SORBtimeline _lowres.pdf.

_____. 2011a. *Plan 2040 Regional Development Guide.* Available at http://documents.atlanta regional.com/plan2040/docs/lu_plan2040_development_guide_0711.pdf.

_____. 2011b. *Regional Snapshot: ARC's County and Small-Area Forecasts: What the Future Holds in the Atlanta Region.* Available at www.atlantaregional.com/File%20Library/Info%20Center /Newsletters/Regional%20Snapshots/Forecasts/RS_Feb2011_Forecasts.pdf.

_____. 2011c. *Regional Travel Survey: Final Report.* Available at http://www.atlantaregional.com /transportation/travel-demand-model/household-travel-survey.

_____. 2011d. *Transportation Investment Act Final Report – Approved Investment List Atlanta Round-table Region.* Available at www.metroatlantatransportationvote.com/documents/final_report.pdf.

_____. 2012a. *Regional Snapshot: 2012 Regional Population.* Available at www.atlantaregional .com/File%20Library/Info%20Center/Newsletters/Regional%20Snapshots/Population/RS _August_2012_Pop.pdf.

_____. 2012b. *The Atlanta Regional Commission and the Transportation Investment Act of 2010.* Available at www.metroatlantatransportationvote.com/documents/ARC_and_TIA2010_JJ.pdf.

_____. 2012c. *2012 Transportation Factbook.* Available at www.atlantaregional.com/File%20 Library/Transportation/Resources/tp-transportation-fact-book-2012.pdf.

_____. 2013a. *FY 2012 Comprehensive Annual Financial Report.* Available at www.atlantaregional .com/File%20Library/About%20Us/History%20Funding%20Membership/2012_CAFR.pdf.

_____. 2013b. "Tri-State Water Wars." Available at www.atlantaregional.com/environment /tri-state-water-wars.

Atlanta Regional Commission and Piece by Piece. 2012. *Neighborhood Stabilization Program: Overview of NSP1 Implementation and Best Practices in Metro Atlanta.* Available at http://atlantaregional housing.org/pbp/docs/NSPReport_PBP_ARC.pdf.

Atlanta Regional Council for Higher Education. 2008. *The Atlanta Region: National Leader in Higher Education.* Available at www.atlantahighered.org/default.aspx?tabid=627&Report=5&xmid=557.

Atlanta Urban Design Commission. 1987. *Atlanta's Lasting Landmarks.* Atlanta: Atlanta Urban Design Commission, U.S. National Park Service, and Georgia Department of Natural Resources.

Badertscher, Nancy. 2012. "Georgia Failed to Count Thousands of High School Dropouts." *The Atlanta Journal-Constitution*, August 19. Available at www.ajc.com/news/news/local/georgia-failed-to -count-thousands-of-high-school-d/nRMLL/.

Barr, Bob. 2010. "A Streetcar Named Nowhere." *AJC.com, The Barr Code*, November 19. Available at http://blogs.ajc.com/bob-barr-blog/2010/11/19/a-streetcar-named-nowhere/.

Basmajian, Carlton W. 2008. "Planning Metropolitan Atlanta? The Atlanta Regional Commission, 1970–2002." Ph.D. diss., University of Michigan Ann Arbor.

Baxter, Tom. 2013. Personal conversation with David Pendered, August 7.

Bayor, Ronald H. 1996. *Race, Atlanta and the Shaping of Twentieth-Century Atlanta.* Chapel Hill: University of North Carolina Press.

Beatty, Mike (commissioner, Georgia Department of Community Affairs). 2013. Personal communication with David Pendered, July 25.

Bierig, Aleksandr. 2009. "SCAD Comes to the Rescue of Atlanta's Ivy Hall." *Architectural Record*, May 26. Available at http://archrecord.construction.com/news/daily/archives/090526scad.asp.

Blau, Max. 2013. "Council Oks Community Benefits Plan for Falcons Stadium Neighborhoods." *Creative Loafing*, December 3. Available at http://clatl.com/freshloaf/archives/2013/12/03/council-oks -community-benefits-plan-for-falcons-stadium-neighborhoods.

Blowers, Andrew, ed., 1993. *Planning for a Sustainable Environment: A Report by the Town and Country Planning Association.* London: Earthscan.

Bluestein, Greg. 2012. "Business Boosters Admit Atlanta in 'Crisis' Amid Effort to Boost City's Economy." *Atlanta Journal Constitution*, June 27. Available at www.ajc.com/news/news/local/business-boosters -admit-atlanta-in-crisis-amid-eff/nQWmg/.

Bluestein, Greg, Bill Rankin, and Scott Trubey. 2013. "High Court Grants Georgia Water-Wars Victory." *The Atlanta Journal-Constitution*, July 26. Available at www.ajc.com/news/news/local/high-court-grants -georgia-water-wars-victory/nQWmm/.

Blythe, Robert W., Maureen A. Carroll, and Steven H. Moffson. 1994. *Martin Luther King, Jr. National Historic Site Historic Resource Study.* Atlanta: National Park Service, U..S. Department of the Interior.

Boone-Heinonen, Janne, Penny Gordon-Larsen, David K. Guilkey, David R. Jacobs, and Barry M. Popkin. 2011a. "Environment and Physical Activity Dynamics: The Role of Residential Self-Selection." *Psychology of Sport and Exercise* 12 (1): 54–60.

Boone-Heinonen, Janne, Ana V. Diez Roux, Catarina I. Kiefe, Cora E. Lewis, David K. Guilkey, and Penny Gordon-Larsen. 2011b. "Neighborhood Socioeconomic Status Predictors of Physical Activity Through Young to Middle Adulthood: The CARDIA Study." *Social Science & Medicine* 72 (5): 641–649.

Boston, Thomas D. 2005. "The Effects of Mixed-Income Revitalization and Residential Mobility on Public Housing Residents: A Case Study of the Atlanta Housing Authority." *Journal of the American Planning Association* 71 (4): 393–410.

_____. 2011. *Impact of Mixed-Income Revitalization of Grady Homes: Atlanta Housing Authority.* Atlanta: Atlanta Housing Authority and U.S. Department of Housing and Urban Development.

Botchwey, Nisha, and Matthew Trowbridge. 2011. "Training the Next Generation to Promote Healthy Places." In *Making Healthy Places: A Built Environment for Health, Well-Being, and Sustainability*, edited by Andrew L. Dannenberg, Howard Frumkin, and Richard J. Jackson, 321–334. Washington, D.C.: Island Press.

Bowen, John T. 2010. *The Economic Geography of Air Transportation: Space, Time, and the Freedom of the Sky.* New York: Routledge.

Bradley, Mark. 2013. "Stunning News: Atlanta Braves Moving to Cobb." *Atlanta Journal Constitution*, November 11. Available at www.ajc.com/weblogs/mark-bradley/2013/nov/11/stunning-news -atlanta-braves-moving-cobb/.

Braubach, Matthias, and Jon Fairburn. 2010. "Social Inequities in Environmental Risks Associated with Housing and Residential Location—A Review of Evidence." *The European Journal of Public Health* 20 (1): 36–42.

Braveman, Paula A., Catherine Cubbin, Susan Egerter, Sekai Chideya, Kristen S. Marchi, Marilyn Metzler, and Samuel Posner. 2005. "Socioeconomic Status in Health Research." *Journal of the American Medical Association* 294 (22): 2879–2888.

Brown, Eric. 2013. "The Atlanta Braves' Move To Cobb County Is About Race, Not Transportation," *International Business Times*, November 14. Available at www.ibtimes.com/atlanta-braves-move-cobb-county-about-race-not-transportation-1470814.

Brown, Robbie. 2009. "Atlanta Is Making Way for New Public Housing." *The New York Times*, June 20. Available at www.nytimes.com/2009/06/21/us/21atlanta.html?_r=0.

_____. 2011a. "Ambitious Plans for a Building Where Sears Served Atlanta." *The New York Times*, August 16. Available at www.nytimes.com/2011/08/17/realestate/commercial/in-atlanta-big-plans-for-a-big-former-sears-center.html.

_____. 2011b. "Atlanta Finds Its Identity as Tree Haven Is Threatened." *The New York Times*, July 21. Available at http://www.nytimes.com/2011/07/22/us/22trees.html.

_____. 2013. "Now Atlanta Is Turning Old Tracks Green." *The New York Times*, Feburary 1. Available at www.nytimes.com/2013/02/15/us/beltline-provides-new-life-to-railroad-tracks-in-atlanta.html.

Brubaker, Elizabeth. 2001. *The Promise of Privatization.* Toronto: Energy Probe Research Foundation.

Buckhead CID (Community Improvement District). 2013. "Projects: GA 400/MARTA Pedestrian Bridge." Available at www.buckheadcid.com/projects/marta-bridge/.

Bullard, Robert D., Glenn S. Johnson, and Angel O. Torres, eds. 2000. *Sprawl City: Race, Politics, and Planning in Atlanta.* Washington, D.C.: Island Press.

Buron, Larry, Susan J. Popkin, Diane K, Levy, Laura E. Harris, and Jill Khadduri. 2002. *The HOPE VI Resident Tracking Study: A Snapshot of the Current Living Situation of Original Residents from Eight Sites.* Washington, D.C.: U.S. Department of Housing and Urban Development.

Cagle, Farris W. 1991. *Georgia Land Surveying History and Law.* Athens: University of Georgia Press.

CAP (Central Atlanta Progress, Inc.). 1971. *Central Area Study I.* Available at www.atlantadowntown.com/_files/docs/cas1.pdf.

_____. 1988. *Central Area Study II.* Available at www.atlantadowntown.com/_files/docs/cas2.pdf.

_____. 2000. *Central Atlanta Action Plan.* Available at www.atlantadowntown.com/_files/docs/ca2p.pdf.

_____. 2004. *Imagine Downtown.* Available at www.atlantadowntown.com/_files/docs/imagine_report_final_low_es.pdf.

_____. 2007. *The Green Line: Downtown Atlanta.* Available at http://www.atlantadowntown.com/_files/GreenLineFullReport.pdf.

_____. 2009. *Imagine Downtown: ENCORE, 2009 Update.* Available at www.atlantadowntown.com/_files/docs/imagineencorereport_web.pdf.

_____. 2013a. "History." Available at www.atlantadowntown.com/about/history.

_____. 2013b. "Fairlie-Poplar Historic District Streetscape Improvements." Available at www.atlantadowntown.com/initiatives/transportation-improvements/fairlie-poplar-streetscape.

_____. 2013c. "About Economic Development." Available at www.atlantadowntown.com/business.

_____. 2013d. "Center for Civil and Human Rights." Available at www.atlantadowntown.com /initiatives/center-for-civil-and-human-rights.

_____. 2013e. "Atlanta Streetcar." Available at www.atlantadowntown.com/initiatives/atlanta -streetcar.

_____. 2014. "Downtown Atlanta At-a-Glance." Available at www.260peachtree.com/PDFs /downtown/downtown_atlanta_fact_sheet.pdf.

Carlson, Daniel. 1995. *At Road's End: Transportation and Land Use Choices for Communities.* Washington, D.C.: Island Press.

Carson, O.E. 1981. *The Trolley Titans.* Glendale: Interurban Press.

Carson, Rachel. 1962. *Silent Spring.* New York: Houghton Mifflin Company.

Carter, Jimmy (former president of the United States and governor of Georgia). 1983. Meeting with Barbara Faga, September.

_____. 1992. *Turning Point: A Candidate, a State, and a Nation Come of Age.* New York: Times Books.

Carter Center, The. 2013. "Timeline of the Carter Center." 2013. Available at www.cartercenter.org /about/history/chronology.html.

Cassidy, Christina A. 2013. "Nathan Deal, Kasim Reed Forge Rare Partnership." *The Huffington Post,* June 8. Available at www.huffingtonpost.com/2013/06/08/nathan-deal-kasim-reed_n_3408320.html.

Cervero, Robert. 2013. *Suburban Gridlock II.* New Brunswick: Transaction Books.

Chamberlain, Lisa. 2006. "Building a City Within the City of Atlanta." *The New York Times,* May 24. Available at www.nytimes.com/2006/05/24/realestate/commercial/24atlanta.html?pagewanted=1&_r=2.

Chambliss, Julian C. 2008. "A Question of Progress and Welfare: The Jitney Bus Phenomenon in Atlanta, 1915–1925." *Georgia Historical Quarterly* 92 (4). Available at http://scholarship.rollins.edu/cgi /viewcontent.cgi?article=1095&context=as_facpub.

Chaskin, Robert J., Mark L. Joseph, Sara Voelker, and Amy Dworsky. 2012. "Public Housing Transformation and Resident Relocation: Comparing Destinations and Household Characteristics in Chicago." *Cityscape* 14 (1): 183–214.

Christopherson, Susan, and Jennifer Clark. 2007. *Remaking Regional Economies : Power, Labor, and Firm Strategies in the Knowledge Economy.* New York: Routledge.

_____. 2010. "Limits to 'The Learning Region': What University-Centered Economic Development Can (and Cannot) Do to Create Knowledge-Based Regional Economies." *Local Economy,* 25 (2): 120–130.

Chetty, Raj, Nathaniel Hendren, Patrick Kline, and Emmanuel Saez. 2014. "Where Is the Land of Opportunity? The Geography of Intergenerational Mobility in the United States." White paper, Harvard University, University of California, Berkeley, and National Bureau of Economic Research. Available at http://obs.rc.fas.harvard.edu/chetty/mobility_geo.pdf.

Clark, Jennifer. 2013. *Working Regions: Reconnecting Innovation and Production in the Knowledge Economy.* London: Routledge.

Clark, Jennifer, and Susan Christopherson. 2009. "Integrating Investment and Equity: A Critical Regionalist Agenda for a Progressive Regionalism." *Journal of Planning Education and Research* 28 (3): 341.

Clemmons, Jeff. 2012. *Rich's: A Southern Institution*. Charleston: The History Press.

Cleveland Foundation, The. 2013. *Cleveland's Greater University Circle Initiative: Building a 21st Century City through the Power of Anchor Institution Collaboration*. Available at http://community-wealth.org /sites/clone.community-wealth.org/files/downloads/Cleveland%27s%20Greater%20University%20Circle%20Anchor%20Initiative.%20Case%20Study.pdf.

Cloues, Richard. 1996. "Crescent Avenue Apartments." Nomination form on file at the Historic Preservation Division of the Georgia Department of Natural Resources, Atlanta, Ga.

CLPHA (Council of Large Public Housing Authorities). 2013. "HOPE VI." Available at www.clpha.org/hopevi.

Coffee, Neil T., Tony Lockwood, Graeme Hugo, Catherine Paquet, Natasha J. Howard, and Mark Daniel. 2013a. "Relative Residential Property Value as a Socioeconomic Status Indicator for Health Research." *International Journal of Health Geographics* 12 (1): 22.

Coleman, Kenneth, ed. 1977. *A History of Georgia*, 2nd ed. Athens: University of Georgia Press.

Collins, Patricia A., Michael V. Hayes, and Lisa N. Oliver. 2009. "Neighbourhood Quality and Self-Rated Health: A Survey of Eight Suburban Neighbourhoods in the Vancouver Census Metropolitan Area." *Health & Place* 15 (1): 156–164.

Costello, John O. 2003. *Georgia's Chattahoochee River: An Overview for the American Institute of Hydrology*. Atlanta: Georgia Department of Natural Resources.

Cougherty, Conor. 2013. "Welcome to Rockford, the Underwater Mortgage Capital of America." *The Wall Street Journal*, September 8. Available at http://online.wsj.com/news/articles/SB100014241278 87324324404579043300994815702.

Cousins, Tom. 2013. Telephone interview with Maria Saporta, June 7.

Cove, Elizabeth, Xavier De Souza Briggs, Margery Turner, and Cynthia Duarte. 2008. *Can Escaping from poor Neighborhoods Increase Employment and Earnings?* Washington, D.C.: The Urban Institute.

Crimmins, Timothy J., and Dana F. White. 1989. "Looking for Atlanta." In *The New Georgia Guide*, by the Georgia Humanities Council, 238. Athens: University of Georgia Press.

Cummings, Scott. 2007. "The Emergence of Community Benefits Agreements." *Journal of Affordable Housing and Community Development Law* 17 (2): 6–7.

Dagenhart, Richard, Nancey Green Leigh, and John Skach. 2006. "Brownfields and Urban Design: Learning from Atlantic Station." *Transactions on Ecology and the Environment* 94.

Davidson, Ethan (director of communications, Atlanta BeltLine, Inc.). 2013. Meeting with Alexander Garvin, September 3.

Davis, Billy. 2013. Phone conversation with Barbara Faga, October 13.

Davis, Janel. 2012a. "GA: Transit Tax Opposition Getting Louder in Cobb County." *Mass Transit*, May 23. Available at www.masstransitmag.com/news/10720335/ga-transit-tax-opposition-getting-louder -in-cobb-county.

Davis, Stephen. 2012b. *What the Yankees Did to Us: Sherman's Bombardment and Wrecking of Atlanta*. Macon: Mercer University Press.

DeepRoot Canada Corportation. 2013. "Toronto Captures Rain on Downtown Streetscape: Underground Rain Gardens Line Six Blocks Of Bloor Street." Available at www.deeproot.com/silvapdfs /caseStudies/BloorStreetCaseStudy.pdf.

DeSousa, Christopher, and Lily-Ann D'Souza. 2013. "Atlantic Station, Atlanta, Georgia: A Sustainable Brownfield Revitalization Best Practice." White paper, Institute for Environmental Science and Policy, University of Illinois at Chicago. Available at www.uic.edu/orgs/brownfields/research-results/documents /AtlanticStationCaseStudyFinalforposting1-3-13.pdf.

Dewan, Shalia. 2006. "The Greening of Downtown Atlanta." *The New York Times*, September 6. Available at www.nytimes.com/2006/09/06/arts/design/06belt.html?_r=0.

Dills, James E., Candace D. Rutt, and Karen G. Mumford. 2012. "Objectively Measuring Route-To-Park Walkability in Atlanta, Georgia." *Environment and Behavior* 44 (6): 841–860.

Dobbins, Michael. 2013. Telephone interview with Brian Leary and Barbara Faga, October 25.

Dorsey, Hattie B. 2013. "Atlanta Can Get Stadium Right This Time with Community Benefits Agreement." *SaportaReport*, May 5. Available at http://saportareport.com/blog/2013/05/atlanta-can-get -stadium-right-this-time-with-community-benefits-agreement/.

Dreier, Peter, John Mollenkopf, and Todd Swanstrom. 2001. *Place Matters: Metropolitics for the 21st Century*. Lawrence: University Press of Kansas.

Druid Hills (Druid Hills Civic Association, Inc. v. Federal Highway Administration, The National Trust for Historic Preservation v. Federal Highway Administration). 1985. 772 F.2d 700 23 ERC 1663,15 Envtl. L. Rep. 21,082.

Du Bois, W.E.B. 1899. *The Philadelphia Negro: A Social Study*. Philadelphia: University Of Pennsylvania Press.

_____. 1903. *The Souls of Black Folk*. Chapel Hill: Project Guttenberg.

Dusenbury, George. 2013. Meeting with Barbara Faga, September 10.

Ellis, John, and Stuart Galishoff. 1977. "Atlanta's Water Supply, 1865-1918." *The Maryland Historian* 8 (1): 5–22.

Engle, Sam Marie. 1999. "The Olympic Legacy in Atlanta." *University of New South Wales Law Journal* 22 (3): 902–906.

Engles, Friedrich. 1845. *The Condition of the Working Class in England*. Leipzig: Otto Wigand.

Essential Economy Council, The. 2013. *Report of Findings: State of Georgia*. Available at www .essentialeconomy.org/wp-content/themes/trim/documents/ee-report-2.21.13.lowres.pdf.

Essig, Alan (executive director, Georgia Budget and Policy Institute). 2013. In-person conversation with David Pendered, March 13.

Etienne, Harley F. 2012. *Pushing Back The Gates: Neighborhood Perspectives on University-Driven Revitalization in West Philadelphia*. Philadelphia: Temple University Press.

Faga, Barbara. 2006. *Designing Public Consensus*. Hoboken: John Wiley & Sons, Inc.

Fair, Gordon Masker, John Charles Geyer, and Daniel Alexander Okun. 1966. *Water and Wastewater Engineering: Volume I: Water Supply and Wastewater Removal*. New York: John Wiley & Sons, Inc..

Fisherer, George W., ed. 1971. *Studies of Appalachian Geology: Central and Southern*. New York: Interscience Publishers.

Fitzpatrick, Tom. 2010. "How Modern Land Banking Can be Used to Solve REO Acquisition Problems." In *REO & Vacant Properties: Strategies for Neighborhood Stabilization*, by the Federal Reserve Banks of Boston and Cleveland and the Federal Reserve Board, 145–150. Available at www.federalreserve .gov/newsevents/conferences/reo_20100901.pdf.

Foote, Shelby. 1974. *The Civil War: A Narrative, Volume Three, Red River to Appomattox*. New York: Random House.

Fox 31 News Team. 2013. "School Bus with Students Runs Off Road." *Fox31onLine*, March 28. Available at www.mysouthwestga.com/news/story.aspx?id=877723#.UkN8quBQbVM.

Fox Theatre, The 2013. "The Fox Story." Available at http://foxtheatre.org/the-fox-story/.

Franklin, Shirley (CEO, Purpose Built Communities and former mayor of Atlanta). 2013. Telephone interview with Maria Saporta, June 12.

Freaney, Margie. 1997. "In Search of the True Story Behind 'Atlanta Population Now' Sign." *Atlanta Business Chronicle*, September 29. Available at www.bizjournals.com/atlanta/stories/1997/09/29/editorial3.html?page=all.

Freedom Park Conservancy. 2013. "History of Freedom Park." Available at www.freedompark.org/fpc/about/history/.

Freemark, Yonah. 2009. "Chicago Olympics May Depend on Better Transit – But Where's the Commitment?" *The Transport Politic*, September 10. Available at www.thetransportpolitic.com/2009/09/10/chicago-olympics-may-depend-on-better-transit-but-wheres-the-commitment/.

French, Steven P., and Disher, Mike E. 1997. "Atlanta and the Olympics: A One-Year Retrospective." *Journal of the American Planning Association* 63 (3): 379–392.

Frey, William H. 2012. *Population Growth in Metro America Since 1980: Putting the Volatile 2000s in Perspective*. Washington, D.C.: The Brookings Institution.

Friends of the High Line. 2013. "Frequently Asked Questions." Available at www.thehighline.org/about/faq.

Fulmer, Ann. 2010. *Burning Down the House: Mortgage Fraud and the Destruction of Residential Neighborhoods*. National Criminal Justice Reference Service. Washington, D.C.: National Institute of Justice.

Fulton County (Georgia). 2011. "Transportation Accessibility." Available at www.fultoncountyga.gov/fced-about-fulton-econ/fced-transportation.

Fussell, Elizabeth, Narayan Sastry, and Mark VanLandingham. 2010. "Race, Socioeconomic Status, and Return Migration to New Orleans After Hurricane Katrina." *Population and Environment* 31 (1-3): 20–42.

Galloway, Tammy, H. 2004. "Ivan Allen Jr. (1911-2003)." *New Georgia Encyclopedia*. Available at www.georgiaencyclopedia.org/nge/Article.jsp?id=h-1382.

Garrett, Franklin M. 1954. *Atlanta and Environs: A Chronicle of Its People and Events, 1820s–1870s, Volume1*. Athens: University of Georgia Press.

Garvin, Alexander. 2004. *The BeltLine Emerald Necklace: Atlanta's New Public Realm*. San Francisco: The Trust for Public Land.

Georgia Cities Foundation. 2013. "Community Improvement Districts." Available at www.georgiacitiesfoundation.org/Resources.aspx?CNID=28756.

Georgia Department of Transportation. 2009. *Mileage of Public Roads in Georgia by Surface Type for 2009*. Available at www.dot.ga.gov/informationcenter/statistics/RoadData/Documents/441/DPP441_2009.pdf.

Georgia General Assembly. 1831. "1832 (Seventh or Gold) Land Lottery in Georgia." Available at www.georgiaarchives.org/research/1832_gold_lottery.

Georgia (State of). 2013. *The Governor's Budget Report, Fiscal Year 2014*. Available at http://opb.georgia.gov/sites/opb.georgia.gov/files/related_files/document/Governors%20Budget%20Report%20FY%202014.pdf.

_____. 2013. "Georgia Election Results." Available at http://sos.georgia.gov/elections/election
_results/default.htm.

Georgia State University. 2008a. *Georgia Regional Transportation Authority Rider Survey*. Atlanta: Georgia
State University Andrew Young School of Policy Studies.

_____. 2013. *Quick Facts*. Available at www.gsu.edu/factsheet.html.

Georgia Trust for Historic Preservation. 1999. *Window on the Past: Door to Our Future*. Atlanta: Georgia
Trust for Historic Preservation.

Georgia World Congress Center. 2013 "About the Authority." Available at www.gwcc.com/about
/Default.aspx.

GGTCFC (Georgia Government Transparency and Campaign Finance Commission). 2013a. "Campaign
Disclosure Report: Citizens for Transportation Mobility, Inc." Available at http://media.ethics.ga.gov
/search/Campaign/Campaign_Name.aspx?NameID=7075&FilerID=NC2010000025&Type
=committee.

_____. 2013b. "Campaign Disclosure Report: Deal, Nathan." Available at http://media.ethics.
ga.gov/search/Campaign/Campaign_Name.aspx?NameID=5753&FilerID=C2009000086
&Type=candidate.

Gibson, Campbell, and Kay Jung. 2005. "Historical Census Statistics on Population Totals by Race, 1790 to
1990, and by Hispanic Origin, 1970 to 1990, for Large Cities and Other Urban Places in the United
States." Working Paper No. 76, U.S. Census Bureau. Available at www.census.gov/population
/www/documentation/twps0076/twps0076.html.

Gittlesohn, John and Healther Perlberg. 2013. "Blackstone Buys Atlanta Homes in Largest Rental Trade."
Bloomberg.com, April 25. Available at www.bloomberg.com/news/2013-04-25/blacktone-buys
-atlanta-homes-in-largest-bulk-rental-trade.html.

Goodwin, Amy (principal planner, Atlanta Regional Commission). 2013. E-mail communication with David
Pendered, August 2.

Gournay, Isabelle. 1993. *AIA Guide to Atlanta*. Athens: University of Georgia Press.

Grable, Stephen. 1979. "Applying Urban History to City Planning: A Case Study in Atlanta." *The Public
Historian* 1 (Summer): 45–59.

Grillo, Jerry. 2013. "Growing Jobs, Growing the Economy." *Georgia Trend*, August. Available at www
.georgiatrend.com/August-2013/Growing-Jobs-Growing-The-Economy/.

Gross, Julian, Greg LeRoy, and Madeline Janis-Aparicio. 2005. *Community Benefits Agreements: Making
Development Projects Accountable*. Washington, D.C.: Good Jobs First and the California Partnership
for Working Families.

Guhathakurta, Subhrajit, and Ying Cao. 2011. "Variations in Objective Quality of Urban Life Across a City
Region: The Case of Phoenix." In *Investigating Quality of Urban Life*, edited by Robert W. Marans and
Robert J. Stimson, 135–160. Netherlands: Springer.

Guttentag, Jack. 2007. "The Good That Subprime Loans Do." *The Washington Post*, September 8. Available
at www.washingtonpost.com/wp-dyn/content/article/2007/09/07/AR2007090700015.html.

Gwinnett County (Georgia). 2009. *2030 Unified Plan*. Available at www.gwinnettcounty.com/portal
/gwinnett/Departments/2030UnifiedPlan.

Han, Jung Hoon, Naomi Sunderland, Elizabeth Kendall, Ori Gudes, and Garth Henniker. 2010. "Chronic Disease, Geographic Location and Socioeconomic Disadvantage as Obstacles to Equitable Access to E-health." *Health Information Management Journal* 39 (2): 30–36.

Hardy, Eric M. 2011. "Policy Drought: Water Resource Management, Urban Growth, and Technological Solutions in Post–World War II Atlanta." Ph.D. diss., Georgia Institute of Technology.

Harlan, Louis R., ed. 1974. *The Booker T. Washington Papers, Volume 3: 1899–95.* Urbana: University of Illinois Press.

Harmon, David Andrew. 1996. *Beneath the Image of the Civil Rights Movement and Race Relations: Atlanta, Georgia 1946–1981.* New York: Garland Publishing.

Harnik, Peter. 2013. Telephone interview with Barbara Faga, August 13.

Harris, Art. 1982. "Road to Carter Center is Paved with Protest." *The Washington Post,* July 6.

Harrop, Lee (program management officer, Atlanta BeltLine, Inc.). 2013. Interview with Alexander Garvin, September 6.

Hart, Ariel. 2010. "Pricey Streetcar Won't Ease Traffic." *The Atlanta Journal-Constitution,* November 7. Available at www.ajc.com/news/news/local/pricey-streetcar-wont-ease-traffic/nQmk5/.

_____. 2011. "Mass Transit: A Must-Have or a No-Win?" *The Atlanta Journal-Constitution,* April 21. Available at www.ajc.com/news/mass-transit-a-must-919165.html.

Hart, Ariel, and Shannon McCaffrey. 2012. "Business Behind Sales Tax Push." *The Atlanta Journal-Constitution,* July 24. Available at www.ajc.com/news/news/state-regional-govt-politics/business-behind-sales-tax-push/nQXSb/.

Hartley, Daniel A. 2010. "Blowing It Up and Knocking It Down: The Effect of Demolishing High Concentration Public Housing on Crime." Working paper, Federal Reserve Bank of Cleveland. Available at www.clevelandfed.org/research/workpaper/2010/wp1022.pdf.

Hartsfield Atlanta International Airport. 2000. *Hartsfield Atlanta International Airport Competition Plan.* Available at www.atlanta-airport.com/docs/Facilities/airport_complan.pdf.

Hartsfield-Jackson (Hartsfield-Jackson Atlanta International Airport). 2013. "Fifth Runway." Available at www.atlanta-airport.com/Airport/Construction/Fithrunway.aspx.

_____. 2014. "Navigate to 2030: ALT Master Plan." Available at www.atlanta-airport.com/Airport/MasterPlan/the-study.html.

Havard, Sabrina, Séverine Deguen, Denis Zmirou-Navier, Charles Schillinger, and Denis Bard. 2009. "Traffic-related Air Pollution and Socioeconomic Status: A Spatial Autocorrelation Study to Assess Environmental Equity on a Small-Area Scale." *Epidemiology* 20 (2): 223–230.

Hein, Virginia. 1972. "The Image of 'A City Too Busy to Hate': Atlanta in the 1960s." *Phylon, The Atlanta University Review of Race and Culture* 33 (3): 205–221.

Henderson, Jason. 2004. "The Politics of Mobility and Business Elites in Atlanta, Georgia." *Urban Geography* 25 (3): 193–216.

Hendricks, Gary. 1999. "Hartsfield Plans for the Millennium, Two Extra Airstrips Envisioned." *The Atlanta Journal-Constitution,* January 28.

Henry, Scott. 2010. "Burbs or Bust: The Atlanta Journal-Constitution Has Left Atlanta—Literally and Figuratively—in Its Quest for Suburban Readers." *Creative Loafing,* November 17. Available at http://clatl.com/atlanta/burbs-or-bust-the-ajc-has-left-atlanta/Content?oid=2364218.

Hetter, Katia. 2013. Where Is the World's Busiest Airport? *CNN*, September 13. Available at www.cnn .com/2013/09/04/travel/worlds-busiest-airports-2012/index.html.

Hill, Elizabeth, Dorfman, Jeffrey H. and Elizabeth Kramer. 2010. "Evaluating the Impact of Government Land Use Policies on Tree Canopy Coverage." *Land Use Policy* 27 (2): 407–414.

Hill, Melvin B. 1994. *The Georgia State Constitution: A Reference Guide.* Westport: Greenwood Publishing Group.

Hirshman, Dave. 2006. "Cleared for Landing: Atlanta Toasts Airport's Fifth Runway; Strip to Cut Delays, Boost Flight Capacity." *The Atlanta Journal-Constitution*, May 17.

Historic District Development Corporation. 2013. "About Us." Available at https://sites.google.com/site /historicdistrictdevelopment/.

Holmes, Bob, Mitch Moody, Andy Hill, Cheryll Hardson-Dayton, Nykia Green, Rashid Herd, Elias Sisya, and Jeffrey Williams. 2003. *The Capitol Homes Hope VI Evaluation Baseline Study.* Atlanta: Atlanta Housing Authority.

Hooks, George (former regent, University System of Georgia and former member, Georgia Legislature). 2013. Personal conversation with David Pendered, March 8.

Hooper, Hartwell, and Susan Hooper. 1999. "The Scripto Strike. Martin Luther King's 'Valley of Problems': Atlanta, 1964–1965." *Atlanta History* 43 (3): 5–34.

Hornsby, Alton. 2004. *Southerners, Too? Essays on the Black South, 1733–1990.* Lanham: University Press of America.

Howard, H.D. 1982. "Resale of Surplus Right of Way Along I-485." *Right of Way Magazine*, October. 4–7.

Humphreys, Jeffrey M. 2012. "The Economic Impact of Georgia's Deepwater Ports on Georgia's Economy in FY2011." White paper, Terry College of Business, The University of Georgia.

Immergluck, Dan. 2013. "The Role of Investors in the Single-Family Market in Distressed Neighborhoods: The Case of Atlanta." Working paper, Joint Center for Housing Studies of Harvard University. Available at www.jchs.harvard.edu/sites/jchs.harvard.edu/files/w13-2_immergluck.pdf.

Invest Atlanta. 2013a. "About Us." Available at www.investatlanta.com/about-us/.

_____. 2013b. "Tax Allocation Districts." Available at www.investatlanta.com/builders-developers /tax-allocation-districts/.

_____. 2014. "Housing Development." Available at www.investatlanta.com/builders-developers /housing-development/.

Inwood, Joshua F.J. 2009. "Contested Memory in the Birthplace of a King: A Case Study of Auburn Avenue and the Martin Luther King Jr. National Park." *Cultural Geographies* 16 (1): 87–109.

Jacobs, Jane. 1992. *The Death and Life of Great American Cities.* New York: Vintage Books.

Jehl, Douglas. 2003. "As Cities Move to Privatize Water, Atlanta Steps Back." *The New York Times*, February 10. Available at www.nytimes.com/2003/02/10/us/as-cities-move-to-privatize-water-atlanta -steps-back.html.

Johnston, James Houstoun. 1931. *Western and Atlantic Railroad of the State of Georgia.* Atlanta: Georgia Public Service Commission.

Jourdan, Dawn, Shannon Van Zandt, and Nicole Adair. 2010. "Meeting Their Fair Share: A Proposal for the Creation of Regional Land Banks to Meet the Affordable Housing Needs in the Rural Areas of Texas." *Journal of Affordable Housing & Community Development Law* 19 (2): 147–159.

Karkaria, Urvaksh. 2011. "Porsche Unveils $100M Atlanta HQ Plans." *Atlanta Business Chronicle*, May 12. Available at www.bizjournals.com/atlanta/news/2011/05/12/porsche-unveils-100m -atlanta-hq-plans.html.

Keating, Dennis. 2011. *Cuyahoga County Land Reutilization Corporation: The Beginning, The Present, and Beyond, 2009–2011.* Available at www.cuyahogalandbank.org/articles/CCLRC_2009_2011 _Report.pdf.

Keating, Larry. 2000. "Redeveloping Public Housing: Relearning Urban Renewal's Immutable Lessons." *Journal of the American Planning Association* 66 (4): 384–97.

_____. 2001a. *Atlanta: Race, Class, and Urban Expansion.* Philadelphia: Temple University Press.

_____. 2001b. *Strengthening a Valuable Resource: The Fulton County/City of Atlanta Land Bank Authority.* Washington, D.C.: Fannie Mae Foundation.

Keating, Larry and Carol A. Flores. 2000. "Sixty and Out: Techwood Homes Transformed by Enemies and Friends." *Journal of Urban History* 26 (3): 275–311.

Keating, Larry, Max Creighton, and Jon Abercrombie. 1997. "Community Development: Building on a New Foundation." In *The Olympic Legacy: Building on What Was Achieved*, edited by David Sjoquist. Atlanta: Research Atlanta, Inc.

Keith, Janet. 2013. Telephone interview with Barbara Faga, August 16.

Kiernan, Colleen. 2011. "Metro Atlanta Turning Winning Transit Season into Losing One." *SaportaReport.com*, October 9. Available at http://saportareport.com/blog/2011/10/metro-atlanta-turning -winning-season-for-transit-into-a-losing-one/.

Kirk, Patricia. 2007. "Restoration Project Jump-Starts Neighborhood Revitalization in Atlanta." *Urban Land* 66 (1): 32–33.

Kissel, Carrie. 2012. "Georgia Votes on Regional Sales Tax Initiative for Transportation Funding, with Mixed Results." National Organization of Development Organizations, August 14. Available at www.nado .org/georgia-votes-on-regional-sales-tax-initiative-for-transportation-funding-with-mixed-results/.

Knight Foundation (John S. and James L. Knight Foundation). 2010. "What Attaches People to Their Communities?" Available at www.soulofthecommunity.org/.

Konrad, Miriam. 2009. *Transporting Atlanta: The Mode of Mobility Under Construction.* New York: State University of New York Press.

Kramer, Elizabeth, Michael J. Conroy, Matthew J. Elliot, Elizabeth A. Anderson, William R. Bumback, and Jeanne Epstein. 2003. *A Geographic Approach to Planning for Biological Diversity: The Georgia Gap Analysis Project.* Athens: Georgia Cooperative Fish and Wildlife Resources, Warnell School of Forest Resources, U.S. Department of Interior, and U.S. Geological Survey.

Kruse, Kevin M. 2005. *White Flight: Atlanta and the Making of White Conservatism.* Princeton: Princeton University Press.

Labovits, Steven. 1999. "Privatization of the City of Atlanta's Water System: A Cost Savings Initiative and a Plan for the Future." In *Preparing for the 21st Century, Proceedings of the 29th Annual Water Resources Planning and Management Conference*, edited by Erin M. Wilson, 1–16. Reston: American Association of Civil Engineers.

LeGrand, Adelee (vice president, AECOM). 2013. Telephone conversation with Barbara Faga, August 15.

Leinberger, Christopher B., and Mason Austin. 2013. *The WalkUP Wake-Up Call: Atlanta* . Available at www.atlantaregional.com/File%20Library/Land%20Use/WalkUPs/WalkUP_Atlanta_final.pdf.

Lenskyj, Helen. 2000. *Inside the Olympic Industry: Power, Politics, and Activism.* Albany: SUNY Press.

Leslie, Katie. 2013. "19.5 Million Dollar Deal Lands Stadium Church." *The Atlanta Journal-Constitution.* August 6. Available at www.ajc.com/news/news/mayor-to-announce-stadium-news-tuesday -councilman-/nZF3D/.

Livable Buckhead Community. 2013. "Special Public Interest District 12." Available at http://livable buckhead.com/community/land-use-planning-2/special-public-interest-district-12/.

Lohr, Kathy. 2011. "The Economic Legacy of the Atlanta Olympic Games." *National Public Radio,* August 4. Available at www.npr.org/2011/08/04/138926167/the-economic-legacy-of-atlantas-olympic -games.

Lomax, Michael L. 1997. "The Arts: Atlanta's Missing Legacy." In *The Olympic Legacy: Building on What Was Achieved,* edited by David Sjoquist. Atlanta: Research Atlanta, Inc.

Longwell, Todd. 2013. "Vampire Diaries,' 'Hunger Games' Fuel Peachy Georgia Production Scene." *Variety,* September 24. Available at http://variety.com/2013/biz/news/georgia-games-competitors-with -tax-incentives-1200668497/.

Lyon, Elizabeth A. 1975. "Change and Continuity: Atlanta's Historic Business Buildings." In *The American Institute of Architects Guide to Atlanta,* edited by Kenneth B. Marsh, 20. Atlanta: Atlanta Chapter of the American Institute of Architects.

MARTA (Metropolitan Atlanta Rapid Transit Authority). 2008. *General Riders, Half-Fare Program, Mobility Program Demographics and System Usage Profiles.* Atlanta: Metropolitan Atlanta Rapid Transit Authority.

Martin, Harold H. 1978. *William Berry Hartsfield: Mayor of Atlanta.* Athens: The University of Georgia Press.

Martin, Jean. 1975. *Mule to MARTA, Volume 1.* Atlanta: Atlanta Historical Society.

Mason, Wayne. 2013. Telephone interview with Maria Saporta, June 12.

McDearman, Brad, Ryan Donahue, and Nick Marchio. 2013. *Export Nation 2013.* Washington, D.C.: The Brookings Institution.

McGuckin, Nancy, and Nandu Srinivasan. 2005. *The Journey-to-Work in the Context of Daily Travel.* Paper presented at the Census Data for Transportation Planning Conference, Irvine, CA, May 11–13.

McKaughan, Joe. 2004. "Fox Theatre." *New Georgia Encyclopedia,* March 4. Available at www .georgiaencyclopedia.org/articles/arts-culture/fox-theatre.

McMath, Robert C., Ronald H. Bayor, James E. Brittain, Lawrence Fostor, August W. Gielbelhaus, and Germaine M. Reed. 1985. *Engineering the New South: Georgia Tech, 1885–1985.* Athens: University of Georgia Press.

McPhee, John. 1983. *In Suspect Terrain.* New York: Farrar, Strauss and Giroux.

McPherson, Greg, James R. Simpson, Paula J. Peper, Scott E. Maco, and Qingfu Xiao. 2005. "Municipal Forest Benefits and Costs in Five US Cities." *Journal of Forestry* 103 (8): 411–416.

Melosi, Martin V. 2011. *Precious Commodity: Providing Water for America's Cities.* Pittsburgh: University of Pittsburgh Press.

Meridan Record. 1960. "Furtive Dynamiters Blast Big Atlanta Negro School." *Meridian Record*, December 13. Available at http://news.google.com/newspapers?id=lsVHAAAAIBAJ&sjid=Mf8MAAAAIBAJ& pg=2597,4967787&dq=english+avenue+atlanta&hl=en.

Metro Atlanta Chamber. 2006. *Atlanta MSA Growth Statistics.* Atlanta: Metro Atlanta Chamber. Available at http://web.archive.org/web/20070927062537/http://www.metroatlantachamber.com /macoc/business/img/MSAGrowthStatsReport2006.pdf.

_____. 2013. "Metro Atlanta Is the Best Place to Nurture Your Business, Whether You're a Fortune 500 or an Innovative Startup." Available at www.metroatlantachamber.com/business.

Metropolitan North Georgia Water Planning District. 2009. *Water Supply and Water Conservation Management Plan.* Available at www.northgeorgiawater.org/plans/water-supply-and-water-conservation -management-plan.

Metropolitan Planning Commission. 1952. *Up Ahead: A Regional Land Use Plan for Metropolitan Atlanta.* Available at https://smartech.gatech.edu/bitstream/handle/1853/45672/Up_Ahead .pdf?sequence=1.

_____. 1954. *Now...for Tomorrow: A Master Planning Program for the Dekalb-Fulton Metropolitan Area.* Available at https://smartech.gatech.edu/bitstream/handle/1853/45273/dekalb-fulton -plan.pdf?sequence=1.

Mendheim, Susan. 2013. Telephone interview with Maria Saporta, June 7.

Myers, Dowell. 1988. "Building Knowledge about Quality of Life for Urban Planning." *Journal of the American Planning Association* 55 (3): 347–358.

Miami-Dade Water and Sewer Department. "Water Rate Comparison." Available at www.miamidade. gov/water/rate-comparison.asp.

Midtown Alliance. 2013. "Bringing a Blueprint to Life." Available at www.midtownatl.com/about /programs-and-projects/planning-and-urban-design/midtown-blueprint.

Milazzo, Paul Charles. 2006. *Unlikely Environmentalists: Congress and Clean Water, 1945–1972.* Lawrence: University Press of Kansas.

Miller, Matthew D. 2012. "The Impacts of Atlanta's Urban Sprawl on Forest Cover and Fragmentation." *Applied Geography* 34: 171–179.

Mincey, Sarah K., Schmitt-Harsh, Mikaela, and Richard Thurau. 2013. "Zoning, Land Use, and Urban Tree Canopy Cover: The Importance of Scale." *Urban Forestry & Urban Greening* 12 (2): 191–199.

Mollenkopf, John H. 1983. *The Contested City.* Princeton: Princeton University Press.

Mollenkopf, John H., and Manuel Castells. 1991. *Dual City: Restructuring New York.* New York: Russell Sage Foundation.

Monroe, Doug. 2012. "Where It All Went Wrong." *Atlanta Magazine*, August 1.

Morris, Aldon D. 1984. *Origins of the Civil Rights Movement: Black Communities Organizing for Change.* New York: The Free Press.

Morris, Marya. 2006. *Integrating Planning and Public Health: Tools and Strategies to Create Healthy Places* (Planning Advisory Service Report 539/540). Chicago: American Planning Association.

Murphy, Sherry, Jiaquan Xu, and Kenneth D. Kochanek. 2013. *Deaths: Final Data for 2010.* Washington D.C.: Centers for Disease Control and Prevention.

Myers, Dowell. 1988. "Building Knowledge about Quality of Life for Urban Planning." *Journal of* the American Planning Association 55 (3): 347–358.

National Commission on Severely Distressed Public Housing. *The Final Report of the National Commission on Severely Distressed Public Housing.* Washington, D.C.: National Commission on Severely Distressed Public Housing.

National Housing Law Project. 2002. *False Hope: A Critical Assessment of the HOPE VI Public Housing Redevelopment Program.* Oakland: National Housing Law Project.

National Park Service. 1985. *General Management Plan Development Concept Plan and Environmental Assessment of the Martin Luther King Jr. National Historic Site.* Washington, D.C.: U.S. Department of the Interior.

_____. 2013. "Selma-to-Montgomery March." Available at www.nps.gov/nr/travel/civilrights /al4.htm.

National Trust for Historic Preservation. 2013. "Sweet Auburn Historic District." Available at http:// savingplaces.org/treasures/sweet-auburn-historic-district.

Nellenbach, Michelle. 2013. "Governor Nathan Deal and Mayor Kasim Reed Working Together to Bring Jobs to Georgia." Available at http://bipartisanpolicy.org/blog/2013/06/governor-nathan-deal -and-mayor-kasim-reed-working-together-bring-jobs-georgia.

Newman, Harvey K. 1999. *Southern Hospitality: Tourism and the Growth of Atlanta.* Tuscaloosa: University of Alabama Press.

_____. 2001. "Historic Preservation Policy and Regime Politics in Atlanta." *Journal of Urban Affairs* 23 (1): 71–86.

_____. 2002. "The Atlanta Housing Authority's Olympic Legacy Program: Public Housing Projects to Mixed Income Communities." Atlanta: Research Atlanta, Inc.

Nowak, David J., Daniel E. Crane, Jack C. Stevens, Robert E. Hoehn, Jeffrey T. Walton, and Jerry Bond. 2008. "A Ground-Based Method of Assessing Urban Forest Structure and Ecosystem Services." *Arboriculture and Urban Forestry* 34 (6): 347–358.

Nowak, David J., and John F. Dwyer. 2007. "Understanding the Benefits and Costs of Urban Forest Ecosystems." In *Urban and Community Forestry in the Northeast,* edited by John E. Kuser. Netherlands: Springer.

O'Mara, Margaret Pugh. 2005. *Cities of Knowledge : Cold War Science and the Search for the Next Silicon Valley.* Princeton: Princeton University Press.

Pace, David. 1999. "Atlanta Agrees to Another $700,000 Fine to Settle Water Pollution Suit." *Associated Press,* August 4. Available at http://onlineathens.com/stories/080499/new_0804990017.shtml.

Padgett, Richard, and James R Oxendine. 1997. "Economic Development: Seeking Common Ground." In Sjoquist, David L. et al. 1997. *The Olympic Legacy: Building on What Was Achieved.* Atlanta: Research Atlanta, Inc.

Patton, Carl V. 1997. "Downtown: The Heart and Soul of Atlanta." In *The Olympic Legacy: Building on What Was Achieved,* edited by David Sjoquist. Atlanta: Research Atlanta, Inc.

Pendered, David. 2012. "Transportation Sales Tax Backers Chide Tea Party Leaders as Part of Steady Campaign Aimed at July 31." *SaportaReport,* June 14. Available at http://saportareport.com /blog/2012/06/transportation-sales-tax-backers-chide-tea-party-leader-as-part-of-steady-campaign/.

_____. 2013a. "A Relation Between Stadium Deal and Stalled MARTA Bill? Who's to Say." *SaportaReport*, March 19. Available at http://saportareport.com/blog/2013/03/a-relation-between-stadium-deal-and-stalled-marta-proposal-whos-to-say/.

_____. 2013b. "Atlanta Mayor Kasim Reed's Fundraising Accelerates in 2013, Latest Report Shows." *SaportaReport*, April 9. Available at http://saportareport.com/blog/2013/04/atlanta-mayor-kasim-reeds-fundraising-accelerates-in-2013-report-shows/.

_____. 2013c. "PATH Foundation Named in Ga. 400 Trail, Latest of Its $55 Million Projects." *SaportaReport*, May 12. Available at http://saportareport.com/blog/2013/05/path-foundation-memorialized-in-ga-400-trail-the-latest-of-55-million-in-projects/.

Pendergrast, Mark. 2007. *For God, Country, and Coca-Cola*, 2nd ed. New York: Basic Books.

Peper, Paula J., E. Gregory McPherson, James R. Simpson, Shelley L. Gardner, Kelaine E. Vargas, Qingfu Xiao, and Fiona Watt. 2007. *New York City, New York: Municipal Forest Resource Analysis*. Albany, Ca.: Pacific Southwest Research Station, U.S. Forest Service.

Perry, Egbert (CEO of the Integral Group and former president of H.J. Russell & Company). 2013. In-person interview with Maria Saporta, June 6.

Pickett, Kate E., and Pearl, Michelle. 2001. "Multilevel Analyses of Neighbourhood Socioeconomic Context and Health Outcomes: A Critical Review." *Journal of Epidemiology & Community Health* 55 (2): 111–22.

Piper, Valerie. 2005. *Case Study Atlanta*. Washington, D.C.: The Brookings Institution.

Poole, Shelia M. 2012. "Sweet Auburn District Listed as Endangered." *The Atlanta Journal-Constitution.*, June 12. Available at www.ajc.com/news/news/local/sweet-auburn-district-listed-as-endangered/nQWLT/.

Popkin, Susan P., Bruce Katz, Mary K, Cunningham, Karen D. Brown, Jeremy Gustafson, and Margery Austin Turner. 2004. *A Decade of Hope VI: Research Findings and Policy Changes*. Washington, D.C.: The Urban Institute.

Pousner, Howard. 1986. "Jimmy Carter: Why That Grin Is Back Again." *The Atlanta Journal-Constitution*, September 26. Available at www.ajc.com/news/news/local/jimmy-carter-why-that-grin-is-back-again/nQkf9/.

Portman, John. 2013. Telephone interview with Maria Saporta, May 21.

Powers, Mary B., and Debra Rubin. 2003. "Severed Atlanta Water Contract Was Tied to Unclear Language." *Engineering News-Record* 250 (5): 14.

Preston, Howard L. 1979. *Automobile Age Atlanta: The Making of a Southern Metropolis, 1900–1935*. Athens: University of Georgia Press.

Preuss, Holger. 2002. *Economic Dimension of the Olympic Games*. Barcelona: Centre d'Estudis Olympics.

Pritchett, Amy R. 2013. "Hartsfield-Jackson Atlanta International Airport." *New Georgia Encyclopedia*, December 6. Available at www.georgiaencyclopedia.org/articles/business-economy/hartsfield-jackson-atlanta-international-airport.

Public Citizen. 2003. *Water Privatization Fiascos: Broken Promises and Social Turmoil*. Washington, D.C.: Water for All Campaign.

Puentes, Robert, and Adie Tomer. 2011. *Transit Access and Zero-Vehicle Households*. Washington, D.C.: The Brookings Institution.

Quesenberry, Preston. 1996. "The Disposable Olympics Meets the City of Hype." *Southern Changes* 18 (2): 3–14.

Rails to Trails Conservancy. 2013. "About Rails-to-Trails Conservancy." Available at www.railstotrails.org /aboutUs/index.html.

Rainey, J. Lynn. 2013. "Community Improvement Districts." Available at www.raineyandphillipslaw.com /community-improvement-districts.html.

Raja, Samina, Changxing Ma, and Pavan Yadav. 2008. "Beyond Food Deserts: Measuring and Mapping Racial Disparities in Neighborhood Food Environments." *Journal of Planning Education and Research* 27 (4): 469–482.

Reuter, Dan (manager, Community Development Division, Atlanta Regional Commission). 2013. Personal conversation with David Pendered, July 30.

Rice, Bradley R. 1981. "The Battle of Buckhead: The Plan of Improvement and Atlanta's Last Big Annexation." *Atlanta Historical Journal* 25 (Winter): 5–22.

————. 2014. "Maynard Jackson." *New Georgia Encyclopedia*, July 26. Available at www .georgiaencyclopedia.org/articles/government-politics/maynard-jackson-1938-2003.

Risley, Ford. 1991. "National Notebook: Atlanta; Sears Center Bought by City." *The New York Times*, June 2. Available at www.nytimes.com/1991/06/02/realestate/national-notebook-atlanta-sears-center -bought-by-city.html.

Robert, Stephanie A. 1998. "Community-Level Socioeconomic Status Effects on Adult Health." *Journal of Health and Social Behavior* 39 (1): 18–37.

Robert, Stephanie A. 1999. "Socioeconomic Position and Health: The Independent Contribution of Community Socioeconomic Context." *Annual Review of Sociology* 25: 489–516.

Rome News Tribune. 1972. "Carter Says Toll Road Will Not Be Constructed." *Rome News Tribute*, December 15.

Rose, Michael. 2001. *Atlanta: Then and Now*. San Diego: Thunder Bay Press.

Ross, Catherine. Forthcoming. *The Architecture of the Megaregion*. Washington, D.C.: Federal Highway Administration.

Ross, Catherine, ed. 2009. *Megaregions: Planning for Global Competitiveness*. Washington, D.C.: Island Press.

Roth, Darlene, and Andy Ambrose. 1996. *Metropolitan Frontiers: A Short History of Atlanta*. Atlanta: Longstreet Press.

Roughton, Bert. 1991, "Atlanta Olympics Update '91: On Journey to '96, Atlanta Aims to Stage Great Games and Improve Itself." *The Atlanta Journal Constitution*, July 21.

Rutheiser, Charles. 1996. *Imagineering Atlanta: The Politics of Place in the City of Dreams*. London: Verso.

Rybczynski, Witold. 2000. *A Clearing In The Distance: Frederick Law Olmsted and America in the 19th Century*. New York: Scribner.

S&P Dow Jones Indices and CoreLogic. 2013. "S&P/Case-Shiller Home Price Indices." Available at http:// us.spindices.com/index-family/real-estate/sp-case-shiller.

Salama, Jerry J. 1999. "The Redevelopment of Distressed Public Housing: Early Results from Hope VI Projects in Atlanta, Chicago, and San Antonio." Housing Policy Debate 10 (1): 95–136.

Salkin, Patricia, and Amy Lavine. 2008a. "Negotiating for Social Justice and the Promise of Community Benefits Agreements: Case Studies of Current and Developing Agreements." *Journal of Affordable Housing and Community Development Law* 17 (2): 113–144.

Salkin Patricia, and Amy Lavine. 2008b. "Understanding Community Benefits Agreements." *Practical Real Estate Lawyer*, July: 19–34.

Sanchez, Thomas W., Rich Stolz, and Jacinta S. Ma. 2003. *Moving to Equity: Addressing Inequitable Effects of Transportation Policies on Minorities.* Cambridge, Mass.: The Civil Rights Project at Harvard University.

Sang, Sunhee, Morton O'Kelly, and Mei-Po Kwan. 2011. "Examining Commuting Patterns Results from a Journey-to-Work Model Disaggregated by Gender and Occupation." *Urban Studies* 48 (5): 891–909.

Saporta, Maria.1998. "Midtown Plan Thwarts Proposed Parking Lot: First Union's Proposal Runs into Midtown Plan." *The Atlanta Journal-Constitution*, January 27.

————. 2013. "As Historic Buildings Disappear, Atlanta Losing Its Sense of Place." *SaportaReport*, March 25. Available at www.saportareport.com.

Saporta, Maria, and Amy Wenk. 2013. "New Falcons Stadium Price Tag 'Rises Up' $200M." *Atlanta Business Chronicle*, October 28. Available at www.bizjournals.com/atlanta/news/2013/10/28/new-falcons-stadium-price-tag-jumps.html?page=all.

Sassen, Saskia. 2001. *The Global City: New York, London, Tokyo.* Princeton: Princeton University Press.

Schrank, David, Tim Lomax, and Bill Eisele. 2011. *2011 Annual Urban Mobility Report.* College Station: Texas Transportation Institite. Available at http://d2dtl5nnlpfr0r.cloudfront.net/tti.tamu.edu/documents/mobility-report-2011-wappx.pdf.

Schuder, Rex (recreation planner, Gwinnett County). 2013. E-mail interview with Ellen Heath, April 1.

Severson, Kim. 2012. "For Transit Relief, Congested Atlanta Ponders a Penny Tax." *The New York Times*, July 15. Available at www.nytimes.com/2012/07/16/us/atlanta-area-residents-to-vote-on-tax-for-transportation.html?pagewanted=all.

————. 2013. "In Atlanta, Two Churches Lie in New Stadium's Path." *The New York Times*, April 21. Available at www.nytimes.com/2013/04/22/us/in-atlanta-two-churches-lie-in-new-stadiums-path.html.

Shelby, James. 2013. In-person conversation with Leon Eplan, September 15.

Shepherd, Anne, and Christi Bowler. 1997. "Beyond the Requirements: Improving Public Participation in EIA." *Journal of Environmental Planning And Management* 40 (6): 725–738.

Sherer, Paul M. 2003. *The Benefits of Parks: Why America Needs More City Parks and Open Space.* The San Francisco: Trust for Public Land. Available at www.eastshorepark.org/benefits_of_parks%20tpl.pdf.

Shingleton, Royce. 1985. *Richard Peters: Champion of the New South.* Macon: Mercer University Press.

Silva, Diana A. 2011. "Land Banking as a Tool for the Economic Redevelopment of Older Industrial Cities." *Drexel Law Review* 3 (2): 607–640.

Sinderman, Martin. 2013. "Baxter, Caterpillar are Big Scores for Georgia," *Atlanta Business Chronicle*, March 1. Available at www.bizjournals.com/atlanta/print-edition/2013/03/01/baxter-caterpillar-are-big-scores-for.html.

Sjoquist, David L. 2000. *The Atlanta Paradox.* New York: Russell Sage Foundation.

Sjoquist, David L., ed. 1997. *The Olympic Legacy: Building on What Was Achieved.* Atlanta: Research Atlanta, Inc.

Skinner, Jim. 2013. *The Atlanta Region: A Demographic and Economic Discussion.* Atlanta: Atlanta Regional Commission.

Smith, Harold. 2010. *Historic Smyrna: An Illustrated History.* Smyrna: Smyrna Historical and Genealogical Society.

Smith, W. Eugene. 1968. "Lanier's 'Folly' Grimly Real." *The Atlanta Journal*, January 11.

Spartanburg Herald, The. 1971. "Atlanta Road Work Suspended." *The Spartanburg Herald*, November 18.

Stirgus, Eric. 2011. "Is Atlanta Drowning in the Nation's Highest Water Bills?" *PolitiFact Georgia*, September 23. Available at www.politifact.com/georgia/statements/2011/sep/23/carla-smith/atlanta-drowning-nations-highest-water-bills/.

Stone, Clarence. 1989. *Regime Politics: Governing Atlanta, 1946–1988.* Lawrence: University Press of Kansas.

Stone, Clarence. 1993. "Urban Regimes and the Capacity to Govern: A Political Economy Approach." *Journal of Urban Affairs* 15(1): 1–28.

Storper, Michael. 1997. *The Regional World: Territorial Development in a Global Economy.* New York: Guilford Press.

Summers, Lawrence. 2012. "Building Blocks for America's Recovery." *Financial Times*, October 28. Available at www.ft.com/cms/s/2/94197118-1ed0-11e2-be82-00144feabdc0.html#axzz2sHN8FlzA.

Tappendorf, Julie A., and Brent O. Denzin, 2011. "Turning Vacant Properties into Community Assets Through Land Banking." *Urban Lawyer* 43: 801–814.

Tarr, Joel. 1996. *The Search for the Ultimate Sink: Urban Pollution in Historical Perspective.* Akron: The University of Akron Press.

Terrazas, Michael. 1996. "Let the Arts Begin: The Cultural Olympiad." *Georgia Tech Alumni Magazine Online,* Summer.

Thomas, Jane. "Margaret Mitchell (1900–1949)." *New Georgia Encyclopedia*, September 27. Available at www.georgiaencyclopedia.org/articles/arts-culture/margaret-mitchell-1900–1949.

Tierney, Mike. 2012. "Falcons Seek New Dome, Not Atlanta Fixer-Upper." *The New York Times*, December 15. Available at www.nytimes.com/2012/12/16/sports/football/atlanta-falcons-not-interested-in-fixer-upper-seek-a-new-stadium.html?pagewanted=all&_r=0.

Time. 1961. "Education Milestones." *Time*, September 8.

Toon, John D. 2007. "Metropolitan Atlanta Rapid Transit Authority (MARTA)." *New Georgia Encyclopedia*, October 20. Available at www.georgiaencyclopedia.org/nge/Article.jsp?id=h-1023.

Trees Atlanta. 2013. "History: From Seedlings, A Forest Can Grow – The Path to a Vibrant Tree Canopy for Atlanta." Available at http://treesatlanta.org/who-we-are/history/.

Trubey, J. Scott. 2013. "The Past is Past Atlantic Station Owners Say." *The Atlanta Journal-Constitution.* July 20. Available at www.myajc.com/news/business/the-past-is-past-atlantic-station-owners-say/nYs96/?icmp=ajc_internallink_textlink_apr2013_ajcstubtomyajc_launch_

_____. 2013. "Tyler Perry Plans 'Huge Expansion' of Atlanta Studios." *The Atlanta Journal-Constitution*, April 10. Available at www.ajc.com/news/business/tyler-perry-plans-huge-expansion-of-atlanta-studio/nXHj4/.

Trust for Public Land, The. 2013. "Atlanta, GA ParkScore Index." Available at http://parkscore.tpl.org/city.php?city=Atlanta.

_____. 2013. "Parks for People." Available at www.tpl.org/our-work/parks-for-people.

Turbov, Mindy, and Valerie Piper. 2005. *HOPE VI and Mixed-Finance Redevelopments: A Catalyst for Neighborhood Renewal.* Washington, D.C.: The Brookings Institution.

UK Government and Mayor of London. 2013. *Inspired by 2012: The Legacy from the London 2012 Olympic and Paralympic Games.* London: Crown. Available at www.gov.uk/government/uploads /system/uploads/attachment_data/file/224148/2901179_OlympicLegacy_acc.pdf.

U.S. Bureau of Economic Analysis. 2013a. "Economic Growth Continues Across Metropolitan Areas in 2011." Available at www.bea.gov/newsreleases/regional/gdp_metro/2013/pdf/gdp _metro0213.pdf.

_____. 2013b. "State Personal Income, 2012." Available at www.bea.gov/newsreleases/regional /spi/2013/spi0313.htm.

U.S. Bureau of Labor Statistics. 2012. *May 2012 Metropolitan and Nonmetropolitan Area Occupational Employment and Wage Estimates, Atlanta-Sandy Springs-Marietta, GA.* Washington D.C.: U.S. Department of Labor.

_____. 2013a. "The Employment Situation – March 2013." Available at www.bls.gov/news.release /archives/empsit_04052013.pdf.

_____. 2013b. "Atlanta Area Employment – November 2012." Available at http://www.bls.gov /ro4/cesatl.pdf.

U.S. Census Bureau. 1990. "American FactFinder, DP-1: Profile of General Demographic Characteristics." Washington, D.C.: U.S. Census Bureau.

_____. 2000. "American FactFinder, DP-1: Profile of General Demographic Characteristics." Available at http://factfinder2.census.gov/faces/nav/jsf/pages/index.xhtml.

_____. 2010. "American FactFinder, DP-1 - Profile of General Population and Housing Characteristics." Available at http://factfinder2.census.gov/faces/nav/jsf/pages/index.xhtml.

_____. 2011. "American FactFinder, DP-03: Selected Economic Characteristics." Available at http:// factfinder2.census.gov/faces/nav/jsf/pages/index.xhtml.

_____. 2012. "American Community Survey 5-Year Sample, 2007–2011." Available at www.census .gov/acs/www/#.

_____. 2013. "Overview." (Decennial Censuses of 1970, 1980, 1990, 2000 and 2010.) Available at www.census.gov/history/www/through_the_decades/overview/.

U.S. Department of Housing and Urban Development. 1994. *Audit Report: Housing Authority of the City of Atlanta Public Housing Management Operations.* Atlanta: Atlanta Regional Office, U.S. Department of Housing and Urban Development.

_____. 2013a. *Public and Indian Housing Revitalization of Severely Distressed Public Housing (HOPE VI).* Available at http://portal.hud.gov/hudportal/documents/huddoc?id=rev-of-sev-distress.pdf.

_____. 2013b. "State of the Cities Data System (SOCDS)." Available at www.huduser.org/portal /datasets/socds.html.

U.S. Department of the Interior. 2009. "NLCD 1992/2001 Retrofit Land Cover Change Product." Available at www.mrlc.gov/nlcdrlc.php.

U.S. Department of Transportation. 2009. *High-Speed Rail Strategic Plan.* Washington, D.C.: Federal Railroad Administration.

U.S. Environmental Protection Agency. 2013a. "Public Involvement Policy and Related Documents." Available at www.epa.gov/pubinvol/public/.

————. 2013b. "Atlantic Station (Atlantic Steel Site Redevelopment Project)." Available at www.epa.gov/smartgrowth/topics/atlantic_steel.htm.

U.S. General Accounting Office. 2006. *Olympic Games: Federal Government Provides Significant Funding and Support.* Washington, D.C.: General Government Division, U.S. General Accounting Office. Available at www.gao.gov/assets/160/156989.pdf.

U.S. Geological Survey. 2006. *Georgia's Surface Water Resources and Streamflow Monitoring Network, 2006.* Atlanta: U.S. Geological Survey Georgia Water Science Center. Available at pubs.usgs.gov/fs/2006/3084/pdf/fs2006-3084.pdf.

U.S. Internal Revenue Service. 2013. "SOI Tax Stats-Migration Data." Available at www.irs.gov/uac/SOI-Tax-Stats-Migration-Data.

Vaeth, Elizabeth. 1998. "1996 Olympics: A Defining Moment in Atlanta's History: Was It Worth It?" *Atlanta Business Chronicle,* June 15. Available at www.bizjournals.com/atlanta/stories/1998/06/15/focus17.html?page=all.

Vargo, Jason, Habeeb, Dana, and Brian Stone Jr. 2013. "The Importance of Land Cover Change Across Urban-Rural Typologies for Climate Modeling." *Journal of Environmental Management* 114 (5): 243–252.

Warhop, Bill. 2007. "City Observed: Power Plants." *Atlanta Magazine,* June 7. Available at http://web.archive.org/web/20070607192757/http://www.atlantamagazine.com/article.php?id=207.

Weather Channel, The. 2014. "Monthly Averages for Atlanta, GA (30326)." Available at www.weather.com/weather/wxclimatology/monthly/graph/30326.

Weisman, Steven, R. 1990. "Atlanta Chosen Over Athens for 1996 Olympic Games." *The New York Times,* September 19. Available at www.nytimes.com/1990/09/19/sports/atlanta-selected-over-athens-for-1996-olympics.html.

Wheatley, Thomas. 2012. "DeKalb NAACP Calls Transportation Tax Racist." *Creative Loafing,* April 19. Available at http://clatl.com/freshloaf/archives/2012/04/18/dekalb-naacp-calls-transportation-tax-racist.

Williams, John (CEO of Corporate Holdings, LLC and founder and former CEO of Post Properties, Inc.). 2013. Telephone interview with Maria Saporta, June 12.

Williams, Louis. 2014. "William B. Hartsfield (1890–1971)." *New Georgia Encyclopedia,* August 12. Available at www.georgiaencyclopedia.org/articles/government-politics/william-b-hartsfield-1890-1971.

Willoughby, Lynn. 1999. *Flowing Through Time: The History of the Lower Chattahoochee River.* Tuscaloosa: University of Alabama Press.

Wilson, William J. 1985. "The Urban Underclass in Advanced Industrial Society." In *The New Urban Reality,* edited by Paul E. Peterman, 126–160. Washington, D.C.: The Brookings Institution.

————. 1987. *The Truly Disadvantaged: The Inner City, the Underclass, and Public Policy.* Chicago: University of Chicago Press.

————. 1991a. "Studying Inner-City Social Dislocations: The Challenge of Public Agenda Research: 1990 Presidential Address." *American Sociological Review* 56 (1): 1–14.

_____. 1991b. "Another Look at Truly Disadvantaged." *Political Science Quarterly* 106 (4): 639–656.

_____. 2009 *More Than Just Race: Being Black and Poor in the Inner-City*. New York: W.W. Norton & Company.

Wolf-Powers, Laura. 2010. "Community Benefits Agreements and Local Government: A Review of Recent Evidence," *Journal of the American Planning Association* 76 (2): 1–19.

Wolfe, Tom. 1998. *A Man in Full*. New York: Farrar, Straus & Giroux.

World Health Organization. 1948. *Constitution of the World Health Organization*. Geneva: World Health Organization.

Wormer, Lisa, Dan Carlson, and Cy Jilberg. 1995. *At Roads End: Transportation and Land Use Choices for Communities*. Washington, D.C.: Island Press.

WSB-TV. 2011. "Atlanta May No Longer Be 'The City In a Forest.'" *WSB-TV*, July 22. Available at www .wsbtv.com/news/news/atlanta-may-no-longer-be-the-city-in-a-forest/nDLGr/.

Yang, Xiojun. 2002. "Satellite Monitoring of Urban Spatial Growth in the Atlanta Metropolitan Area." *Photogrammetric Engineering and Remote Sensing* 68 (7): 725–734.

Youngblood, Mtamanika. 2012. "Razing May Threaten Sweet Auburn Status." *The Atlanta Journal-Constitution*, March 14. Available at www.ajc.com/news/news/opinion/razing-may-threaten-sweet-auburn -status/nQSCL/.

Zuehlke, Kai. 2009. *2008 Regional On-Board Express Bus Survey*. Atlanta: Georgia Regional Transportation Authority.

CONTRIBUTORS

Frank S. Alexander is the Sam Nunn Professor of Law at Emory University School of Law and co-founder of the Center for Community Progress. His work has focused on homelessness and affordable housing, and he has served as a fellow of the Carter Center of Emory University and as a commissioner of the State Housing Trust Fund for the Homeless.

Douglas Allen was professor emeritus of architecture at the Georgia Institute of Technology, where he taught courses in landscape architecture, urban history, and urban design. He previously served as interim dean and associate dean of the College of Architecture.

Jennifer Ball is vice president of Planning and Economic Development for Central Atlanta Progress, Inc., where she manages land use and transportation planning efforts, economic development initiatives, and implementation projects within Downtown Atlanta.

Thomas D. Boston is a professor of economics in the Sam Nunn School of International Affairs at the Georgia Institute of Technology. He has served as president of the National Economic Association, editor of *The Review of Black Political Economy*, senior economist to the Joint Economic Committee of Congress, and economic advisor to four mayors of Atlanta.

Nisha Botchwey is an associate professor in the School of City and Regional Planning at the Georgia Institute of Technology. Her research focuses on health and the built environment, community engagement, and health impact assessment.

Michael Carnathan is a senior researcher at the Atlanta Regional Commission and at Neighborhood Nexus, a data hub for metropolitan Atlanta area decision makers, where he provides data and develops tools to help leaders at all levels make better decisions. Prior to this, he worked in the auditor's office of Athens-Clark County.

Jennifer Clark is an associate professor in the School of Public Policy and director of the Center for Urban Innovation in the Ivan Allen College at the Georgia Institute of Technology. Her research focuses on regional economic development, manufacturing, industrial districts, and innovation.

Benjamin R. DeCosta has over 20 years of executive experience in airport leadership, including positions as aviation general manager of the Hartsfield-Jackson Atlanta International Airport and general manager of Newark International Airport. He also currently provides consulting services to the aviation industry.

Michael Dobbins, FAICP, is a planner, urban designer, architect, and teacher who has practiced mainly in the public sector over the last 40 years. He has directed planning and urban design agencies in New York City, New Orleans, Birmingham, Berkeley, and Atlanta. He presently is a professor of practice in the School of City and Regional Planning at the Georgia Institute of Technology.

Jim Durrett is executive director of the Buckhead Community Improvement District. Previously, he was vice president of environmental affairs at the Metro Atlanta Chamber, founding executive director of the Urban Land Institute Atlanta, and founding executive director of the Livable Communities Coalition.

Leon S. Eplan, FAICP, heads Urban Mobility Consult, Ltd., an Atlanta planning firm specializing in rail and bus passenger transportation in urban areas. He is a former professor and director of the Program (now School) of City and Regional Planning at the Georgia Institute of Technology and past president of the American Institute of Planning (now the American Institute of Certified Planners). He was Atlanta's commissioner of planning and development during the 1970s and again in the 1990s.

Harley F. Etienne is an assistant professor of urban and regional planning at the University of Michigan. He teaches in the areas of urban community development, inner-city revitalization, neighborhood change, urban poverty, and qualitative research issues in planning. His research focuses primarily on the intersection of social institutions and processes of urban neighborhood change.

Barbara Faga has over 35 years of consulting experience with AECOM, EDAW, and the cities of Atlanta and Alexandria, Virginia. She is an urban designer who has directed large, complex projects, including resorts, parks, and downtown revitalization. In 2011 she was named an AECOM Fellow and is currently completing a Ph.D. at the Georgia Institute of Technology.

Shirley Franklin served as Atlanta's mayor from 2001 to 2009, the first African American female mayor of a major southern city. She is now the Barbara Jordan Visiting Professor in Ethics and Political Values in the Lyndon B. Johnson School of Public Affairs at the University of Texas at Austin. She also serves as chair of the board and CEO of Purpose Built Communities.

Alexander Garvin has a combined career in urban planning and real estate. He is president and CEO of AGA Public Realm Strategists, Inc. and adjunct professor of urban planning and management at Yale University, where he has taught continuously for 46 years.

Subhro Guhathakurta joined the Georgia Institute of Technology in 2011 as the director of the Center for Geographic Information Systems and professor in the School of City and Regional Planning. He was previously associate director of the School of Geographical Sciences and Urban Planning at Arizona State University and among the founding faculty members of the School of Sustainability.

Eric M. Hardy is an historian of technology who specializes in the urban environment. He has taught courses at Loyola University New Orleans since 2010 in the history and sociology departments and the Environment Program. He has also taught courses in U.S. history and the history of technology at the Georgia Institute of Technology and Georgia Tech-Lorraine in Metz, France.

Ellen Heath, FAICP, is a principal and vice president of AECOM Design and former principal and vice President of EDAW. She is also a former president of the Georgia Planning Association.

John Heath, AICP, served for 28 years in the City of Atlanta's Bureau of Planning. He was responsible for coordinating the city's participation in the 1990 and 2000 decennial censuses, as well as coordinating the preparation of the annual Comprehensive Development Plan.

Paul B. Kelman, FAICP, retired from his position as executive vice president of Central Atlanta Progress, Inc. in 2010 after 22 years with the organization. He served as planning director of Gwinnett County, Georgia, chief of environmental planning for the Atlanta Regional Commission, principal environmental planner for Miami-Dade County, and a commissioned officer in the U.S. Public Health Service in Chicago. He also taught city planning for ten years at the Georgia Institute of Technology as an adjunct professor.

Elisabeth Kulinski is with Ernst & Young's Indirect Tax practice in Los Angeles focusing on credit and incentives. She was formerly a budget and policy advisor for economic development with the Georgia General Assembly and a consultant with Cushman & Wakefield's business incentives practice in Atlanta.

Brian Leary is the managing director of Jacoby Development and oversees the Atlanta-based national developer's mixed use, walkable urban and retail activity. Prior to this, he was president and CEO of Atlanta BeltLine, Inc. Before leading the BeltLine team, he oversaw the design and development of Atlantic Station, an urban brownfield redevelopment project, and he worked for Central Atlanta Progress.

Susannah Lee is a visiting researcher at the Center for Geographic Information Systems at the Georgia Institute of Technology. She is interested in practitioner-oriented research that drives community improvement efforts. She concurrently works at the Midtown Alliance, an Atlanta business improvement district, where she manages GIS and urban development projects.

Audrey Leous is a research scientist at the Center for Quality Growth and Regional Development at the Georgia Institute of Technology. She has also worked at the U.S. Green Building Council on the development of online resources for green building continuing education and at the Community Foundation for Greater Buffalo.

Joseph G. Martin Jr. is now a member of the Peace Corps in Macedonia. He was previously the president of Park Central Communities, the Atlanta Economic Development Corporation, the Underground Festival Development Corporation, the Summerhill Neighborhood Development Corporation, the Capitol Hill Neighborhood Development Corporation, and the Atlanta Board of Education.

Laurel Paget-Seekins is a research fellow at the Bus Rapid Transit Centre of Excellence and Centre for Sustainable Urban Development at Pontificia Universidad Católica de Chile in Santiago.

David Pendered is an Atlanta journalist with 30 years of experience reporting on the region's urban affairs. Since 2008, he has written for print and digital publications, and advised on media and governmental affairs. Previously, he spent more than 26 years with The Atlanta Journal-Constitution.

Randal Roark is a planner and architect practicing in Atlanta for the past 42 years. He is associate professor emeritus in the School of Architecture and Planning at the Georgia Institute of Technology, where he was the undergraduate program director in architecture and founder and director of the Urban Design Workshop. He was the director of planning and design for the Corporation for Olympic Development in Atlanta.

Catherine Ross is the Harry L. West Professor of City and Regional Planning and director of the Center for Quality Growth and Regional Development at the Georgia Institute of Technology. She has served on committees of the National Academies and the University Transportation Centers and on the board of directors of the Eno Center for Transportation.

Maria Saporta has been a business and civic journalist in Atlanta for nearly 33 years. She worked with the Atlanta Journal-Constitution and now writes for the Atlanta Business Chronicle and SaportaReport.

Leslie N. Sharp is the assistant vice provost for Graduate Education and Faculty Affairs at the Georgia Institute of Technology, where she teaches historic preservation. Previously she was an associate research professor in history at the Center for Historic Preservation at Middle Tennessee State University.

Jason Vargo is a fellow with the Center for Sustainability and the Global Environment and the Global Health Institute at the University of Wisconsin-Madison. His research examines the influences of the built environment on healthy behaviors among residents in Bogotá, Colombia, and the U.S.

Harry L. West was a professor of practice of quality growth and regional development in the School of City and Regional Planning at the Georgia Institute of Technology. Prior to this, he held a senior position with Parsons Corporation. He was also the executive director of the Atlanta Regional Commission for 27 years.

Mtamanika Youngblood is the president of Sweet Auburn Works, a non-profit organization working to revitalize the Sweet Auburn commercial corridor in Atlanta. She is chair of the board and past president of the Historic District Development Corporation. She also served as president and CEO of Sustainable Neighborhood Development Strategies, Inc., and was the founder and president of The Center for Working Families, Inc.

CREDITS

Figure 13.7   Nisha Botchwey

Figure 13.8   Nisha Botchwey

Figure D.1   Harley Etienne

Figure 16.1   Hartsfield-Jackson Atlanta International Airport

Figure 16.2   Hartsfield-Jackson Atlanta International Airport

Page 197   Central Atlanta Progress

Figure 18.3   Alex Garvin & Associates

Figure 22.3/   The S&P/Case-Shiller Atlanta Home Price Index and the S&P/Case-Shiller 10-City
Figure 22.6   Composite Home Price Index are proprietary to and are calculated, distributed and marketed by S&P Opco, LLC (a subsidiary of S&P Dow Jones Indices LLC), its affiliates and/or its licensors and has been licensed for use. S&P® is a registered trademark of Standard & Poor's Financial Services LLC; Dow Jones® is a registered trademark of Dow Jones Trademark Holdings LLC and Case-Shiller® is a registered trademark of CoreLogic Case-Shiller, LLC. © 2013 S&P Dow Jones Indices LLC, its affiliates and/or its licensors. All rights reserved.

Page 212   Alex Garvin

Page 214   Alex Garvin

Figure E.1   Georgia World Congress Center

Figure F.1   Harley Etienne

INDEX